REDEEMING THE REVOLUTION

THE MEXICAN EXPERIENCE
William H. Beezley, series editor

REDEEMING THE REVOLUTION

The State and Organized Labor
in Post-Tlatelolco Mexico

JOSEPH U. LENTI

UNIVERSITY OF NEBRASKA PRESS   LINCOLN AND LONDON

Portions of chapter 2 previously appeared in Joseph U.
Lenti and Amelia M. Kiddle, "Co-opting Cardenismo: Luis
Echeverría and the Funeral of Lázaro Cárdenas," in *Populism
in Twentieth-Century Mexico: The Presidencies of Lázaro
Cárdenas and Luis Echeverría*, ed. Amelia M. Kiddle and
María L. O. Muñoz (Tucson: University of Arizona Press,
2010), 174–89. © 2010 by the Arizona Board of Regents.
Reprinted with permission of the University of Arizona Press.

Portions of chapter 4 previously appeared in "'A
Revolutionary Regime Must Put the Interests of the Majority
First': Class, Collectivism, and Paternalism in Post-Tlatelolco
Mexican Tripartite Relations," *Latin Americanist* 54, no.
4 (Winter 2010): 163–82. Reprinted with permission.

Library of Congress Control Number: 2017940996

Set in Garamond Premier Pro by Rachel Gould.
Designed by N. Putens.

To the most honorable workers
I know, my mother and father,
Helen and Umberto Lenti

In Mexico there are unions but there is no unionism.... And there is no workerism although there are workers.... Fifty years of white unionism, white with the pallid look of cowardice and betrayal, have exhausted our workers of their class-consciousness.... Each trembles with fear just at the thought of dismissal or the exclusionary clause.... On the first of May the day of labor is celebrated.... But when is the day of the laborer? ... All of this derives, mainly, from the capitulation of their leaders.... If they had an Olympiad of vanity, corruption, and uselessness, the labor leaders would take all the gold medals.... There is a mystery that puzzles me: they say that the Revolution has gotten down from its horse.... Why, then, are there still so many many *charro* leaders?

Editorial, *El Heraldo* (Saltillo, Coahuila), October 7, 1970

CONTENTS

PHOTOGRAPHS

Following page 176

ACKNOWLEDGMENTS

It is a cliché to say that a scholar accrues many debts while researching and writing, although in this case the adage applies. This book, and more broadly, my education, was completed only through the generosity of droves of people who have supported me during the span of my careers at the University of New Mexico and Eastern Washington University. Originating from a seminar paper written at UNM in 2005, this project grew and saw its development nurtured and often corrected by Linda B. Hall, she who has been a true friend and mentor to me since I began graduate school in 2002. Through her edits and revisions of my work, her advice and ideas, our countless excursions, sporting events, and lunches in the United States and Mexico, and her endless generosity in writing letter after support letter on my behalf, Linda guided me along the academic path and made my journey to the ranks of the professional historian a rich and joyful experience.

My work, as well as my sanity, also benefited from a revision or two offered by Brad Shreve, Erik Loomis, Kathleen McIntyre, Colin Snider, Margarita Ochoa, Nydia Martínez, Brian Stauffer, Will Veeder, Yann Kerevel, Lucy Grinnell, Chris Vigil, Meg Frisbee, Danielle Scott, Frank Salazar, Frank Alvárez, and Brandon Morgan, at UNM, some of whom read parts of the dissertation but more generally were the kind of friends any human being needs to endure. Judy Bieber, Manuel García y Griego, Greg Crider, Jürgen Buchenau, Michael Snodgrass, Amelia Kiddle, María L. O. Muñoz, Annemarie Frohnhoefer, and the late Adrian Bantjes—all of whose work I admire greatly—offered valuable comments on selected chapters. John Hart, to whose fan club I also subscribe, read the complete manuscript and offered important revisions. John's known hatred of "acrobabble" (i.e., the overuse of acronyms) and his commitment to making great history read like great literature have inspired my writing since the beginning. Last, folks at the University of Nebraska Press, Bridget Barry, Emily Wendell, Sara Springsteen, and Joy Margheim in particular, have been generous in their support of this project, and its quality is all the better because of it.

Thank-yous are also due to friends in Washington, and in particular to Estéban and Elisa Rodríguez, Majid and Sheki Sharifi, Christina and Martín García, Joe and Diana Sperry-Navarro, Matt and Priscilla Rabinovitch, Ann Le Bar, Bob and Riva Dean, Larry and Renee Cebula, and Elisha Miranda and Alex Ramírez, who shared their laughter, homes, food, and plenty of wine with me while I've resided in the great Northwest. The same can be said for each and every member of the Department of History at Eastern Washington University—a group I've enjoyed the camaraderie of for the past seven years. Thank you Liping Zhu, Michael Conlin, Bob Dean, Ann Le Bar, Nydia Martínez, John Collins, Larry Cebula, Ed Slack, Laura Hodgman, Kathleen Huttenmaier, Monica Stenzel, Bill Youngs, and Valerie Burnett for being the kinds of colleagues all budding teachers require to grow and thrive. In the same vein I have benefited from the vitality and knowledge of Mayra Villalobos, Michael Edwards, Samantha de Abreu, Tomás Shalloe, Nicolle Southwick, Ian Pettus, Logan Camporeale, and Ronald Scheck—all former students and themselves budding Latinamericanists. Special mention should also be made of Douglas and the incomparable baristas at The Mason Jar in Cheney, a coffeehouse at which I wrote a significant portion of this book. Last but not least, Vickie Rutledge Shields, the former dean of the College of Social Sciences at EWU, has been indispensable to this project, heaping encouragement and funding on me that has allowed short-term trips to Mexico.

Fellowships I've won from the National Endowment for the Humanities and the Latin American and Iberian Institute at the University of New Mexico have funded extended stays in Mexico filled with adventures, missteps, and triumphs worthy of their own book-length studies. In nearly every research setting I've been blessed with assistance from excellent people, and standing out among the scores of archivists, librarians, phototechnicians, and other professionals who've aided this project are Diego Castillo Collins, Alma del Carmen Vásquez Morales, Erika Gutiérrez, Máximo de Jesús Méndez, and Edgar Paul Ríos Rosas—all at the Archivo General de la Nación. I am also grateful to María Luisa Izquierdo, who shared her expertise and home with me one summer, and Virginia Morales, a former student who helped me locate images in Mexican institutions in 2015. A special mention must also be made of Linda Arnold, not an employee of the AGN per se, but an institution unto herself who has over the course of decades compiled an electronic catalog that is indispensable for anyone interested in writing the history of Mexico. Although not included formally in this book's bibliography, the "Guía Arnold" was perhaps its most important resource.

Several years of researching in Mexico have also allowed me to get to know people there quite intimately. To all of you, but especially to my *familia amiga*—Raul and Fabiola Flores, Ritchie and Mayra López, Noemi and Juan Andaluz, little Paulina, Magali, and all of the extended members of the family in the colonias Santa María la Ribera, Pantitlan, and Narvarte—thank you immensely for helping me navigate the streets and norms of México, D.F. I will always appreciate the way you have invited me into your homes and entertained my many rants about the eccentricities and marvels of *la onda chilanga*.

Call it a cliché again for those who research abroad, but the most important gift I received from this experience was a family. Thank you Jennyfer, Sebastián, and Bianca (who arrived to the world near the end of this process) for succoring me during this long and taxing process. Your love and support is something I will always cherish. Finally, I thank my parents and brothers—Helen and Umberto, Frank and Andrew—and other family members, my Uncle John and Auntie Ann in particular, for the enduring support they've shown me over the years. To each of you and to so many family members and friends in Massachusetts, Italy, and elsewhere: I love you and miss you all very much. None of this was possible without you.

Casa: House of the World Worker (Casa del Obrero Mundial)

CCE: Business Coordinating Council (Consejo Coordinadora Empresarial)

CFE: Federal Electric Commission (Comisión Federal de Electricidad)

CNOP: National Confederation of Popular Organizations (Confederación Nacional de Organizaciones Populares)

CONASUPO: National Popular Subsistence Company (Compañia Nacional de Subsistencias Populares)

CROC: Revolutionary Confederation of Workers and Peasants (Confederación Regional de Obreros y Campesinos)

CROM: Mexican Regional Labor Confederation (Confederación Regional de Obreros de México)

CT: Congress of Labor (Congreso del Trabajo)

CTM: Confederation of Mexican Workers (Confederación de Trabajadores de México)

DGIPS: General Directorate of Political and Social Investigations (Dirección General de Investigaciones Políticas y Sociales)

FAMOSA: Factories of Monterrey (Fábricas Monterrey S.A.)

FAT: Authentic Workers' Front (Frente Auténtico del Trabajo)

FSTDF: Federation of Federal District Workers' Unions (Federación Sindical de Trabajadores del Distrito Federal)

FSTSE: Federation of Public Sector Workers' Unions (Federación de Sindicatos de Trabajadores al Servicio del Estado)

FTNL: Nuevo León State Workers' Federation (Federación de Trabajadores de Nuevo León)

HYLSA: Monterrey Tin and Sheet Metal (Hojalata y Lámina de Monterrey S.A.)

JFCA: Federal Conciliation and Arbitration Board (Junta Federal de Conciliación y Arbitraje)

JLCA: Local Conciliation and Arbitration Board (Junta Local de Conciliación y Arbitraje)

NLFT: New Federal Labor Law of 1970 (Nueva Ley Federal del Trabajo)

PAN: National Action Party (Partido de Acción Nacional)

Pemex: Mexican Petroleum (Petróleos Mexicanos)

PRD: Party of the Democratic Revolution (Partido de la Revolución Democrática)

PRI: Institutional Revolutionary Party (Partido Revolucionario Institucional)

SME: Mexican Electricians' Union (Sindicato Mexicano de Electricistas)

STERM: Mexican Electrical Workers' Union (Sindicato de Trabajadores Electricistas de la República Mexicana)

STFRM: Mexican Railway Workers' Union (Sindicato de Trabajadores Ferrocarrileros de la República Mexicana)

STPRM: Mexican Petroleum Workers' Union (Sindicato de Trabajadores Petroleros de la República Mexicana)

STPS: Secretariat of Labor and Social Welfare (Secretaría de Trabajo y Previsión Social)

SUTERM: United Electric Workers' Union (Sindicato Único de Trabajadores Electricistas de la República Mexicana)

TD: Democratic Tendency (Tendencia Democrática)

UNAM: National Autonomous University of Mexico (Universidad Nacional Autónoma de México)

USD: U.S. dollars

REDEEMING THE REVOLUTION

Introduction

A Revolution to Redeem the Nation

Redeemers and prophesies of redemption have been central to the Mexican narrative. Choosing from among many, the predicted return of Topiltzin, the Toltec lord who was shamed and exiled in the tenth century, and the expected resurrection of Emiliano Zapata, the revolutionary who was ambushed and killed in 1919, were visions that effected historical change in Mexico long after the redeemers had exited the stage. Redeemers walk among Mexicans even today, we are told, as scholars apply this label to Subcomandante Marcos and Andrés Manuel López Obrador, both of whom endured political or personal setbacks in their lives and whose expected revivals factor into the modern Mexican drama.

Redeemer and *redemption* are concepts that need political contextualization. Being terms that originated in a Latin world of Christians and pagans, the verb *redeem* and the noun *redeemer* connote religious meanings by definition. "To redeem," according to the dictionary of the Real Academia Española, has several interrelated definitions, as it can mean: (a) to rescue or free from slavery by means of payment; (b) to buy back something that had been sold, possessed, or owned for some reason;

(c) to free from an obligation or to settle it; or (d) to put an end to some humiliation, pain, distress, or other adversity or discomfort.[1] History informs us that the act of redeeming was carried out by members of religious communities that were designated to rescue Christian captives from the Saracens, Syrian tribesman who lived on the edges of the Roman Empire and held people for ransom. A redeemer, then, was one who paid the ransom and freed a fellow believer from slavery and perdition. The same dictionary defines *redeemer* quite simply as "something that redeems," although the *redemption* definition elaborates by explaining that the redeemer par excellence, Jesus Christ, was he who "redeemed human kind by means of his passion and death."[2]

Given that Christ is understood by most Spanish-speaking Catholics as the arch redeemer, it is not surprising that Mexicans have frequently bestowed that honorific upon religious figures: Topiltzin, whom commoners prophesized would return to rescue them from their oppressive Aztec overlords, and the Virgin of Guadalupe, who would rescue them from their idolatry, being prime examples. What is surprising, on the other hand, and ironic, is that the concept of redemption has also been ascribed to the modern nation's seminal event, the Mexican Revolution, that which substantially weakened the Roman Catholic Church and displaced it as the country's primary institution. Scholars have noticed this paradox and have mutually ascribed religious overtones to the movement. Historians Enrique Krauze and Marjorie Becker, for example, have shown that the processes of education and land reform undertaken in the 1920s and 1930s by José Vasconcelos and Lázaro Cárdenas, respectively, were viewed like campaigns of religious conversion by individuals who saw in the ideology of the Mexican Revolution (and not Christ) the source of their people's salvation.[3] The redemption concept also extended beyond schoolteachers and peasants in revolutionary Mexico, as unionists who assembled at annual First of May parades in the 1910s and thereafter railed against the almost biblical oppression they suffered at the hands of their employers and speculated about the power of the Revolution to save them from it. Partisans of the revolutionary regime in Mexico, history reveals, felt little compunction about applying religious imagery to a secular movement waged with overt anticlerical goals.

This book links the Mexican state's ongoing quest for redemption with the changing status of organized workers in the twentieth century. State builders beginning in 1917 acted to make two paradigms—the nation and the Mexican Revolution—analogous in order to redeem the former concept and show organized workers that the regime that emerged from the latter could be a force of good and a deliverer of social justice. The resulting nation-Revolution metonym established the ruling regime's legitimacy, solidified workers' loyalty toward it, and bolstered its authority thereafter. This process was effective but yielded diminished returns as time passed.

Above all, this book demonstrates how the Mexican Revolution, an institution that itself came to require redemption, was rescued after 1968 by demonstrating to organized workers how much it had done for them and how much more it could deliver. Causation is established by linking the killing of hundreds of student protestors in the Tlatelolco district of Mexico City on October 2–3, 1968 (an event indirectly related to the labor movement) with the creation of the New Federal Labor Law of 1970, the participation of millions of workers in mass political events, and the altered form of relations among the state, organized labor, and business in the ensuing period. Ultimately, the ways that the Tlatelolco massacre moved the Mexican state to counter a crisis of legitimacy that beset it by redeeming (meaning both to restore and to cash in on) its revolutionary credentials with a prominent social sector are assessed herein. But while a restored alliance with the state benefited unionists and challenged business interests in substantive ways, this book also reveals that conflict ensued when workers criticized the chasm between rhetoric and reality and tested their leaders' limits of toleration.

Before tackling this study's central question—*Why was the Mexican Revolution in need of redemption after 1968 and how was it redeemed?*—some historical prefacing is required. Mainly, one must ask, *What did the Mexican Revolution originally redeem?* The following sections assess how the movement of 1910–17 created a national system markedly different from those that preceded it and how that revolutionary state formed lasting bonds with organized workers, a crucial and privileged part of the Mexican working class.

"Institutions and Laws" to Redeem the Nation

When outgoing president Plutarco Elías Calles implored in his last annual address on September 1, 1928, for Mexico to "move, once and for all, from being a 'country ruled by one man' to 'a nation of institutions and laws,'" he issued a demand to a people who were skeptical about the power of the nation to better their lives.[4] Only six weeks earlier, on July 17, President-Elect Álvaro Obregón, the towering revolutionary, had fallen victim to an assassin's bullet, and this while Mexico was embroiled in an ongoing civil war waged by Catholic zealots to overturn anticlerical laws and the government that enforced them. If that was not enough, the dust of the previous decade's epic revolution had barely settled in Mexican society, suggesting to many that government was more a force of division and destruction than unity and progress. In a country accustomed to viewing politics as a process where bullets were more powerful than ballots, little was inspirational about the president's call. Mexico's turbulent experience with nationhood did not permit such optimism.

Truthfully, the national institution had not been an important presence in people's lives in the time since Mexico won its independence from Spain in 1821—except for when they were called upon to fight for or against it. Regionalism prevailed in the postindependence period, as presidents came and went, holding office for only months, or even days, thus preventing the federal government from implementing programs. Dizzying turnover also meant that the national institution was overshadowed by the caudillos—typically, creole landowners with strong regional constituencies, much power in the army, and aspirations to federal office. Caudillos tended to preserve the localized patron-client networks that had benefited them prior to independence and distributed government jobs, pensions, and public works to friends and followers in reward for their loyalty. Even the dictatorial regime that the country endured under

Porfirio Díaz (1876–1911), which brought an end to foreign invasion, civil war, and dismemberment, did not eliminate the regionalism that characterized Mexico. Caudillos remained powerful throughout the Porfiriato and people remained subject to the peculiarities of local-, parish-, and hacienda-level laws. The people of Mexico, particularly those in the working class whose patriotism was so often called upon in battle, thus had little use and even less regard for a nation that demanded much from them while offering little in return.

Calles led a regime that aspired to change all of that. The federal government born in 1917 of popular revolution had already delivered to its people in the way of public education, land redistribution, and labor reform, but the gains were piecemeal and touched relatively few people. And many others, quite frankly, wished it had not touched them at all—a fact evidenced by the explosion of rebellion in 1926 by armed Catholics who judged their government "godless" by virtue of its ban on parochial education, its restriction on clergy, its disentailment of church lands and buildings, and, most recently, its efforts to create a "national" church to rival the Roman Catholic institution. Moreover, the killing of Obregón and the ongoing revolt suggested that chaos was still the norm after more than a decade along the path of revolutionary consolidation. Further action was required. Only in the "institutions and laws" that Calles desired could one foresee the redemption of the national concept and Mexico itself in the hearts and minds of the masses.

Redemption with zealous Catholics not being a viable path to pursue, the government worked to form alliances with other social sectors. Organized workers had a recent history of partnering with the regime, and they were a social group that required redress more than others. Mexico's historical regionalism and the era of the caudillos had injured workers in myriad ways. Laws dating from the nineteenth century conveyed traditional civil law notions of private property that saw employers and employees as free parties able to offer employment or sell their labor under conditions of their choosing. The Constitution of 1857 emphasized individual rights and guaranteed workers' freedoms in important ways, but this theoretical "freedom of labor" kept the basic terms of industrial relations outside the purview of the federal government. The state's invisibility in the workplace meant that even the constitution's minimal workers' protections went unenforced. Debt peonage, for instance, which was constitutionally prohibited, continued in practice and was even sanctioned by Díaz, who feared that its abolition would disrupt the production of crucial export commodities like henequen.

Piecemeal legislation and court rulings made at state levels to indemnify workers whose rights had been violated revealed a gradual movement toward the acceptance of employer liability, but the matter of what role the federal government could play in the regulation of business and industry was still decades away from settlement. No federal options existed for the glass worker in Nuevo León, for instance, who although hurt on the job had no recourse to challenge a state-level statute passed in 1906 that limited an employer's liability for on-the-job injuries. The workplace dangers glass workers faced, however, paled when compared to the perils that confronted their brethren in the mines, a group that generally toiled with no safety net whatsoever. Miners and other workers of the time became increasingly conscious of their shared plight through the pages of *Regeneración*, the newsletter of the Mexican Liberal Party, led by Ricardo Flores Magón, and many began to agitate for rights. Important strikes waged by miners at Cananea (1906) and textile workers at Río Blanco (1907) exerted pressure on the Díaz government, which responded in 1908 by proposing accident compensation at a national level. The proposal was deemed bad for business by foreign owners, however.

Astute legal history offered by William Suarez-Potts helps contextualize business owners' opposition to such laws. Turn-of-the-century discourse about employers' responsibilities, he writes, produced new ideas about social legislation built around transcendental principles and social duties, not merely traditional civil law notions of private property.[5] Faced with a fashionable paradigm of social law, irate employers clung to traditional liberal tenets that they believed precluded them from having to abide by workplace regulations. The constitutionally guaranteed "freedom of labor," they argued in litigation, meant that their employees could opt not to work in their establishments if they were uncomfortable with the conditions. By the end of the century this fiction was being debunked by Supreme Court rulings and even by the Catholic Church, which in the 1891 encyclical *Rerum Novarum* criticized the exploitation of workers caused by industrialization and the lack of a minimum wage and working-hour regulations.[6] Yet these juridical, philosophical, and even religious debates over workplace relations yielded limited benefits and only on a case-by-case basis. A major social movement would be required to effect change at a national level and liberate the Mexican working class from the continued abuses it endured.

The Mexican Revolution of 1910–17 permanently changed the nature of governance in Mexico. Unlike regimes that had previously governed the country, the revolutionary state that took power after 1917 endeavored to reduce regional challenges to its authority. Local warlords who had managed patron-client networks in previous times were less and less tolerable in a state system that increasingly endowed its leader with autocratic powers. Wielding immense power, including the ability to handpick their successor every four (later six) years, postrevolutionary presidents stood in contrast to the quixotic caudillos that Mexicans had previously associated with rule.[7] The Mexican Revolution thus signaled the end of the age of the chaotic, local, and personalistic caudillo and the dawn of the stable, national, and bureaucratic presidential regime.

Revolutionary consolidation, however, took time, and little semblance of stability, peace, or centralization occurred while the bullets flew. In truth, the workers' plight was never the primary thrust of the movement, despite the influence that the Mexican Liberal Party exerted on Francisco I. Madero, the originator of the military movement against Díaz. Madero's Plan de San Luis Potosí denounced the regime for violating the constitution and ignited the Mexican Revolution but did not speak directly to the question of labor reform. His ancillary rhetoric, however, promised constitutional protection for workers, and he did permit them to form trade unions once he held provisional power. As president, Madero oversaw important developments that benefited the workers' cause further still. A Workers' Law was passed in 1912—the only bill Congress passed during his administration—and the president took steps to increase the state's regulatory power over workplace conditions and conflicts. All of this made Madero appear a solid ally of the working class.

To workers' great dismay, the putative "Father of the Mexican Revolution" did not live to see these modest reforms realized. Ousted and assassinated in a military coup, Madero did not witness workers marching in the nation's first International Day of Labor parade. Organized by the recently formed House of the Workers of the World (Casa, for short) on May 1, 1913, and carried out in Mexico City, the parade was designed to urge Congress, now under the thumb of General Victoriano Huerta, to legislate the eight-hour day, mandate compensation for work-related accidents, and legally recognize labor organizations. None of these objectives were realistic while the "usurper" Huerta commanded Mexico, and the nascent workers' movement and the Casa in particular experienced Porfirian-like repression during his rule.

Workers' hatred for Huerta moved them to support the cause led by Venustiano Carranza, a wealthy landowner from the northern state of Coahuila. Like the Plan de San Luis Potosí offered by Madero, Carranza's Plan de Guadalupe initially lacked a labor component. But as did Madero, Carranza later amended his program to include labor reforms meant to create "equilibrium" in the productive process and to balance the interests of workers and employers. Carranza's faction ultimately drove Huerta from power in July 1914, and this, along with the demonstrated support he showed for labor, made Carranza and his general, Álvaro Obregón, attractive to working-class organizations around the nation. Eager to woo urban workers to his side in the incipient civil war against Francisco "Pancho" Villa in the north and Emiliano Zapata in the south, Carranza gave the Casa semiofficial status, allowed it to organize, channeled funds to it, and sided with it against foreign employers.[8] A pact signed on February 15, 1915, solidified the Casa-Carranza alliance, affirming that the "House of the Workers of the World [adhered] to the constitutionalist government headed by Citizen Venustiano Carranza" and pledging to "give their collaboration with the constitutional cause." Clauses 2 and 7 of the pact demonstrated the Casa's gratitude to a faction it felt indebted to and committed it to a military and political alliance with the government in the future. They read, respectively,

> [Second.] The workers of the House of the Workers of the World, for the purpose of hastening the triumph of the constitutionalist revolution and intensifying as far as possible the unnecessary shedding of blood, put on record the resolution they have taken to collaborate in an effective and practical manner for the triumph of the revolution and to take up arms either to garrison towns that are in the possession of the constitutionalist government or to fight the reaction.
>
> [Seventh.] The workers shall establish revolutionary centers or committees in all the places they judge convenient to do so. The Committees, besides the propaganda work, shall supervise the organization of labor groups and their collaboration in favor of the constitutionalist cause.[9]

The most immediate and most important outcome of this pact was the creation of the Red Battalions, an army of some six thousand Casa members that helped tip the balance in favor of Carranza in his battles against Villa and Zapata in 1915. By 1916 the supremacy of Carranza and the Constitutionalist faction was indisputable. The power to rescue the Mexican working class via labor reform and a new constitution was theirs alone.

Carranza ascribed his victory in war to the nation's workers. Once president, though, he flashed his natural conservative colors and was hardly an ally of the working class. In 1916 he demobilized the Casa and authorized military and police crackdowns on other anarcho-syndicalist organizations that rejected hierarchy and adhered to "direct action," meaning strikes in place of government-mediated negotiations. Still, labor advocates in his regime and in the military wielded enough power to pressure him to include significant labor provisions in the constitution, as did an ascendant socialism in the nation. By the time a constitutional convention was convened in Querétaro in January 1917 the pressure to enact labor reform had reached a crescendo. Delegates worked for ten days on a labor program that ultimately became law with the promulgation of the federal constitution on February 5, 1917. Undoubtedly, the progressive nature of Article 123 of the constitution stunned many in the workers' movement, who had expected far fewer of their priorities to be affirmed. Within the article's thirty paragraphs were clauses that mandated an eight-hour workday, a mandatory day of rest, postpartum leave for women, health and safety standards in the workplace, an "adequate" minimum wage, equal pay regardless of sex or nationality, overtime pay, low-cost and employer-provided housing, profit sharing and social insurance for old age and involuntary termination of work, and occupational injury, illness, or death compensation.

Article 123 also responded to the demands of organized labor as it guaranteed workers and employers the right to unionize, guaranteed workers the right to strike and employers the right to lock out their employees, protected unionized workers from discharge without cause and guaranteed them three months' severance pay, and, declared all strikes licit (except those by munitions factory workers and some public employees) that had as an objective the attainment of equilibrium between the factors of production.[10] Also called for within the article's text was the creation of a system of conciliation and arbitration boards composed of business, labor, and state representatives that could rule on the legality of strike or lockout actions and adjudicate disputes that emerged in the workplace. Finally, Article 123 prohibited hot-button practices that had sparked workers' militancy at Cananea and elsewhere, including an inhumane workday, debt peonage, employers' retention of wages, and the mandatory use of the company store.

Workers did not universally acclaim Article 123 upon its introduction. Casa members, for example, bristled at the decisive role it afforded the government in labor arbitration. Neither were *patrones* (employers) thrilled with it. In response they formed themselves into the National Confederation of Industrial Chambers in December 1917 in order to protect property rights that they believed Article 123's profit-sharing and social insurance provisions encroached upon. Patrones, in fact, held good cards in this deal, as Mexico was a country where federal labor prescriptions that were on the books rarely resembled conditions that were present on the shop floor. To their delight and to workers' dismay, this historical de jure and de facto differential remained in place even after 1917, and the newly created Secretariat of Industry, Commerce, and Labor was inaugurated lacking any real power to enforce federal labor law in areas where state law superseded it. The federal labor law's lack of jurisdiction in the states was no oversight; delegates to the constitutional convention feared treading on the political autonomy of local governors, many of whom had recently been generals and still commanded the allegiance of large numbers of armed men. This trepidation ultimately gave labor law in Mexico a familiar federal and local distinction that created a bureaucratic mess employers easily took advantage of.

With the de jure and de facto differential rearing its ugly head yet again, the onus fell on workers to compel enforcement through pressure tactics at the state level. Strikes increased markedly after 1917, and particularly in crucial industries like petroleum, railroads, textiles, and mining. In some instances, strikers were brutally dispersed, forcing them to the realization that Presidents Carranza and then Obregón, to whom so many workers had given their loyalty and some their lives in battle, were hostile to a strong and assertive labor movement. In other cases, strikes were undercut by jurisdictional conflicts that emerged between federal and local authorities who bickered over who had the authority to mediate strikes and negotiate contracts. Conflicts in industrial areas with interstate scopes such as railroad transportation were particularly contentious, as employers shunned local laws in favor of federal norms (or vice versa) depending on which law benefited them most. Often when workplace disputes arose they were settled in the home state's civil court and by judges who were generally conservative and friendly to business interests.[11] Despite these institutional challenges, worker militancy continued undeterred and eventually forced state legislatures to enact some ninety laws and decrees to codify the provisions of Article 123 by 1928.

To overcome the absence of a federal labor law codifying Article 123 a number of states created local conciliation and arbitration boards in accordance with the article's paragraph 20. In most cases the boards functioned as the courts of last resort in conflicts over which they had jurisdiction, and they heard both individual and collective labor disputes. Initially, after 1918, the boards were hamstrung by Supreme Court decisions that deprived them of binding authority and did not let them resolve individual worker grievances, only collective conflicts. These positions were reversed in 1924 at the behest of President Obregón, who pushed through the change to strengthen relations with the Mexican Regional Labor Confederation, then the nation's largest and most influential labor organization. President Calles, pursuant to his centralizing mission, later created the Federal Conciliation and Arbitration Board (JFCA) in 1927 and gave it authority to resolve questions that arose in pivotal industrial sectors. The JFCA benefited the organized labor movement as a whole, as the tripartite composition of the boards gave workers representation in the administration of labor justice and provided them with an important channel for the resolution of disputes outside of the workplace. Moreover, by removing employee-employer conflicts from the judicial system and giving government officials a deciding role in their resolution, the federal conciliation and arbitration boards increased the labor movement's ability to translate its growing political importance into workplace gains. Finally, the JFCA operated outside of the regular judicial system—a boon for a Mexican working class that saw the civil courts as historically aligned with business interests.

Most importantly, perhaps, the creation of the JFCA in 1927 formed part of a trend that increased the federal government's capacity to intervene in the regulation of the Mexican economy. This was a trend that the major organized labor players of the 1920s applauded and a trend further developed with the creation of the 1931 Federal Labor Law. Prior to its passage, proponents of the law argued that a unified federal labor code was necessary for two reasons: first, to codify basic rights granted to workers in the 1917 Constitution, and second, to regulate labor matters under a single federal law. The former goal was accomplished, though the latter largely failed to eliminate idiosyncrasies that persisted in the application of labor law at the state and municipal levels. Patrones, as they had done after 1917, again coalesced to oppose the proposed

legislation by forming themselves in 1929 into the Mexican Employers' Confederation, or COPARMEX, which became the nation's largest
employer organization and hence the most powerful counterweight the
employer class had against state and organized labor priorities. Ownership's opposition notwithstanding, the proposed legislation passed and
served the federal government and the ruling National Revolutionary
Party because it increased the power the government had over deciding
labor-capital disputes and inspired unions to smooth out kinks in their
relationships with state authorities. The postrevolutionary state's labor
establishment had not yet concluded its gestation, however; the Autonomous Department of Labor was established in 1932 and became the
precursor to the Secretariat of Labor and Social Welfare, a cabinet-level
ministry created in December 1940. Both bodies, ostensibly "autonomous" from presidential oversight, would answer to a higher power and
become key cogs in the processes of postrevolutionary state formation
and national redemption thereafter.

State and Organized Labor Collaborationism

One could have honestly concluded by 1932 that Calles's reformist goals
for the nation were being implemented vis-à-vis the Mexican working
class. Much had been accomplished in the four years since he had outlined his vision, as there were laws on the books to enforce Article 123's
labor prescriptions and government institutions in place to regulate
workplace conditions and mediate conflicts. Just as crucial for the realization of Calles's dream was the establishment of the official party in
1929, a process that he personally commandeered. The official party was
created when Calles (who still lorded over Mexico although no longer
president) summoned a motley group of local elites, agrarian chiefs,
labor bosses, and presidents of small parties to a meeting in Querétaro
wherein they founded the National Revolutionary Party. Upon their
initiation into the party, Mexico's chief caudillos "brought with them ...
their entire network of followers, people whose personal loyalty was
assured through one or another element of the sacred triad of personal
relationships consisting of family, friendship, and god-parenthood."[12]

Thus the official party became a flexible confederation of power brokers who could ameliorate disputes between rivals and diffuse potential threats from newcomers by incorporating their agendas into its own. As importantly, the official party provided the federal government a sophisticated national network to distribute spoils to supporters in exchange for their political support and activism.[13]

With the christening of this "revolutionary family" (as the official party was frequently dubbed) the ruling regime had a classic corporatist structure within which to pursue both the goals of redemption and the subordination of the working class. Certainly workers had been organized and even co-opted before by the government, but the kind of consolidation that Calles had in mind at that moment was not a process that would suffer the autonomous and unruly trade unionism practiced by the Casa of Carranza's time, nor even the collaborationist but strident unionism recently employed by the CROM, the Mexican Regional Labor Confederation.

The CROM was formed in May 1918 when a group of unionists defected from the Casa over its rejection of Article 123, which it believed afforded the government too much power over labor arbitration. Led by Luis N. Morones, a mechanic employed by the Mexican Light and Power Company, adherents to the CROM believed that the constitution was sufficiently "pro-worker" and that the labor movement should reject ideological rigidity and embrace tactical flexibility.[14] Moreover, the CROM sought to overcome organized labor's tactical and numerical weaknesses by building political alliances with elite groups, a strategy that led Morones in August 1919 to forge a secret pact with presidential candidate Álvaro Obregón in which he promised to mobilize the union's full support for him in the 1920 election in exchange for privileged political access, the creation of (and CROM influence over) a separate labor ministry, and presidential support for labor legislation codifying the provisions of Article 123.[15] These developments and the formation of the Mexican Labor Party in 1919 signaled organized labor's definitive entrance into national politics and marked the end of its independence from the state. With this, the pipeline of collaborationism—a tight and reciprocal relationship between the regime and the dominant segments of the trade unionist movement—had been laid and there was no place for oppositional currents in its flow. Suddenly, the anarcho-syndicalist position that had defined the Casa and dominated the workers' movement only five years earlier was judged antinational and counter to the goals of the Mexican Revolution.

The CROM and Mexican Labor Party were crucially important sources of mass support for a still fragile regime in the 1920s, and the CROM, although it falsely claimed two million members in 1928, was by the late 1920s the largest and most politically influential labor organization in Mexico.[16] Its stature enabled it to win real benefits for its members, including the first collective contract in the history of the country, as well as for Morones, whose eccentric tastes and lavish lifestyle are now the stuff of legend in Mexican history.[17] Additionally, the CROM created national federations in industries in which none had previously existed, namely among teachers, printers, and textile, sugar, and port workers. CROM dominance in the Mexican workplace, however, was never absolute, and the organization did not establish a strong presence in the strategic railroad transportation, electricity generation, and petroleum industries, wherein workers maintained strong anarchist influences that compelled them toward democratic governance and political independence.[18] Nevertheless, the CROM proved crucial in the process of state consolidation, as it helped the regime co-opt the rhetoric of the workers' movement and absorb it into its own discourse of national redemption by means of revolution.

Although the CROM was a crucial partner of the state in the 1920s, state-labor collaborationism was not predicated on equality. Just like a corpus had one head, the revolutionary family had one father—and it was not Luis Morones. By 1927 the influence that the boisterous Morones (who also served as secretary of industry) exerted over the government threatened Calles and, by extension, the stability of the regime. Calles, we can presume, was thinking of Morones (as well as the slain Obregón) when he cautioned against a "country ruled by one man," and the president probably rejoiced in the downfall of his rival after he was implicated in the assassination of the president-elect. Morones's troubles damaged the CROM, whose power was staked to the political influence and connections of its leader. But even with this development, the success via subordination blueprint for large labor confederations in the postrevolutionary period had been sketched. The prospects for future collaborationism and mutually beneficial relations between large organizations and the state were good, though new threats emerged to threaten the supremacy of that dynamic.

The ascension of Lázaro Cárdenas to the presidency in 1934 marked the end of Calles's ten-year lordship over the political establishment and ruptured the collaborationist pipeline. As president, the former Michoacán governor manifested a position toward organized labor and economic development markedly different from those of his predecessors. Whereas Calles, according to Myrna Santiago, subscribed to a capitalist development project that minimized class conflict through state management, the one-time Calles protégé Cárdenas encouraged workers to push to achieve the oft-referenced "equilibrium" via the inclusion of worker comanagement and profit-sharing clauses in their collective contracts with employers. Furthermore, Calles compromised with capital and squeezed labor in the interest of reaching a balance between the factors of production that he felt was optimal to the nation's industrialization goals. Cárdenas, on the other hand, believed equilibrium could be reached only by guaranteeing workers' rights and by permitting workers to pursue (via strikes) a "level of 'equity and social justice'" needed to produce the stability that true development required.[19]

By 1935 the rift between Cárdenas and Calles forced the political establishment to a point of introspection. Calles operated behind the scenes encouraging violent fascist organizations, including the Gold Shirts, to harass groups of radical and, specifically, communist, Jewish, and Chinese workers. Speaking on the floor of the Mexican Senate on June 11, 1935, against a backdrop of unprecedented labor agitation—there were 642 recorded strikes that year, involving 145,212 workers—Calles voiced positions that forced any remaining neutral parties to take sides.[20] He insisted that the National Revolutionary Party reign in its "nonconformists" if it wished to prosper and advance. The identity of the nonconformists was not a mystery; they were those radicals who formed themselves into the "left wings" of the political spectrum and whose actions were driving the nation to ruin. "Soldiers of the Revolution," Calles determined, were required to defend its cause against these threats.[21]

Calles's words on the Senate floor provoked the great fervor of the legislative body that heard them and heartened the CROM, which stayed loyal to its governmental benefactor. Conversely, Calles's speech alienated him from other portions of the workers' movement for good. The threatening and censuring tone of the speech turned the majority of workers' organizations against Calles and guaranteed the triumph of the Cárdenas position on labor. Responses were immediate. A joint declaration signed by the Mexican Electricians' Union, Mexican Mining and Metalworkers' Union, National Union of Telephone Workers, Mexican Railway Workers' Union, and other important non-CROM-affiliated unions appeared in Mexican newspapers the following day, June 12, 1935. Its highlights read,

> Mexico's organized worker and peasant movement . . . protests energetically against the declaration of General Calles . . . and declares that it will defend the rights of the working class . . . those that it itself obtained . . . and will not rest in advocating for the economic and social betterment of the salaried workers . . . ; The strike movements condemned in these declarations, [those that] respond to a collective malaise and a state of social injustice, are phenomena that occur on high by those who represent the capitalist interests. The strikes will stop when the bourgeois system in which we live is transformed . . . ; Mexico's organized worker and peasant movement . . . declares that it will oppose any transgression of its rights, using, at the necessary moment, the general and nation-wide strike as its mode of defense against the possible implantation of a fascist regime in Mexico.[22]

Groups adhering to the ideas published in the response convened shortly after to form the National Committee for Proletarian Defense, the immediate precursor to the Confederation of Mexican Workers (CTM) formed in February 1936. The genesis of the CTM had immediate ramifications; most importantly, it supplanted the CROM as the nation's primary labor front and ended the political careers of Calles and Morones, both of whom were charged with conspiring to blow up a railroad, arrested, and deported to the United States on April 9, 1936. Moreover, the creation of the CTM presaged the erasure of the collaborationist model of state-labor relations, for the organization's Declaration of Principles explicitly precluded a partnership with the government and opposed the intervention of "third parties," meaning the conciliation and arbitration boards, in labor disputes.[23]

These radical stances, however, would never truly be taken by the CTM despite the heavy dose of anarcho-syndicalism injected into its foundational rhetoric. The CTM's initial strategy mixed idealistic principles with pragmatic action, and while its official motto called for a "Classless Society" and its members demanded "the abolition of the capitalist system," appended language described the necessity of combating imperialist domination and achieving political and economic freedom in the country before pursuing those ends. Its Declaration of Principles also pointed out that the CTM did not seek to abolish private property, nor was it communist. What the CTM was, according to its leaders, was an organization that had to cooperate with progressive elements to combat the forces of creeping fascism and pursue a form of national development that would allow it to secure its long-range goals. Together these factors suggested that even while the CTM was in its gestation it was already embarking on a new, albeit slightly revised, course of collaboration with the government that subsequent congresses would ratify into its central principles.

The CTM's reluctance to pursue true autonomy from the state was due to the real friendship it enjoyed with the president during the Cárdenas administration. Organized workers, in general, enjoyed state favoritism with Cárdenas and became, according to one labor historian, a "senior partner" in the nation's corporatist political regime.[24] These were heady days for unionists, who won repeated victories over employers in their mobilizations. Raw statistics paint a clear portrait. An average of 478 strikes per year were waged during the years 1934–40, involving 61,422 workers annually. Of the strikes that reached the federal arbitration phase and were ruled upon, 1,596 (79 percent) were won by employees and only 434 (21 percent) by employers.[25] The joys of material gains won by workers were enhanced by the respect and reverence they felt for Cárdenas, who greatly differed from Calles, he who had once called striking oil workers "ingrates" and "traitors." Unionists were eager to show their support for their ally in Mexico City, and many felt a personal connection to him. A type of syndicalism that historian Michael Snodgrass calls "revolutionary unionism" thus emerged wherein large trade unions guaranteed their members patronage from the state in exchange for their functions as "vehicles of cultural engineering and political integration."[26] These "so-called revolutionary unions," he has written, also became schools for the making of "a new Mexican working class, one that was like General Cárdenas himself—hardworking, clean living, patriotic, and loyal to the National Revolutionary Party."[27] Here the mission of the Cárdenas state to reshape Mexican culture took on another aspect, for just as peasants learned in rural schools about the historical manipulations of the clergy and *hacendados* (large estate owners), so too did industrial workers receive instruction on the government's mission to pursue equilibrium and defend them from the abuses of patrones.

Revolutionary unionism, though it conveyed a more proworker feel than had been the norm since 1917, was still collaborationism, meaning it was still a pact predicated on labor's deference to state goals. The CTM was the most important political ally the Cárdenas state and official party had after 1936, and its ability to mobilize its members proved crucial in discouraging action on the part of those who opposed the oil expropriation act of March 18, 1938. Furthermore, the CTM supported Cárdenas's chosen successor, Manuel Ávila Camacho, and its conduct in the heated presidential contest of 1940 set the precedent for its role in future elections.[28] In this way the CTM replaced the CROM as the primary political ally for the governing elite, causing hard-liners to surface within the new labor bureaucracy to question the organization's independence. Even Vicente Lombardo Toledano, he who had formerly broken from the CROM in order to free the labor movement from state control, embraced a close relationship with the Cárdenas regime while serving as the CTM's first secretary general from 1936 to 1941. His stance angered the most radical parts of the CTM and convinced the Mexican Electricians' Union to secede from the organization in November 1939. Lombardo's vision of collaborationism, however, was guarded and put him at odds with the majority of CTM leaders, who desired even closer ties with the government. Inevitably, Lombardo was replaced by Fidel Velázquez, who, while at the helm of the CTM for much of the next six decades, set the organization on a course of government adherence that branded the specific form of state-labor collaborationism that this study focuses on.

Come 1936 Plutarco Elías Calles, the former president who more than anyone else impelled the creation of the postrevolutionary state, found himself bested by his protégé, vilified by the working class, and ultimately banished from Mexico. But in spite of his categorical defeat perhaps we may imagine that Calles felt a tinge of satisfaction that the clarion call he issued in 1928 had been heeded. Mexico, both because of and in spite of him, had become by the mid-1930s a nation with laws inscribed in the Constitution of 1917, Article 123, and the 1931 Federal Labor Law, and with institutions embodied by the federal ministries, the official party, and a large labor confederation that functioned under the auspices of the regime. Mexico circa 1936 was by no means a place devoid of powerful individuals; arguably, "Tata" Lázaro commanded the allegiance of Mexicans as firmly as had the Jefe Máximo (as Calles was branded) or don Porfirio (Díaz) before him. Yet other trappings of modernity had assuredly arrived. Everything was in place, it seemed, in this Mexico of "institutions and laws" to redeem the nation for its past sins against the working class.

Theory and Method

Redemption, however, would not be easily maintained, for reasons explained in the next chapter. The challenge of maintaining stability and control would preoccupy policy makers throughout the middle decades of the twentieth century, although the specter of a return to nineteenth-century-style factionalism and civil war never loomed large.

Kevin Middlebrook's concept of postrevolutionary authoritarianism helps us makes sense of the state's success in this regard by showing how a regime that emerged from a cataclysmic revolutionary scenario ultimately flourished by including mass actors in the ruling coalition, espousing an ideology linked to the revolutionary experience to legitimate its control, and working to develop a hegemonic party and a bureaucracy to serve its interventionist agenda. Once having cemented its control, the regime then set about looking for allies and found in the organized labor movement an easily mobilized mass actor. Subsequently the government oversaw the creation of an alliance with several of the nation's most powerful (though certainly not all) labor organizations, rooted in the reciprocal exchange of material and legal favors from the state and political loyalty from the unions.[29] Middlebrook's model, in essence, yielded the arrangement that I term *collaborationism* and understand herein as the historical tendency of the state and organized labor toward a symbiotic relationship that strengthens their respective positions by seeing legislation and other union-friendly conditions handed on down from high in exchange for wild, "spontaneous" shows of mass politics percolating up from below.[30]

The attention this study affords to episodes of mass politics that occurred over five decades after the end of revolutionary bloodshed reinforces the belief that hegemony is a perpetual process that is never truly concluded. Hegemony, to quote Florencia Mallon, is "a set of nested processes, constant and ongoing, through which power relations are contested, legitimated, and redefined at all levels of society." "Hegemony," she clarifies, "is hegemonic process: it can and does exist everywhere, at all times."[31] Mallon's thesis applies nicely to a political climate in post-1917 Mexico wherein a dialog of national redemption was "constant and ongoing" and wherein shows of mass politics surfaced "everywhere, at all times." That this version of political domination proved so durable and, arguably, successful testifies to the power of the nation-revolution metonym as well as the effective manipulation of the revolutionary legacy by the government and its civil wings. Although incidents of resistance and rebellion were unceasing during the period 1929–68, rifles and tanks were seldom needed to assert the will of the regime. One might surmise, then, that a process described by E. P. Thompson as "cultural hegemony" took root wherein elites who lacked iron-clad control over the lower classes effectively employed a system of "pomp and public ritual" to create consent and maintain hierarchy.

Episodes of mass politics that funneled mass actors onto jammed streets and plazas to conduct demonstrations, march in parades, hand out leaflets, or distribute charitable items in support of the ruling regime held powerful sway in determining the course of political life in twentieth-century Mexico. Popular mobilization was a class bargaining tactic that empowered both the political elites who benefited from the public displays of support and the unionists who filled public plazas with their voices, placards, and bodies. In this regard I mimic the position expressed by Michelle Dion, who considers how popular mobilization forced the creation of welfare programs that benefited the average Mexican. As she sees it, organized mass actors who mobilized in the twentieth century influenced the choice of the new executive. Once in power, he was hence reliant on this cross-class coalition and was likely to reward his supporters with new or reformed social programs. Dion's formula is applicable in the state-labor equation, and it is not difficult to imagine collaborationism in the following scenario: "In such instances, subordinate classes need not force the state's hand or be the most powerful member of the ruling coalition; to renegotiate the terms of regime support, they need only threaten to destabilize the coalition or its legitimacy through public mobilization or private withdrawals of support. At times, the demands of subordinate classes can be broad and extensive, and political elites may concede to only some of those demands. This is part of class bargaining, but the fact that political elites have conceded to any demands reveals that a bargain took place."[32]

All of this is not to say, however, that the tactics of popular mobilization employed by the regime and the organized labor sector did not yield diminishing returns as time passed. They did—and one may see evidence of reduced enthusiasm on the part of the mobilized across the 1950s, 1960s, and 1970s in the increasing reliance on *acarreados*, or "those carried-in," to pack the crowd and inflate the appearance of popular support for state or union goals. Despite this, mass politics formed a central part of the collaborationist bargain and produced benefits as much for state as union actors—a contention this book aspires to prove for the post-1968 period.

The reliance on mass politics and ritualized public spectacle by the regime to foment consent also suggests the presence of *dictablanda*, a kind of "soft authoritarianism" that substitutes "hard" force with "soft" measures that require some degree of public support. Essays in a 2014 volume edited by Paul Gillingham and Benjamin Smith internalize the paradigm on hegemonic process articulated by Mallon, Thompson, and others and effectively use the dictablanda framework to show that mid-twentieth-century Mexico was a polity in which people recognized the government's shortcomings but accepted them in exchange for patronage or other benefits. Debunking once-entrenched notions about Mexican authoritarianism and governance during a historically stable and prosperous period, the essays in the volume highlight the mechanics of negotiated rule in a nation that lacked the coercive power of strong states and relied on dictablanda as a practical necessity.[33] By including this concept in my own study I hope to further illustrate the tendency of the post-Tlatelolco state to appease organized labor via rhetoric, legislation, wage increases, political positions, bribes, and other forms of patronage.

Additionally, this is a study concerned with language. More than anything else, perhaps, it is an examination of the rhetorical "culture wars" waged, according to Christopher Clark and Wolfram Kaiser, to determine the supremacy of values and collective practices of modernity and fought using a range of instruments, but most commonly words and images. Invariably, say Clark and Kaiser, these conflicts unfold with the combatants voicing increasingly radicalized rhetoric, the purpose being on both sides to "define one's own cause and the values espoused in its support, and to define the 'enemy' in terms of the negation of those values." So extreme and all-pervasive can this process of rhetorical inflation be that it can come to constitute a kind of "virtual reality, quite independent of the complex and nuanced relationships" that actually exist between the opposing sides.[34]

Clark and Kaiser's framework, although developed using the Catholic and anticlerical milieu of nineteenth-century Europe, is easily applied to a post-1968 Mexican stage whereupon two well-defined civil sectors—*sindicalistas* (unionists) and *patrones* (employers)—did battle in the press, on workshop floors, and behind picket lines to win over the public and make allies in the Mexican regime. Analysis of *la prensa obrera* (the workers' press), composed of the publications of state-allied labor organizations, is crucial in this regard, for it conveys an editorial alliance with the government that promoted mutually shared goals and belied the independent current that frequently ran through a union's membership. This project also listens to the voices of the disenchanted segments of the workers' movement by reviewing magazines that diverged from the union journals, which tended to be strongly in favor of state positions and policies. Use of daily newspapers of all political stripes is similarly central to this work, both for and in spite of the heavy doses of subjectivity they contained.

Finally, this study uses unpublished archival records to deduce the government's objectives and construct a general chronology of its efforts to monitor and, on occasion, repress unsanctioned labor activity. Thousands of reports produced by agents of the General Directorate of Political and Social Investigations, one of the two major domestic intelligence bureaucracies that operated in Mexico in the late 1960s and 1970s, inform this analysis, closely chronicling the movements of agents as they observed union assemblies and even infiltrated union halls in their missions to root out subversion and preserve state security. Moreover, hundreds of labor suits and collective contracts filed with the labor ministry and not hitherto reviewed are considered in this book, in the process demonstrating how the New Federal Labor Law of 1970 empowered workers to assert newly acquired rights on an individual and collective level.

Structure and Style

The following chapters narrate a story of sin and redemption. Chapter 1 demonstrates the salience of the modern nation's "original sin," the massacre of Tlatelolco, on the ensuing relationship between the state and organized labor. This discussion shows how unionists' opposition to the student movement and their support for the government's repressive actions revived a dialogue of collaborationism that bolstered their position and yielded the New Federal Labor Law of 1970—a landmark piece of legislation that shaped future state, organized labor, and business relations. Chapters 2 and 3 continue the theme of redemption, focusing on the presidential campaign waged by Luis Echeverría, the death of Lázaro Cárdenas, and government measures to increase state control over the oil, copper, and electrical power industries as processes that further restored historical bonds with workers and helped the government regain legitimacy it had lost from prolonged social unrest.

Chapters 4 and 5 analyze alterations made to the revolutionary corpus and the discontent these changes provoked. Chapter 4 shows how revolutionary-era conceptions of class, collectivism, and paternalism returned to official and popular discourse and altered the terms of tripartite relations after Tlatelolco. Focusing on the expansion of federal social services, this chapter reveals that labor leaders supported an invigorated paterfamilias at the head of the corporatist structure, believing it to be an asset that increased their leverage in negotiations with employers. Chapter 5 uses case studies in Monterrey to reveal the ferocity of labor conflict in that hub of industry and supports the notion that business owners were useful rhetorical adversaries in the regime's quest for redemption.

Chapter 6 demonstrates how the New Federal Labor Law of 1970 altered basic terms of workplace relations by expanding the right to strike. Reforms in the new labor code pertaining to employers' health and safety requirements are also scrutinized, as are the findings of federal labor authorities that ruled on personal indemnification and unlawful termination suits. Following this the chapter considers the power of the collective contract in contemporaneous labor relations, testing both employers' and labor leaders' assertions that workers were the darlings of a reinvigorated revolutionary regime. Chapters 7 and 8 continue this discussion of rhetoric versus reality, assessing how mass actions carried out by female unionists and rogue electrical workers to free themselves from "*charro*" control, while unsuccessful, represented an insurgency that tested the fabric of collaborationism and weakened the hegemony of the regime at large.

Finally, chapter 9, the conclusion, and the epilogue end the narrative on the themes of tribulation, death, and resurrection. Taken together, chapter 9 and the conclusion describe the perilous "populist" path trodden by Luis Echeverría during his late presidency to salvage his and his government's reputations, ultimately proving that despite the real economic decline endured by the working class in those years the campaign waged by the Mexican state after 1968 largely appeased organized labor and redeemed its revolutionary credentials with that pivotal sector. Subsequent history recounted in the epilogue, however, shows how revolutionary ideals were reinforced, then abruptly abandoned by succeeding presidential administrations, casting doubt on whether the brand of collaborationism restored after Tlatelolco brought any real and permanent benefit to its actors. Resurrected once again in 2012 with its recapture of the presidency, the present Institutional Revolutionary Party (PRI) regime's quest to redeem the Mexican Revolution, one might surmise, is as alive today as it was in the post-1968 period.

CHAPTER I

Tlatelolco!

The Need for Revolutionary Redemption

The year 1968 was one of opportunities and challenges for the Mexican state. While some in government busied themselves with preparations for the games of the Nineteenth Olympiad, to commence on October 12, others focused on diffusing unrest that had festered on the nation's campuses and was threatening to spread to the streets. In the interest of preserving civil order and conveying an image of stability in Mexico, authorities opted to confront dissent firmly. Fearing that outsiders would view political agitation as evidence of institutional weakness, officials more often chose a hard line over compromise in their dealings with protesters. Prolonged political agitation by student groups that summer moved the government, and particularly Secretary of Internal Affairs Luis Echeverría, who was charged with preserving domestic security, toward increasingly severe action as the start of the Olympics approached. Relations between the state and student groups grew worse after July 22, when street clashes first broke out between police and rioters. Subsequent confrontations between Mexico City student groups and military and police elements on July 26, 27, and 29 were violent and resulted in several deaths, numerous injuries, and the imprisonment of student demonstrators. Echeverría sought to pacify the situation and proposed on August 22 a closed-door dialogue with leaders of the movement. The National Strike Committee rejected his proposal, demanding that talks be public and conducted with the media present.

The extent of the movement's size and strength was put on full display on August 27 in a four-hundred-thousand-person demonstration that dominated the capital's most visible thoroughfares. Protesters assembled at the National Anthropology Museum and at about 4:40 p.m. began their march along Paseo de la Reforma toward the city center, carrying banners that detailed their cause. Upon arrival at the Plaza de la Constitución, the gargantuan central square of Mexico City better known as the Zócalo, the marching mass was joined by some fifteen thousand youths who awaited them. Some who entered the adjoining Metropolitan Cathedral negotiated with the parish priest, Jesús Pérez, who gave them permission to ring the church's bells at 6:50 p.m. and turned the façade lights on to illuminate the plaza for their proceedings, which were certain to last through the night. At about 7:20 p.m., when the rear guard of the march had still not departed from the museum, a group of marchers hoisted up the plaza's flagpole a *bandera rojinegra*, the red-and-black flag of protest and the international symbol of workers' militancy.

With the flag raised the meeting was convened and a poem by Isaías Rojas, one of the more than eighty students then confined in Lecumberri, Mexico City's downtown penitentiary, was read to set the tone for the evening. Near the end of the meeting the multitude voted to demand that a dialogue be held on September 1, in the Zócalo and under the control of the student brigades, which planned to remain stationed there until then. Later that evening a group of about two hundred departed the plaza on foot en route to Lecumberri, intent upon freeing their comrades confined in the nearby prison. Matched up against military tanks and other armed vehicles, the liberating force was turned away by about 11:20 p.m. Security personnel who repelled unarmed protestors at Lecumberri were then dispatched to the Zócalo, where they would be stationed for the night. By 1:15 a.m. the overwhelming military force, composed of two infantry battalions, twelve armored cars, four fire trucks, about two hundred police cars, and four troops of transit police, succeeded in largely vacating the plaza. Intelligence briefs produced by the General Directorate of Political and Social Investigations throughout the evening report that "students were not only dislodged, but also pursued along the streets of the historical center."

With the plaza largely empty and the student threat mostly neutralized, government attention turned to lowering the bandera rojinegra, a symbol the authorities viewed as an act of provocation. At about 10:00 a.m. Federal District workers were mobilized to remove the "seditious" and "communist" flag from the nation's most sacred civil space. Although city workers were heckled with cries of "acarreados" and "sheep" by the small contingent of demonstrators who stilled milled about in the plaza, they succeeded in lowering the flag without incident. Harder-line measures ensued, nevertheless, and by morning's end all remaining demonstrators were removed from the plaza—some pursued through downtown streets by soldiers who were met with bottles, flowerpots, and other objects residents hurled at them. In some cases soldiers responded with gunfire, as bullet holes in hotel walls still attest.[1]

Following the events of August 27–28, the repression of the student brigades and the mainstream press's hostility toward the student movement increased substantially. Days later, while giving the annual presidential address on September 1, President Gustavo Díaz Ordaz conveyed his opinion that while freedom of expression was guaranteed in Mexico, political dissent was unwise because it threatened the nation's stability. Speaking to critics on all sides, Díaz Ordaz declared, "We have been so tolerant that we have been criticized for our excessive leniency, but there is a limit to everything, and the irremediable violations of law and order that have occurred recently before the very eyes of the entire nation cannot be allowed to continue."[2] Those unsympathetic to the student cause applauded; their president had expressed a firm position at long last. Members of the National Strike Committee, on the other hand, strongly objected. They considered the president's message scolding and a blatant threat.

Protest continued in the following month, emboldened by the president's warning. On September 17 a National Strike Committee missive asserted that the movement, which was originally raised to protest the unlawful incursion of government forces in the nation's university life, had evolved into an authentic and popular social struggle waged to reestablish rights guaranteed by the Mexican Constitution. With this language, federal authorities deemed the student challenge too dangerous to tolerate less than one month before the eyes of the world would be fixed upon Mexico.

The following day, September 18, soldiers invaded Ciudad Universitaria, home of the National Autonomous University of Mexico (UNAM) and the national command center of student activism. Dozens of students, professors, and university employees were detained in actions that drew even the ire of some *priístas* (members of the PRI) who sympathized with the protests voiced by the university's rector, Javier Barros Sierra. The government's aggressive actions and blatant violation of the constitutional guarantee of university autonomy convinced Barros Sierra that his position was no longer tenable. On September 22 he announced plans to resign but days later was convinced by university leaders to rescind his resignation. On September 24 violent street clashes waged between students and soldiers left several dead and wounded on the streets of the northern Mexico City neighborhood of Santo Tomás. These actions propelled military forces to occupy the nearby installations of the National Polytechnic Institute. More violence ensued on campus and students and faculty were detained en masse. Once again, the principle of university autonomy was violated and the propensity of the government to violently quash dissent confirmed its repressive nature.

Mexican soldiers left Ciudad Universitaria on October 1 after thirteen days of occupation. In a spirit of conciliation, National Strike Committee leaders were asked to call an end to the student strikes at UNAM, the National Polytechnic Institute, and other schools and return to classes. They rejected these pleas and instead planned a meeting for the afternoon of the following day, October 2, to be held in the Plaza de las Tres Culturas, a public square in the downtown district of Tlatelolco that derived its name from the convergence of ancient Aztec ruins, a colonial Spanish church, and modern, Mexican-era apartment buildings that abutted it. National Strike Committee representatives met with Barros Sierra and government emissaries at the rector's home at ten that morning to try to set terms for negotiation. They asked specifically for the immediate withdrawal of troops from university facilities, the cessation of violence, and liberty for all those apprehended during the army's occupation of UNAM. Their demands were not accepted. Student organizers then turned their attention to the demonstration planned for later that day.

The following chronology of the events that occurred at Tlatelolco on October 2, 1968, is based on a summary of eyewitness accounts. By 5:15 p.m. a large gathering had assembled in the Plaza de las Tres Culturas. National Strike Committee members could view the mass of people from the terrace of a third-floor apartment in the Chihuahua residential building, which overlooked the plaza. The size of the crowd was estimated at between ten and twenty thousand men, women, and children, with dozens of undercover agents sprinkled among them. Speakers addressed the assembly, but their words were drowned out by the sounds of helicopters that flew overhead. At around 6:15 p.m. a number of army units arrived at the plaza, ostensibly to prevent demonstrators from entering a nearby building that was known to hold political prisoners. Flares appeared in the sky. Everyone looked up. Suddenly, without warning, soldiers advanced on the crowd. Shooting began. The chaos of the scene made it difficult to locate where the first shots came from, though eyewitnesses later confirmed that they originated from military weapons. All hell broke loose in the moments that followed. The crowd scrambled in terror as machine gun and rifle fire zoomed in all directions. Many noticed, some felt, the presence of snipers who were stationed in upper-level apartments and rained gunfire down on the unsuspecting mob. The identity of the snipers is still a controversial question. According to government reports the gunmen were student agitators who served to provoke the military into an armed confrontation. Those supportive of the students' cause argued quite the contrary, that the gunmen were army sharpshooters ordered to incite violence by randomly targeting demonstrators. The bloody scene witnessed in the plaza extended into the crowded halls and tiny apartments of nearby housing units, where several combatants were killed in shoot-outs with military personnel. The terrible confrontation lasted until the dawn of October 3.[3]

The balance of the events of October 2–3, 1968, remains a point of heated contention. Undoubtedly hundreds of demonstrators were detained at Tlatelolco by federal and municipal forces that formed the Olympia Battalion, organized only months earlier. A more polemical topic is the number of casualties that resulted from the events of that afternoon and evening. Officially, the Secretariat of Internal Affairs reported thirty-nine civilian and two military deaths. Forty-one total fatalities is a significant death toll and one that certainly qualifies the events of Tlatelolco as a massacre. Yet the figure of 39 greatly contrasts with that of 325 civilians that government opponents alleged were killed. The exact total remains unknown to this day, but the great disparity in the evaluations of the size and scope of the events is crucial in contextualizing the difference in understanding about their impact. In the days that followed, the Díaz Ordaz government resorted to old habits and blamed the confrontation on provocation by communist youth groups. Talk was heard about a temporary suspension of individual liberties, but no such drastic action could be taken on the eve of Olympic festivities. The student representatives, at least those who remained alive and unconfined, were shell-shocked and scared. Some regrouped in the days that followed and announced on October 9 an "Olympic Truce" to be observed for the two-week duration of the games. It was in this climate of violence, fear, and shock that the Mexico City "Olympiad of Peace" was convened by President Díaz Ordaz on October 12, 1968.

The role of organized workers in the events described above is difficult to discern at first glance. Nonetheless, this book views the massacre perpetrated on October 2–3, 1968, as the fulcrum upon which relations between the state and organized labor in Mexico subsequently hinged. The sequence of events that culminated at Tlatelolco represented a decisive moment that altered the nation's modern political culture. Student protests called into question the revolutionary credentials of the Mexican state and its legitimacy as rightful heir to that legacy, but those protests did not occur in a vacuum. Political reform implemented after Tlatelolco also conveyed the Mexican state's desire to counter deeper-seated threats to its authority that emanated from other societal sectors, most importantly from organized workers who had militated at heightened levels since the late 1950s. The seeds of unionists' discontent that would grow and flower simultaneously with the budding of student activism in the late 1960s are outlined forthwith.

Economic and Social Decline during the Midcentury "Miracle"

Mexico witnessed extraordinary economic expansion in the post–World War II decades, sustaining gross domestic product growth rates averaging 6 percent annually during the so-called Mexican Miracle from 1941 to 1980.[4] To unionists, this period of unprecedented growth owed to the tripartite labor system established by Article 123 and perfected during the Cárdenas presidency (1934–40). In this arrangement workers felt central to the processes of development and saw their salaries rise concomitantly with corporate profits while reaping social benefits. The role of organized labor in the nation's industrialization process was thus understood as determinant, and union leaders ensured workers that their priorities were at the top of the federal agenda.[5]

To their dismay, however, union leaders saw their sector's status relative to capital decline as the Mexican Miracle reached full maturity in the 1950s. Economists trace this loss of standing directly to the state's adoption of import substitution industrialization, an economic strategy that aims to reduce a nation's foreign dependency by increasing its production of industrialized products but often requires the kind of massive capitalization not achievable domestically. The implementation of import substitution industrialization, although it oriented the state toward greater intervention in the economy, kept Mexican development dependent on foreign capital. Recognizing their advantages, domestic and foreign investors negotiated favorable terms that put little pressure on them to accommodate the demands of labor. Unprecedented economic growth rates were touted, while rising inequities between corporate earnings and workers' salaries were masked. Labor leaders told workers to celebrate the efforts of their unions, which continued to win wage increases and other economic incentives, but worker joy rang hollow as real wages fell and purchasing power plummeted. Figures endorsed by the Fondo de Cultura Económica demonstrate that the real average daily wage (adjusted for inflation) attained by the Mexican worker during the period 1954–63 paled in comparison to what was earned by those working a decade earlier. Workers' daily wages reached a nadir of just 18.86 pesos in 1956, though the average figure otherwise hovered between 44.61 (in 1955) and 57.98 (1962) during the decade referenced above.[6] Men and women feeling the pain of their declining economic status gradually became conscious of their shared malaise, and by the late 1950s a discourse pervaded shop floors alleging the government's preference for employers over workers. The fiscal inadequacy of the midcentury state also compounded problems, it appeared, as Mexico accrued less federal tax revenue than any other Latin American nation because of a regressive tax code, an insufficient collection infrastructure, and frequent tax strikes. The ensuing lack of revenue, concludes Benjamin Smith, reduced the coercive and co-optive powers of the state and made *dictablanda*—that is, the exertion of soft power—a practical necessity for the government in its dealings with increasingly wealthy employers.[7] Worker chatter about the government's (and their unions') coziness with business threatened the survival of the collaborationist norm that had guided relations between the state and organized labor since the 1920s. Under a state system that derived authority directly from its perceived legitimacy as inheritor of a revolutionary legacy, such doubts threatened the hegemony of the state and official party.[8]

In the decade that preceded the tumult of 1968 unionized workers in diverse sectors demanded better wages; safety, medical, and housing provisions; and the right to elect union leaders. Sometimes their efforts were rewarded. Relative worker income rose markedly after 1961, though typically their voices were silenced; in contrast to the days of Cardenismo, the percentage of strike petitions approved at the federal level reached historical lows during the presidential periods 1958–64 and 1964–70, phenomena elaborated upon later in this chapter. The resurgence of popular labor unrest, and the government's quashing of it, hinted at the contradictions inherent in the state's development strategies and cancelled the relative labor peace that had characterized the prior two decades. Worker militancy, in contrast to student activism, posed a real threat that might topple the regime. By the late 1960s the state was required to respond. It was organized workers, therefore, the sector most ascribed with historical symbolism and most capable of destabilizing the regime, that became the chief target of state rhetoric and the primary beneficiary of reform after Tlatelolco. It would be the nation's organized workers, therefore, who would be assigned the most rigorous curriculum on revolutionary redemption. Fortunately for them, they had a capable instructor.

Fidel Velázquez and the Birth of Conservative Nationalism

No one is more essential to the tale of state-organized labor collaborationism in twentieth-century Mexico than Fidel Velázquez, a man who after first taking control of the CTM in 1941 controlled the nation's most important labor organization for fifty-four of the next fifty-seven years. Neither is anyone more controversial. A tireless advocate for and redeemer of Mexico's working class to some, Velázquez is remembered as an enemy of it by others, the kind of man whose death on June 21, 1997, provoked scathing words in his obituaries, like "Fidel Velázquez, head of the CTM, did more than any other single individual to keep Mexican workers in a position of subordination to the Mexican government, the PRI and the employers."[9] The facts of his upbringing, his politicization, and his rise to the summit of the Mexican labor bureaucracy are inextricable from the story of collaborationism, conflict, and redemption told herein.

Fidel Velázquez Sánchez was born on May 12, 1900, in San Pedro Azcapotzaltongo (today Nicolás Romero), State of Mexico. He was the fifth of seventeen children born to Gregorio Velázquez and Herlinda Sánchez, seven of whom died as children. Fidel's father, Gregorio, was the administrator of a small ranch and was one of the most respected men of the village, taking the post of municipal president on several occasions.

Young Fidel was put to work at an early age cutting alfalfa and tending to the family's five cows. He was educated only until the end of primary school. "The rest," he once remarked, he "learned from life." He lived this way until the age of fourteen, when the violence of the Revolution forced his family to flee their home for the capital in search of safety. The family's stay in Mexico City did not last long, for Gregorio, a "man of the field," was not accustomed to city life and quickly moved the family to Tlaxcala and later Puebla when he found work on a timber ranch. There Fidel worked alongside his father as a machine assistant until Gregorio was killed in 1918 in the crossfire of renewed violence that pitted forces loyal to Carranza, then the Mexican president, against those loyal to Obregón, who was formerly Carranza's top general and had taken up arms against his one-time patron.[10]

With the death of his father, Velázquez, who was injured in the same skirmish, returned to the capital and took a job at a milk factory in the neighborhood of Azcapotzalco, which required him to deliver milk to residents by mule. It was in this humble position that young Fidel attended Casa meetings and first immersed himself in the world of working-class syndicalism. In 1921 he voiced anarcho-syndicalist rhetoric sprung straight from the already-defunct Casa's handbook in a failed attempt to organized the factory's eight hundred workers into a company union. He learned from his failure, and by 1923 he had already eschewed radicalism in favor of an approach that touted the advantages that workers could garner through a government alliance. His unionization efforts this time brought his dismissal from the company, although his real political clout convinced the owners to rehire him shortly thereafter. After regaining his job, Fidel set about organizing the Union of Dairy Industry Workers, a company union with the propitious acronym UTIL, meaning "useful." By leading UTIL, he became its union representative in the larger Federation of Federal District Workers' Unions (FSTDF), then affiliated with the CROM. From that moment onward he understood that the strength of his group and his continuity at the head of it depended upon government support. It was then, according to José Luis Trueba Lara, that Fidel Velázquez began to learn the secrets of Morones, the tricks of power that would enable him and the workers he led to mutually prosper with the government.[11]

The implication of Morones in the 1928 assassination of Obregón rocked the halls of the labor bureaucracy and sent his subordinates scurrying to distance themselves from their disgraced leader. In February 1929 a group of five led by Velázquez published a manifesto entitled "Why we separated from the CROM" wherein they launched various charges at Morones and hurled the epithet of "DINOSAUR!!" at him because of his long reign at the head of the organization. Morones responded to the attack on April 30, 1929, defiantly contending that "the CROM," having "all the characteristics of a corpulent oak, of strong and large roots and a gigantic trunk," was a tree from which "five miserable worms" emerged. One supporter, Luiz Araiza, disagreed with the characterization made by Morones. These "worms," Araiza retorted to Morones, were not traitors but *cinco lobitos*, or "five little wolves" that "soon, very soon, were going to eat all the hens in your corral." Thus were born the five little wolves, with Velázquez dubbed the "prodigal little wolf" for leading the break with Morones.[12] Paradoxically, all of the five little wolves were of working-class origin except Velázquez, who originated in the peasant class.

The defection of the Velázquez junta likely did not rankle Morones too much initially. The defecting twelve unions were relatively insignificant, as they were, aside from Velázquez's dairy workers, mere trolley car operators, soft drink workers, and workers of the Panteón Español—an elite cemetery located in Mexico City. Much more damaging to the CROM than the loss of these minor unions were the spots on the newly formed Federal Conciliation and Arbitration Board given to Velázquez and the others by President Emilio Portes Gil, who was greatly appreciative of their break with Morones. From these positions the five little wolves exerted great influence in determining the legality of strikes and in the drafting of the 1931 Federal Labor Law. Moreover, each little wolf used his position to effectively recruit members and unionize workers from diverse industries.[13] Velázquez capitalized on his post most of all, using it as a platform to advocate for positions that appealed to workers and *patrones* alike, including the institution of shorter days and wage-salary reductions to create new jobs. Velázquez also pushed for the creation of a national labor confederation, a goal that when realized in 1933 via the birth of the Federal District Chamber of Labor and its insertion into the National Revolutionary Party signaled his arrival as a national-level politician.

Despite the status of Lombardo as the intellectual author of the CTM, the dominant figure in the history of the organization was Velázquez. While serving as the CTM's secretary of organization from 1936 to 1941, Velázquez used that crucial post to build a network of state and regional federations loyal to him. Backed by President Ávila Camacho, Velázquez won the election and succeeded Lombardo as CTM secretary general for the first time in March 1941. He ran for reelection in 1944, won, and upon resuming office violated the basic postrevolutionary tenet of no reelection, just the first of nine times he would do so. He held the mantle of leadership until 1947, when he was replaced by Fernando Amilpa y Rivera, an occasional rival of Velázquez but someone ultimately committed to maintaining a close state-CTM alliance. Returned to power in 1950, Velázquez would never again relinquish control, winning reelection eight more times and holding the secretary general position consistently from 1950 until his death in 1997.[14]

The Velázquez CTM, in other words, the post-1941 CTM, jettisoned the brand of collaborationism that typified the Cárdenas-Lombardo years. The era of revolutionary unionism thus appeared an interregnum in the story of postrevolutionary state-labor relations, for organized labor had not prior to 1934, and would not after 1940, enjoy the level of autonomy it maintained during those years, while still remaining politically potent. A more pliant labor bureaucracy emerged after 1940, but not because of personal weakness on the part of its leader. Velázquez was an arch pragmatist who developed his own brand of politics by personally observing the fate that befell others who butted heads with the revolutionary elite. He witnessed the terrific crash of Morones when he challenged Calles, who commanded Mexico under the guise of the Portes Gil administration, and he stood nearby as Lombardo embraced communism and regretted the CTM's ever-increasing subordination to the state, thus alienating himself from party and union leaders. These were firsthand lessons that instilled in Velázquez an ideology appropriately described as conservative nationalism, a political strategy that committed him to realizing the Revolution's egalitarian goals within the established order and made him deeply loyal to the "party of the revolution."[15]

As such Velázquez was hesitant to challenge presidential administrations and was an avowed anticommunist. His loyalty paid dividends for the CTM via seats for its members in the PRI, the Mexican Congress, federal and local conciliation and arbitration boards, and a bevy of other political posts. These seats, accurately referred to "positions" because they were not won in elections, were in effect political subsidies paid to the CTM for its loyalty to the ruling regime. Subsidies also came in the form of hard currency. State-allied labor organizations in twentieth-century Mexico were tied both financially and politically to the government. The CTM, like the CROM before it, was formed initially of small company- and plant-level unions organized into heterogeneous state and regional federations. This decentralization severely hindered its capacity for mobilization when it was forced to compete against more powerful unions of oil, railway, and electrical workers. Substantial funds were required to connect distant networks of workers, and union dues, when they were actually collected, proved woefully insufficient. For the CTM to stay potent and keep its leverage over unionists in the most powerful sectors, outside support was necessary. Thus emerged as early as 1936 a tight financial bond between the Mexican state and the CTM, among other state-allied labor confederations and unions. The state's subsidization of this portion of the organized workers' movement increased with time, and although exact numbers are impossible to obtain, some observers estimated that by the 1970s direct government financial subsidies to the CTM ranged from 500,000 to several million pesos annually.[16]

The positions and monies given to unions from the state gave them great bargaining power but kept them dependent on a government benefactor. The Mexican state's sponsorship of the labor bureaucracy, however, was not a sign of its benevolence; political and financial subsidies were part of a collaborationist bargain that benefited both sides of the arrangement.

The government's immense "investment" in the CTM greatly improved the prospects of its social and industrial development goals. The dramatic change in its developmental direction after 1941 could have been derailed had an unwilling labor bureaucracy opposed it. Instead the Velázquez CTM supported President Ávila Camacho's industrialization program wholeheartedly despite the ways it tightened procedural requirements for strike petitions and modified federal labor law to limit workers' right to strike. For its loyalty the CTM was rewarded with thirty-two seats in Congress and received funds badly needed to finance the confederation's nationwide operations.[17]

Conservative nationalism was in vogue by the early 1940s and in June 1942 Mexico's most important labor organizations, including the CTM, CROM, Confederación General de Trabajadores, and Mexican Electricians' Union affirmed that strategy by pledging to avoid strikes, limit wage demands, and increase productivity during the wartime emergency. The details of this agreement, called the Worker Unity Pact, flew in the face of the most basic ideals of direct action and further alienated the radical elements that remained in the labor bureaucracy. Ironically, the number of legally recognized strikes in the federal-jurisdiction industries rose sharply in 1943 and 1944, largely due to wartime inflation and the imposition of restrictions on collective actions that reduced workers' efficacy in bargaining with employers.[18] Nonetheless, conservative nationalism was firmly entrenched by this point and new shows of state-labor collaboration were forthcoming. The Industrial Labor Pact reached in 1945 between the CTM and the National Chamber of Manufacturing Industries declared labor and capital's shared goals of avoiding strikes, restraining inflation, and attracting foreign investment. Loudly assailed by Lombardo, who was prone to histrionics when decrying organized labor's capitulation to business, the Industrial Labor Pact proved that national priorities had changed and that the regime of the Revolution was more committed to the cause of industrial development than it was to addressing social issues.[19] In this change of focus, it similarly appeared, the Mexican state had a powerful but amenable labor partner to work with.

Charrismo and the Railway Workers' Challenge

The conservative nationalism shown by the labor bureaucracy in the 1940s consolidated the labor establishment of the era into the form that it would maintain in subsequent decades. Pragmatic collaboration was henceforth the norm, though its durability continued to be tested— and often on the nation's iron rails. In a real sense postrevolutionary state-labor collaborationism was forged on Mexico's railroads, for it was a conflict among *ferrocarrileros*, or railway workers, in 1927 that moved Calles to create the JFCAs and thus establish federal jurisdiction in resolving workplace conflicts in that crucial industry. Similarly, it was the resolution of another melee among railway workers nearly two decades later that ushered in near complete government control over that industry's workforce.

The nation's most important railroad company, Ferrocarriles Nacionales de México, was nationalized in 1937, although workplace conflict continued between members of the Mexican Railway Workers' Union (STFRM) and state-appointed administrators who ran the system. Worker militancy inside a state-owned industry put the CTM, with which the STFRM was affiliated, in an awkward position. Ideological tension inside the confederation reached a boiling point by January 1947, with STFRM members clamoring for direct action and resumed radicalism inside the organized workers' movement as a whole. The radical-moderate division pushed the STFRM to secede from the CTM in late February. Elections held the following month to choose CTM leadership drew the ire of the STFRM representatives, and for good reason; prior to the election, CTM leaders had manipulated voting procedures so that each member union of the CTM was afforded one vote, thus reversing the statutory requirement that affiliated unions' accredited votes equaled their total membership. The electoral strength of large national unions like the STFRM hence was greatly diminished; the importance of the small but numerous company- and plant-level unions that formed the Velázquez faction's base of support, on the other hand, was enhanced. In this way Velázquez was able to guarantee the victory of the moderates' preferred candidate, Fernando Amilpa, and the loss of the radicals' choice, STFRM secretary general José Luis Gómez Z.

The CTM under Amilpa continued the collaborationist course set by Velázquez and even tightened relations with the government by requiring that all CTM members join the official party (renamed the PRI in 1946) or face expulsion from their unions. Reformed rhetoric further proved the CTM's change in direction. "For a Classless Society," the CTM's official motto since its inception in 1936, was changed to "For the Emancipation of Mexico," a slogan that removed the class-based component from its mission and better expressed its purpose to aid in the industrialization of the nation and reduce its dependence on imported goods.[20] Opponents of the Amilpa-Velázquez faction did not take these changes lying down. Led by Gómez Z., a mass of organized workers coalesced into the Coalition of Worker and Peasant Organizations, which by mid-1948 boasted over eight hundred thousand members and rivaled the CTM as the most important labor organization in the country.[21]

The status of the new coalition as a viable alternative to the CTM, however, was challenged by internal divisions within its most important union—the STFRM—and the tenuous control Gómez Z. had over the union's ninety thousand members. Additionally, because the coalition swam against the current of the labor establishment, it was forced to operate according to rules set by its adversaries in the Secretariat of Labor and Social Welfare (STPS), the federal labor ministry. An election was held for control of the STFRM in which Jesús Díaz de León, the state's preferred man, was declared the unofficial winner. Workers were outraged and resisted, though Díaz de León seized control of union offices with the help of STPS allies. Díaz de León then set about altering internal procedures in ways that consolidated decision-making power within the union in his own hands. Labor opponents and radicals were purged from the STFRM, some arrested. He waged a vicious smear campaign against Gómez Z. that tarnished his reputation with the union's rank and file. Statutes passed in September 1949 altered the process of electing union leaders from a direct format into an indirect one in which union members voted only for their corresponding local and national representatives. Moreover, the tradition of secret balloting that had been in place in Mexico since the union's founding in 1933 was replaced with open balloting, a system wherein union members voted on ballots they were required to sign.

Together, Díaz de León's actions were referred to as the *charrazo* in reference to his enthusiasm for Mexican popular rodeos and horsemanship (*charrería*). Díaz de León hence formed the prototype for subsequent *charros*, a term that literally means "dudes" or "cowboys" but in the context of organized labor connotes a union boss who is in the service of the state and is open to bribes or other forms of inducement. The practical consequences of the charrazo for the once famously democratic union ensured that the new political order rested on state power. Naturally, the new state-allied version of the STFRM became a reliable supporter of the PRI and after 1952 saw its top officials receive coveted political posts while simultaneously directing the union.[22] Overall, the charrazo resulted in the STFRM becoming a top-down and undemocratic union similar to thousands of other run-of-the-mill outfits that formed the CTM in the 1950s.

By 1950 the CTM's place at the pinnacle of the organized labor movement in Mexico was undisputed, though other national confederations arose (some sponsored by the state itself) to challenge its supremacy.[23] Boasting a membership of 1.6 million workers—70 to 90 percent of all the nation's unionized workers, according to one estimate—grouped into some forty-two hundred unions, the CTM roll featured twenty-one national unions, including the STFRM, the Mexican Telephone Workers' Union, and the Mexican Petroleum Workers' Union (which rejoined the confederation in 1954). The inclusion of these unions on the CTM's rolls gave it a new presence in heavy industrial sectors in addition to its traditional bastion of support in the light manufacturing, communication, tourism, and entertainment sectors.[24] With the CTM guiding the movements of so much of the nation's workforce, episodes of labor agitation sharply declined and an average of only 108 strikes were witnessed annually during the six-year presidential administration of Miguel Alemán (1946–52), and 248 during the term of Adolfo Ruiz Cortines (1952–58).

Such numbers represented a significant drop when compared to those seen during the Cárdenas and Ávila Camacho administrations, which saw 478 (1934–40) and 387 (1940–46) strikes annually, respectively.[25] Reduced worker activism in the postwar era, however, stemmed from more than CTM domination; government authorities exercised their power to intervene in union affairs and presided over conciliation and arbitration boards in ways that diffused potential labor conflicts before they could reach the strike stage. These legitimate functions on the part of state officials sometimes complemented extralegal actions they took to employ strikebreakers to discourage antiestablishment positions and generally keep unions "in line."[26]

Wartime unity pacts, the co-optation of historically independent unions of railroad and petroleum workers, and the ascendancy of the CTM after World War II yielded a labor serenity difficult to sustain. Worker activism rates showed a sharp uptick during the presidency of Adolfo López Mateos, spiking to an average of 403 strikes annually during the years 1958–64. Most workers of the time mobilized against spiraling inflation, though many others protested the repressive and undemocratic nature of the labor bureaucracy that ruled their working lives. Railway workers once again led this fight, for it was they who had been most trammeled by the leaders of organized labor. The charrazo of the late 1940s had enraged this most radical segment of the trade union movement then, and many held a grudge.

By 1958 the railroad industry's rank and file clamored that they were grossly underpaid. This gripe further rankled the average railway workers, who also believed that their union officials did not act with their best interests in mind.[27] An ad-hoc commission to address these issues was formed in June 1958, and Demetrio Vallejo, a well-known union activist from Oaxaca and former member of the Mexican Communist Party, was elected to lead it. Vallejo assailed STFRM leadership and demanded the ouster of charros he claimed had been bought by Ferrocarriles Nacionales de Mexico, the state-owned railroad company. Vallejo's position garnered wide support, and when a demand for a salary increase of 350 pesos per month was not met by the company, workers began a series of escalating strikes, beginning with a partial "sit-down" on June 26 and culminating with a general strike on June 28, which found the support of unionized petroleum workers, teachers, and students across the nation. The general strike caught the attention of President Ruiz Cortines, who succeeded in having the strike lifted that same day by coaxing the opposing sides to agree to a 215-peso-per-month salary increase.

The salary increase abated tension temporarily, but the vexing question of union governance remained. On July 12 STFRM members held a special convention and elected Vallejo secretary general of the union. The vote was not accepted by the STPS, which had the sole legal authority to certify union elections. Dismayed but not disheartened, workers called for a strike on July 31 in defiance of the labor ministry's ruling. The strike lasted two hours and again provoked solidarity strikes by sympathetic unionists. Subsequent harassment and intimidation failed to sway the workers' from their position, forcing the government to agree to hold new elections for the union's leadership position. On August 6 the workers' choice was indisputable; Vallejo won in a landslide.[28]

Vallejo's tenure as head of the union was destined to be rocky, as he was committed to rooting out *charrismo*, specifically the co-optation of union leaders by state and company officials in the union's upper echelons. Furthermore, Vallejo vowed to pressure the company to further increase wages and provide housing and medical benefits to railway families. Two strategies that Vallejo proposed to raise revenue were raising passenger rates and terminating subsidies given by the state to U.S. mining and metal companies. Hearing their demands ignored, STFRM members resumed militancy in March of the following year, 1959. A March 25 strike moved first-year president Adolfo López Mateos to order the military and police in to break up strike activities with tear gas and clubs. Approximately ten thousand workers were fired and eight hundred prisoners taken, many on the grounds that they were communist agitators.[29]

The harsh repression and arrest of striking workers in August 1959 effectively ended the railway workers' challenge to the labor establishment. Of those arrested, Vallejo was among the most harshly punished, as he was convicted of violating Article 145 of the penal code—the infamous

Law of Social Dissolution—and sentenced to eleven years and four months in prison. With the defeat of the railroad worker insurrection the primary grassroots threat to the collaborationist norm in state-labor relations was stamped out. Subsequent years saw a further crystallization of this dynamic into the institutional norm, though a rebellious streak continued to burn in the chests of unionized workers. Into the 1960s the CTM held its place at the head of the labor bureaucracy, and federal and local conciliation and arbitration boards discouraged workers from undertaking strike actions in most instances. The resurgence of worker activism seen during the López Mateos administration thus appeared to be an anomaly by the latter part of the decade, as only 124 strikes were waged annually during a Díaz Ordaz administration (1964–70) that saw the government curb worker militancy by rejecting strike petitions at historic levels and controlling their unions via their near-total dependence on the labor ministry for funding and other political subsidies.[30]

Another crucial development during this period was the formation of the Congress of Labor (CT) in February 1966. The establishment of the CT achieved the long-standing goal of the labor establishment to unite organized labor into a single organization closely tied to the PRI. The CT, which in 1973 grouped more than thirty of the nation's most important labor confederations and federations into a single entity, hence was the embodiment of collaborationism, as it was the principal vehicle for conveying the "official" labor movement's political and economic demands.[31] The CT also provided the government and PRI an enormous support base easily mobilized for elections or other episodes of mass politics. Not surprisingly, the CT was heavily influenced by the CTM, which claimed between 2.5 and 3 million members by 1970.

Even with the consolidation of the labor establishment nearly completed, the resurgence of labor activism in the late 1950s and 1960s hinted at the contradictions inherent in the state's development strategies. Charros, mindful not to bite the hand that feeds, defended the state's development program and tried to quash rank-and-file dissent by painting it with red brushstrokes. When speaking about the railway workers' challenge in 1958, Fidel Velázquez was curt and revealing. In his view, the communist pedigree of Vallejo in the context of Cold War politics put the nail in his coffin. Organized labor's maximum leader sounded positively Calles-esque when he judged that "Vallejo and his associates only want to create a create a climate of agitation in benefit of their communist theories; already there is no doubt that they are Communist because they themselves have removed the mask and have let everyone see their red-ness; they are seditious because Valentín Campa, Demetrio Vallejo, Dionicio Encinas, Othón Salazar, Agustín Sánchez and others have said in distinct tones that they are not in agreement with the present regime but instead, they are against it."[32] The position of Velázquez, in short, was that to fight your union was akin to fighting your nation. To the aging veteran of the syndical wars of the 1920s and 1930s, the Mexican state and the large confederations of working-class trade unions were one and the same. Collaborationism, in his mind, was a simple equation that required each element, on occasion, to show unconditional support for the other's side. The government would fight to defend its labor partner when it was attacked, much as the CT or CTM would mobilize to defend the regime when its status was threatened. The watershed year of 1968 and the challenges it presented to the Mexican state and labor bureaucracy would create new opportunities for each partner in the relationship to prove its commitment to the collaborationist cause.

Collaborationism in the Workers' Press

The horrific confrontation at Tlatelolco did not extinguish student activism in Mexico. Still, after October 2 the Mexican student movement would never again count on the popular force and numbers it had possessed prior to the killing and imprisonment of hundreds of its core members. In the months that followed students returned to classes at the nation's major universities and did not, in general, resume the kind of aggressive activism that had become commonplace that summer. In this regard, Mexican authorities could find some solace in knowing that harsh repression succeeded in limiting radical militancy to the margins of the movement. Furthermore, the use of military force to quash protest on the eve of the Olympics was a measure that pleased the leadership of organized labor, which had for months prior to October 2 called for decisive force to combat dissent.

Strong support for the federal government was expressed on the pages of the workers' press, that is, the publications of state-allied trade unions and labor confederations, in the weeks that preceded and followed October 2. The position of the CTM prior to the massacre was made crystal clear via a letter to the editor that appeared in *Tribuna Obrera*, the weekly newspaper of the Congress of Labor. In its "Manifesto to the Nation," first published in September, the CTM summarized its understanding of student activity and explained that the organization, as "a product of the Revolution that professes only the body of ideas of that social movement of 1910," could not remain indifferent before the grave threat that undermined peace and stability in Mexico. Indifference, it elaborated, would be contrary to the nature of an organization that was "a permanent factor in the progressive action of national life." The CTM, therefore, driven by perceived historical obligations and, very likely, by resentment over the recent appropriation of the red-and-black strike flag by student protesters in the Zócalo, felt obliged to counter those "foreigners," "bad Mexicans," and "communist agents" who had manipulated students into attacking the regime. Enemies were advised that the organization would use syndical action to whatever extent necessary to put an end to the antijuridical and anarchic climate that they wanted to bring to the nation. All adversaries were warned that the CTM, in firm alliance with President Díaz Ordaz, would "unmask and destroy native or foreign agitators" who wanted to harm the nation by corrupting its youth.[33]

The CTM's pledge of solidarity with the government pressured other pillars of the establishment to make similar shows of deference. The September 19 missive entitled "To the People of Mexico" issued a unified condemnation of student dissent by the three official sectors of the PRI. Writing as the self-proclaimed "representatives of the majority forces of the nation," union leaders of the rural, worker, and popular and professional sectors expressed their support for the government's decision to dispatch the army to seize control of the UNAM campus. Authors of the document reasoned that it was the leaders of political groups of diverse ideologies inside the university, and not government officials, who were guilty of violating university autonomy, for they were the ones who had occupied buildings and turned the campus into a center of operations against the institutions of the nation. It was these agitators who had impeded the renewal of classes and prevented "real students" from pursuing an education. This kind of action could not be tolerated, for it contributed to "idleness" and was "a waste of resources and time." It also risked producing a "scientifically, technically, and personally inept generation" that would not be able to fulfill the functions that the nation demanded.[34] The decision to invade, the letter's authors concluded, was taken only after all lawful recourse had been made available to, and rejected by, students, teachers, and employees of the university. The army's occupation of UNAM hence was not an act of force or a violation of the tenet of university autonomy. It was, according to the nation's political establishment, a necessary measure to reestablish the true function of the university.

Pieces printed in the workers' press in 1968 confirmed that labor leaders mostly encouraged the aggressive tactics used by the state to counter student protest. Government repression at a relatively small scale was generally condoned. But even when mass violence finally arrived in Mexico organized labor remained nonplused. The October 7, 1968, edition of *Tribuna Obrera* made no mention of the violence that had occurred at Tlatelolco just days before. The following week the newspaper ran several stories that made reference to October 2, though not directly. One piece reported that the executive committee of the CTM met on October 6 to discuss "violent disturbances" that had recently occurred. At the meeting committee members unanimously responded to the call for unity made by CTM leaders Fidel Velázquez and Jesús Yurén Aguilar and agreed to hold meetings at state levels to reinforce the working class's "firm unity around the Revolutionary regime over which Licenciado Gustavo Díaz Ordaz presides."[35] In that edition's editorial section, Congress of Labor opinion makers also ran a piece entitled "Mission Accomplished" wherein they praised the successful inauguration of the Olympic Games as proof of the nation's current state of civil and economic stability. They congratulated Mexico's leaders for bringing the world's most important sporting event to the nation. Organizers, they reasoned, could not have chosen a better day to inaugurate the games—October 12, after all, being the Día de la Raza (Day of the Race) in Mexico. Neither could they have picked a better venue than that of Olympic Stadium at UNAM, making a perhaps not-ironic reference to the site of so much government repression. These triumphs, editors concluded, were achieved "in spite of the inconsequential and insidious vociferations of elements that tried to disparage the success of the Olympics." Mexicans, they assured, held no rancor toward those who tried to disgrace the nation. Rather, they now basked in the glory of overcoming "innumerable obstacles" and the achievement of turning Mexico into "an oasis of peace" and the sporting capital of the world.[36]

Worker periodicals heaped praise on Mexican leaders for successfully bringing the Olympics to fruition and defusing threats that endangered the nation's forward advancement. The messages printed in the workers' press echoed those run in the majority of mainstream publications. One need only scan the coverage of the events of 1968 to notice an overwhelming journalistic and editorial bias for the government's cause over that of the students. With few exceptions, contemporary periodicals defended the military occupation of the universities and opposed the right of students to counter police force. Certain periodicals provided venues for dissenting opinions, though typically these spaces were available only for purchase and not freely provided. This was the case with the Mexico City daily *El Día*, which received payment for publishing a September 19 letter to the editor entitled "To the President of the Republic," condemning the "shameful" and "unconstitutional" military occupation of UNAM and signed by two hundred well-known painters, poets, musicians, actors, architects, scientists, photographers, and writers.[37]

On October 3 few newspapers published memorials to commemorate those fallen at Tlatelolco, as was commonly done following the death of prominent individuals. An important exception was seen in *Excélsior*, the large Mexico City daily that distinguished itself from its competitors through relatively impartial reporting of events. Readers saw on the front page of that newspaper's October 3 edition only a black rectangular graphic with the Spartan caption "*¿Por Qué?*" (Why?) This image by cartoonist Abel Quezada Rueda has haunted observers ever since. Nevertheless, *Excélsior* at the time could not be labeled antiestablishment. Neither it nor any other major newspaper reported casualty figures on October 3 that greatly diverged from official state figures. *El Día* showed itself particularly apologetic of civil violence. It reported that the military and police elements responsible for the killings were provoked by agitators and that federal legislators fully justified the use of force to combat "the participation of national and foreign elements that pursue anti-Mexican objectives."[38]

A strong condemnation of government action at Tlatelolco was found in *Por Qué? Revista Independiente. Por Qué?* was published weekly and sold at the low cost of two and a half pesos (roughly three times the cost of a subway ticket) in order to maximize its availability to the popular classes. The magazine proved itself to be a political factor during this period to the extent that it often saw its runs looted or its staff members assaulted by state partisans. For this reason, many of its contributors wrote using pseudonyms, some notable exceptions being Demetrio Vallejo, Federico Emery U., and Mario Menéndez Rodríguez, each of whom wrote articles from their prison cells in the notorious Lecumberri Federal Penitentiary. Menéndez, who was jailed in 1970 for being editor of the controversial magazine, continued to edit *Por Qué?* while imprisoned. The tone of the magazine was, without exception, critical of the regime, and its articles were devoted to exposing corruption, relating the plight of political prisoners, criticizing foreign monopolies in Mexico, alleging CIA influence in foreign relations, challenging the independence of the mainstream press, ridiculing the electoral system, and bringing attention to the repression of civil rights, demographic explosion, inflation, and hunger in Mexico. *Por Qué?* was also committed to exposing unlawful connections between the government, businesses, and trade unions.

Unlike those who wrote in mainstream papers, reporters and editorialists who filled the pages of *Por Qué?* were not ambivalent in labeling the events of October 2–3 as they saw them—"genocide." Writing on November 29, 1968, Menéndez cautioned that if the massacre witnessed at Tlatelolco was denied, Mexico risked becoming an immense "Plaza of Graves."[39] In the same edition, Urbano Cortés concluded that the repression that climaxed at Tlatelolco demonstrated the corrosion of the nation's formal government structure. "The official apparatus is bankrupt," he wrote, and added that finally, with the people's eyes wide open, it had become apparent that the only thing 'institutionalized' by the Institutional Revolutionary Party was "the indefinite permanency of the cabal the forms the 'revolutionary family.'"[40] Issues run in subsequent months struck similar notes of urgency. A headline announced that the "Constitution Has Died," and one writer pondered whether the state of fear, lawlessness, and repression that currently gripped Mexico put the nation and its people on the brink of a new 1910.[41]

Combating strong government criticism of the ilk found in *Por Qué?* was a concern of the government but did not constitute its primary media mission. Syndical propagandists of the time devoted far more energy toward dictating the discourses that would fill the workplaces, classrooms, or kitchens of those individuals they considered to be the "true Mexican people," be they loyal unionists, law-abiding students, or patriotic housewives. Journalistic obedience to government regulators was essential for the maintenance of state authority and legitimacy in the period, as scholars have demonstrated, yet the underreporting of Tlatelolco by the mainstream press cost it credibility with the public by exposing the intricate connections that linked it with the Mexican state.[42] A similar contention is more difficult to make when assessing the nature of coverage in workers' press publications. Very likely the clear government bias evident on the pages of organized labor's major periodicals appealed to the readers of those publications. Who was the typical reader of *Ceteme*, for example? He or she was one of the nearly 2.5 million workers organized into a union that was affiliated with the nation's largest labor confederation, the CTM. In addition, *Ceteme* was read by the spouses, children, siblings, or any one of the millions of relatives of union members, who may have found in its pages information about government social programs that directly impacted their lives. The typical reader of *Ceteme* or *Tribuna Obrera*, therefore, was a unionist and thus a member of a class in Mexican society whose fate was directly tied to the success of the Mexican government. History had dictated that the well-being of the organized workers' movement was linked to the well-being of the government that emanated from the Mexican Revolution. And the reverse was advertised as similarly true; the Mexican state could not prosper without the support of its most important societal sector. As such, the reader of union literature probably did not empathize with the struggle raised by Mexican students in the summer of 1968.

The question of who, exactly, instigated the movement of 1968 is pivotal. The student activism that culminated that summer did not occur in a vacuum; unionists and peasants had militated for rights at heightened levels since the late 1950s. However, the episodes of July–October 1968 were specifically the domain of the Mexican student movement. As a rule these actions were taken by largely middle-class, youthful members of the nation's privileged classes. They were not typically the product of organized worker or peasant activism, nor did they emerge from the masses of the urban poor. This distinction is crucial in the way that it absolved the Mexican state in the hearts of many for the harsh repression it inflicted upon the movement's participants. Federal forces acted to crush the movement brutally, but in their actions large and important segments of society saw necessary measures to counter a threat that endangered the overall progress of the nation. Government partisans saw in those protagonists killed on the nation's campuses and on October 2 mostly subversive elements. Either they were foreign or domestic proponents of strange ideologies who acted at home to undermine nationalist goals or they were remnants of the unpatriotic bourgeois class who had somehow managed to survive the mass cleansing process inflicted upon them by the Mexican Revolution so long ago. In any case, they were dangerous and needed to be dealt with.

The lack of sympathy shown toward the student activists did not come from differences in priorities; students, after all, demanded political reforms meant to benefit the great majority of Mexicans. Unionists were told by their leaders that the essence of student demands did not matter. Their cause was waged illegally and was thus illegitimate. This talking point was hammered home by Fidel Velázquez on July 26 when he echoed the government's position by criticizing the "professional agitators" who were using the increased publicity that surrounded the upcoming Olympics as an opportunity to embarrass the nation. On July 31 he convened the Executive Committee of the CTM and declared the organization's support for the demands of the student class, just so long as they were submitted through adequate channels. Mexico's students, therefore, were determined to be acting unlawfully by not respecting the channels of dissent provided by the law. Importantly, Velázquez also saw them as petulant and privileged. "It is not admissible in any way," he concluded, "that select social groups try to break established social order by using privileges that the rest of the population does not enjoy."[43]

In addition to the movement's illegality, union officials stressed the elitist and foreign character of the student cause. Alfonso Sánchez Madariaga, one of the five little wolves, was quoted in the September 14 edition of *Ceteme* and could not hide his disdain. He pledged, "The CTM will impede the penetration of extremists that try to sow disunity in the country." "It was foreign elements," he lamented, who "constructed [rebellion] in the style of Paris," and now, as he saw it, "not only did Paris send us feminine fashion, but also the subversive elements that [now] barricade themselves in the street with urban service buses." The CTM's position that a large proportion of the Mexican student population had been manipulated by nefarious elements that were foreign, and apparently "feminine," was not altered after October 2. Velázquez was unmoved by the carnage of Tlatelolco. He declared on October 5, "The events of Tlatelolco demonstrate that more than just subversion, the rebellion is against progress and the general development of the nation. There is not a student problem, rather, there exists an intent at rebellion or subversion that must be stopped at its origins." The CTM chief was not the only labor official to find a measure of satisfaction in bloodshed. Sugar workers' leader José María Cruz seemed to relish the raw display of government force. "To the assault of the agitators," he warned, "we will answer with the closed fist."[44]

The words of Velázquez, Cruz, and others suggested that a strong affinity bound members of the labor bureaucracy with those in the federal government. In the pride they exhibited over raw power labor officials hinted that they saw the use of state force as an affirmation of their own strength. By typecasting all of those who participated in demonstrations, campus sit-ins, and street skirmishes as communist pawns or elitist youth, labor scribes played to the nationalist and class-conscious tendencies of the average Mexican worker. Velázquez employed both of these tropes when he spoke on November 4. The events of the past summer had confirmed his feeling that Mexican youths were "not apt to acquire the vote at age eighteen, proof of that being that they let themselves be dragged along by subversive elements that engendered the student movement."[45] To Velázquez, student activists possessed unfavorable qualities that Mexican workers did not. They were criminals who did not respect the spaces for political action provided by their government. They were elitist and unpatriotic because they were seduced by foreign and anti-Mexican ideologies. And they were young and impressionable, which meant that they lacked the maturity to resist being dragged into criminality by subversive elements. In each of these ways, they contrasted with Mexican workers—those who found strength through loyalty, an identity through class, history through the legacy of the workers' struggle, and pride through a love of nation. With so little in common, apparently Mexican workers were hard-pressed to sympathize with the cause of student activists. The dead did not matter. What mattered above all was the preservation of the one-party system that had been formed by a revolution waged precisely to protect the interests of Mexican workers and their families.

Velázquez did not speak for the entirety of the labor movement in Mexico, as much as he wished to. Several influential individuals and organizations gave student demonstrators qualified support. Perhaps most important was the rhetorical support students received from the Mexican Electricians' Union (SME), a CTM affiliate but an organization with a left-leaning reputation that was historically established. On August 24 the union released a statement that declared, "We agree with the students when they reject any foreign infiltration (of whatever persuasion), as in the case of the CIA, that tries to create the myth that Mexico is saturated with Communists."[46] Strong personal motives likely drove electricians' union leaders to make these remarks, as their union was accused of harboring communists in its ranks. Furthermore, the SME echoed the positions of the National Strike Committee on the topics of nationalization and increased state control of industry. These points of commonality convinced the SME to formally express its support on September 4 for a movement that it determined pursued political and social causes beyond those related to university life in Mexico.

Some workers from the electrical, petroleum, and other industrial sectors marched in solidarity with students in 1968, although on their own accord. One image from a Mexico City march in September shows young, slender men hoisting a banner that reads "Oil Workers are in Solidarity with the Popular Movement." The iconic derrick of Petróleos Mexicanos (Mexico's sole oil company) is featured on the sign but the *siglas* (initials) and *escudo* (shield) of the Mexican Petroleum Workers' Union, the STPRM, are not displayed.[47] In the same column an image shows a contingent of men hoisting a banner that reads "Electrical Workers Demand the Repeal of Article 145 and Liberty for Political Prisoners," making reference to two of the student movement's most impassioned causes, and another that flung labor-specific demands around: "*Electricistas*. Death to Syndical *Charrismo*! We Support the Students."[48] Here again, imagery gives the impression that there was some congruence between the causes of organized labor and the student movement. Yet the workers' refusal, or more likely, their inability to include any electrical union's initials or shield on their banners, demonstrates that substantial syndical support for the student cause was not forthcoming.

Still there were unionists who saw past syndical prohibitions and formally expressed their solidarity with those who agitated for political rights. Shows of nonconformity toward the government's hard-line repression emanated from even the most elite corners of the labor bureaucracy. Just prior to the Tlatelolco massacre, Díaz Ordaz received a letter from a group of petroleum workers who expressed their disapproval of government action. The letter, which was signed collectively (and thus anonymously), contrasted with the official line of support adhered to by the leaders of the STPRM, the union to which the letter's authors belonged. But even within that elite niche of organized labor there were signs of unease. Juan José Ortega Loera, secretary general of the union, was personally moved by the killing of several of his members' children by army and police authorities. He wrote Díaz Ordaz after October 2 and expressed his feeling that it was "useless to destroy the lives of young Mexicans who represent the future of Mexico."[49] Jesús Reyes Heroles, who then served as director general of Petróleos Mexicanos, the national oil company, likely shared Ortega's grief. He attended the funeral of a daughter of a *petrolero* killed at Tlatelolco.

Organized labor's endorsement of government repression, though not unanimous, was overwhelming. A similarly supportive position was taken by the PRI. In the months prior to the tragedy, the Mexican Congress became the epicenter of rhetorical opposition to student agitation. Scores of priísta legislators used their turns at the podium to hiss venom at known members of the National Strike Committee or to launch accusations against faculty or administrative sympathizers of the movement, including Heberto Castillo and Javier Barros Sierra. In their invectives legislators cast student demonstrators as traitors and seditious pawns of a foreign conspiracy. Their actions were "anti-Mexican" and required that harsh reprisals be meted out to guarantee the peace and stability of the nation. Harsh reprisals, to say the least, were imminent, and when they finally arrived on October 2 leaders of the Mexican political and labor establishments cooed approvingly. On October 4 members of the lower house of the Mexican Congress approved a resolution proposed by deputies of the PRI and the Authentic Party of the Mexican Revolution that endorsed the measures taken by the executive "to guarantee the peace" and against "subversive action."[50] Members of the minority National Action Party and Popular Socialist Party abstained from signing the document.

The official support by the nation's organized labor and political institutions for the government's actions did not silence criticism. Concern over the government's violent tack was shown by none other than Lázaro Cárdenas, the former president of the nation and leader emeritus of the PRI. In a speech on October 5, Cárdenas issued a plea to state and university authorities alike to bring an end to the conflict, though he specifically condemned government repression of student demands. Cárdenas was certainly not the only political or labor insider who believed that the merciless execution of youths by the state was not the proper course of action. Unionists did, after all, hold the right to organize and the right to voice their concerns militantly close to their hearts. Many as well, and particularly those who took part in the railway workers' strikes of 1958–59, had seen government repression close up and could empathize with the cause of the students and university workers who now made demands similar to those they had voiced a decade before. To those who felt this way, the events of the past year resurrected questions about the government's democratic qualities. Moreover, the government's credentials as a "revolutionary" body were also called into question because of its affinity for using "guerrilla" tactics to repress even lawful forms of dissent. In a relatively brief time, the student mobilization that transpired that summer and autumn not only challenged federal authority but also raised questions about the very legitimacy of the ruling regime.

But while many roiled with anger toward the government, Mexico's typical unionist largely kept quiet during the tumultuous summer and autumn months of 1968. Judging from official statistics, 1968 was a year of historical tranquility on the organized labor front. In his investigation of labor records of the period, Kevin Middlebrook counted only 145 strike petitions filed that year at the federal level, though he notes the possibility that information on federal-jurisdiction strikes may be incomplete for 1968. If accurate or even semiaccurate, the volume of federal strike petitions filed in 1968 starkly contrasts with what preceded it (1,661 in 1967) or followed it (1,361 in 1969), further confirming 1968 as anomalous in the labor history of the period.[51]

The New Federal Labor Law of 1970

Organized labor's loyalty during the trying months of 1968 would be rewarded in due time. In December 1968, a few weeks after the successful completion of the Olympics, Díaz Ordaz submitted a presidential initiative to Congress announcing his intention to replace the 1931 Federal Labor Law with an updated code. Union excitement over the initiative was palpable in the months that followed. A cartoon run in *Ceteme* on January 11, 1969, showed a worker standing under the banner of the "New Federal Labor Law." A sledgehammer rested on his shoulder, ready to fend off any who dared threaten his rights. Threats were omnipresent. Men in suits were depicted hiding behind a rock wall. They appeared crawling on their bellies, and one held a pistol while he prepared himself to pounce on the worker. The caption read, "In spite of all the ownership maneuvers, the workers will defeat them."[52]

In truth *cetemistas* (members of the CTM) had good reason to be confident that they would prevail; even by that early date, the passage of a new labor law was a foregone conclusion in what was functionally a one-party system.[53] Nevertheless, it fell upon party leaders to remind workers that they were crucial in the legislative "fight" that would ensue. PRI president Alfonso Martínez Domínguez spoke to unionists gathered for the CTM National Committee's Seventy-Fourth Regular General Assembly on February 26 and reminded them about the party's historical labors on their behalf. The PRI, he stressed, "is the party of workers' rights and of the working class, [it] is the party of unity and revolutionary struggle; it is the party that has brought, brings, and will bring the transformation of Mexico. It is the party of *Mexicanidad* [Mexican-ness], of national sovereignty, of justice and peace. It is the party of the people that unites all Mexicans by their most positive acts and insists on extending the conquests of the peasants, the middle class, and the workers, opening the channels so that all the country is served by the ideology of the Mexican Revolution."[54] Recognizing in turn workers' place in the revolutionary family, Martínez declared, "We know—the whole country recognizes— that the working class, that the CTM, in its long life, has carried forward a permanent history of loyalty to the institutions of the revolution, to its doctrine, and to its men." As for the labor matter that was pending in Congress, Martínez was unequivocal: "The PRI determinedly supports Mexican workers and the CTM in their fights and in their aspirations to achieve a new Labor Law," a priority that he called "a step forward" and "a sign of the imperative" need for workers to enjoy a greater portion of the national wealth.[55]

Strong shows of PRI support for a new labor code heartened cetemistas, who cherished their ally's position in government. The practical political domination exerted by the PRI cancelled the system's ostensible pluralism in a way that compelled other parties to accede to labor reform. Members of the Authentic Party of the Mexican Revolution and the Popular Socialist Party, some independent legislators, and even members of the National Action Party (PAN) who feared appearing antiworker and alienating potential voters ventured to CTM headquarters in the following months to put their public support on record. With the passage of a new labor law a fait accompli, these meetings brought together politicians and labor and business leaders to negotiate certain controversial details, such as profit sharing, behind closed doors.

Nearly a year after its introduction in December 1968, the presidential initiative had finally worked its way through the negotiation process and morphed into bill form. Hundreds of unionists packed the balconies and spilled into the antechambers of the Mexican Congress building to hear the bill's first reading on October 30, 1969. A train of speakers filed to the podium to support the proposed legislation. Included among the proponents of the bill were union officials as well as representatives of the powerful business advocacy groups the National Commerce Confederation and the National Confederation of Industrial Chambers, many of whom either spoke or submitted written briefs in support of it. Seemingly all who spoke that day agreed with the initial rationale of the president that passage of the proposed legislation was desperately needed to institute a national labor code that would be more dynamic and better for workers and employers.[56]

Of the 889 articles included in the proposed bill, some of the most significant changes proposed involved the workweek and employee compensation.[57] Time limits were imposed on shift lengths, although the forty-hour workweek was not established. The workday would continue to be eight hours during the day but was limited to seven hours at night. Employees were guaranteed one day of rest during the workweek and were granted mandatory double-time pay if they chose to work on their day off. Employees who opted to work on Sunday were guaranteed time-and-a-quarter pay. Also proposed was an expansion of the table that listed the possible infirmities (from forty-nine to sixty) that the worker could claim as job related. Stipulations also increased indemnifications for workers who contracted the listed sicknesses. The reformed labor code also endeavored to expand the scope of its protections to new segments of the workforce. Article 331 of the bill afforded full federal protections to domestic workers and entitled them to basic rights such as breaks.[58] Inventors were protected under the new law and were offered arbitration rights in the contentious arena of royalties.[59] Even the interests of professional soccer players as workers were heeded. Article 295 of the bill prohibited the transfer of *futbolistas* from club to club without the athlete's consent.[60]

While the legislation was being read, Luis M. Farías, the top priísta in the Chamber of Deputies, spoke to the press and mocked the concerns voiced by some businessmen that the new law would hinder industry and force investors to flee the nation. These fears he likened to those expressed in 1931 on the eve of the passage of the original labor code. As he saw it, the new law—like its predecessor—would stimulate the economy of Mexico, for as the condition of the worker improved so too would that of the consumer. This sentiment was echoed by CTM officials, who saw historical precedent in ownership's current opposition to the bill. On November 8 *Ceteme* ran the headline "1936: History Repeats Itself," making a reference to the famous confrontation witnessed that year between the Nuevo León employer class and Mexican president Lázaro Cárdenas. In that conflict, business leaders grouped into the powerful Junta Patronal de Monterrey countered a glassworkers' strike that was ruled legal by the state's conciliation and arbitration board by halting production across the state. The lockout provoked a visit by Cárdenas to the industrially crucial region. He listened to representatives of labor and capital and after hearing both sides issued the following reprimand to local businessmen: "Those owners that feel fatigued by the social struggle can deliver their industries to the workers or to the government. That would be patriotic; the work stoppage, no."[61]

Clearly, CTM opinion makers saw similarities between ownership's intransigent positions of past and present. They wrote that the business sector had historically countered workers' rights "by reflex," wielding the same tired old arguments and warnings that industry would flee the nation if such "excessive" privileges were granted to workers. "The same whimpers of poorly paid professional mourners" were now being heard within coalitions that had formed inside Congress against the passage of the law. They would fail, editors proclaimed, because like their predecessors who faltered in the proworker climate of Cardenismo, they now faced a Mexican state that supported the workers' cause. With the worker-friendly provisions included in the proposed labor code, the "whipping" that Cárdenas had given the owners of yesteryear seemed destined to be repeated.[62]

May 1, 1970

The New Federal Labor Law (NLFT) was approved by Congress on December 23, 1969, and put into effect on May 1, 1970, El Día del Trabajo (Labor Day). The government and the PRI had complied. Labor's bosses were now obliged to return the favor. To show their gratitude, upward of one million Mexican workers took part in parades, demonstrations, speeches, and strike activities in cities stretching the length and width of the republic: in Guadalajara, Puerto Vallarta, and Ciudad Guzmán in the west; in Minatitlán and Orizaba in the east; in Hermosillo in the north; and in numerous central and southern cities, including Salamanca, Ocotlán, Toluca, Ameca, and most notably, in Mexico City— the nation's capital. All who participated, it was reported, took to the streets to commemorate the eighty-fourth anniversary of the strike in Chicago, to show solidarity with the worker struggles of the past and present, and to thank president Díaz Ordaz for having delivered them the NLFT—a new and comprehensive labor code meant to rewrite the terms of workplace relations in Mexico.[63]

Coverage of the day's events in Mexico City described the actions of participants and those of the Mexican president almost heroically. Readers of the nation's major newspapers were told that at 9:40 a.m. Díaz Ordaz had hoisted the national standard up the flagpole of the Zócalo.[64] Díaz Ordaz then marched half the length of the plaza until he reached the doors of the National Palace, viewing along his walk workers dressed in their union colors and many toting a symbolic NLFT under their arms.[65] He ascended to the balcony of the palace. From there, flanked on his left by Fidel Velázquez and Salomón González Blanco, secretary of labor and social welfare, and on his right by Edgar Robledo Santiago, president of the Congress of Labor, and Alfonso Martínez Domínguez, president of the PRI, he could view the assembly gathered below. From that perch the principal figures of the nation's labor establishment also saw the banners that draped the walls of the buildings that abutted the Zócalo's four sides. In the enormous print of the hanging signs they likely felt their efforts to appease Mexico's working class validated, as they could read the following phrases: "The New Federal Labor Law, one more conquest of the regimes of the Revolution deserving of the applause and recognition of the workers of the Federal District," "Thus are honored the Martyrs of Chicago," "Thus it [the regime] complies with Mexico," and "Thank you President Díaz Ordaz."[66]

After a few congratulatory words imparted from above, the parade commenced at 10:03 a.m. The massive procession organized itself into five columns led by thirty-nine female marchers dressed in white and bedecked in the Mexican flag. This troop of "beautiful little ladies," according to one reporter, formed a sort of "feminine war band," with one marcher for every labor confederation, federation, or union affiliated into the Congress of Labor. Trailing this group were five compact columns of workers, two representing national unions, the Federation of Public Service Workers' Unions and the Union of Cinema Production Workers, and three from national confederations: the CTM, the CROM, and the CROC, the Revolutionary Confederation of Workers and Peasants.[67] Sprinkled throughout these columns were large placards that conveyed the collective gratitude of these important labor players. Marchers leading the Congress of Labor's contingent carried a placard that read, "In honor of Pro-Worker President Gustavo Díaz Ordaz for having bequeathed us a better, more just, and more dynamic labor law. May 1, 1970." Members of the FSTDF hoisted a sign that stated, "Yesterday Juárez the Reformer; Today Díaz Ordaz the Fulfiller." Members of the union's Local 4 tap-danced on "showy rhythmic tables with canes." Cetemistas echoed the theme of the president's revolutionary compliance. They marched in the parade and conveyed in large print the message that "the best homage to those who struggled for social justice is the New Federal Labor Law that is today brought to life by the loyal interpreter of the Mexican Revolution, Licenciado Gustavo Díaz Ordaz."[68]

Several unions distinguished themselves through the creativity of their displays. Local 1 of the Union of Cinema Industry Workers fashioned a placard in the form of a filmstrip and sustained the image with balloons that kept it at a regular height. The sign simply thanked the Mexican president for bringing the NLFT to fruition. The National Education Workers' Union, Mexico's single-largest trade union, with over a quarter of a million members, presented a large and orderly contingent that, to once again borrow the nomenclature of local reports, was led by "beautiful little ladies" who carried green, white, and red flags. Some unions built floats in addition to painting placards. The Mexican Petroleum Workers' Union displayed a car in the shape of the March 18 refinery located in the Mexico City district of Azcapotzalco. Employees of the Federal Electric Commission built a platform on a trailer with a replica of *Apollo 11* and two satellite tracking towers. When the trailer stopped in front of the balcony of the National Palace, two men dressed as astronauts emerged from the module and saluted the executive cadre of onlookers above.[69]

At 1:20 p.m. that afternoon the parade finally concluded. Observers commented that the massive procession, at more than three hours long and involving approximately 750,000 people, was the most brilliant First of May parade witnessed in Mexico since the first one in 1913.[70] The immense enthusiasm and participation were attributed to the realization among workers about the new rights the NLFT would grant them as well as a desire on their part to thank the law's principal author, President Díaz Ordaz. Díaz Ordaz felt the adulation of Mexico's organized labor hierarchy in person in a postparade ceremony held in the National Palace. In a speech, Edgar Robledo Santiago, president of the Congress of Labor, called the president a "soldier of the national dignity."[71] The NLFT, Robledo felt, was the "the best instrument of our struggles" and "the cleanest flag of social justice created by the Mexican Revolution." Its realization he attributed to the wise direction of Gustavo Díaz Ordaz—a vigorous and patriotic defender of the Revolution's institutions.[72] Later Robledo awarded the president gold and silver medals and presented him with a plaque on behalf of the more than three million workers affiliated with the organization. It read, quite succinctly, "Gustavo Díaz Ordaz: Pro-Worker President of Mexico."

Díaz Ordaz appeared visibly moved by these gestures. He received the gifts with modesty and profusely thanked the members of the Congress of Labor for the "undeserved honors" they had always granted him. He proceeded to state that his *oberismo* ("worker-ism") was not electoral propaganda; it was, he alleged, a product of the "revolutionary conviction" that he manifested for "a healthy, vigorous, and autonomous trade union-ism."[73] Directing his message at the patrones in the room, he commended them for permitting the creation of the new law and thanked them for their future cooperation in complying with its provisions. He spoke to labor leaders next, extending them a similar request for responsibility. "While a gun is more powerful," he cautioned them, "with more feeling of responsibility it must be managed, with more care it must be used, with more nobility it must be harnessed."[74]

Díaz Ordaz's optimism that workplace relations in Mexico would benefit from the NLFT set the tone for subsequent messages emitted that day in a postceremony press conference. Some labor partisans, however, could not help but doubt employers' commitment to respecting the terms of the NLFT, for much existed in Mexican history to suggest that employers, out of a lack of awareness, or worse, outright antipathy, would not heed the new law and its provisions. These were concerns long voiced by leaders of the CTM, some of whom wrote in the organization's weekly newspaper the following day that although the passage of the NLFT was a positive development for the Mexican people, much remained to be done. The federalization of additional labor tribunals, the promulgation of a new social security code, and the establishment of a forty-hour workweek in Mexico were responsibilities now incumbent upon the regime of the Revolution, the newspaper's editors felt.[75] It thus appeared that despite outward appearances, optimism over the law's ability to alter workplace relations in Mexico was guarded. Concerns expressed by officials inside the presidential cabinet and within the nation's most prominent labor organizations on the very same day that the historic new law was implemented evidenced a lingering mistrust between the factors of production. These concerns also foreshadowed the major battles that would define the terms of labor and capital relations in the years ahead.

Like the 1931 Federal Labor Law and Article 123 before it, the NLFT served important redemptionist purposes as it elevated organized labor's primary demands to a legal level. Workers were congratulated in speeches and in editorials that their longstanding battles with patrones and against injustice were over and that their cause had been taken up by a powerful ally—the regime of the Mexican Revolution. A piece entitled "What is the Institutional Revolutionary Party?" appeared in *Ceteme* on May 30, 1970, and reminded workers once more about the revolutionary nature of the regime.[76] A story in the same issue of *Ceteme* expressed how even disgruntled workers were required to put the interests of the nation before their own by delaying a strike they were planning so as not to conflict with another high-profile sporting event that Mexico was set to host—in this case, the 1970 World Cup, scheduled for May 31–June 21 of that year. All bus drivers grouped into Local 14 of the FSTDF, according to section leader Joaquín del Olmo, were unanimous in agreeing "that the nation is first" and that they would not "make a spectacle before the eyes of the world"[77] With the best interests of the nation in mind, the bus drivers agreed to file their strike petition after the tournament concluded.

This chapter narrates a story suggesting that although university students and other parts of the popular and professional sectors of Mexican civil society voiced the loudest demands for rights and reforms, it was organized workers who benefited most directly from their efforts. After Tlatelolco, the government and the PRI desired to restore the fabric of important social pacts that could solidify their standings. In this context, peace with the nation's militant university students was not the top priority. The size and scope of their cause was mitigated in the mainstream press and almost entirely ignored in union publications. And when dissent was described, reporters slandered protesters outright or used verbal cues to suggest they harbored foreign or seditious agendas. Few practical measures were taken in 1969 to appease student agitators; they did not yet factor into the one-party state's mission to rehabilitate the genetic strands of the postrevolutionary corpus.

Unionists, on the other hand, who had shown so little sympathy for the student cause while the nation's security forces worked to crush it, were essential to the task of restoring the government's legitimacy. To them, the government offered the New Federal Labor Law that went into effect on May 1, 1970. More was required, though. Nothing less than a total transformation in governing ideology was needed to convince the most ardent revolutionary unionists that they were the government's priority after decades of neglect; nothing less than the complete restoration of the Mexican Revolution would regain worker trust and loyalty. In 1970, an election year, the political airwaves were jammed with rhetoric that promised Mexican workers these things and more.

CHAPTER 2

On the Redeemer's Trail

Luis Echeverría and the Campaign of the Revolution

"Upward and Onward!"

Events that occurred at Tlatelolco on October 2, 1968, finally removed the shroud of state infallibility in civil society. Due to the conflicting nature of reports produced by official and nonofficial sources the facts of what occurred that day are difficult to ascertain. Speculating about the impact of those events on political society is similarly difficult, although the reformist character of the Echeverría candidacy launched barely one year later suggests that the student movement shaped the nation's political discourse and forced the state to alter its political conduct. This is not to say, however, that the state's tack of reform derived only from pressures exerted by student protests. It did not. Rather, political reform in the post-Tlatelolco period represented the state's attempt to counter a much larger and deeper-seated threat to its authority emanating from other societal sectors. The government's repression of the student movement fueled an already incendiary situation, but as the previous chapter explains, the seeds of Tlatelolco were planted well before the questions of university autonomy and democratization first began to burn on Mexico's campuses. It is in this context that the Mexican state entrusted Luis Echeverría with redeeming the Mexican Revolution and combating the crisis of legitimacy that beset it.

Luis Echeverría Álvarez was born on January 17, 1922, in Mexico City. Yet Echeverría was the product of an affluent family with deeply entrenched Mexican roots extending the length of the country, from Sonora to Jalisco to Oaxaca. He also had a direct connection to the modern nation's formative event, as his father, Rodolfo, was paymaster to General Rodolfo Sánchez Taboada, who fought under Obregón in the Mexican Revolution.

A practicing Roman Catholic, the teenager considered entering the seminary but opted against it, instead deciding to attend public schools and attain a law degree from the National Autonomous University of Mexico in 1945, where he taught for a short stint. That same year he married María Esther Zuno Arce, whom he had met five years earlier, reportedly at the home of Diego Rivera and Frida Kahlo, the famed artists, whom he greatly admired. His marriage to Zuno, the daughter of a powerful Jalisco politician, proved efficacious, and he began his political career a year later by joining the newly reorganized official party, the PRI. There again familial connections benefited him as he climbed the ranks quickly, working first as director of press and propaganda and then later as private secretary to Sánchez Taboada, the party's president, whom his father had served in the field. In 1952 Echeverría left the PRI and followed his boss to the navy ministry, where he assisted him in the same position until 1954. Well launched on his bureaucratic career, Echeverría then assumed the position of chief of staff to the secretary of public education in 1954 and obtained the same position in the PRI in 1957. In 1958 he was named by President Adolfo López Mateos as undersecretary of internal affairs, a position he held until November 19, 1963, when he replaced Gustavo Díaz Ordaz, who left to campaign for president, at the top of the ministry. Echeverría continued to serve as secretary of internal affairs under Díaz Ordaz and held the post until assuming the presidency on December 1, 1970.[1]

Echeverría's bureaucratic career followed conventional Mexican lines of political patronage, but his climb to the presidency was unique. As secretary of internal affairs he occupied the most important cabinet position and a natural springboard to the presidency; four out of the five presidents holding office in the period 1946–76 held this position in the cabinet of their predecessor.[2] Neither Miguel Alemán, Adolfo Ruiz Cortines, Adolfo López Mateos, nor Gustavo Díaz Ordaz, however, arrived at the presidency through strictly bureaucratic channels—as did Echeverría. These men, unlike Echeverría, held elected offices and had national reputations prior to commencing their presidencies.

Even with his long record of federal service and the infamy he attained for his role in the repression of 1968, Echeverría was a little-known national figure when he was selected by Díaz Ordaz to succeed him as president. Since mainstream Mexican society had little exposure to the political insider Echeverría, his selection by Díaz Ordaz called for a grander-than-usual *destape* (meaning, literally, the "uncovering" or "revealing" of the sitting president's pick for his successor), to be performed on October 21, 1969, on the stage of the country's most prominent political theater, the Zócalo. Dozens of little flags with the candidate's face and the simple message "Bienvenido" (Welcome) hung from streamers draping the square's light poles. Red, white, and green confetti rained down on the plaza as crowds cheered the arrival of Echeverría, the man almost certain to be their next president. Newspaper coverage the following day was similarly festive as writers praised Díaz Ordaz's selection of Echeverría. Reports claimed that widespread shows of celebration could be seen around the country and that the nominee spent many of the following days receiving a train of well-wishers who went to his office to congratulate him in person. *El Universal* editor Antonio Lara Barragán wrote that business owners concurred with the selection of Echeverría, evidenced by the numerous verbal statements expressing support for the nominee given by leaders of the National Confederation of Chambers of Commerce, the National Confederation of Industrial Chambers, and other business organizations.[3] Other *El Universal* staffers covered the events and did not hide their approval. Demetrio Bolaños Espinosa wrote that the forty-seven-year-old Echeverría, he of the "brilliant revolutionary career" and "strong political personality," had so impressed the great majority of the nation that they nominated him to the highest office.[4] José Rigoberto López described jubilation in the capital over the fact that for the first time a native son of the Federal District was on track to become president of the republic.[5] Jorge Coca P. felt that Echeverría's personal qualities inspired confidence in his ability to lead. The nation, he surmised, would be in good hands under his stewardship, for he was, after all, a family man who had raised eight children with his loving wife, María Esther Zuno.[6] Finally, Elias Chávez reported that the overwhelming feeling among those he interviewed was that "He is the best," although he could not help but note that some were concerned about the "student problem" he would surely face.[7]

Following the ceremonial destape Echeverría sought to reverse his relative anonymity by carrying out a campaign that astonished observers as much for its determination to reach remote audiences as for the candidate's effort to distance himself from his predecessor. The energetic and athletically built candidate of above average height tirelessly criss-crossed Mexican territory over a nine-month period, visiting each of the country's twenty-nine state capitals and traversing thirty-five thousand miles in the process. It was while he was on campaign that the press first began referring to Echeverría as "the preacher," because he was talkative, opinionated, and felt the need to speak directly to the public on a regular basis.[8] The nickname stuck, and Echeverría continued this tendency as president, often taking to the road to explain his positions in a manner reminiscent of the circuit-rider priests who once rode the hinterlands of the Spanish Empire on horseback to bring Christianity and salvation to the pagan masses.

Echeverría's circuit riding also harkened back to the more recent campaign of redemption undertaken by Cárdenas when he campaigned for president in 1933–34. To reinforce that connection Echeverría referred to the former president on a daily basis, all the while affirming his resolve to change the direction of the nation over the next six years.[9] The reformist character of the campaign represented the Mexican state's grudging acceptance of the nation's turbulent social climate and desire for change. Echeverría was well aware that there were some who did not approve of his candidacy and from the start he tailored his campaign to meet these challenges. His early campaign rhetoric signaled a drastic change in the direction of government policies. When speaking to the international press corps for the first time as a candidate, on October 21, 1969, Echeverría was asked to define his political position. His answer was concise: "La Revolución Mexicana y la Constitución de 1917: ¡Arriba y Adelante!" (The Mexican Revolution and the Constitution of 1917: Upward and Onward!)[10]

Echeverría thus inaugurated his campaign by referencing one of the two major tenets that would become hallmarks of his administration: an intention to redeem the Mexican Revolution by restoring the primacy of the Constitution of 1917 in government. In his first speech as a precandidate (he still lacked the PRI's official nomination), Echeverría addressed an organization steeped in revolutionary significance—the National Peasants' Confederation. Speaking before the delegation, Echeverría asserted that the first stage of agrarian reform had been realized; the redistributive phase of the Revolution was complete and peasants had attained land. The current task, he stressed, was to implement a second stage of agrarian reform: the exportation of production.[11] Throughout the campaign, Echeverría excited peasants with rhetoric that echoed their sacred mantras and paid homage to their heroes. In Anenecuilco, Morelos, birthplace of Emiliano Zapata, Echeverría tailored his message accordingly. He stated that there, in the home of the social crusade for the oppressed peasant class, his revolutionary convictions were confirmed.[12] The peasants of Morelos had ignited the struggle that enshrined in Mexican society the hallowed principle that the land belonged to those who worked it. They were the true protagonists of the Mexican Revolution. By preaching the primacy of agrarian issues and reiterating that the principal debt of the Mexican state was to the peasants of the nation, Echeverría gained widespread support from the official agrarian sector. This support would prove crucial early in his presidency, as most peasant unions supported the passage of the Federal Agrarian Reform Law in April 1971.[13]

Echeverría's stance that it was necessary to reestablish the centrality of revolutionary ideology in a state system that had strayed from its

principles had appeal beyond the agrarian sector. In his effort to recon-
nect with the ideology of Cárdenas, Echeverría made bold and symbolic
overtures to workers as well. When speaking before miners and railway
workers, Echeverría customized his message, often remarking that their
predecessors at Nacozari, an important copper-mining area in Sonora
since before the Revolution, were the original protagonists of change.
Speaking to members of the Mexican Railroad Workers' Union Echeverría
reasoned that since the Revolution was fought on rails and railway workers
contributed to its greatest and most significant phases, the Mexican state
owed them a historical debt.[14]

The theme of compensating workers for their role in Mexico's development was referenced ad nauseam throughout the campaign, and to good
effect. Before trade unions Echeverría emphasized the need to restore
social justice in the productive process, in the process incorporating into
his message organized labor's long-favored watchwords of *equilibrium*
and *harmony*. A huge headline in the October 25, 1969, issue of *Ceteme*
announced, "Luis Echeverría: A Candidate of the *Cetemista* Workers."
There it was reported that Echeverría was designated precandidate for
president at the assembly of the PRI National Council held on October
22, and editors confidently predicted that the PRI, "Our Party," would
officially nominate him to the presidency—a safe bet given that over
one-fifth of the five-thousand-plus delegates in attendance who would
attend were CTM members.[15]

CTM support for Echeverría was not unconditional, but enthusiasm
for the candidate seemed genuine. To Fidel Velázquez, Echeverría "harbored a spotless patriotism that complemented his revolutionary core,
strong personality, absolute commitment to defending the well-being
of the nation, and above all, a close connection to the workers of whose
problems he understood"[16] Speaking before the Coordinating Council
of the Congress of Labor, an organization over which Velázquez then
also presided, the candidate reiterated his position that the upward
march of the workers' movement could not be detained, nor could the
advancement of new agreements governing relations between labor and
capital be halted. This was a pledge he wanted to stress in the event he

arrived at the presidency. Satisfied, Velázquez did not delay in formally declaring CT support for Echeverría in a stirring speech laden with historical symbolism and redemptionist rhetoric.[17]

The nation's primary labor organizations heaped constant support on Echeverría during the period of his precandidacy. In an editorial entitled "Luis Echeverría, el hombre," *Ceteme* editorialists opined that "with Licenciado Luis Echeverría, the CTM renews its pact with the Revolution, a pact that it fundamentally tries to advance more quickly and more extensively so that it achieves unrealized goals and accelerates social justice." Echeverría, they believed, was endowed with the qualities of a redeemer, one who would "decisively and bravely bear the standard of the holy cause of the Revolution." The CT expressed its official backing for Echeverría as well via a full-page advertisement in *Ceteme*. In the ad CT scribes presented a history of the workers' movement in Mexico that positioned Díaz Ordaz, who was currently working to bring the New Federal Labor Law to fruition, at the culmination of a heroic narrative celebrating the deeds of "the intrepid warriors" who fought against the Porfirian reaction, the brave members of the House of the World Worker, and the "patriot" Venustiano Carranza.[18] Only with a man with revolutionary credentials as firmly established as Echeverría's, they concluded, could this story be advanced and the socially just reforms that the working class deserved be achieved.

The ringing endorsement given Echeverría by the pillars of organized labor sparked syndical enthusiasm. Support for his nomination appeared via half- and quarter-page advertisements placed in the October 25, 1969, edition of *Ceteme* by unions of irrigation, road, construction, meat, public sector, cinematographic, liquor, sugar, and petroleum workers. On October 26 Echeverría addressed an "impassioned" assembly of workers gathered for the VIII General Congress of the Federal District Workers' Federation. Flanked by Velázquez and the union's secretary general, Jesús Yurén Aguilar, he spoke to the crowd of over one-half million that filled the Felipe Carrillo Puerto Auditorium and spilled into the nearby Plaza de la República. First he referenced a recent attempt to explode dynamite on the steps of CTM headquarters: "I felt it as if it had been on the doors of my home." He then sought to clarify his worker credentials, claiming that although he was not "of pure worker extraction" nor had he had a long "political life" (experience in elected office), he harbored a deep personal connection to workers, developed over twenty-four years of following in the footsteps of Velázquez and Yurén in their struggles for workers' rights. Echeverría concluded by declaring his revolutionary resolve. The fundamentals of the Constitution of 1917, he maintained, were still valid, and he ended his speech with a promise to continue the perpetual fight of the "Old Constituents of 1917" for the well-being and progress of the Mexican worker.[19]

Addressing worker, peasant, and popular and professional unions had long been the meat and potatoes of politicking in Mexico. Echeverría continued and expanded this tradition by working exhaustively to win syndical support prior to receiving the party's nomination. Over the course of barely three weeks, from October 21 to November 13, 1969, Echeverría made the rounds of society's three major sectors: meeting with unionized peasants in Morelos, Puebla, and the Federal District; with popular and professional groups, including the nation's umbrella organization, the National Confederation of Popular Organizations, the National Charro Federation, students, university faculty and other intellectuals, federal senators, teachers, state employees, taxi drivers, and economists; and most notably with an impressive array of labor organizations, including the CTM, the Revolutionary Workers Confederation, the Mexican Railroad Workers' Union, the Mexican Petroleum Workers' Union, the Puebla State Workers' Federation, workers of the Refinería 18 de Marzo, and others. No faction of civil society was deemed too insignificant. Echeverría spoke to groups outside the traditional sectoral framework, including Mexican citizens residing in the United States; working-class urban neighborhood associations; members of the Mexican Legion of Honor, the National Matadors' Union, and the Nisei Association of Mexico; and members of the national soccer team, no doubt in anticipation of the 1970 World Cup scheduled for the following June and hosted by Mexico.

Upon accepting the nomination on November 15, 1969, Echeverría spoke before the members of the PRI's National Executive Committee and repeated the message he had perfected in union halls. He assured party leaders that he was committed to adjusting the priorities of the Mexican state and altering the course of national economic development. He admitted that the Mexican Miracle was flawed and that macroeconomic gains were offset by socioeconomic inequality. To remedy the situation he announced that the time had come to build a more just structure on the Revolution's broad foundations. The task, although not easy, could be achieved by calling on capitalists to be "nationalist businessmen with a social vision." Those who refused this call and lacked a clear idea of their social responsibility, he contended, were not true men of business. As for foreign investment, it would continue, but capitalists would hence have to respect the laws and customs of Mexico by reinvesting their profits into new fields of domestic production.[20] With these words Echeverría made official his reformist call for social justice and renewed nationalism. The following day, November 16, 1969, he officially launched the "Campaign of the Revolution" with the full weight of the party and official sectors behind him.

Beginning in Querétaro the campaign endorsed the continuity of the revolutionary regime while simultaneously arguing for the necessity of reform. Development would continue, but the direction of industrialization would follow a more socially responsible policy. The Mexican state would also reorient its strategy of financing development; new sources of foreign capital would still be sought but the goal was to move toward eventual self-financing. By promising reform of the nation's development policies, Echeverría appealed to the most symbolic sectors of Mexican civil society, namely, peasants and workers. Their centrality to the campaign's focus was evident from its rhetoric, which promised a new stage of agrarian reform for peasants based around new partnerships between agriculture and industry as well as housing, social security, and other benefits for workers.

Revolutionary references appealed to other sectors of the populace and notably to those sympathetic to the student movement. Seeking to mend fences with the Mexican youth, Echeverría spoke at the Universidad Nicolaita de Michoacán and called for a moment of silence to honor those killed at Tlatelolco. This gesture enraged not only students, many whom blamed Echeverría personally for the massacre, but also the secretary of defense, General Marcelino García Barragán, who expressed the discontent of the army to President Díaz Ordaz. From that point on each subsequent moment of silence called for by Echeverría was prefaced with the disclaimer that it honored killed military personnel as well as students.[21]

The Revolution was used by the Echeverría campaign for various ends but not always for conciliatory purposes. For some, the promised ubiquity of the Revolution in future state operations was not a welcome prospect—a common opinion, certainly, among those who listened to the candidate during a campaign swing through Nuevo León in April 1970. In Monterrey, the northern hub of Mexican industry, Echeverría paid homage to the city's industrious citizens but ascribed the region's overall affluence to the Revolution and the work of the Mexican people as a whole. In a speech to owners who had formed themselves into the famous Grupo Monterrey, which had challenged Mexican state hegemony over industrial policy in the age of Cárdenas and periodically again after 1940, Echeverría remained on point. He stated that modern private enterprise in Mexico was born of the Revolution and was hence subject to its social mandate. It was the Revolution that "cancelled our feudal past, salvaged our natural resources, and put in motion the productive forces that established and firmly maintained the favorable conditions and ample guarantees for investment." Therefore, it was not inappropriate to require its primary beneficiaries (i.e., *patrones*) to share its rewards. Unbridled profits and the unequal distribution of wealth via the absence of profit sharing were anachronistic to the causes of national and social development. Should he have the honor of being president, Echeverría promised, his administration would rectify the situation by proceeding with the strictest adherence to a revolutionary morality that stressed the common good and pursuit of social justice.[22]

Echeverría's revolutionary rhetoric and call for sacrifice threatened the business sector but endeared him to organized labor—both its leadership and the rank and file. Women organized into the PRI's Female Assembly gave their vigorous endorsement to the candidate on June 10, believing him to be a "bulwark and standard-bearer" of the Mexican Revolution in whom the hopes of the women of the labor, peasant, and popular sectors rested.[23] Still, worker cynicism emanating from decades of government neglect was pervasive. Worker discontent was a factor CTM leadership recognized and moved to combat. In the days prior to the election of July 5 CTM leaders exhorted members to turn out in support of Echeverría. At a breakfast hosted by the CT, Velázquez addressed the delegates and members of the press in attendance with a message of confidence: "The Mexican workers will respond at the voting booth and with political support to the call made by our candidate, Licenciado Luis Echeverría Álvarez. As always, the Mexican worker accepts the responsibility that is afforded him in the revolutionary process of the country. Not a single Mexican worker will refuse the call to unity and action made by Luis Echeverría Álvarez, candidate for the Presidency of the Republic."[24] Echeverría issued a similar call to civic duty in a television spot aired on election eve. In a message full of optimism, he argued that political apathy weakened the force of the citizenry and halted the progress of the nation. "There is neither liberty nor progress," said Echeverría, "without the integration and direction of the majority." Nothing was worse than apathy, he felt, and he preferred that one cast a vote against him rather than not vote at all.[25]

In spite of the unified refrain issued by organized labor and Echeverría, Mexicans opted not to vote in the 1970 presidential election in record numbers, as only 42 percent of voters went to the polls. Voters' abstention proved distressing to Echeverría, whose electoral victory was never realistically in doubt. Certainly the candidate was aware he had opponents, though he may have underestimated the extent of popular cynicism about the political process. That the modern Mexican state was illegitimate and antipatriotic was a sentiment frequently expressed in dissident literature of the period. An article run in the antiestablishment magazine *Por Qué?* on the eve of the election and titled "Why it is useless to vote" expressed these feelings quite concisely. Casting a ballot was useless, wrote Carlos Arreguín, "because national elections were farcical pageants designed to convince foreign powers that the crimes perpetrated in Mexico were committed by legitimately elected authorities." One could deny the government bureaucracy legality by abstaining and thus impeding "new 'tlatelolcos,' new robberies of the country, new repressions and new jailings."[26]

Even some members of the National Action Party, usually a moderate oppositional force, found themselves voicing radical rhetoric in the run-up to the election. Five hundred members of the Baja California state party met in Tijuana on May 4, 1970, and heard speeches decrying the "dictatorial processes" of the PRI and the "torrent of new blood" that it had inflicted upon eighteen-year-olds who had only wanted to "revolutionize" Mexico and do away with the country's dictators and ignominy.[27] In the same vein, on July 2, just days prior to the election, young members of the PAN drove the streets of Tuxtla Gutiérrez warning citizens through a megaphone that a vote for Echeverría would "ensure a new massacre like that of Santiago Tlatelolco."[28] This message strongly contrasted with the image of the future president adhered to by loyal *priístas* in Chiapas, one of whom told the press on June 7 that with Echeverría "the flags of the PRI" and the "programs of the Revolution" would be in "clean hands."[29]

Opposition to the regime, although intense, was not strong enough to derail the PRI machine. Echeverría emerged victorious—and with ease. He defeated Efraín González Morfín of the PAN by a margin of better than six to one, garnering 11,970,893 votes to his rival's 1,945,070.[30] But while it is true that the election demonstrated the continued electoral force of the PRI, whose candidate also captured the nominations of diverse groups, including the Popular Socialist Party and Authentic Party of the Mexican Revolution, continued control of the nation's political system was not the only goal of Echeverría's quest. The Campaign of the Revolution, which according to government figures saw Echeverría over the course of 226 days visit over 1,000 localities and deliver 859 speeches before 34 million people, had a more ambitious agenda: to redeem the Mexican Revolution and restore the state's ideological sway over the populace.[31] By actively promoting a reformist message that emphasized the centrality of the Revolution in modern life, the state and PRI hoped to appeal to vast segments of the masses who clung to the legacies of Madero, Carranza,

Zapata, and Cárdenas. In the opinion of many workers, peasants, teachers, students, and others, the contemporary state had diverged from the principles of the Revolution and its heroes. This position was shared by the party's standard-bearer, Echeverría, who in spite of his best efforts failed to convince the voting public that the return of revolutionary ideology was imminent. Widespread voter apathy in the election of July 5, 1970, confirmed the great disenchantment among the masses toward government and indicated to the state that its mission to reestablish itself as legitimate heir to the legacy of the Mexican Revolution remained incomplete. It was in this context that the death of the great redeemer and last surviving hero of the Mexican Revolution, Lázaro Cárdenas, on October 19, 1970, presented the government a golden opportunity to stride toward its objective.

The Death and Myth of Lázaro Cárdenas

The death of Cárdenas precipitated a national outpouring of emotion. Thousands of citizens participated in the events honoring the fallen president that culminated on Wednesday, October 21, a national day of mourning, when fifty thousand people gathered in Mexico City to bury his remains beneath the southeast column of the Monument to the Revolution in the Plaza de la República. There he joined presidents Francisco Madero, Venustiano Carranza, and Plutarco Elías Calles in both literal and figurative containment. The official management of the Cárdenas funeral reveals the Gustavo Díaz Ordaz government's desire to control the ways in which his memory could be used by promoting the idea of the revolutionary family and the linear progression of the Revolution. It also signaled to President-Elect Luis Echeverría the strength of the populist alliance Cárdenas had been able to construct during his period in office. At the time of his death, Cárdenas retained the allegiance of broad sectors of the population, and Echeverría saw that by appealing to the traditional supporters of Cardenismo he might be able to attract a similar base of support.

The loss of Cárdenas was an emotional blow many in the nation felt personally. *Ceteme* conveyed the emotion of the union member simply:

"The Fatherland in Mourning."[32] Workers' despondence was understandable in light of the historical role Cárdenas played in furthering the cause of organized labor in Mexico. Letters of condolence poured in from unions around the country and filled the pages of newspapers in the weeks following his death. *Ceteme* published several eulogies summarizing the impact of Cárdenas on the nation's workers. One recalled that it was Cárdenas's support for labor that enabled the birth of the CTM in February 1936. Equally important, they added, was the intrepid defiance he showed toward the business sector while in office. This attitude was best exemplified in his decision to seize possession of foreign petroleum assets on March 18, 1938. Editors reminisced that he, "serene, but determined, expropriated for Mexico the petroleum during a period when there was fear of confronting the power of foreign monopolies and enormous economic pressure from abroad." Cárdenas did it, they exclaimed, and in the process he achieved the economic independence that produced the industrialized Mexico of today and tomorrow.[33]

The positions of the labor bureaucracy as conveyed in *Ceteme* did not belie the profound sense of loss felt by the average union member, many thousands of whom journeyed to the Plaza de la República to pay their respects. The death of Cárdenas caused great sadness but also presented the Mexican state and Echeverría an opportunity to mobilize the former president's supporters. In an editorial that appeared in *Excélsior*, Froylan M. López Navarez pointed out that the death of a leader did not necessarily mean the death of a cause.[34] In his comments to reporters on the night of Cárdenas's death, Alfonso Martínez Dominguez, president of the PRI, called on all sectors of society to keep the memory of Cárdenas alive by continuing the progressive march of the Revolution.[35] He offered a justification of the administration's policies as the linear progression from, and inheritor of, Cardenismo, echoing the line frequently used by Echeverría during his campaign.

Various aspects of the ceremonies organized by the government reveal its efforts to comfort distraught Cardenistas and demonstrate its revolutionary credentials and legitimacy to the masses. The photos that show Cárdenas's coffin surrounded by former presidents reinforced his place in the revolutionary family, and those that pictured Díaz Ordaz and Echeverría flanking the coffin symbolically expressed their desire to show the legitimacy of the progression of leadership in the PRI's one-party system.[36] Other elements of the state funeral were also didactic. In recognition of the significance the nationalization of the oil industry had for the country, the first honor guard to stand at attention beside Cárdenas's coffin comprised members of the Mexican Petroleum Workers' Union. Bearing the organization's standard, they stood silently beside the coffin of the president whose decision to nationalize the oil industry remained, in the eyes of the people, a symbol of the pursuit of sovereignty and social justice. Meaningful not only to oil workers, the relevance of the expropriation transcended social categories; a middle-class woman waiting in line to pay her respects at the Chamber of Deputies recalled that she had given her jewelry to the government in 1938 to help pay for the indemnification of foreign oil companies.[37]

In both words and actions, there was no mistaking the fact that Echeverría wanted to channel the memory of a unifying political figure to help mend a fractured nation. Once in office, Echeverría continued the practice he had begun while campaigning and referenced the national hero Cárdenas on a near-daily basis. Echeverría also wanted to emulate the common touch his predecessor enjoyed with the masses. In order to confirm his nationalism he ordered that Mexican foods replace foreign dishes and wines at state functions. Los Pinos, the presidential residence, was redecorated with art and handicrafts brought in from the village of Tlaquepaque to present a more Mexican vibe.[38] To fashion himself a man of the people he often removed the business suit and donned the popular guayabera shirt; his wife, María Esther Zuno, commonly wore folkloric dresses à la Frida Kahlo, sparking great ridicule in the press.[39] In a similar vein, to connect with the Mexican working class Zuno spurned the title of First Lady, preferring instead to be called *compañera*—a term that means comrade when applied in the work or political spheres.[40] These aesthetic efforts by "the preacher" and the "compañera" were largely unconvincing, and many resented the Echeverrías for their ambitious efforts to replace their beloved patriarch.

Others resented the president for different reasons. To those on the extreme left, Echeverría's attempt to resurrect Cárdenas and connect with the left was misguided because in their eyes, not even the fallen president was immune to attack. Writing in *Por Qué?* on November 5, 1970, Rafael Tinoco presented an obituary of Cárdenas diametrically opposed to those that appeared in mainstream and workers' periodicals. Tinoco felt obliged to narrate the origins of the "myth" of Cárdenas and identify the erroneous sources of his near-deification in society. He wrote, lamentingly,

> Lázaro Cárdenas has been elevated to the status of upper-level saint on the iconographic altar of the dominant class and its government. . . . As such, the oligarchic bureaucracy calls him: "creator of the new Mexico," "reformer of the nation's basic structures," "defender of the humble," "Paladin of the peasants," "he who gave the land," "defender of the workers," "the only one who could solve the problems of the people," "sacred *Tata* of the poor," "dispenser of all possibility of life and work," "enemy of the powerful," "anti-imperialist," "liberator of the economy," "expropriating nationalist," "undisputed chief of the Mexican people's struggle for liberation," "kind hearer of the dishonorable," "he who could obtain freedom for political prisoners," and on and on endlessly. . . . That is the myth of Lázaro Cárdenas, of the Army General, of the ex-president, of the ever-loyal government functionary.[41]

The author then remarked that the false praise heaped upon Cárdenas had devastating effects upon society. First, ritualistic belief in the myth that Cárdenas was a sort of messiah, a "miraculous saint" to whom all social advancements could be attributed, succeeded in transforming someone who had been a mere "government functionary" into the masses' only hope for salvation. Such blind devotion, he added, made citizens into "impotent spectators and beggars waiting in hope that their problems be solved 'from the heavens.'" An accompanying photograph showed President Cárdenas heading a group of Mexican and North American army engineers surveying a piece of terrain. The caption defied a strong and independent Cárdenas, reading: "General of the oligarchy's army, Cárdenas has been the governmental bourgeoisie's most loyal servant."[42]

An even more injurious outcome of the "myth of Cárdenas" to Tinoco was its power to "castrate" Mexican politicians, in effect turning them into "dirty servants" and "silent accomplices" of the "powerful and disciplined instruments of repression." As Tinoco saw it, the Mexican state and the PRI had appropriated the revolutionary legacy and co-opted the nation's history to pursue its own bourgeois-inspired ends. The memory of Cárdenas was a prime player in this process of manipulation, and as such could not be held beyond reproach if true democracy and social justice were to be pursued.

The lack of reverence that some showed Cárdenas guaranteed that his ideological devotee and heir apparent to the redeemer position would receive similar rebuke. Add the fact that Echeverría was among those most singly associated with the Tlatelolco massacre and icy relations between the state and dissident groups were guaranteed. In fact, many on the left tied Echeverría even more closely to the bloodshed of October 2 than Díaz Ordaz, for Echeverría, who was then the secretary of internal affairs, was believed to have ordered the Olympia Battalion, which was under his command, to provoke the crowd at Tlatelolco, in the process contravening the orders of army soldiers (under the command of the secretary of defense, General Marcelino García Barragán), who were directed not to fire on the plaza.[43] True or not, the widely held belief that Echeverría acted independently cast him as the primary villain of Tlatelolco and an even more odious figure than Díaz Ordaz. Regular pieces run in *Por Qué?* and other publications hostile to the regime were thus skeptical of the "assassin," constantly challenging the candidate's democratic rhetoric and his promises to restore an equilibrium and social justice to society. These writers were not moved by his diatribes against powerful capitalists and the forces of first-world exploitation, nor were they impressed by his promises to restore the ideals of the Mexican Revolution to government. A comic strip by Barreto run on December 4, 1969, concisely iterates popular skepticism. The tongue-in-cheek piece entitled "Mexico Enjoys a Current Revolution!" begins by showing a fiery Echeverría offering a promise and a disclaimer. "Sure, there remains much to do!," the caption reads, prompting Echeverría to say with chagrin, "Well, we are not all supermen." He regains his composure in the next panel, though, employing pyrotechnics and proclaiming with a fist held high, "Nor are we vulgar demagogues to hide it!"[44]

Opening the strip by mocking Echeverría's penchant for hyperbole enabled the artist to illustrate other tragic similarities between pre-revolutionary society and post-Tlatelolco Mexico. Virtually all the ills suffered by the nation in the late Porfiriato were given parallels in the present day. The strip reasons that the land problem, ostensibly solved by agrarian reform, had actually endured, evidenced by the image of a greedy *latifundista* in modern attire grinning broadly while smelling new land opportunities: "$nif, $nif, $nif." The notion that the Revolution had brought an end to outside exploitation of Mexican resources is also mocked, and emblems of Ford, DuPont, Kodak, Union Carbide, and General Electric call attention to the plethora of powerful foreign companies then operating in Mexico. Next, the question of workers' rights is contested. Prior to the Revolution workers had no voice, "Nor did unions exist," it states, prompting a character wearing a sombrero and bearing the unmistakable visage and trademark dark glasses of Fidel Velázquez to respond, "Unless they were *charros*." "I've returned" he then snarks malevolently. Finally, the strip challenges the authenticity of the democracy created by the Revolution. A panel reads, "Those [Porfirian] government workers needed thirty years to become rich," to which a young boy responds, "Today they only need six," referring to the number of years in a presidential term and conveying the cynicism of the day with a particular poignancy.[45]

The above-referenced pieces articulated radical and openly angry positions toward the one-party state and its representatives, past and present. Another incendiary take on the candidacy of Echeverría offered by Demetrio Vallejo was printed in *Por Qué?* on December 18, 1969. In the piece, titled "Echeverría Speaks: Demagoguery or Reality?," Vallejo raises doubts about Echeverría's commitment to restoring revolutionary values and scoffs at the slogan "¡Arriba y Adelante!" The PRI's continued effort to validate its existence by positing a living connection to past heroes irked Vallejo even more. In his words,

Our heroes have been converted into a myth by "revolutionaries" that we hope do not bite their tongues upon pronouncing their names. It is true that we have to respect them, invoke them, venerate them, and imitate their grand virtues, but [we must do so] for what they did, not for what they left to do. They were revolutionaries in their own time. Today the world is divided into two systems: capitalist and socialist. These two opposing realities have created a distinct situation from the world in which they lived and fought. To invoke our heroes in the spirit of continuing to realize what they did as "revolutionaries" is anachronistic and jingoist. For that reason the students are right when they invoke Lenin, Che Guevara, and others alongside our heroes, because those figures represent not only the ideals and aspirations of a nation, but rather of all humanity. The doctrine that they sustained was and continues being internationalist. That is the difference.[46]

Vallejo's critique tapped into an increasingly vocal current that challenged the legitimacy of the state and PRI as rightful heirs to power by way of their political descent from the Mexican Revolution. In his message he made the case for internationalism and in doing so ironically hinted at the *tercermundista* ("third-worldist") rhetoric often espoused by Echeverría. *Tercermundismo* stood alongside revolutionary redemption as one of the two rhetorical tenets of Echeverría's campaign. In short, tercermundismo was a populist strategy employed by the candidate during his campaign (and afterward) to broaden his base of support. His third-world advocacy surely garnered him some votes and subsequent support, as it appealed to a minority of allied-professional groups—teachers, most importantly—and others with established leftist tendencies. But few who opposed the regime were persuaded by the themes repeated ad nauseam by the candidate. Aside from the occasional paean offered to socialist icons like Che Guevara and Mao Zedong, there was little practical meat to substantiate Echeverría's self-proclaimed leftism. The persistent attacks launched against Echeverría in the pages of *Por Qué?* hindered his efforts to show ideological solidarity with the independent left.

Words levied by Vallejo proved particularly injurious, for he, along with Valentín Campa, was the face of the railway workers' strike of 1958–59 that laid bare the vast chasm in priorities that divided rank-and-file workers from organized labor's leadership. As described previously, Vallejo's efforts to detach the Mexican Railroad Workers' Union from the grasp of government-backed charros and his procommunist politics led to his arrest in 1959. Charged with various crimes, including sedition, Vallejo was sentenced to serve over eleven years in federal prison. From his confinement in Lecumberri Federal Penitentiary, Vallejo kept contact with the outside world by writing a near-weekly column for *Por Qué?* wherein he maintained a vigilant critique of the Mexican state and its routine violations of workers' rights. Vallejo's undeniable political and cultural significance convinced President-Elect Echeverría to intervene to procure early release on August 13, 1970, for Vallejo and Campa, who had by then become living martyrs and icons of the student and independent workers' movements.

Echeverría took to the campaign trail, courting popular and leftist support. With Cárdenas's death in October 1970, he intensified his effort. By the time Echeverría took office that December his message had been fine-tuned into a new ideological paradigm that, although impossible for some to stomach, greatly appealed to those most closely linked to Mexico's historical legacy. Leaders of peasant and worker organizations applauded the candidate's message of reform, for it heralded a new identity for Mexico, one that positioned it in stark contrast to its recent self. The source of Mexico's "new identity," however, was not new but rather quite old: it was the Mexican Revolution. Speaking at his inauguration on December 1, 1970, Echeverría confirmed this orientation in an address that was well received for its uncharacteristic brevity and clarity. As he had stated countless times before, social development in Mexico would continue but would thenceforth follow a direction guided by ideals of fairness and social justice. In the speech's key passage, the new president reasoned, "To encourage the conservative tendencies that have surged from a long period of stability equated a denial of the heritage of the past. To repudiate conformity and accelerate general evolution, on the other hand, is to maintain the energy of the Revolution."[47] Thus concluded the

Campaign of the Revolution, but the one-party state's rhetorical effort to improve its reputation with the organized working class of Mexico would continue.

The Democratic Opening and Organized Labor

Echeverría channeled the intense energy he demonstrated on the campaign trail effectively to the National Palace, making his first year in office a monumental period of legislative activity and reform. During this time he maintained a "killing pace of activity," to the amazement of the press and the exhaustion of his aides. His pace never slackened, apparently, and he astonished even foreign spies, one of whom wrote in 1975 that his "unflagging energy is truly astounding" in working "16 hours or more per day, seven days a week."[48] His stamina impressed many, as did his rhetorical commitment to reforming the Mexican political system from the roots. There were few nooks or crannies of the national life in which he did not intend to intervene.

Unlike Díaz Ordaz, Echeverría made substantial efforts to respond to the sectors most directly associated with the events of 1968. During his first year in office he opened a dialogue with disenchanted intellectuals and students and acceded to some of their demands, including a limited version of university autonomy and the release of a number of high-profile political prisoners. Government conciliation with the left formed a central part of Echeverría's much-heralded *apertura democrática* ("democratic opening")—a rhetorical strategy that, according to historians Héctor Aguilar Camín and Lorenzo Meyer, was not intended to undermine the "essential goodness of the Mexican 'legacy'" but rather attempted to reform mentalities and practices inside the government that social unrest had exposed as outmoded. The democratic opening, they explain, "was a response to the demands of 'updating' the legacy, in order to preserve whatever was preservable. The idea of 'letting things change so that everything remains the same' went hand in hand as an attitude and a perception, with the very anachronism of some of the major governmental policy decisions."[49]

However, as was witnessed inside the agrarian sector, the initial gains produced by the democratic opening did not placate everyone. Scathing journalistic attacks launched against the regime never ceased while Echeverría held office, and the persistence of antiestablishment rhetoric in the early years of his administration convinced the Mexican government that aggressive measures to oppose dissent were still necessary. By 1971 student activism had resumed, although it did not match its pre-Tlatelolco level of intensity. It was deemed threatening to state stability, nonetheless, and government repression revealed that the democratic opening had a real ceiling of toleration.

In this regard the impact of 1968 was acute, for as realization about the massacre spread, so too did society's general uneasiness about ruthless government repression. In post-Tlatelolco Mexico, consequently, the state was forced to employ subtler measures to counter groups and individuals it deemed subversive. The General Directorate of Political and Social Investigations (DGIPS), a dependency of the Secretariat of Internal Affairs, was vastly expanded and dispatched thousands of agents to observe and report on student meetings and union proceedings in a way that represented a quieter (and probably more effective) way to defuse potential threats than deploying antiriot squads or strikebreakers. Students, unionists, and other astute observers cried foul and identified government moles in their midst. The Mexican state denied these activities, publicly trying to appear tolerant and to regain a measure of legitimacy that had been lost over more than a decade of discord.[50]

Paramilitary groups also sprung to life in this period, most notably in the form of the Halcones (Falcons), who violently met student protestors on the streets of Mexico City on June 10, 1971. On that day some thirty thousand students assembled in the downtown Tlaxpana neighborhood of the city and marched in solidarity with students who were protesting repression at the University of Monterrey. In actuality, Eric Zolov tells us, conflicts at that university had already been resolved, but a splinter group of radical students from UNAM decided to go forward with the unauthorized march to show the continued validity of street protest. The goals of the march were muddled but the enormous scale of the crowd affirmed that anger still simmered at the political system. As the march began, scores of policemen stood idly by. The tension was raised when members of the Halcones arrived and attacked the unarmed protesters (many of high school age) with spiked boards, baseball bats, and guns.[51] The clash left between nine and fifty demonstrators dead (depending on which report one accepts) and hundreds more wounded. The violence evoked painful memories of 1968 but also demonstrated a new breed of tactics the government would use to indirectly counter dissent and, in effect, wage a "dirty war" against its citizens.

Seeking to offset public outcry over yet another brutal crackdown against civil protest in Mexico, Echeverría summoned his preacher instincts and responded quickly. Appearing on television that evening, he calmly promised that those responsible for the violence would be punished. To many observers his anger and commitment to free expression seemed genuine as he acted in the following days to remove a slew of officials from power, including Alfonso Martínez Domínguez, former president of the PRI and the current regent of Mexico City.[52] "Whoever falls, falls," confirmed Echeverría in a nationally televised interview he gave to television journalist Jacobo Zabludovsky.[53] Subsequent action in the following months, however, disappointed those who demanded justice. The government's investigation was inconclusive and no perpetrators were charged. Ultimately, as was the case in the last months of 1968, basic questions went unanswered. The public was left only to speculate: Who were the Halcones and where did they come from? Many assumed that in spite of his public recriminations, Echeverría knew of their existence and had approved of their use against the demonstrators. Contrasting rumors circulated that the Halcones were linked with industrialists in Monterrey, some of whom criticized Echeverría's pledges to redistribute wealth and were resolved to embarrass him by discrediting his democratic opening. Other theories held that the Halcones were in fact formed and funded by the CTM, an allegation that provoked Fidel Velázquez to famously respond, "The Halcones do not exist because I don't see them."[54] Department of Federal Security documents that surfaced in 1998 proved that the first explanation was most accurate. The Halcones were a paramilitary group composed of fifteen hundred recruits who had been trained at the

Police Academy of the Federal District and taught Japanese martial arts for the purpose of quelling riots. They were paid for their service.[55]

No fingers yet pointed to the president in the days following the bloody episode. Hoping to guide public perception and avert a strong social reaction against the regime, party delegates met at PRI headquarters and decided to jolt the machinery of mass politics into high gear. A massive demonstration was planned to show the "conscientious support" and solidarity of the "revolutionary social sectors" for the government of Luis Echeverría and against the "declared enemies of Mexico, be they Mexicans or otherwise." Delegates belonging to the CTM affirmed their support for the actions taken against students whom they judged to "have zeal for nothing except the subversion of order." Velázquez elaborated on his organization's position in an address to the assembly. He said that the position of the CTM would be identical to that it had adopted when it faced "similar occurrences" in 1968; it would energetically condemn disturbances provoked by "agitators who have taken possession of the conscience of certain student groups." Adding that there was no justification for disturbing the peace during a time when Mexico's "rhythm" of growth was the fastest in its history, Velázquez believed that the workers' movement could not be "contemplative" against those who threatened peace, justice, and progress, nor would it continue supporting higher education with financial subsidies—an amount he estimated at 600 million pesos annually—while students opted to pursue violent acts instead of their studies.[56]

Photographs taken of the June 15 demonstration confirm that it was indeed massive and possibly the largest of its kind ever held up to that point, as Velázquez asserted. Demonstrators packed the Zócalo from end to end, waving placards indicating their union affiliation and expressing their opposition to "foreign agitation" in Mexico. Scanning the photographs featured in *Ceteme* and major Mexico City dailies one sees the predominance of cetemistas in the crowd and specifically members of the Federal District Workers' Federation. One also sees significant contingents from the peasant, popular, and professional sectors expressing their support for the Mexican president.[57]

Speeches were given by the leaders of the PRI's three wings to remind unionists about the remarkable slate of reforms enacted by their president in just over six months in office. Alfredo Bonfil, secretary general of the National Peasants' Confederation, cited the passage of the Federal Agrarian Reform Law two months earlier and emphasized that more than ninety thousand hectares of land had been distributed to date—an allotment that he believed benefited more than 1,500 rural workers. Jorge Preisser, speaking on behalf of the National Confederation of Popular Organizations, followed Bonfil at the podium and listed recent developments that benefited those in his sector. Importantly, he endorsed the kind of repression recently witnessed on Mexico City's streets. "In a city as large as this," he reasoned, "peace by means of a firm hand of government is essential." "What is it that the agitators want?" Preisser quizzed the audience. "To break the march of progress? To compromise the national interest and security?" None of that could be tolerated, he declared, if social reforms and economic development were desired in Mexico. In this regard Mexico's organized workers similarly pledged their loyalty to Echeverría. Speaking for the Congress of Labor, Arturo Romo guaranteed the president that workers were cognizant of the clear dangers that such nationalistic and revolutionary work implied, and all were committed to do their part to preserve law and order on the nation's streets. Workers, Romo assured, were with "Mexico and with President Echeverría!" United, they were "against provocateurs and extremists!"; they were "against those who sowed disorder and anarchy to interrupt the revolutionary process of Mexico!"[58]

Of all of the day's speeches, of course, none was more anticipated than that of Echeverría—the political figure who stood to lose (or gain) the most from the recent events. In a real sense the prestige of Echeverría's entire political program was at stake, for the June 10 incident challenged his government's purported tolerance for dissent. He spoke to critics who mocked his commitment to a democratic opening in Mexico, explaining, "I have never solicited unconditional applause from my compatriots. The right of the people to dissent and demand that their leaders adhere to the Constitution and the laws is the essence of democracy." Free expression, he nevertheless felt, needed limits and could not be condoned when voiced by clandestine groups, provocateurs, and reactionary politicians merely to sow discord. Any one of these groups, one could infer, might have been behind the violence perpetrated on June 10. Their actions would not be tolerated. Echeverría concluded his address to a friendly audience with rhetorical flourishes and promises. "Mexico will not back down!," he thundered. "It would be unforgivable if we permitted a handful to cancel the national hope. Those who have provoked or unleashed the violence are enemies of harmony and progress. Against them is risen the people's indignity!"[59]

Echeverría's speech was in a sense exculpatory but was far from a formal denial of personal or state involvement in the incident. The tone of his speech, filled with revolutionary rhetoric but ultimately vague on the topic of culpability, confirmed the purpose of the demonstration. The PRI did not convene the massive gathering to counter assumptions (which were accurate) about Echeverría's involvement in the events of June 10. Rather, the demonstration showed the party's solidarity with the president regardless of his role in the incident. Each of the day's speakers deflected criticism away from the regime by either impugning the motives of the victims of the assault (the student demonstrators) or slinging accusations at outside groups (foreign and/or domestic industrialists) who may or may not have perpetrated the tragedy.

The PRI's giant public spectacle and Echeverría's unseating of officials (which implicated them but did not confirm anyone's guilt) did not suffice for those who demanded that culprits be convicted and that prison time be served. Such demands frequently appeared in the press, wherein the incident was referred to as the Corpus Christi Massacre or, on occasion, the "little October 2," in reference to the larger massacre perpetrated at Tlatelolco nearly three years earlier. Ultimately, the political fallout from Corpus Christi weakened Echeverría by questioning the sincerity of his democratic opening. Moreover, finger pointing in his administration and within the PRI exposed severe rifts that had formed inside the revolutionary family as a whole. Echeverría's "Campaign of the Revolution" and the death of Lázaro Cárdenas presented the government and the PRI golden opportunities to rekindle populist alliances like the ones that had served Cárdenas decades before. Major reforms were implemented and old relationships restored to a real degree in just the first six months of the Echeverría administration. With the debacle of June 10, 1971, however, the new government's grace period was ended and a more hostile climate, less conducive to social and political reform, took root. To avert crisis, the government and PRI activated the machinery of popular mobilization and compelled its organized rank and file to demonstrate their solidarity with the Mexican state and its embattled leader to the nation at large. One show of mass political theater did not avert a crisis, although it helped. Organized labor—as it had in 1968—complied again. The operator's manual of collaborationism required the revolutionary state to return the favor.

CHAPTER 3

"The Government of the Republic Thus Pays Its Debt"

"Mexicanizing" the National Patrimony

Jesús Reyes Heroles, Oil, and the National Patrimony

The Mexican state confronted the crisis of legitimacy that the Corpus Christi massacre created much like it did the one created by Tlatelolco—in an indirect manner. It did not tackle the problem head on by negotiating with students, intellectuals, youths, and other disgruntled sectors. Rather, it redoubled efforts to redeem its revolutionary credentials by appealing to its most dependable constituency—organized labor. Previous chapters demonstrate that the state's efforts to cement alliances with organized labor began immediately after the Tlatelolco massacre and bore fruit by the early 1970s. Organized labor's strong support for the state was made evident through frequent and sizable shows of mass politics like those witnessed on May 1, 1970, and June 15, 1971. The political arm of the Mexican state, the PRI, was also crucial in redeeming its revolutionary credentials with its working-class constituents. Alfonso Martínez Domínguez (before being scapegoated for blood spilled on June 10 and ousted by Echeverría as regent of Mexico City) served as PRI president from 1968 to 1970 and had credibility with workers due to his status as former head of the Federation of Public Service Workers' Unions. His successor, Manuel Sánchez Vite, echoed his predecessor's worker-friendly rhetoric but did not receive the same warm embrace from workers due to his lack of labor credentials; he had been a law professor and then governor of Hidalgo before leading the party from 1970 to 1972. His successor, in contrast, although also a former law professor, aroused the kind of union excitement desperately needed by a political system reeling from another public relations disaster.

Jesús Reyes Heroles was sworn in as PRI president on February 21, 1972. In his speech upon taking the PRI's reins he promised to purify the party and reignite revolutionary processes that would enable *priístas* to confront "provocateurs . . . who try to unleash forces to justify a rigid state of capitalism."[1] Instantly, it appeared, those who called for the restoration of a revolutionary economy found a new friend in government. Fidel Velázquez, perpetual leader of the CTM, brimmed with optimism about the new party chief, feeling Reyes Heroles to be "intellectually one of the most valuable treasures Mexico has" and "one of the best exponents of the ideology of the Mexican Revolution."[2] Opinions expressed in the mainstream press conveyed similarly hopeful notes. Editors at *Excélsior* embraced Reyes Heroles's "activist" character while those at *El Universal* hoped that his proposed changes would fix "contradictions" some believed existed in the party.[3]

The pleasure Velázquez and others showed over the appointment of Reyes Heroles surged from the latter's long and proven commitment to revolutionary idealism. Since he first joined the official party in 1939 Reyes Heroles had articulated a kind of ultranationalism that endeared him to ideologues in the party's labor sector. His early radicalism did not diminish over the next three and a half decades and it colored a stretch of public service during which he represented his home state of Veracruz in the Chamber of Deputies and held high-level positions in the Labor and Presidential Ministries, Ferrocarriles Nacionales de Mexico, the Mexican Social Security Institute, and Petróleos Mexicanos (Pemex), the state-run oil company. In each of these roles, and through extensive teaching and writing, Reyes Heroles excited passions by advocating reform and articulating notions of nationalism and class consciousness derived directly from the Mexican Revolution. Upon assuming the presidency of the PRI in 1972, Reyes Heroles in effect assumed the role of ideologue in chief, a position his character and professional pedigree made him well suited for.

Reyes Heroles's long political life gave his supporters much to relish but provided his detractors plenty of material as well. In truth, his past relationship with organized labor had been tumultuous. Reyes Heroles battled constantly with the oil workers' unions while serving as director general of Pemex (technically the nation's largest employer) from 1964 to 1970. *Petroleros* (oil workers), knowing that oil revenue enabled the Mexican state to overcome insufficiencies in its tax revenue, recognized their strength and mobilized at elevated rates in the 1960s to pursue "revolutionary" priorities that increased national control of the industry, among other things. Other conflicts, interestingly, were born from the Mexican oil industry's state of hyperprosperity, and the issue that divided petroleros was not expansion of the industry but rather at what rate to expand it. Reyes Heroles was by no means opposed to increasing Mexico's oil-producing capacity; as head of Pemex he installed three major facilities—two on land in Chiapas and one off the coast of Campeche—that increased the total production of basic petrochemicals from 397 million tons in 1964 to 1.933 billion tons in 1970. Yet Reyes Heroles butted heads with union leaders because he implemented a strategy designed to pace the extraction of the resource in order to extend its supply period. While Reyes Heroles saw this "rationalization" as a long-term strategy that could assure Mexico's self-sufficiency in the future, unionists saw only a hesitancy that hurt Mexican workers by denying them employment opportunities in the present.

Moreover, Reyes Heroles advocated an efficiency and modernization position that put him at odds with oil workers' unions. As Reyes Heroles contended, Mexico's oil company was simply inefficient, and he produced figures showing that Pemex occupied five to ten workers in the production of each barrel of crude oil, whereas other international businesses occupied only two to four. This inefficiency meant higher production costs, something the Pemex chief was committed to reducing through salary cuts and workforce reductions.[4] He counseled petroleros to temper their zeal for personal gain for the good of the nation. He reasoned that just as the administration would not skimp on providing benefits to workers that they rightfully deserved, neither should workers impede the growth of a socially important industry with excessive labor demands. Such patriotic discourse, however, had little sway over well-entrenched unions whose power and influence derived from the size of their ranks. Though they listened intently to Reyes Heroles's messages they heard only the inevitability of job cuts. Workplace conflict frequently ensued, and in the end Reyes Heroles's pro-nation rhetoric did not preclude confrontations between petroleros and the state. Upwards of one-third of all unions that constituted the STPRM raised labor suits against Pemex while Reyes Heroles ran the company.[5]

But even while relations stayed consistently rocky between Pemex and petroleros, Reyes Heroles maintained the support of the STPRM, the nation's umbrella oil workers' organization. His sharp political acumen and his drive to clean out corruption inside the company's administration earned him respect from rank-and-file oil workers, the majority of whom were aware of the rampant embezzlement in the industry and the illegal sale of contracts by Pemex officials to union bosses. Called *venta de plazas*, this practice was so widespread that in 1969 leaders of the STPRM began a purification campaign to remove corrupt officials guilty of eliciting kickbacks.[6] Reyes Heroles was on the hunt as well, and his "moralizing" mission incited strong confrontations, the most famous with a functionary known as "don Five Percent" who demanded that percentage for each contract he granted to oil workers' unions.[7]

Campaigns Reyes Heroles launched to reduce foreign capital in the oil industry solidified his status with petroleros. Before describing the details of these campaigns, though, a quick preface about the importance of economic nationalism in the sphere of the Mexican oil industry is required. Mexican workers, according to anthropologist Emma Ferry, historically understood natural resources as inalienable possessions of the kingdom (later nation) and viewed property as patrimony to be held intestate by the monarch (later president) and passed on to future generations through inheritance. Patrimony, Ferry explains, denotes collective, exclusive ownership by a social group, often organized or conceptualized as a patrilineal kin group. To describe something as patrimony places limits on its exchange by classifying it as *inalienable*; such patrimonial possessions are meant to remain within the control of the social group that lays claim to them and usually to be passed down intact from generation to generation. This desire to preserve the patrimony, though it had been a "highly charged 'root metaphor'" in place in Mexico since the colonial period, was articulated with the experience of the Mexican Revolution.[8] Workers in postrevolutionary society understood petroleum as constituting one of those "inalienable" resources over whose control was crucial toward preserving the national patrimony—a fact evident in the language of Article 27 of the Constitution of 1917. Consolidating domestic control over the nation's oil supply hence formed the basis of postrevolutionary nationalism and bolstered arguments against foreign penetration in the industry.

Historian Myrna Santiago has illustrated this process clearly. Petroleros of the 1920s and 1930s, she explains, understood the Revolution as an episode undertaken primarily to vindicate the cause of the Mexican worker. Oil workers at El Aguila and other foreign-owned companies struck often to force the hand of their employers, and in doing so "turned nationalism into a synonym of class struggle, reaffirming the class nature of the Revolution itself and the role of labor in forging it." Their actions were motivated by their sense that the "revolutionary ideal" was fading in the face of oil companies' belligerence and the state's failure to enforce constitutional provisions on labor (Article 123) and state control of natural resources (Article 27).[9] Oil workers' militancy reaped rewards. By March 1938 incessant labor-capital conflict and the persistence of foreign oilmen in flaunting Mexican law moved President Cárdenas to side with the cause of the workers. His March 18, 1938, announcement declaring that the "machinery, installations, buildings, pipelines, refineries, storage tanks, means of communication, tankers, distribution stations, ships, and all other properties of the foreign companies" were hence property of the Mexican state was the expropriation decree that validated the decades-long struggle of the Mexican oil worker.[10] "It was in this context," says Ferry, "that languages of patrimony acquired particular efficacy in mobilizing labor in support of the postrevolutionary state and the PRI."[11]

The actions of Reyes Heroles in the arena of oil, though hardly as dramatic as those of Cárdenas some thirty years earlier, were also pleasing to organized labor. To the unionist of the 1970s as much as those of the 1930s, Mexico's natural resources (and particularly its oil) were part of the national patrimony. State control over these assets was the preferred condition. Being only a parastate, or partially state-owned, company, Pemex's viability depended on private investment that could constitute as much as 49 percent of its total capital. Moreover, many of Mexico's social programs—its education system, for example—were directly funded by Pemex profits. Reyes Heroles recognized the centrality of private (even foreign) investment in the oil industry to the realization of Mexico's social development and did not attempt to eliminate it entirely. He did, however, reduce the level of foreign capital in the sector by purchasing petroleum assets from foreign-owned companies. Pemex spent USD 225 million in June 1969 to purchase three North American–owned companies. The measure was widely acclaimed in political circles, though it met with standard cynicism from the left. Responding to the purchase, *Por Qué?* columnist Carlos Ortega G. asked scathing questions: "Wasn't the oil already ours?; Were we all duped in believing that we owned the oil after Lázaro Cárdenas decreed the expropriation of the holdings of all foreign companies that exploited the subsoil of Mexico?" Ortega granted that legal maneuvers implemented after 1940 had enabled foreign capital to reinfiltrate the Mexican industry, yet he did not concede that these developments negated the validity of Article 27, which did not require Mexico to compensate foreign entities for the "reclamation" of its natural resources. "Did Jesús Reyes Heroles, director of Pemex and 'ideologue' of the Revolution, forget what Article 27 of the Constitution ordered?" he inquired sardonically. Was the recent sale of North American companies to Pemex, Ortega queried, a "fraudulent nationalization"? Was it just another political ploy to impress upon the Mexican people a false image of a sovereign and brazen "revolutionary family"?[12]

Leftist skepticism aside, Reyes Heroles's leadership of Pemex enabled

Mexico to exert a degree of control over its petroleum resources not seen for decades. In addition to directing Pemex's purchase of foreign-owned resources Reyes Heroles oversaw the annulment of long-standing legal agreements that had enabled foreign investment to return to prominence in the Mexican oil industry. Desperate for foreign capital, Pemex during the presidency of Miguel Alemán signed a series of contracts in 1949–51 that permitted mostly North American companies to build and operate offshore drilling installations, in return promising them full reimbursement for their initial outlays and 15 percent of their proceeds for a period of twelve to fifteen years. These so-called *contratos riesgos* ("risk contracts") also required Pemex to sell all or part of that facility's production to the investing company. The legality of the risk contracts was hotly debated. Proponents of the reform argued that Cárdenas had authorized the creation of what were called "shared profit contracts" between Pemex and private companies as early as 1938, though none had yet been realized. Opponents countered that any state association with private capital subverted the nationalization cause. The intentions of Cárdenas were thus left open to debate, even with the former president available to clarify his position.[13] Cárdenas revoked his support for the contracts, but only privately, and opponents were successful in pressuring the government to cancel only twelve of the original seventeen contracts within a few months of their signings. Five risk contracts survived and governed Pemex's relations with foreign companies for the next two decades.

The surviving risk contracts were odious to nationalists who operated in the post-Tlatelolco climate of revolutionary redemption. They lobbied against them using well-founded legal and symbolic arguments, contending that the risk contracts granted concessions to foreign companies in clear violation of the terms set forth in the 1958 Governing Law to Article 27 and injured national pride by increasing foreign control over Mexico's most prized resource. Reyes Heroles agreed wholeheartedly, and he did not hide his pleasure when he announced the annulment of the remaining five contracts on February 27, 1970. With their elimination, he declared, pressure "emanating above all from the United States" to permit the return of foreign capital in the oil industry had been relieved. With legal arrangements that had for twenty years appeared as "an opprobrious stain inside the nationalized industry" finally removed, Reyes Heroles proclaimed the days of foreign manipulation of Mexican oil to be over.[14]

In overseeing the reduction of foreign capital and influence in Pemex, Reyes Heroles pursued objectives that helped restore a piece of the national patrimony to the Mexican corpus. His nationalist credentials were, except in the opinion of those on the implacable left, beyond reproach, and in spite of his numerous tussles with oil workers' unions he was by 1972 the logical choice to spearhead the PRI's campaign to redeem the ideology of the Mexican Revolution. Furthermore, Reyes Heroles conveyed the Mexican state's economic strategy writ large in the post-Tlatelolco period by advocating increased state control of the nation's oil resources while permitting some private capital investment. This mixed (public-private) economic philosophy fit neatly into Echeverría's *tercermundista* framework because it positioned Mexico inside a movement that saw governments worldwide increase control over their national economies. The reach of this system extended beyond the planned economies in place in the Soviet Union, China, and Cuba into remote corners of Asia, Africa, and Latin America, even penetrating Western Europe and North America. Measures implemented by President Rafael Caldera in another ascendant petroleum player, Venezuela, paralleled those enacted in Mexico and helped his government exert greater control over its petroleum resources.

Yet merely implementing mixed economies in Mexico and Venezuela did not constitute nationalism in the opinion of those on the vocal Latin American left. And it certainly was not socialism—the only acceptable path to social justice, some believed. Highly dismissive of the Mexican state's nationalist credentials in the late 1960s was Eduardo Galeano, a Uruguayan writer who in 1971 produced *Open Veins of Latin America*, a *longue durée* history chronicling the leeching of the region's natural resources by outsiders since European-Native contact in 1492. According to Galeano, it was no longer Spanish conquistadors who threatened the people and lands of Latin America but rather businessmen emanating primarily from the United States. These modern conquerors wielded investment capital in place of swords and they exploited the region's lands and subverted its peoples' sovereignty at the invitation of purported nationalists. Mixed economic systems Galeano viewed as "fig-leafed imperialism," and he criticized "mexicanization" for permitting (not preventing) the penetration of foreign capital into new economic sectors.[15] "Big foreign concerns" in Mexico, he wrote, "now control more than half the capital invested in computers, office equipment, machinery, and industrial equipment; GM, Ford, Chrysler, and Volkswagen have consolidated their power over the auto industry and its network of auxiliary factories; the new chemical industry belongs to DuPont, Monsanto, Imperial Chemical Industries (British), Allied chemical, Union Carbide, and Cyanamid. In all foreign capital participates overwhelmingly in the production of cement, cigarettes, rubber, housewares, and assorted foods."[16] *Open Veins of Latin America*, although rejected by economists for its clear Marxist orientation, sold millions of copies worldwide and disseminated an anti-imperialist (and anti-Yankee) message that was influential in the formal and informal dialogues of Mexican party leaders, policy makers, and unionists of the 1970s.

The type of state economic intervention pursued in Mexico, albeit not sufficient in the view of hardline Marxists, responded not only to international trends but also to pressures that had been exerted at home for the better part of a decade. The history of economic policy in Mexico warrants discussion, for 100 percent control of an industry by the state had neither been achieved nor even attempted in practice. The political economies of both pre- and postrevolutionary Mexico featured mixed systems wherein two well-defined public and private sectors coexisted to invest in the production, sale, and regulation of a good. "Since the time of the Aztecs," the economist Fernando Paz Sánchez explained, government in Mexico had been involved in economic matters through a direct investment in industry and through the channeling of private resources to drive social development. In terms of the first function, the government acted as a minority partner with private capital, rarely fronting more than one-third of the total capital invested in an industry. With regard to the latter function, government in Mexico considered its intervention in the economy integral to the fulfillment of its social objectives. This historical mandate, Paz Sánchez believed, was articulated with even greater clarity by the Mexican Revolution, a momentous event that encouraged the government to exert increased control over basic industries it deemed crucial to the national well-being, albeit always inside the "variables of a capitalist economy."[17]

The above-described position was the official line of the PRI in the post-Tlatelolco period but was nonetheless controversial. Arguments that ensued focused on the degree to which the Mexican state was required to exert "control" over a resource in order to be revolutionarily compliant. Politicians, economists, and lawyers of the 1970s searched for historical corroboration in their efforts to support one position or another. Those who argued for a limited government role in the economy found backing in a memorandum from 1911 emitted by none other than Francisco I. Madero, after he took the reins of the presidency. Submitted to the governments of the United States and several other nations on February 15, 1911, the Madero memorandum offered guarantees of protection for, not threats against, foreign properties and interests upon the recipient nation's recognition of the revolutionary government.[18] The document, said Juan Sánchez Azcona, who penned it on Madero's behalf, was designed to assuage international fears and was well received by foreign chancelleries. The economic philosophy that it conveyed, however, did not resemble that which was written into law in 1917. Sánchez later recalled that Madero never harbored nationalist ambitions on economic matters, and his memorandum, which accurately expressed the political economy of the "father of the Mexican Revolution," was intentionally suppressed by a Mexican state that ascribed to a more hands-on method of managing the economy.

The Mexican state's increasingly nationalist posture on questions of land and resource control after 1917, contends historian Arnaldo Córdova, was due in part to its ties with organized labor, a pivotal ally during the military phase of the Revolution. Eager to keep organized labor in the progovernment camp, state officials spouted rhetoric that stressed anti-imperialism and social justice even while implementing an industrial development program imbued with modernist and Fordist ideals some deemed "openly dehumanizing." Organized labor's acceptance of an official party (and its concomitant subordination to politicians) required similar finagling but ultimately came in 1929 as the National Revolutionary Party created a social organization that established labor's centrality to the productive process.[19] In this way collaborationism through compromise became the status quo state-organized labor relationship in postrevolutionary Mexico and, save for six years during Cardenismo (1934–40) when revolutionary unionism prevailed, informed future syndical activity while the state enacted policies that mixed public with private investment and waffled between support for protectionism and an unabashed love of free enterprise. To those touting a "miracle" in Mexico there was no question that the state's haphazard economic course yielded results; the nation's industrial capacity expanded monumentally between 1940 and 1970. But the level of discontent present in 1968—on a scale not seen since the late 1920s—also confirmed that the promise of national advancement did not allay the anger of large segments of society that did not reap the rewards of macroeconomic expansion.

One of the most disenchanted groups, ironically, was organized labor, a sector that should have experienced the benefits of industrial growth most directly. The sources of union discontent in the 1960s were diverse but sprung in part from business's fortified position and organized labor's reduced standing vis-à-vis the state. The establishment of the maquiladora (originally, minority-owned foreign corporations, typically assembly plants) system on the U.S.-Mexican border sharpened the pain that accompanied the perceived demise of collaborationism in important ways. First, it caused union bosses to groan about the tendency of border-area factory owners to employ female laborers, believing that they required lower wages, were more easily controlled, and were less likely to unionize. Studies have demonstrated that a degree of unionization in female-dominated industries did occur, but the evolution of the maquiladora sector progressed largely apart from an organized labor movement that presented a history and collective ethic that was quintessentially male. Second, the rise of the maquiladora sector suggested to unionists the practical abandonment of economic nationalism as a philosophical priority in the nation's industrial development philosophy. An examination of the legal evolution of the system supports the latter conclusion. Consider the following chronology:

1966 The Border Industrialization Program authorized minority-owned foreign corporations to establish plants in the border region to assemble products for export.

1971 Maquiladora Industry Legislation permitted maquiladoras to operate all over the nation and abolished the requirement that installations be majority-owned Mexican entities.

1975 Acuerdo 101-1001 permitted 100 percent foreign ownership of corporations operating inside Mexican territory, except in the textile industry, and removed administrative and fiscal stipulations deemed as hindrances to investment in Mexico.[20]

Unquestionably, the gradual loosening of legal restrictions produced stunning growth in the sector. During the Díaz Ordaz administration, twenty-four maquiladoras were in operation employing 3,866 workers. Legislation passed in 1971 eliminated the requirement that Mexican-based capital compose the majority of investment and enabled the industry to balloon to 364 establishments employing 52,473 workers. Growth rates accelerated in the following years and new and ever more liberal legislation eschewed any protectionist pretensions. Mexican policy makers celebrated the rapid expansion of an industrial sector that reached 542 establishments and 658,069 workers during the administration of José López Portillo (1976–82).[21]

But even while the maquiladora sector advanced in its growth, Mexican policy makers clung to a rhetorical strategy that pursued revolutionary redemption through economic nationalism. How could they do otherwise? Calls for an expanded role of government in the management of the economy were routinely made in left-leaning and workers' periodicals.[22] An article that appeared in *Ceteme* on May 2, 1970, however, pulled few punches by workers' press standards. In a piece entitled "Our Economy Is Heading toward Monopoly," Arturo Romo wrote ominously that rising prices were the product of the growing domination of industry and markets by an exclusive club of owners. This monopolization of the economy, he feared, was a problem not solvable through mere salary increases. The only way to fix defects of the system like price gouging was by drastically altering the nation's political, social, and economic structures to permit the Mexican Revolution and the Constitution of 1917 to flourish. What Romo desired, in plain language, was for state officials to take the flow of basic goods out of the hands of private investors and place it in their own. A complete reshuffling of the nation's political economy, beginning with the state's seizure of the banking sector, was required to make commerce compliant with the tenets of the Mexican Revolution as he understood them.[23]

Organized labor's dedication to economic nationalism influenced party leaders and informed the rhetorical platform adopted by the PRI during the Echeverría sexenio. Gathering a week before the presidential election in the Mexico City suburb of Naucalpan de Juárez, elite priístas reached the conclusion that the industrialization of Mexico would maintain the Mexican Revolution as its point of departure. They agreed that the Constitution of 1917 established a juridical mark that still governed the country's "nationalist economic development and [its] balance between the public and private sectors." Continuing, party members affirmed that the state, as a "legitimate product of the Mexican Revolution," began the constructive phase of nation building with perfectly defined ideas to utilize the nation's natural resources for the benefit of all and asserted that those resources, especially nonrenewable resources, constituted one of the bases of current and future development. For that purpose they reckoned such resources needed to be exploited in a rational manner by the state in conjunction with private capitalists who had, since the implementation of policies of import substitution, responded nobly to the government's stimulus to industrialize Mexico within a framework of national protection.[24]

Mexicanization and the Debt Repaid

The PRI's restored commitment to a mixed economic system contradicted state actions in certain industrial (mainly maquiladora) settings but still promised organized labor benefits that were more than merely symbolic. In truth organized labor stood to benefit from increased state intervention in commerce because an expanded parastate apparatus inserted government, and by extension the entire labor establishment, deeper into the workings of the economy. From that privileged position powerful state-allied organizations like the CTM could exert great influence over economic questions of tariffs, trade quotas, and price controls as well as pressure the state more effectively on labor matters concerning wages, benefits, and collective contracts. There were also benefits to be had by the state in this arrangement. Assuring organized labor a seat at the economic negotiating table meant restoring a relationship of symbiotic reciprocity. Organized labor, grateful as it would be, would then pledge its allegiance to the regime, in the process reestablishing the important bonds of collaborationism that had formerly profited both elements.

Echeverría understood this equation and he tried to rally workers by promising to maintain or increase state management of vital petroleum, electricity, iron and steel, and mining resources. While campaigning for president he pledged that these industries formed part of the "national being" and would remain in Mexican hands. Referring specifically to the mining industry, he spoke in Monclova, Coahuila, on April 20, 1970, and stated, "The Mexican state, the revolutionary state of our country, will continue encouraging all efforts to mexicanize the mining industry [through] the acquisition of businesses, because before all, and above all the interests and investments that [these measures] promote, their linkage with workers will be the factor that lets them maintain a social policy in accordance with the greater interests of the nation."[25] This clear government preference for nationalization pleased workers but concerned capitalists, many in North America, who feared that the favorable investment climate that Mexico had hosted since 1940 was changing.

But for all of his rhetorical bluster, Echeverría was not preparing to implement in Mexico large-scale economic change to the degree that was occurring elsewhere. Most famously, such changes were taking place in Chile, where President Salvador Allende was constructing a "Chilean path to socialism" with the revenue gained through the 1971 confiscation of the Chuquicamata copper mine, a North American holding. In a speech announcing the nationalization of Chuquicamata, Allende linked the necessity of resource control to national sovereignty when he exclaimed, "Today the iron is ours, the salt-peter is ours, the coal is ours, the steel is ours, the copper is ours. Today we separate from copper more gold, more silver, more rhenium, and more tungsten, riches that used to leave without leaving a footprint for us. For that, we have rescued from the hands of foreign capital those basic riches that should have always been ours and that the oligarchical and reactionary groups delivered to the foreign businesses."[26] Echeverría, though frequently prone to mimicking Allende's anti-imperialist rhetoric, understood that a Chilean-style conversion of the economy was not possible in a country where strict state control and management of the economy did not jive with the terms of political economy established by its Revolution. Additionally, Echeverría's actions were constrained by his awareness that organized labor, having established its historical preference for a mixed economic system, simply would not have approved. Echeverría pursued a course of action that showed he was driven less by a desire to turn Mexico into a socialist bastion and more by a need to prove to the nation's most ideologically centrist sectors his government's commitment to revolutionary compliance. Probably the lack of drastic economic reform on Echeverría's agenda prevented a military coup d'état from appearing in Mexico à la the one that toppled Allende's government in September 1973. The transitions of companies or entire industries to partial state control during his administration were cordial and largely uncontentious.

In this regard, the nationalization, or rather, the "mexicanization," of the copper industry in 1971 is emblematic. To clarify, the term *mexicanización* was used when the state acquired majority control, meaning a minimum of 50.01 percent, of a company's or an industry's holdings. National Patrimony Secretary Horencio Flores de la Peña addressed the press on August 27, 1971, and announced that the government had entered into negotiations to purchase a controlling interest, 50.98 percent, in the Cananea Mining Company, a subsidiary, like Chuquicamata, of the Anaconda Copper Mining Company. He explained that upon "mexicanizing" the company the government would then oversee the sale of roughly half of the acquired assets to small, domestic investors, 9.81 percent to

Cobre de México, another 9.81 percent to Banco Nacional de México, and 5.88 percent to Cananea Mining Company employees. The deal's completion, he predicted, was imminent and once completed would put a basic product under the control of Mexican-owned companies that would hence be able to access the best export markets and modern technologies. Furthermore, domestic operation of the company promised increased production, and he outlined a program to invest billions of pesos to boost the company's annual output from 42,000 tons of copper to over 140,000 tons in the next five years.

Alongside being ideologically in line with the Echeverría state's economic philosophy, the mexicanization of the company had great symbolic significance, Cananea being the location of the 1906 miners' strike that ignited the national organized workers' movement in 1912 and was an important precursor of the revolution. With history in mind, it seemed fitting to Flores de la Peña that the state now acted to complete a revolutionary process of reducing foreign control of Mexican resources in a location where some believed the Revolution began. The mexicanization of the company, he contended, "achieved a fundamental advance in the historic process by means of which Mexico and Mexicans have recovered their subsoil riches," for Cananea remained until that day "the only important mining company in the country wherein national capital was not the majority."[27]

The significance of the action to workers was similarly emphasized. Most unionists were versed in the legacy of Cananea, and more than miners celebrated the first show of militant unionism against the exploitation of Mexican workers by foreign industrialists. Flores de la Peña recognized this fact and integrated it prominently into his message: "Cananea is historically linked with the Mexican Revolution and the with the workers' movement. The government of the Republic thus pays its debt with the initiators of the Revolution and organized labor, recognizing that it [the working class] must be the basis of an economic development policy imbibed with social justice, because the redistribution of revenue is an economic mirage if it does not support an authentic labor movement, strong, independent, and conscious of its class and social responsibility."[28]

By arguing that workers had built modern Mexico in alliance with a supportive state and that such an alliance was in need of renewal if future prosperity and growth were desired, Mexico's secretary of national patrimony made a civic call to arms that was espoused with increased frequency after Tlatelolco. Unionized workers could then see in the labor establishment a defender of their cause and an ally in their battles with business. Officials pointed to government purchases of strategically important and symbolic companies like that in Cananea to verify this condition of renewed collaborationism. With mexicanization, miners were judged rewarded.

Media sources suggest that the government argued its case convincingly to the public as well as to owners. The Mexico City daily *El Universal* reported on August 28, 1971, the day following the announcement, that the state's acquisition of 51 percent of the company provoked spontaneous demonstrations of joy seldom seen before in the state of Sonora. To the townspeople of Cananea, apparently, the mexicanization was the single most important development in the past sixty-five years (or in all the time elapsed since their ancestors waged the historic strike against foreign exploitation in 1906).[29] Roberto Elzy Torres, mayor of Cananea, summarized the significance of the action for local residents with a joyous front-page announcement printed in *El Heraldo de Cananea*.[30] Three days later, on September 1, the same newspaper opined that the positive repercussions of the president's decision to mexicanize the Cananea Mining Company would benefit the nation "by opening the doors to Mexican investment in mining on a large scale."[31] Other supporters of the action referenced the positive impact it had on resolving tense labor negotiations between members of Local 65 of the Mexican Mining and Metalworkers' Union and management and producing a collective contract that would govern workplace relations for the next two years.[32]

Local members of the business community were equally pleased, and they publicly expressed support for the action. Writing in their September newsletter, members of the Cananea Chamber of Commerce stated that they "greatly applauded the measure of the President" and believed that it constituted "one of the most positive acts of the first year of the government." For their part, the businessmen elaborated, they would continue to insist that federal authorities establish a refining plant in Cananea so as to further enjoy the benefits of "our mineral" (meaning copper) as well as prepare for the future mining of areas in nearby Nacozari.[33]

Mine owners supported the action as well, believing that mexicanization had the potential to eliminate certain obstacles that hindered the industry's development. Just prior to the Cananea announcement, Jorge Larrea, president of the Mexican Chamber of Mining, spoke to a gathering of mining industry professionals and touted the benefits of mexicanization, some of which included improved access to new technological resources, stable and moderated prices, and increased profits. Public and private partnerships in the sector, Larrea believed, could bring even more benefits to owners, and he called on the state to drastically increase investment to stimulate industrial growth and enhance production to increase exports.[34] Larrea's desire to increase exports was justified; financial statistics from 1970 show that the Mexican mining industry as a whole was underproductive in the area of exportation, reaping a total of just 3.2 billion pesos (about USD 256 million) from sales abroad. The paucity of this figure, stunningly low for a nation as mineral rich as Mexico, was reflected in the performance of copper, which represented just 2.2 percent of the nation's total mineral exports for 1970.[35] It was in this context that the words pronounced by Flores de la Peña only weeks later must have been encouraging to the nation's miners and mine owners alike.

Even some foreign mine owners were on board with mexicanization—at least publicly. Anaconda president John B. Place went on record and stated that the decision to sell the Cananea Mining Company to the Mexican state was entirely that of the company. Citing the company's sound financial situation—it had recorded profits of around USD 60 million the previous year—Place understood why some were puzzled by the sale. He answered inquiries by explaining that Anaconda directors found it economically attractive to take on the Mexican government as a financial partner to cofund the company's future restructuring plans. When asked if the process was similar to the forced acquisition of his company's assets in Chile, Place's answer was unequivocably no. The difference, he told reporters, "was like night and day."[36]

Place was correct to conclude that Anaconda's experiences in Chile and Mexico had little in common. Yet subsequent company history suggests that his summary of the company's motivations were, at best, incomplete. With the confiscation of its assets in Chile earlier that year, Anaconda lost two-thirds of its total copper production. Losses from the Chilean takeover, coupled with a concurrent decline in the world price of copper, weakened the company's financial position and caused it to move its operations into other mining areas, namely coal. Together these factors likely encouraged Anaconda to consent to a friendly (and profitable) "takeover" by the Mexican government.

Electrical workers did not get as much rhetorical credit as miners, but they too had written important chapters in the narrative of organized labor in Mexico. It was electrical workers, after all, who formed the SME in 1914—the oldest of the major national unions and one of the most influential in determining the outcome of the revolutionary conflict. But unlike workers in other primary economic sectors, electrical workers never unified into a single national union, and as a result rival unions competed bitterly for public and private contracts even as rapid development created employment for most workers in the sector. Separate agreements that awarded the SME and the National Electrical Industry Workers Union exclusive rights to labor contracts created by the Central Light and Power Company and the Federal Electric Commission (CFE), respectively, quelled confrontations in the sector temporarily. Mexicanization of the electrical industry by President Adolfo López Mateos on September 27, 1960, however, reignited friction by bringing Central Light and Power under majority state management and forcing the SME to brush up more closely with its adversaries, the newest foe being the Electric Workers' Union of Mexico—an organization created by the consolidation of fifty-two unions and headed by the ardent nationalist Rafael Galván Maldonado. The subsequent decade was riddled with *electricista* conflict, and battles waged within the CFE by members of the two prevailing unions proved particularly hot. Unfortunately for the SME, its two competitors agreed to sign a unity pact and join their ranks into a single organization called the United Electric Workers' Union (SUTERM) on October 26, 1972. The creation of the SUTERM represented an alliance of the SME's two primary rivals and threatened its bargaining position even further. And although the SME and the SUTERM would not cease to militate alongside one another inside the CTM, their rivalry burned intensely and demonstrated the richness and complexity of the organized workers' movement in the post-Tlatelolco period.

Both being members of the CTM and firmly fastened to revolutionary tradition, the SME and the SUTERM mutually lobbied the Echeverría state for increased government intervention in the economy. On this topic the SUTERM was unequivocal. Mexicanization was simply not enough; nothing less than 100 percent government control of the nation's electrical power assets would suffice. This position was regularly expressed by union leaders in the first year of the organization's existence. According to the editors of its monthly publication, the importance of state intervention in the economy was a fact confirmed in Mexican history. Nationalization, as they understood it, was the outcome of a revolutionary equation that factored the "deep-seated nationalist sentiment of workers, peasants, and the poor" on one side against "the inexistence of a national bourgeoisie strong enough to confront imperialism and exploit the nation's resources" on the other. Fortunately, they believed, the problem was solved by the presence of a "nationalist-revolutionist state" that, *by necessity*, turned itself into the principal economic manager. State control of the economy did not erase every trace of imperialism from the national reality, they conceded, although it ended the "long colonial night" by charting Mexico on its own path toward national development. State nationalization policies, therefore, were part of the nation's very "physiognomy" and were too important to tamper with. No discussion of policy reversal via privatization could be tolerated. "¡Ni un paso atrás . . . !" (Not a single step backward on the matter of nationalizations!) they declared, borrowing one of Echeverría's favorite catchphrases. More, not less, government control of industry was needed to truly put industry at the service of the nation and its masses of workers, peasants, and the poor. And less, not more, foreign control of industry was required to safeguard the nation's critical resources against outside manipulation. Only steps forward to nationalize new industries would prevent the breach that imperialism had created in Mexico from widening.[37]

On these basic principles, SUTERM and SME members were largely in agreement. Old grudges, however, died hard, and the two primary unions of electrical workers kept bitter relations during the Echeverría sexenio. One point of contention was the ownership status of the SME's primary employer; Central Light and Power was a parastate and not a fully nationalized company like the CFE. To *sutermistas*, therefore, their *compañeros* in the SME served a questionable master and hindered the cause of industry-wide unification. This was a message the SUTERM leaders delivered in person to Echeverría and to José López Portillo, the CFE director, when they came to inaugurate the union's national head-quarters on May 8, 1973. SUTERM secretary general Francisco Pérez Ríos elaborated that the Central Light and Power Company was objectionable not just because of its semiprivate status but also because the company maintained a degree of foreign ownership. In fact, only 4.5 percent of the company's shares in 1973 were owned by foreigners—Canadians, mostly—but state acquisition of those shares was a big deal to SUTERM leaders, who called the measure urgent and argued that as long as Central Light and Power operated as a mixed business it violated Article 27 of the Constitution, which reserved for the nation exclusive domain over the electrical power industry.[38]

Echeverría and López Portillo heard these arguments and nodded approvingly. López Portillo raised the subject again at a press conference weeks later and confirmed to reporters that a small percentage of Central Light and Power shares were owned by non-Mexicans and that their presence in the nation's electric industry was indeed unconstitutional. The situation, however, was one he believed could be easily remedied and the entire industry "honestly mexicanized" in the next two months. Yes snags to nationalization existed, he admitted, mainly in the form of a disagreement over share prices that challenged negotiations. But nothing, the future president of Mexico declared, would deter Mexico from its goal; the Central Light and Power Company would be part of the national patrimony by summer's end. Such a method would both honor the man who had charted the course thirteen years before (former president López Mateos) and help further "dilute the image of an expropriating Mexico."[39]

López Portillo's grand pronouncement, like so many others he made in his political career, did not come to fruition. Nonetheless, the future president's rhetoric fit the post-Tlatelolco state's economic model to a T. The Echeverría regime increased state control over of the economy but did so by observing the rules of business. It tread lightly along the fine line of nationalization, simultaneously celebrating the government's sovereignty when reducing the level of foreign investment in the oil industry or reclaiming majority control over the copper or electrical power industries while confirming its economic liberalism when touting the benefits of a mixed economy and compensating owners for the purchase of their assets. Walking this fine line enabled government and party officials to refute any dangerous linkages one could infer between their actions and nationalizations undertaken in Mexico in 1938 or more recently in Allende's Chile. In most cases, owners did not cry "Communism!" in response to mexicanization, and foreign capital accumulated in 1970s Mexico like it had during the previous decade. Only the most impassioned capitalist opponents of the regime believed that Echeverría, Reyes Heroles, Velázquez, or other nationalists were directed by Moscow, and no one took extensive steps to topple the regime and install a Chilean-style junta in Los Pinos.

Nonetheless, the Echeverrista economic strategy increased oversight and control of private industry by the state. It was a model that, although not socialism, was also not unbridled capitalism nor even the tempered-liberal economic model established by the Constitution of 1857. It was a mixed economic model whose character as a product of the revolutionary experience in Mexico was authentic. The promotion and implementation of this model in the period represented another effort on the part of the state to rekindle revolutionary-era norms and revive a species of collaborationism reminiscent of an earlier time. State-allied unions, it was believed, would benefit from mexicanization as whole industries came under complete or partial state control. Seated more prominently at the negotiating table, trade unionists would wield more power in their dealings with *patrones* and, theoretically, exert greater control over their lives. Mexican policy makers promoted such messages and in doing so spoke directly to the wants and needs of a sector they were desperate to woo back into the fold of compliance.

CHAPTER 4

Restoring the Revolutionary Corpus

Unity, Class, and Paternalism in Tripartite Relations

Jesús Reyes Heroles's ascension to the top of the Institutional Revolutionary Party in 1972 unnerved Mexican *patrones*, and for good reason. As demonstrated in the previous chapter, the former head of the state-owned oil company Petróleos Mexicanos advanced strong nationalist notions that many business owners imagined was bad for business. Reyes Heroles's introductory rhetoric as PRI president required no use of the imagination; it was overtly hostile to private investment. He took the reins of the PRI on February 21, 1972, with a speech that rooted the modern Mexican state's interventionist position deep in history. As he viewed it, the official party had since its origin in 1929 always worked with the government to direct the economy and bring order to a nation where "many Mexicos, ranging from the Mexico of hunger to the Mexico of lavishness, have formed." This made sense, he deduced, in a land where an "entrepreneurial state" had traditionally made public investments and promoted private industries that benefited society as a whole. Public enterprise thus remained a "transformative factor of the national reality"; it played a "decisive role" in modern national development.[1]

Summum Bonum and the Revolutionary Corpus

In truth, the new PRI president brandished a political economy with roots reaching far deeper than those laid down by Mexico's twentieth-century revolutionary experience. His advocacy for state management of the economy dated back to fifth-century Europe, to a nascent Christian culture formed around the pursuit of the summum bonum, or the common good, described by Augustine of Hippo in *City of God* as the standard for all worldly activity. Reyes Heroles's language was also grounded in the writings of Thomas Aquinas, the thirteenth-century Dominican friar who internalized Augustine's notions and explained the dangers of pursuing one's private interest at the expense of the public's. The two interests, Aquinas wrote in *On Kingship, to the King of Cyprus* in 1267, were incompatible, for while one made selfish demands, the other moved one toward commonality. While one caused people to fall apart, the other brought them together. Ultimately Aquinas believed that "the particular interest and the common good [are] not identical. We differ in our particular interests and it is the common good that unites the community."[2]

Together, the prescriptions of Augustine and Aquinas, repeated from the pulpit and in papal encyclicals and royal edicts, formed the traditional reference point of Catholic politics. Their instructions on how to rule morally and how to obey virtuously proved so integral to the maintenance of societies of the early and high Middle Ages that they were awarded sainthood after their deaths. The philosophies of Augustine and Thomas remained relevant into the early modern and modern periods and exerted as much influence over the decisions of the monarchs who reigned over the New World as over the chieftains who developed the states of Latin America in the nineteenth century. Writing in 1974 and well aware of the political reforms afoot in contemporaneous Mexico, political scientist Glen Dealy opined that modern Latin Americans remained essentially Thomists in their outlook and they clung to an ancient form of political organization called monism that saw the "lords of the land" centralize and control potentially competing interests.[3] Ample evidence gave merit to Dealy's conclusions. The Thomist maxims quoted above emphasizing the common good over individual interests read precisely like slogans printed on PRI leaflets or on the pages of any publication of the 1970s workers' press. And more than just Mexican politicians and unionists bought into them, as was revealed by a study of political attitudes taken in Mexico in the previous decade. Of 1,295 persons polled by North American researchers in 1963, 1,190 (92 percent) agreed that "The individual owes his first duty to the state and only secondarily to his personal welfare." Conversely, a mere sixty-two disagreed and forty-three responded that they did not know.[4]

Alongside a belief in the primacy of the common good, another priority of monistic government was unity achieved through strong (even "strong-man") leadership. According to Aquinas, "The most important task for the ruler of any community is the establishment of peaceful unity." Only through the attainment of unity by a virtuous monarch could the welfare and safety of a society be ensured. The alternative to unity, he believed, was perilous. "Nearly every pluralistic regime," he warned, "has ended in tyranny."[5] The pursuit of political and cultural unity through strong leadership preoccupied medieval Catholic rulers as much as the founding fathers of Latin America who built new governments following the removal of Spanish authority from the region. Speaking at Angostura in 1819 Simón Bolívar, the great "Liberator" and champion of American independence, sounded every bit the monist that Aquinas had been when he stated, "Unity, unity, unity must be our motto in all things. The blood of our citizens is varied: let it be mixed for the sake of unity. Our Constitution has divided the powers of government: let them be bound together to secure unity." Bolívar may have raised hackles among his peers by bucking the Republican current and advocating for an absolutist-like unity, but he was far from the only politician to be skeptical of multivocal rule. Regardless of what his opponents claimed to believe, the postindependence models that were created did not allow for real political pluralism among the branches of government. Such a strong consensus existed around the importance of unity that a true separation of powers in postindependence Latin America seemed nonsensical. Early legislatures, wrote Dealy, saw themselves as "spokesmen for the General

Will and courts became appendages of that national interest, prepared not to deal out an impersonal justice, but to defend the general welfare."[6]

The postindependence world designed by Latin America's first leaders was guided by other traditional conceptions as well, and most importantly, by corporatism—a sociopolitical and religious philosophy that originated in the earliest days of Christianity. The Apostle Paul described in 1 Corinthians 12 an organic form of society wherein all people and components were unified functionally, like the human body. As 1 Corinthians 12:12–16 explains,

> 12: Just as a body, though one, has many parts, but all its many parts form one body, so it is with Christ. 13: For we were all baptized by one Spirit so as to form one body—whether Jews or Gentiles, slave or free—and we were all given the one Spirit to drink. 14: Even so the body is not made up of one part but of many. 15: Now if the foot should say, "Because I am not a hand, I do not belong to the body," it would not for that reason stop being part of the body. 16: And if the ear should say, "Because I am not an eye, I do not belong to the body," it would not for that reason stop being part of the body.

Unified functionally, each part of the Christian corpus was vital to the health of the body as a whole. Each part fulfilled a function complementary to the functions of the other parts, as described in 1 Corinthians 12:17–21:

> 17: If the whole body were an eye, where would the sense of hearing be? If the whole body were an ear, where would the sense of smell be? 18: But in fact God has placed the parts in the body, every one of them, just as he wanted them to be. 19: If they were all one part, where would the body be? 20: As it is, there are many parts, but one body. 21: The eye cannot say to the hand, "I don't need you!" And the head cannot say to the feet, "I don't need you!"

As each part was vital to the functioning of the other parts, and to the health of the corpus as a whole, each part deserved respect. Keeping in line with central Christian values, St. Paul forwarded a message that emphasized the respectability of even the "least dignified" part of the body:

22: On the contrary, those parts of the body that seem to be weaker are indispensable, 23: and the parts that we think are less honorable we treat with special honor. And the parts that are unpresentable are treated with special modesty, 24: while our presentable parts need no special treatment. But God has put the body together, giving greater honor to the parts that lacked it, 25: so that there should be no division in the body, but that its parts should have equal concern for each other. 26: If one part suffers, every part suffers with it; if one part is honored, every part rejoices with it. 27: Now you are the body of Christ, and each one of you is a part of it.[7]

St. Paul's metaphor of the corpus was incarnated in medieval Catholic society, taking its most identifiable form in Europe during the High Middle Ages (eleventh to thirteenth centuries CE). In this period peasants, soldiers, clergymen, and even slaves were organized into corporate groups on the basis of their professions and common interests—agricultural, military, religious, and so on. The Catholic Church sponsored the creation of function-based groups and institutions, including religious brotherhoods, lay Catholic orders, military associations, universities, and guilds for artisans, craftspeople, and merchants in order to facilitate economic collaboration between the professions and foster a mutual respect for one another's talents. Were disputes to emerge, they were to be mediated by a cleric, a local lord, or, if necessary, a powerful but benevolent king who reigned over his kingdom like the father ruled his household. The medieval community thus appeared much like St. Paul's ideal Christian corpus in that it was formed of groups that fulfilled distinct complementary functions and were believed to be indispensable to the health of the community, even if they were not afforded equal compensation or prestige. Elaborate imagery gave shape to this conception and conveyed notions of complementarity and hierarchy simultaneously. The medieval corpus was depicted with peasants who tilled the land forming its legs, tradesmen who built its cities constituting its arms, and noblemen and kings who ruled its people occupying its torso and head.

Corporatism worked well in colonial societies, wherein one's profession, religion, ethnicity, or family history determined one's economic fate. The spread of Enlightenment philosophy and, specifically, the values of free will and individualism, however, undermined the corporatist ethos in the region and proved decisive in the thinking of postindependence leaders. Nineteenth-century Liberals rebuked corporatism as a political model and desired to establish republics formed of individuals free to determine their economic activities and destinies. In this context, traditional corporate organizations like the *ejido* and the guild appeared premodern and were assaulted at the national level. Corporatism was particularly repressed in Mexico, where workers who sought to organize were harassed and trade unions were outlawed during the long rule of Porfirio Díaz (1876–1910).

Mexico's revolution of 1910–17 toppled the dictator Díaz and attacked clerical privileges and Catholic power in the nation, but it also proved anachronistic in that it returned to prominence ancient tenets—for example, the common good—that were rooted in pre-Enlightenment Christianity. Postrevolutionary politicians, legislators, and judges resembled their predecessors by viewing themselves as "spokesmen for the General Will" and "defenders" of the "general welfare." Corporatism too was restored—institutionalized, even—upon the creation of the National Revolutionary Party by Plutarco Elías Calles in 1929. The party assembled selected interest groups and gave them exclusive rights and privileges vis-à-vis the revolutionary regime. The large labor and agrarian confederations that formed in the 1930s (the CTM in 1936 and the National Peasants' Confederation in 1938) fit neatly into the party's structure and, after seeing the benefits of a close alliance with the state, willingly swapped independence for partnership during the administration of Lázaro Cárdenas in the 1930s.

Postrevolutionary corporatism in Mexico, as in medieval societies, implied both pros and cons for organized workers. In exchange for sacrificing independence to the government, the 1931 Federal Labor Law imposed less restrictive constraints on workers' right to strike and gave inducements to unions, including subsidies that were far more generous than those found in labor laws of other countries. Inducements written into the labor code also increased the capacity of unions to provide selective benefits for workers and gave union leadership leverage over rank-and-file members.[8] Moreover, the 1931 code benefited the working class through the solidification of the JFCA, first established in 1927 to uphold workers' rights in industrial sectors deemed strategically vital or having an interstate character.

The foundational language of the JFCA stressed objectivity, and the tripartite structure of the bodies, integrated by an equal number of worker and owner representatives and a government representative, reflected the government's commitment to resolving conflicts within a corporatist framework.[9] Yet the early trajectory of the JFCA suggested a state bias for the cause of employees over employers. Government representatives in the period 1935–40 swung their decisive votes overwhelmingly toward the cause of labor, ruling to approve nearly four out of every five of the more than two thousand strike petitions filed.[10] Unquestionably, JFCA rulings in favor of workers were critical components in the decision of Cárdenas to nationalize the oil industry on March 18, 1938.

So often on the wrong side of JFCA judgments, Mexican employers of the 1930s concluded that the scales of justice were tipped against them in the arena of labor arbitration. The tide appeared to shift with economic expansion in the 1940s, and future labor representatives condemned what they viewed as an observable bias on the part of government for capital over labor. By the late 1960s the glory days of the 1930s when workers enjoyed favoritism from the Mexican state seemed a distant memory. Three decades of probusiness policy and development had extinguished any notion unionists may have entertained about the government's pro-labor persuasion. By 1969 the workers' press openly screamed that a governmental bias toward business infected the labor arbitration process and that dramatic reform was required.[11] With the crisis of legitimacy generated by the events of Tlatelolco organized labor sought again to capitalize on the government's need for redemption.

A National Tripartite Commission wherein workers and owners could sit together and discuss such controversial topics as price gouging, hoarding, and inflation was a state offering meant to appease organized labor by providing a new venue for labor contestation. The planned creation of the commission was announced at a May 17, 1971, meeting that lasted nine hours and brought together an impressive array of worker, owner, and government representatives. Echeverría convened the gathering with a speech that stressed the cooperative and revolutionary aspects of the planned commission, to be composed of ten worker representatives, ten business representatives, and five government officials.[12] In his address he espoused a familiar theme, the importance of *convivencia*, or harmonious coexistence between the factors of production, in a way that displayed his commitment to traditional Thomist values. The proposed National Tripartite Commission could hence facilitate dialogue between employers and employees and form one of several tripartite bodies already in existence to resolve labor-capital disputes, including the National Minimum Wage Commission, the National Profit-Sharing Commission, and the National Human Resource Industrial Development Council, among others. The Echeverría government's proven commitment to providing adverse functional groups a venue within which to compete, always under the watchful guidance of the parent state, proved that a corporatist model was in place to structure government in the period.

Still, the Echeverría state was not a perfect corporatist specimen. Class-conscious rhetoric espoused by the president defied the basic corporatist ethos by sowing bodily discord and injuring the health of the corpus. Most postrevolutionary Mexican leaders utilized tripartism to resolve labor disputes but very few welcomed class conflict at the bargaining table. Calles, we recall, like Carranza before him, saw class and national interests as contradictory, and he subscribed to a capitalist development project for Mexico that minimized class conflict through state management. Cárdenas, on the other hand, believed that the constitutionally established goal of equilibrium between labor and capital could best be achieved by guaranteeing workers' rights and permitting workers to push for the inclusion of worker comanagement, profit sharing, and collective contracts in their dealings with patrones.[13] Manuel Ávila Camacho, who succeeded Cárdenas in 1940, was less supportive of progressive worker demands but wrote tripartite negotiation into the Industrial Labor Pact, a 1945 accord to develop Mexican industry under the rubric of economic nationalism.[14] Post–World War II development demands in Mexico, however, spawned a new modus vivendi in tripartite labor relations. Employers increasingly intervened in labor matters and expanded their influence with the state at the expense of workers. In time, their larger role in determining national economic policy undermined the revolutionary-inspired rhetoric that argued for the benefits of class conflict. What was good for business was advertised as good for the nation at large, representing another message that when naturalized into the discourse further muffled the volume of class identity in labor relations.[15]

Speeches made to announce the creation of the National Tripartite Commission in 1971 suggested a renewed comfort with promoting class identity in labor mediation. Echeverría spoke and instructed business leaders to inject their operations with nationalist and humanitarian sentiments. He repeated campaign slogans and argued that their failure to distribute profits equitably caused economic inequality and halted national progress. With a National Tripartite Commission the government would be able to coordinate the forces of production and eliminate contradictions in the economy that placed the interests of one sector above the interests of the nation. Compliance with these goals demanded from everyone "a decidedly patriotic attitude."[16] Rafael Hernández Ochoa, the secretary of labor and social welfare, followed Echeverría that afternoon and warned that a sustained "prosperity" built upon the sacrifice of the majority would not be permitted by the principles of the Mexican Revolution, as "the well being of the workers is a fundamental requisite of an authentic national development." Without it, he warned, "economic imbalance and social injustice" would continue. He then reminded his audience about one of the principal determinations of Article 123—that work was not an "article of commerce" but rather a right—and scolded them for jeopardizing that right by putting thousands of employees out of work through industrial mechanization. He advised Mexican patrones, unionists, and policy makers to promote worker training and state industrial decentralization strategies to right this wrong and help mitigate the pressing problems of un- and underemployment in Mexico. With these words, the state's leading labor authorities appealed to the nationalism of patrones by asking them to think less of personal profits and more about the communal benefits industry could bring. With the National Tripartite Commission the penchant of recent governments to muffle any mention of distinct class concerns in labor negotiations seemed destined for reversal.

Echeverría's commitment to tripartite negotiations and tolerance for open class contestation heartened organized labor and returned the government closer to the bosom of the Mexican unionist who had shunned it since the late 1950s. For the post-Tlatelolco PRI to do the same, newly installed party chief Jesús Reyes Heroles surmised that it desperately needed purification; it needed to remove from its ranks "infiltrators" who had diverged from the dictates of revolutionary ideology. His first speech as PRI president, given on February 21, 1972, is again exemplary in this regard. Speaking to fellow partisans, the new PRI leader broached the previously taboo subject of class when he announced that "We," as members of the PRI, "have an economic and social line of thinking that convinces us that Revolution and personal economic power are not reconcilable. Neither the economically powerful nor those who serve them have a place in this party!"[17]

This highly polemical statement ignited a firestorm of reaction, as it got to the core of understandings about class, corporatism, and the revolutionary body in modern society. María del Carmen Carreño, a prominent official inside the National Confederation of Popular Organizations, took issue with Reyes Heroles and defended the right of the wealthy to belong to the PRI. In contrast, Fidel Velázquez, secretary general of the Confederation of Mexican Workers, was elated with Reyes Heroles and invited him to address the Eightieth General Assembly of the CTM National Council later that month. There *cetemistas* received

Reyes Heroles with a standing ovation and Velázquez introduced him by declaring his organization's enthusiasm for the new PRI chief's ideas. He turned toward Reyes Heroles and declared,

> It is high time, Sir, as you said in your speech, that the rich leave the Institutional Revolutionary Party. You know well that we did not get along with them, nor did we put them in the PRI. The PRI, we understand, is a party of the people, of the workers, of the peasants, of the middle class, of all those who are identified with the Mexican Revolution. The rich do not have to be there, and not only do we agree that they leave the Party, but also that they leave the public posts that they shamefully occupy under the protection of the Party.[18]

Thus, according to Velázquez, there could be no room in the official party for a class of people who did not share the dictates and ideology of its foundational groups. Excluding them from public life was therefore appropriate.

Reyes Heroles received his ovation and set about putting his money where his mouth was. He altered the party's internal statutes to stipulate that large-scale employers of labor could not belong to it. The practical result of this stipulation meant that business owners could not vote in the PRI's state or national councils or hold positions on the National Executive Committee. Owners of large companies were subsequently prohibited from taking part in the party's internal decision-making processes that guaranteed that the three "revolutionary" sectors of civil society—worker, peasant, and popular and professional—would determine policy in Mexico.[19]

Later Reyes Heroles took to the road to spread the news about the PRI's renewed "revolutionary" character. In speeches he often cited the obstacles that the sin of greed presented to the advancement of Mexican society, and in his rhetoric the question of whose conscience was most stained with guilt was never in doubt. In July 1972 he delivered a speech before two thousand residents of the hardscrabble Mexico City boroughs of Gustavo A. Madero and Azcapotzalco and iterated the official position of the party he led. He informed them that the PRI shared their values and was against those who possessed excess property to the injury of those who lacked it. He listed PRI priorities in a way that resonated with locals. "We want less water for those who waste it, so that there be more here; we want less upscale housing developments so that there by fewer shacks here; we want less expenses and waste so that there be more jobs." Turning to labor-specific issues, he pledged that the PRI would not permit employers to pay workers a wage below that established by law, nor would it let "those who have much" allow those who have little to suffer inadequate education, health, and transportation services.[20]

Collectivism in the Worker Home and Body

The emphasis given to class identity and calls made for personal sacrifice by Echeverría, Reyes Heroles, and other state and party officials in the period attested to their desire to reconstitute certain genetic strands of the revolutionary body. Worker demands for increased state involvement in organized labor-business relations showed a similar desire to reestablish that historical norm. Together, state and organized labor rhetoric that emphasized the importance of class, nationalism, and social justice demonstrated a powerful longing to revive certain principles that had formerly guided state and labor relations, another of which was collectivism.

The brand of collectivism that developed inside the workers' movement in postrevolutionary Mexico was distinguishable by its vertical and hierarchical tendencies. Mexican unions, in general, were not democratic organizations, though members took care of their own when help was needed. Mutual aid funds—collectively administered accounts that had roots in medieval corporatist societies—continued to function and remained dear in the hearts of modern unionists. Historically, mutual aid funds were formed from worker contributions and were administered to help workers and family pay unexpected costs such as medical bills or funeral expenses. Union mutual aid funds in the 1970s maintained that basic function.

The creation of the United Electric Workers' Union, formed by the merger of two rival electrical worker unions in 1972, provoked great consternation among members, who wondered what changes would be made to their union accounts. Members' questions were answered and their fears assuaged in the pages of the union's first monthly newsletter. In May 1973 *SUTERM* no. 1 informed readers that all permanent employees of the Federal Electric Commission, the state-owned company with which the SUTERM had the primary labor contract, were automatically registered in the union's general fund. Retired workers were registered as well, though they had to renew their subscriptions within ninety days. Furthermore, dues would remain the same (10 pesos weekly), as would the amount paid to beneficiaries of deceased workers: 125,000 pesos to relatives of active members; 75,000 pesos to relatives of retired members.[21]

The benefits workers could gain by paying into the mutual aid fund were constantly promoted in the workers' press. *SUTERM* frequently published rolls of deceased electrical workers and listed the amounts paid to their families by the union fund. Oftentimes these lists were accompanied by photographs that showed somber-looking widows receiving checks from union officials. One photo that ran in *SUTERM* no. 2 showed Echeverría handing a check to a very elderly woman, likely the mother of a deceased employee. The caption of the photo, which read, "On the March: The Union's Mutual Fund," actually understated the symbolic value of the image.[22] In this scene a SUTERM member observed nothing less than the president of the republic providing for a coworker's loved one. Perhaps, it was hoped, the worker even saw in the image the head and symbolic father of the Mexican people caring for one his weakest children.

Workers saw in mutual aid funds tangible benefits of collectivism in union life. They saw their leaders collect and organize the funds in a way that guaranteed that their families would not face tragedy alone. In the administration and disbursal of funds workers felt pride and camaraderie, knowing that their efforts would benefit a *compañero* in his or her time of need. Such swells of solidarity were especially comforting to workers in a time as tumultuous as the post-Tlatelolco era. In this context, most (not all) unionized workers rallied around a corporate identity that unified them with their leaders, the state, and each other against their historical enemies in the employer class. In this context of moral and societal flux questions raised about the composition of the Mexican state became more salient than ever. The resulting controversies waged over basic questions, including the appropriateness of permitting wealthy individuals membership in the PRI, were addressed by policy makers, who pleased organized labor with resolutions that showed a renewed state empathy for the plight of the worker.

Questions of moral economy, specifically, debates about the debt owed workers by the Mexican state, pervaded popular discourses carried out in urban settings where politicians advertised their restored commitment to the cause of the unionist. In those locales, however, which had long represented the nuclei of organized labor's power base, official messages reached diverse ears. When Reyes Heroles spoke to the residents of Gustavo A. Madero and Azcapotzalco in July 1972 his words were probably heard by more nonunionized, or "free," workers than unionists. Such individuals were not "workers" by the definition ascribed by labor authorities but instead formed part of a massive laboring underclass that worked part-time or temporary jobs without the benefits and protections of union membership. They puzzled policy makers by operating just beyond the control of the official labor establishment.

In the eyes of labor authorities free workers represented more of a threat than an opportunity because they exhibited little demonstrable drive to unionize during the period under review. Why? The answer was simple: demographics. In 1970s Mexico there were simply not enough union jobs available for those who wanted them. Mexico's population in the postwar period grew disproportionately to the ability of organized labor to incorporate new workers into the movement, causing the rate of unionized workers as a percentage of all workers to plummet from a high of 9.1 percent in 1950 to 7.3 percent in 1969.[23] After Tlatelolco, organized labor's leadership continued to exhort the laboring class to organize. *Ceteme* frequently printed a call to free workers to "defend yourself from owner exploitation, use your constitutional rights, join a union." This demand was invariably followed by language from Article 123, Part XVI, affirming the constitutional guarantee that "workers as much as owners will have the right to join together in defense of their respective interests, forming unions, professional organizations, etc."[24]

CTM-led unionization efforts paid off in the post-Tlatelolco period, although the true extent of success is unclear. Mexican union rolls are notoriously unreliable as historical sources and were typically inflated in order to solicit greater subsidies from the labor ministry. One conservative estimate contends that at least 15.2 percent of the Mexican workforce was unionized in 1970, a figure that even if still too high greatly exceeded the 7.3 percent recorded for 1969 and demonstrated at least minimal growth in the organized workforce during that period.[25]

Even with labor gains, unemployment was a day-to-day reality for much of society in post-Tlatelolco Mexico. Even unionists sat idly by waiting for employment. Such was a natural byproduct of population expansion that greatly outpaced the nation's industrial expansion. For context, consider that during the period 1960–69 Mexico experienced its highest rates of population growth, averaging 3.35 percent annually during that period.[26] This colossal expansion, which increased Mexico's population from just under thirty-five million in 1960 to over forty-eight million by 1970, was celebrated by some as tangible evidence of the nation's economic and social maturation. Optimists saw demographic growth as both the product and source of economic expansion, a rationale that permitted one to conclude that as many as six hundred thousand new jobs would be required annually to meet the needs of an expanding populace.[27] Cynics, on the other hand, feared that the nation approached a critical demographic mass. In the opinion of Jesús Yurén, who ran one of the nation's largest unions, the FSTDF, the demographic question represented one of the fundamental challenges workers of the 1970s faced. In his opinion, rapid population expansion was increasing the size of the economically active population at an unsustainable rate. In 1965 12.5 million citizens were involved in wage-earning activities in Mexico, according to CTM statistics. In 1970 that number had grown to 15 million, and it was projected to surpass 18 million by 1975. As a result, Yurén concluded it was necessary to create new employment for at least 650,000 workers a year, a feat not achievable in his opinion, given that modern industry had failed to sufficiently expand and was guilty of underproduction that hindered the creation of new jobs.[28]

Skeptics like Yurén needed only to look to the fringes of any large urban center to corroborate their concerns. There one saw encampments of recently arrived peasants who had come in search of work. Indeed, industrial development in the cities could not keep pace with the dual phenomena of sky-high birth rates and the methodical flow of migrants from the countryside. In the Federal District alone, inward migration coupled with natural yet unprecedented rates of reproduction meant population expansion that nearly quintupled the capital's population in just three decades, growing from 1.4 million in 1940 to 6.9 million in 1970.[29] In the shantytowns hastily constructed on the defunct ejidos and hillsides surrounding the city hundreds of thousands of unemployed and underemployed persons languished. In their very existence, haphazard and disordered, they called attention to the failures of the postrevolutionary state to provide for the displaced throngs of the countryside. In the necessary lawlessness they employed to survive, they questioned the ability of organized labor to provide gainful employment for all who sought it.

Population explosion and its effect on the power of the Mexican organized workers' movement formed a primary topic of discussion at the CTM's Ninth National Congress, convened on April 21, 1974. Attendees of the three-day congress openly fretted about the effects that rapid population expansion was having on the negotiating power of their unions. In the sea of informal urban settlements they saw a virtually limitless reservoir of cheap and manipulable labor—a legitimate concern for an organized workers' movement that had long derived strength and benefits from its status as an indispensible and irreplaceable component of the production process. Others feared that unionists' wages were being depressed by other trends, particularly the rapid expansion of the labor supply via the growth of urban families. When discussing the issue, cetemistas tapped into a popular contemporary discourse that questioned the morality of transitionally or provisionally employed workers forming families. Media sources from months later confirm that this discourse intensified into a full-fledged campaign with a message to workers that was unequivocal: do not produce more workers if you cannot sustain them. This mandate represented the major effort of organized labor to combat the challenges of a demographic situation that threatened its interests and, in the words of a CTM spokesperson, to preserve the liberty and dignity of the Mexican worker.[30]

Preserving the liberty and dignity of the Mexican worker was not a responsibility entrusted only to the leadership of organized labor; it was also conferred upon the individual worker himself. Appealing to the moral conscience of workers was not new. Since the modern labor movement first sprouted in Mexico from the rocky soils of Cananea, unionized workers had regularly been asked to make personal sacrifices for the good of the proletarian cause. What made this particular directive unique, however, was its intrusive and intimate nature. It fixed the gaze of organized labor's leadership directly into the home and instructed workers, for the first time in the history of the movement, to not reproduce. Such a mandate represented a stark reversal from the confident pronatalist tone that characterized labor and state rhetoric in the headiest years of economic expansion. Unlike their predecessors, unionists of the 1970s were ordered by their leaders to limit the size of their families as a show of "paternal responsibility." This directive, it appeared, was gender specific, as it ordered only the father of the family to abstain from future procreation so that his children might "live in a world where they may find remunerative work and can subsist with dignity and honor."[31]

CTM officials sought to perpetuate the workers' movement in Mexico by instilling their specific brand of parenthood in workers. In pursuit of this goal, family planning conferences were held to remind workers that children brought a financial responsibility. One such conference was sponsored by the Mexican Industrial Petrochemical Workers' Union on February 9, 1975, and convened at CTM headquarters in Mexico City. Manuel Ñique, director of the Family Planning and Development Unit of the Regional Inter-American Organization of Workers frightened the gathering of two hundred by describing an almost doomsday scenario wherein Mexico would have by the year 2000 over 120 million people crammed onto just 11 percent its of inhabitable land. In order to avoid sentencing Mexico's next generation to such a difficult future, Ñique asked parents to contemplate the ramifications of producing children the nation could not support. Do not think to yourself that because "I earn well now and can buy them anything" you should have children, he told his listeners. Rather, tell yourself that "it is more important to think of the world that your children will receive."[32] Children, it seemed to Ñique, were a blessing that should come to the working family in moderation—and only to those who could afford them.

The language preferred by labor leaders, stressing collectivism through personal sacrifice and paternal responsibility, positioned the ethos of organized labor as a corollary to the domestic goals of the state, which, not coincidentally, made waves by distributing condoms in this period. Like the nation itself, which was conceptualized as resembling a corpus with the Mexican president at the head and the sectors of society forming its torso and limbs, so too was the labor movement described as a body. Union literature drew further parallels, stating that just as Echeverría watched over his children—the peasants, schoolteachers, and widows of Mexico—so too did Fidel Velázquez provide for the trolley-car driver and assembly-line worker. In their actions the patriarchs served similar functions: both were fighting to shield their progeny from the evils of the greedy patrón and the deceit of the dastardly foreigner. Strong leaders, morally rooted in the precepts of the Mexican Revolution, were important, but Thomist theory advised that only as a unified whole could the body withstand such threats to its existence. To survive, each constituent part had to eschew individualism in favor of dependence.

The State as Provider

In the language and directives cited above we may read a form of social birth control that the CTM wished to impress upon its members. The interventionist, collectivist, and paternalist tones of the debate reflected the general timbre of political discourse in the period. That the leaders of organized labor moved in this direction during the period was not surprising, given that the Mexican state extended its reach into the personal lives of Mexican workers after Tlatelolco by expanding its power to regulate the nitty-gritty of workplace relations via the New Federal Labor Law of 1970 and the National Tripartite Commission. This tack was part of a larger state campaign to increase its authority in society through the psychological and practical reestablishment of its place at the head of the revolutionary body.

Alongside the efforts it made to increase its influence over the economy and labor dispute resolution, the post-Tlatelolco Mexican state also expanded its social services. Its goals in this process were the same as those for the economy and labor, and efforts to expand its capacity benefited certain societal sectors at the expense of others. The Echeverría state drastically expanded the National Popular Subsistence Company (CONASUPO), a network of government-subsidized popular stores. The popular store was not a new idea. A system of subsidized stores to combat food shortages, end the poor distribution of products, and prevent abnormal fluctuations in the market had been in place in Mexico since the National Distributor and Regulator was organized in 1938. The system survived into the 1940s and financed vendors willing to operate popular stores and sell government-furnished products at a markup of no more than 10 percent. Not surprisingly, the regulator was roundly endorsed by the CTM but opposed by business owners, who argued that the government was instituting price controls by fiat and using the guise of social protection to create monopolies out of companies that could afford to operate at low profit margins. By the mid-1940s budget increases augmented the power and presence of the regulator and raised the ire of the National Confederation of Chambers of Commerce, the nation's umbrella commerce organization, which saw in it "an alarming degree of state intervention in the market and private sector."[33]

The Mexican state's embrace of unfettered industrial development after World War II reversed the trend of paternalism in government economic policy. Policies implemented during the presidency of Miguel Alemán Valdés (1946–52) indicated that a new ethos had emerged opposing price controls and calling for limited government involvement in the realms of food subsidization and distribution. The law was changed in 1947 to permit regulator distribution centers to sell merchandise to any business instead of limiting sales to popular stores. Gradually the government stopped funding the regulator altogether and existing popular stores became independent. Other government institutions evolved along similar lines, always prefaced by the rationale that postwar conditions required the state to facilitate rather than direct the market, as it had done during 1930s. Economic reorientation evoked criticism, notably from Daniel Cosío Villegas, who accused Alemán of abandoning the "very heart of the Revolutionary experience."[34] Years later Echeverría revived the counterrevolutionary claim once lodged by Cosío Villegas. Believing that a "settlement" of ideology had occurred between 1940 and 1968, Echeverría desired to rechart Mexico on a course he felt was more congruent with revolutionary ideals.[35] The expansion of CONASUPO after 1970 therefore represented yet another part of that effort because it demonstrated a renewed state commitment to protecting the nation's most vulnerable (and, not coincidentally, most populous) classes from the caprices of the powerful.

Mexican unionists, however, never represented the nation's most vulnerable class. Nor were they the main targets of federal food distribution programs, which were primarily based in rural areas. Popular stores during the Echeverría administration, however, were primarily established in cities and benefited urban as well as rural workers.[36] Urban workers therefore fit squarely into the post-Tlatelolco state's discourse of paternalism, and customers of CONASUPO stores were unwitting recipients of official propaganda that portrayed them as dependents of a benevolent provider who protected them from dangerous elements bent on exploiting them. CONASUPO was promoted in the pages of the workers' press during the years 1970–76 using familiar social themes. Advertisements in *Ceteme* instructed, "Compañero: Defend Your Salary" by shopping at a "cooperative store and taking advantage of the goods that CONASUPO offers at fair prices." Advertisements then listed the units of sale and prices for basic articles sold at below market rates. Items advertised typically included (with prices, in pesos, corresponding to October 1976) rice, 1 kilogram—$6; sugar, 2 kilograms—$4.60; coffee, 250 grams—$5.80; beans, 1 kilogram—$5.50, evaporated milk, 1 kilogram—$1.25; bread, 40 grams—$0.15.[37] The benefits of CONASUPO were also touted to workers in person. CONASUPO director Jorge de la Vega Domínguez was a regular invitee at labor functions and delivered messages that promoted the organization as a safety net that protected the working classes against market fluctuations and social unrest that was beyond their control.

Workers were moved by these messages but also saw tangible benefits in having their own stores. Unionists worked closely with the federal agency to establish popular stores to service their needs. *SUTERM* describes one such process that was undertaken by electrical workers in Celaya, Guanajuato, in June 1973. According to the report, city residents mobbed a newly opened CONASUPO store and emptied its shelves within four hours. At the time of the article's writing, the store was accruing sales of over 12,000 pesos per day and could not meet the mob's voracious appetite for the low-priced goods. Celaya *sutermistas* seized the opportunity and asked their union's secretary general, Francisco Pérez Ríos, for help in acquiring a piece of land that abutted the location of the current store. Pérez Ríos obliged and issued electrical workers a loan from the SUTERM's Housing and Social Services Fund to purchase the property. Next the workers petitioned CONASUPO for permission to install a store. Their request was quickly granted and accompanied by a startup loan of 250,000 pesos. All 210 members of the Celaya local then pooled their resources to cover the loan, in essence becoming shareholders in the enterprise. The store's future success was deemed a certainty by *SUTERM*'s writers, and the union's National Committee congratulated its Celaya members for "the effort that they make to fight the ever more worrisome cost-of-living increases."[38]

Popular stores, as suggested above, were understood as assets that benefited the worker's wallet and protected the working family against economic chicanery. CONASUPO, as commonly described in official rhetoric, represented a counterweight against the wickedness of hoarders and speculators in Mexican society, who through treasonous acts enriched themselves by manipulating the people's access to basic goods. This very public, class-based discourse echoed common polemics of the period that turned so-called hoarders and speculators into popular boogeymen. Diatribes launched against these shadowy creatures became useful vehicles to curry popular support for labor priorities. And support was palpable, a fact that enabled the CONASUPO system to grow to eleven thousand stores in 1976 from one-tenth that number in 1970.[39]

Still, agencies like CONASUPO fell short of meeting workers' demands in important ways. CONASUPO entrusted government officials to distribute basic goods and imposed earning limits on retailers but did not establish price limits on merchandise. SUTERM leaders cited this omission and called on all unions to unite in their fight against the rising cost of living. Price hikes, they wrote in June 1974, had reached intolerable levels, owing to the structural flaws that weakened the nation's system of product distribution and commercialization. Industrialists and merchants, they alleged, thrived in this corrupted framework and fixed prices at their whim. The prevalence of foreign investment in Mexico also created problems, as it introduced "parasites" into the country that retarded the development of national industry and commerce. Workers, SUTERM leaders warned, could not sit idly by in the face of such a threat. "The time to act has arrived!" they declared. "It is imperative to control prices in a radical and drastic manner." In this task the government had an opportunity to affirm its revolutionary credentials: "A revolutionary regime must put the interests of the majority first."

The SUTERM iterated its demands in a June 7, 1974, manifesto sent to the president and hundreds of peasant and worker organizations. The document began by asking Echeverría to punish those who worked to make the rich richer and the poor poorer. "Enough with abuses and provocations!" union leaders exclaimed. The SUTERM then appealed to the working class to pressure the government to pursue the stated ends. This was an important task; nothing less than the Mexican Revolution demanded it. Finally, the SUTERM manifesto presented a series of demands that constituted a veritable wish list of organized labor. Included were requests that the federal government (a) establish price controls on articles of basic consumption; (b) create a technical commission to study, set, and monitor prices; (c) make the production and distribution of basic articles its exclusive domain; (d) expand the operations of CONASUPO, putting additional supply centers under the control of workers and peasants; (e) liberate all supply centers from monopolistic activities "that the hoarders, shop-owners, and the rest of the sharks carry out"; and (f) immediately revise the price of medicines and nationalize the pharmaceutical industry.[40]

Some of these requests were met to varying degrees of satisfaction. Most notably the Echeverría government implemented a series of prices freezes on basic necessity goods. One plan approved by the National Tripartite Commission on June 24, 1974, presented a fourteen-point strategy to help protect workers' salaries against shifts in the market. Under the plan the commission resolved to create a sliding scale to automatically adjust salaries and pledged to consider additional wage increases in the future. More immediately, the plan listed fifty-three items whose prices would be temporarily regulated by the Secretariat of Industry and Commerce. Among the listed items were food staples, including milk, tortillas, beans, eggs, chicken, vegetable oil, rice, evaporated milk, and bread; kitchen items, including purified water, soap, sugar, salt, soft drinks, matches, cornmeal, and flour; clothing items, including dresses and shoes; and some "nonessentials" like cigarettes and coffee.

Not surprisingly, the prices dictated from on high withered under the pressures of the popular market. In the days that followed reports abounded of merchants who ignored federally established price limits. In Monterrey a merchant had his entire stock of beans—estimated at around eight hundred kilograms—seized by inspectors from the state's Industry and Commerce Department because he had charged customers more than the 6.5-pesos-per-kilo rate set by the government.[41] It was reported that other vendors in Monterrey also disregarded price limits and sold goods, sometimes at two and three times above the established limits, to customers who were panic buying in order to prepare for shortages they deemed imminent. This kind of price gouging could be witnessed even in the city's CONASUPO stores, where vendors commonly sold vegetable oil at elevated prices.[42]

Organized labored clamored for state action to combat rampant inflation, and the Echeverría state responded by expanding CONASUPO and placing temporary price freezes on certain items. Echeverría's assistance was also pivotal in winning substantial wage increases for unionists in

September 1973 and September 1974. These measures pleased workers but were ultimately judged insufficient, as the cost of goods remained tied to fluctuations in the world market and out of the hands of state officials, who were empowered only to regulate their markup and not their base cost. Union officials cited the lack of permanent price controls as a crucial deficiency in tripartite relations. Editors of *Ceteme* worried that in the absence of price controls efforts to control wages would be futile, as workers would be constantly compelled to demand wage hikes to meet ever-escalating costs of living.[43] The desire to write price controls into law drove a good deal of the union activism in the period under review. Organized workers, therefore, may have conveyed satisfaction with the state's efforts to increase its influence over the nation's economic and labor functions, but they remained vigilant to demand more from a government they perceived as sympathetic to their cause.

The realization of the National Tripartite Commission would have to wait until 1974, attesting to the intransigency of Mexican patrones toward the state's intervention in economic affairs. Nevertheless, the commission's eventual creation and the birth of other tripartite boards in the period represented real victories for unionists because they enabled labor representatives to intervene directly in the tackling of economic problems that formerly had been resolved by state-business negotiations conducted in private. The government's renewed tolerance for class identity in political and labor discourses appealed to unionists but disheartened patrones, who felt themselves assaulted on multiple fronts: from their workers, who had begun to mobilize against them armed with a restored class solidarity; from the state, which granted organized labor concession after concession in order to restore collaborationism; and now from the PRI, which worked to win voter loyalty by mimicking the government's prolabor positions. In all, the regime's creation of tripartite commissions and expansion of CONASUPO produced a marked increase in state economic power that benefited organized labor. The renewed credence given to notions of complementarity, harmonious coexistence, and the common good yielded more than philosophical debate, for an invigorated paterfamilias at the head of the corporatist structure was an asset that gave unionists increased leverage in their negotiations with business leaders. After the moral challenges created by Tlatelolco, these ancient Catholic values—revived six decades earlier by a social revolution with a potent anticlerical bent—were themselves in need of redemption. Praise emitted in official syndical rhetoric and literature suggested that the one-party state led by latter-day redeemers Echeverría and Reyes Heroles had, yet again, restored values that Mexican unionists held dear and effectively combated the crisis of legitimacy that beset it. The regime's quest for revolutionary redemption, however, faced greater challenges still.

CHAPTER 5

"Años de Huelga"

Business and State-Organized Labor
Conflict in Monterrey, 1973–74

The Death of Eugenio Garza Sada

Since the mid-nineteenth century no group in Mexico has been more associated with industrialism and prosperity than *los regiomontanos*, or those from the city of Monterrey.[1] And within that group no family has captured the essence of entrepreneurialism and corporate benevolence better than the Garza Sada clan. A true dynasty was born in 1890 with the founding of the Cervecería Cuauhtémoc (Cuauhtémoc Beer Company) by Isaac Garza and Francisco G. Sada. Their business partnership engendered the formation of family ties, and Isaac married Francisco's sister Consuelo. This business and familial partnership had great historical impact, as their heirs branched out into new industrial sectors and formed a powerhouse that impacted the destiny of the city and the entire region.

Eugenio Garza Sada personified the grandeur associated with twentieth-century industry in Monterrey more than anyone else. Born on January 11, 1892, Eugenio was the fourth child of Isaac and Consuelo. The Mexican Revolution upended life when it arrived in the state of Nuevo León in 1913 and forced Eugenio's father to suspend operation of his businesses and move the family to safety across the border in the United States.

This experience proved seminal in the formation of young Eugenio, who, according to one biographer, learned the value of hard work in the United States by holding several odd jobs, including that of movie theater attendant. He then flourished as a student, culminating his education in 1917 with a bachelor's degree in civil engineering from the Massachusetts Institute of Technology. Eugenio returned to Monterrey to join the family business after graduation and with the general cessation of military violence in Mexico. In the decades that followed, Eugenio and his brother Roberto alternated at the head of the family's beer empire while also founding a number of subsidiary and new companies, most notable was the steel giant Monterrey Tin and Sheet Metal (HYLSA) in 1943.

The brothers were also lauded for their social and civic works. Employees of their various businesses took part in company societies that provided them and their family members health benefits and other perks. Workers in the Cuauhtémoc and Factories of Monterrey (FAMOSA) plants and their kin were provided medical services before the creation of the Mexican Social Security Institute in 1946. Similarly, beer, steel, and other employees who formed the Garza legions were furnished with workers' housing beginning in 1957, thirteen years before that provision was mandated in the New Federal Labor Law of 1970 and fifteen years before the government created the National Workers' Housing Institute in 1972. The Garza family also gave generously to support hospitals, schools, sports, and other public programs in Monterrey and around the state. Eugenio sowed perhaps his most lasting legacy in 1943 when he sponsored the creation of the Monterrey Technological Institute to permit Mexican youths to receive a first-class technical education without leaving the country. Tec de Monterrey was indeed excellent and was often referred to by Garza Sada as the "love of his loves."[2] He presided over the institution's Board of Regents until his death.

The Garza family and particularly Eugenio inspired wide admiration and reverence in the Monterrey community. Tragically, regiomontanos were deprived of this favorite son on the morning of September 17, 1973, when the automobile in which he, along with his driver, Modesto Torres Briones, and his bodyguard, Bernardo Chapa Pérez, was traveling along

Quintanar Street in downtown Monterrey was abruptly intercepted by a gray Ford Falcon. DGIPS intelligence reports generated that day document the events meticulously, explaining that at about 9:00 a.m. two armed men, both young, jumped from the Falcon and attempted to apprehend Garza Sada by forcing him from his vehicle, a 1969 Ford Galaxy. One of them, known as El Borrado, brandished a machine gun and entered the vehicle, grabbing hold of the eighty-one-year-old magnate.[3] Shots were then exchanged between the two attackers, the driver, Torres, and the bodyguard, Chapa. A hagiographic biography produced in 2003 contends that during the commotion Garza Sada pulled from his jacket an old pistol and fired off rounds that helped kill the assailants, a fact not corroborated in the DGIPS reports.[4] In any event, crossfire killed everyone in the car, including Garza Sada—the target of the failed abduction. Bullets entered his body, puncturing several vital organs. He died where he sat.[5]

Coverage of the murder of Garza Sada and the manhunt that ensued for the unnamed getaway driver—the only survivor of the assault—filled Monterrey and most national newspapers the following day. The daily *El Norte* conveyed the sense of shock shared by readers. The assault was immediately understood for what it was, a botched kidnapping. *El Norte* reported on September 18 that the assailants were connected to the guerrilla organization known as Liga Comunista 23 de septiembre, a group formed in 1970 and named for actions consummated in Chihuahua on that date in 1965. In the short time the group had been in existence it had orchestrated several high-profile kidnappings as well as the hijacking of a Mexicana de Aviación jet that was en route to Cuba with over one hundred passengers on board, including two children of the governor of Nuevo León. These actions, and in particular the hijacking, which was believed to have been supported by Fidel Castro, proved highly successful for 23 de septiembre. The Mexican government paid the group healthy ransoms for the hostages as well as released political prisoners that the group had named. Garza Sada had known he was in danger. Monterrey police had been aware of plans by criminal organizations to kidnap him since at least 1971.[6]

Newspaper accounts of the incident that brought the death of Garza

Sada were greatly outnumbered by stories submitted to honor his life. Hundreds of letters of condolence addressed to his widow, Consuelo Lagüera, and their eight children and forty-four grandchildren flooded the pages of *El Norte*, *El Sol*, and the other regional newspapers in the days that followed. Letters sent to console the Garza family praised Eugenio's business and social accomplishments, and the vast reach of his business empire was reflected in the diversity of those who purchased newspaper space. Quarter-page ads bought in *El Norte* by Fundidora Monterrey and Banco Comercial Mexicano de Monterrey as well as by U.S. corporate giants like Union Carbide and First National City Bank of New York honored Eugenio, who had been at one time or another a major shareholder or key board member of their companies. Other tributes were purchased and placed by those who worked for him. Separate half-page ads were placed by the corporate unions of workers of the Cuauhtémoc, FAMOSA, and Conductores Monterrey plants, and management at Cuauhtémoc, the company founded by his father in 1890, and HYLSA, the steel giant he created in 1943, purchased full-page ads to commemorate him in the days following his death.[7]

Some who expressed their condolences also used their platform to condemn the acts that caused his demise and take a swipe at the government that did not protect him. Ramiro Flores, writing in *El Norte* on September 18, pointed out that he, although rich, was austere and a man of few words. He was also progressive and "more revolutionary than they say." "Who can doubt," Flores asked, "what he, before anyone else in the Republic, gave to his workers that the government now tries to take from them?" It was Garza Sada, after all, who constructed and sustained the first schools, day care centers, and hospitals for his workers. And it was exactly this proven social commitment that made his murder so disheartening. "It must have been cowards that killed don Eugenio," Ramiro Flores felt, because he was, above all, a *valiente* (a brave or strong man). This fact was corroborated in the writer's opinion by Garza Sada's famous stance against the government's assault on the private sector. "Who can forget the period in which Lázaro Cárdenas, as President of the Republic, openly attacked private industry?" Flores asked. Fortunately "it was . . .

don Eugenio who confronted him [Cardénas]. He confronted him and obliged him to rectify his tendency." Such a valiente did not deserve to die at the hands of "delinquent cowards," the writer concluded.[8]

The incipient anger toward the government noticeable in Flores's piece would grow in Monterrey in the coming days, nourished mainly by inflammatory comments made at Garza Sada's burial. The funeral procession in Monterrey on September 18, 1973, was truly a remarkable event. Those who mourned the deceased began the day by viewing his body as it was laid in state on the campus of his beloved Tec de Monterrey. From there it was taken to the Church of the Purísima where it lay alongside the caskets of Chapa and Torres.[9] After a mass was heard for the departed, a procession was held to transport the remains of Garza Sada for burial. A crowd of between 125,000 and 250,000 sullen men and women joined the funeral procession as it left the church.[10] President Echeverría and two of his ministers were included in the multitude. They trailed the hearse as it reached the Panteón del Carmen cemetery at about 5:30 that afternoon.

There the crowds did not disperse despite a driving rain. Under raincoats and umbrellas, those who had gathered to pay their respects to Garza Sada heard separate eulogies from speakers who had been touched by his life's work. First to speak was Ismael Villa, a student at Tec. He told the bereaved that don Eugenio had seen in the youth of Monterrey all of the hopes of the nation. In his example, Mexican youths could find the path to honor. Next Gerónimo Valdez, leader of the Workers Union of the Cuauhtémoc and FAMOSA Society, spoke. He praised Garza Sada, calling him an "exemplary man," and commended his former boss for always respecting labor rights and for being fair and generous with his employees.[11] Finally, Ricardo Margáin Zozaya, a local businessman and leading member of the Monterrey chapter of the National Chamber of Commerce, remembered Garza Sada from the perspective of the patrón. His speech began with a familiar refrain: don Eugenio was both an industrial magnate and a social visionary. He was wildly successful in business but never let the pursuit of personal gain cloud his indefatigable will to serve his community and the nation.

Margáin then moved into the crucial part of his oration. He told the massive crowd and Echeverría, who listened within earshot of the speaker, that the death of the great man could have been prevented. Criminal elements of the kind present in Mexico, he believed, acted with impunity only "when they have lost respect for authority; when the state has stopped maintaining public order; when it has not only let the most negative ideologies have free reign, but also permits them to harvest their negative fruits of hate, destruction, and death." The repeated attacks waged on the private sector in recent years confirmed this situation, and they had been carried out "without any apparent end other than to foment division and hatred between the social classes." Margáin reminded the government (and its leader, who must have seethed nearby) of its responsibility to stamp out dangerous ideologies, and he recommended it begin this task by cleaning out the universities "that have become a no-man's-land where better guarantees are granted to delinquents than to law-abiding citizens." Until "very simple" albeit painful measures were implemented on the nation's campuses, he fretted, the nation risked being destabilized by criminal activity. The civil unrest Mexico endured was also bad for business, clearly, and he asked the government to foster a political climate friendlier to capital investment. To Margáin and other patrones, we can assume, the death of Garza Sada made clear that the time for firm government action had arrived. Retaliation was "unavoidable"; Mexico's future was at stake.[12]

The significance of the Margáin oration was recognized immediately, if for no other reason than its audacity. The "eulogy" was covered in all major Monterrey dailies on September 19, and it was referenced in varying degrees in other big-city newspapers as well. In many instances its full text was printed in a full-page ad jointly purchased by the Monterrey Chamber and other business advocacy organizations that formed the nucleus of the Nuevo León industrial and entrepreneurial elite.[13]

The following day, Guillermo Rocha, a Mexico City hotel owner and president of a national hotelier association, echoed Margáin's sentiments of and took a jab at the government via a letter addressed "To Public Opinion" and printed in regional newspapers.[14] Rocha berated the government for its preoccupation with the recent assassination of Chilean president Salvador Allende on September 11 and its perceived disinterest in the troubles that currently gripped Mexico's own streets. He wrote, "On this day, September 17, 1973, I put my personal flag at half-mast. Not because of the national mourning decreed by the government or for the death of the President of Chile, Salvador Allende: in any case, there have been more proximate and wrenching reasons in our own country... earthquakes and floods, for example, that were not deemed deserved of the mass expression of solidarity [afforded] from a national mourning."[15] Rocha penned his piece against a backdrop that heard Echeverría boldly condemning the military coup that overthrew Allende and making highly publicized efforts to usher his sympathizers out of the country. Echeverría even sent the national jet to fly the widow Hortencia Bussi de Allende and other members of the Allende family out of Santiago to safety in Mexico City on September 16.[16] None of that mattered to Rocha, however. The life of a great man had been stolen much closer to home. And this man was a countryman with values and achievements that Rocha judged superior to those of the foreign politician. He clarified, "No, my mourning on this day is like that of many other Mexicans who think that it is not a crime to create something, that it is not a crime to create jobs, that it is not a betrayal of the nation to provide one's own effort, imagination, and capital to convert ideas into reality.... My mourning, I mean, is for a man that knew how to embody all of these things while imprinting them with a seal of deep social brotherhood: don Eugenio Garza Sada." Echoing Margáin, he then levied blame at the government for permitting the tragedy to occur. "He was the victim, ultimately, of a government that, at the end of three long years, has been sterile in works but—and this for sure—rich in demagogic declarations that have awakened resentments and caused disunity, jealousy, and mutual distrust among Mexicans." It was this government, he bristled, "that which so energetically labored (from the comfort of six thousand kilometers) in defense of a minority of Chilean people guilty of having brought their country to the deepest political, economic, and social abyss in its history," that now vacillated in protecting the rights, peace, and tranquility of its own citizens who desired to work and prosper.[17] One could thus surmise that it was Garza Sada's very values and achievements that cost him his life, according to Rocha.

Patrones and Corporatist Ambivalence

The sentiment that the government had been ambivalent at best, negligent at worst, in its efforts to counter domestic terrorism rang true with patrones nationwide. Also common was the belief that the Echeverría regime was sympathetic to ideologies, namely socialism, that were antithetical to the Mexican entrepreneur. Furthermore, the Echeverría state was judged guilty of fomenting a class consciousness in workers that was similarly bad for the business owner's bottom line. Through its creation of the National Tripartite Commission and its efforts to nationalize large segments of the economy, patrones feared that the regime was espousing class-based rhetoric that was sparking widespread labor unrest. Some of these fears were well founded, as levels of labor activism spiked sharply in the years 1973–74, the so-called Años de Huelga, or "Strike Years." But heightened agitation in the period should not have surprised anyone who considered it in the context of an increasingly dire economic situation. The great majority of activism in the period was waged over basic meat-and-potatoes issues, such as a forty-hour workweek, alleged contractual violations, and demands for higher wages, not toward ideological ends. Nevertheless, enraged patrones in Monterrey and elsewhere accused Echeverría, as they had Cárdenas four decades earlier, of intentionally inciting workers and creating a contentious business climate.

In this context the botched kidnapping and resulting murder of Eugenio Garza Sada seemed to encapsulate everything that was wrong with the current regime. By 1973 employers had become accustomed to being slandered in government and party rhetoric. As a candidate Echeverría lectured them about their patriotic responsibilities to observe the legal rights of workers and as president he trumpeted the myriad ways the New Federal Labor Law had benefited workers. Speaking on September 1, 1971, Echeverría reported that since the labor code's implementation in May 1970, 195 collective contracts had been revised, the legal contracts that governed the sugar, alcohol, and textile industries had been renegotiated, and various commissions had been created to see worker safety, hygiene, and housing provisions realized, among other benefits.[18] In the same breath he exhorted patrones to comply with the law and fulfill their civic duties. Remarks made by Jesús Reyes Heroles upon taking charge of the PRI in 1972, we remember, provoked a debate that questioned the very right of the rich to belong to the official party, a dialogue that called into question the position of large-scale employers on the metaphorical corpus of Mexican society.

To clarify, patrones of the early 1970s were represented in the PRI as part of the popular and professional sector and organized into the National Confederation of Popular Organizations (CNOP)—an umbrella body composed of more than fifty organizations subdivided into thirteen different branches of activity or profession—but their status was murky. In 1972 the CNOP had membership numbers that rivaled those of the National Peasant Confederation or the CTM and contained large public service and education workers unions, the most notable being the National Education Workers' Union, the country's single largest union, comprising over 266,000 schoolteachers. Teachers, in fact, were doubly represented on the corpus, as they were also part of the workers' sector by means of their union's inclusion in the Federation of Public Service Workers' Unions, an affiliate of the Congress of Labor.[19] The typical industrialist, in contrast, had no similar inroads into the PRI's policy-making machinery, as the thirteen branches delegated by the CNOP afforded representation only to businesses with less than one hundred employees. This restriction meant that the Garza Sadas of the world were not privy to the decision-making conversations of politics, but the typical owner of a small creamery, radio station, restaurant, gas station, or bus company was.

Preventing the inclusion of wealthy patrones in the PRI and granting political access to small-scale entrepreneurs fit the ideological schema of the post-Tlatelolco Mexican state. But although large-scale employers were excluded from official political channels they were not prevented from exerting political power through commerce organizations. The major power players of the Mexican industrial and commercial orb continued to congregate after 1968 inside large organizations like the National

Chamber of the Assembly Industry, the National Confederation of Industrial Chambers, and the National Confederation of Chambers of Commerce to influence the government on questions of prices, wages, tariffs, and trade policy in general. And even some local organizations had clout in dictating national policy. Certainly the priorities of the Monterrey chapter of the National Chamber of Commerce were regarded in policy-making decisions. Likewise for the Mexico City chapter that was almost a century old by 1969 and boasted a membership of over twenty-five thousand associated firms, making it the oldest and one of the most important local commerce organizations in Latin America.

Beyond being relegated to an ambiguous place on the corpus of Mexican civil society, patrones—and particularly those in the state of Nuevo León, because of the exceptionally close ties they maintained with North American investors—had always had to answer charges from politicians and labor leaders that they were stooges of foreign capital. Moreover, the long-standing presence and influence of the Catholic and pro-business National Action Party in the region also called into question the revolutionary credentials and very "Mexican-ness" of regiomontanos—at least in the propaganda of the labor establishment. These accusations multiplied in the 1970s. In their defense, the state's business owners asked critics to consider their successes in channeling foreign investment into corporate profits that were spent to improve workers' conditions and finance development at home.[20]

This retort was valid. The crucial contribution made by the business community of Nuevo León in funding national development in twentieth-century Mexico could not be denied. Nuevo León industrialists responded with statistics to allegations that they were "enemies of progress," lacking in feelings of "social solidarity," or just plain selfish. Figures compiled by the major commerce organizations of the state showed that taxes paid by private initiative in Nuevo León constituted 11 percent of total federal revenue in 1976—a real disparity in light of the fact that the state's residents constituted only 3 percent of the national population. Furthermore, employers argued that there was a disparity in the ratio of return versus contributions they received from the federal government. According to their figures, the government invested 1.54 billion pesos in infrastructural and other improvements in Nuevo León in 1976, a return that represented less than one-fifth of the state's tax payment of 8.14 billion pesos. Federal budget numbers further confirmed Nuevo León's importance to the national economy. Public figures showed that while federal investment increased by 22 percent annually during the period 1970–74, it had risen by an average of only 8 percent in Nuevo León during that period. Citizens of the state of Nuevo León thus had just cause to complain; an 8 percent annual increase when factored against the inflation rate of the period represented a real decrease.[21] Local entrepreneurs were right to juxtapose public investment in their state and other northern states against that in Oaxaca, Guerrero, and Tabasco, southern states that were PRI strongholds and received about two pesos in federal government spending for every peso that they paid in taxes.[22]

By the same token the class-conscious discourse spearheaded by Echeverría and Reyes Heroles made them subject to ideological assaults and drove a wedge between the one-party state and the commercial sector. Few homages were given to Mexico's leaders like the kind Francisco Cano Escalante, president of the National Chamber of Commerce, gave Díaz Ordaz when he attended the inauguration of the organization's new headquarters on October 29, 1969. Cano Escalante lauded the Mexican president for the political economy he had maintained. Those abroad, he assured the president, admired the balance of Mexico's mixed economic system, and he pledged that "we in all sectors," knowing its benefits, would continue to work with the state to guarantee that the Mexican economy kept expanding at a record pace.[23] No similar offer of partnership and collaboration would be extended by patrones to the post-1970 government, and particularly toward its leader, Echeverría, whose propensity to vocalize support for leftist figures like Castro and Allende painted him as a socialist in the eyes of many in the business elite.

The Monterrey Challenge

In no Mexican city was the ideological friction between the labor establishment and patrones more heated than it was in Nuevo León's capital city, Monterrey, as suggested by discourses surrounding Gaza Sada's death and burial. Similarly, anecdotal evidence suggests that in no city was the survival and independence of the small and medium-sized businessman more sacrosanct than it was in Monterrey in the 1970s. Recent national wage battles were interpreted there with disdain and union gains accepted grudgingly. By 1973 it was common to infer open hostility in the words and actions of commerce leaders toward the labor establishment and the cause of organized labor. This hostility was conveyed in the press and particularly in the pages of *El Norte*, the city's largest newspaper and a symbol to some of patronal greed and working-class oppression. A demonstration carried out on September 17, 1973, by some 250 students at a local teaching college was designed to protest the paper for its constant and, in their opinion, unjustified attacks on the Soviet and North Korean embassies in Mexico. The focus of the demonstration shifted dramatically, however, as news of the Garza Sada assassination developed throughout the day. Subsequent speeches implored the paper's editors to resist the temptation of linking the assassination and Nuevo León's prominent guerrilla presence to the Soviet Union and its student and worker partisans in the state.[24] Such requests, time would reveal, were wishful thinking, and by 1974 the state hosted a political climate rife with tripartite acrimony unlike anywhere else in Mexico.

El Norte and most major Monterrey newspapers advocated relentlessly against the government and its labor allies throughout the period under review. On May 1, 1974, *El Norte* observed the International Day of Labor holiday contemptuously, assailing in a front-page editorial "known voices" for using the holiday to "reiterate old lies and half truths" that accused businessmen, producers, and industrialists of manipulating the market and undermining the national economy. Antagonists, the editorial alleged, were also distorting the truth by contending that organized workers were worse off in May 1974 than they had been the previous summer—before they received an across-the-board wage increase of 20 percent. These polemics necessitated a response. *El Norte* editors wrote, "To produce more, in an environment of harmony and confidence, is the only recipe to defeat scarcity and its immediate consequence: an increased cost of living." The source of the nation's inflation problem, therefore, was understood clearly. Economic sickness in Mexico was the result of poor management of the national patrimony by state officials, in spite of what "demagogues" alleged to the contrary. The cure for economic malaise appeared similarly clear: let manufacturers "produce more in a climate of harmony and trust."[25] Editors pleaded for the nation's businessmen to be allowed to remedy the nation's ills by conducting their business free from disruptive state and worker interference.

That the typical Monterrey businessman saw the presence of the executive and the labor ministry in his operations as intrusive was not surprising; the historical development of labor-capital relations in Nuevo León took on a life of its own when viewed in comparison to other industrial centers of the nation. Episodes of syndical militancy in the 1930s did not reorder the industrial power structure of the city to the extent desired by organized labor. Patrones assembled in the Grupo Monterrey continued to dictate the terms of labor-capital relations in the region, though they often did so benevolently. Employers instilled loyalty by awarding their employees wages and benefits that were superior to those garnered by workers in other settings. Corporate propaganda and social programs instilled in workers the perception of the "company as family"—a message that, once internalized, fostered a climate of workplace harmony that tempered discontent and produced strong earnings.[26] The kind of industrial paternalism practiced by Eugenio Garza Sada on the factory floors of Cervecería Cuauhtémoc, for example, enabled area employers to stay in the good graces of workers.[27]

Economic prosperity and the general abatement of employee-employer hostility in Monterrey after 1940 ushered in the end of government interventionism there. Labor-capital relations were hence free to advance independently of any pressures exerted by labor establishment authorities. This is not to imply, however, that unionism did not thrive in Monterrey in the postwar period. It surely did and continued to do so into the 1970s, albeit in a unique way. Of the 504,934 persons classified as economically active in 1976 in the city, an astonishingly high number—309,000, roughly 61 percent—were unionized.[28] A fact equally as astonishing: of that organized labor force, more than two hundred thousand workers—nearly two-thirds of it—militated in the ranks of *sindicatos de empresa* (company unions) that were tightly controlled by corporate executives and unlikely to engage in hostile activities against their employers.

The predominance of company unionism in Monterrey represented a thorn in the side of the labor bureaucracy in the 1970s that it was bent upon removing. Labor leaders slandered company unions in myriad ways. They derided them as *sindicatos blancos* (literally, "white unions," but akin to "ghost unions" in the North American labor lexicon) because they were composed of "ghost" workers who metaphorically abandoned their corporal bodies when they sold themselves to the owner who directed all aspects of their union's operations. They were also understood as "white" as opposed to "red," meaning that they were passive stooges rather than hostile militants.

The canvas of the workers' movement in 1970s Mexico was diverse, and especially so in Monterrey, where company unions remained the major force in labor-capital relations. The historical predominance of company unionism in the Mexican north contrasted with the surging of official unionism in the post-Tlatelolco period and created conflict. The roots of conflict were numerous, but perhaps no cause was more central than a basic divergence in philosophy that pitted the traditional commitment of the area's employer class to corporate autonomy against the labor establishment's newly restored knack for interventionism in the workplace. The NLFT empowered government labor and union authorities to intervene in the internal decision-making processes of companies in numerous and distinct ways. Mandatory profit-sharing provisions, for example, undercut industrial paternalism in ways that rewrote the terms of workplace relations. In Monterrey, where the worker profited from industrial paternalism more so than most, labor reforms were often unwelcome.[29] Clashes were unavoidable.

The Gasolinera Conflict of 1974

Still, not every regiomontano worker pledged allegiance to his employer. In Monterrey state-allied unions exerted influence on the local economy through the presence of nearly one thousand chapters representing upwards of one hundred thousand workers by the late 1970s.[30] Unions classifying themselves as "independent," meaning they were free from Congress of Labor or CTM patronage, or "democratic," that is, opposed to the strict hierarchical structure imposed from above on state-allied unions, were also present and composed the third strand of syndicalism in the region. This strand was relatively small but not insignificant. The boisterous activities of independent unions of miners, university students, and electrical workers exerted pressure on the operations of official labor to the extent that some alleged Fidel Velázquez resorted to sponsoring sindicatos blancos to counter them.[31] These two types of unionists took advantage of newly legislated rights and filed grievances against their employers with federal labor authorities in Nuevo León and elsewhere in unprecedented numbers in the 1970s.

A report printed in *El Norte* on June 22, 1974, summarized the situation in Nuevo León during that period of historical worker activity. A total of 306 strike petitions were filed with the Local Conciliation and Arbitration Board in May alone. Of this number, 80 percent (245) were filed by unions affiliated with the CTM, with the remaining 20 percent acting under the tutelage of other large confederations having union representation in the state. *El Norte*, not surprisingly, understood the CTM's hyperactivity cynically. It reported that strikes were raised to protest matters of salary, collective contracting, and benefits and that they were scheduled to explode in the area's hotels, restaurants, printing shops, bakeries, butcher shops, markets, food-production plants, plumbing and carpentry shops, hardware stores, bookstores, pharmacies, dairy facilities, construction firms, woodshops, clothing stores, and gas stations. This analysis was accurate, but the newspaper saw conspiracy in such panoply of activity. It deduced that the CTM, in pursuit of selfish ends, was threatening the regional economy by holding vast swaths of the private sector hostage to the prospect of the strike. Fortunately, it was relieved to report that much of the CTM's grandstanding was defused before it exploded into action, as 128 of the 306 strike petitions filed with the Local Conciliation and Arbitration Board (JLCA) were declared nonexistent (i.e., invalid) and thus cancelled. Of those that remained, only ten strikes were carried out in May and the remaining hundred-plus files stayed active into June. June, however, brought a new wave of conflict. That month 202 strike petitions were filed with the local board, with the majority filed by CTM-affiliated unions.[32]

The strike hung like a cloud over Nuevo León as the region entered the summer of 1974. Area business owners complained about incessant worker demands for higher wages and improved benefits, while consumers fretted about the decreased access to goods that they deemed would be inevitable with production lapses. For one group—*gasolineros*, owners of gasoline stations—worker intransigence had reached a breaking point and required a response. Gasolineros were resolved to counter what they believed was their workers' "ingratitude" with a show of collective might. Not one of the state's eighty-six gas stations opened on Friday, June 6, 1974. Owners reasoned that the *paro* (lockout) was a necessary measure of defense against the illegal and unjustified strike planned by CTM leaders across the state.[33] Stations, they promised, would be reopened the following day at 5:00 p.m., but they warned of future lockouts if the CTM continued along its insolent track. Addressing the situation, Nuevo León governor Pedro Zorrilla Martínez told reporters that although the lockout was illegal because it was conducted without the approval of state labor authorities, he condoned it as a necessary measure to counter strong-arm tactics adopted in recent months by the Nuevo León State Workers' Federation (FTNL), the CTM's state affiliate.[34] Days later, Zorrilla affirmed his support for the owners' position. He estimated that more than 80 percent of the state's gas station owners adequately covered their responsibilities to workers. They were thus justified in employing bold measures to combat the "extortionist" strategies employed by worker organizations in the state.[35]

Gas stations were reopened as promised the next day, June 7. Owners resumed service at their stations and permitted CTM members to return to work, though plans for a union-wide strike at each of the city of Monterrey's forty-seven gas stations remained in place, scheduled to commence June 11 at noon. As the scheduled strike date approached nervous tension gripped the city's streets. Trains of cars clogged congested thoroughfares on the evening of June 10 as drivers hoped to fill up in anticipation of the impending gas shortage they deemed inevitable. Naturally, the prospect of depriving motorists of gasoline in a city as economically vital as Monterrey caught the attention of federal authorities. Pemex director general Antonio Dovalí Jaime weighed in. He instructed Monterrey gasolineros that the lockout they had carried out days earlier was illegal, as it was implemented without Pemex approval and was thus a violation of their contractual terms with the national oil company. Any future lockouts, he warned, would force Pemex to retract generous fiscal concessions that gasolineros currently enjoyed.[36]

The scolding given gas station owners by the Pemex boss did not intimidate them. Manuel García, head of the Monterrey Chapter of the National Union of Pemex Distributors, affirmed that the gas station owners were resolute in their position. He told the press on June 10 that even if a single *bandera rojinegra*, the red-and-black flag signaling a workers' strike, was hung at one of their establishments, Monterrey's gasolineros would hold an indefinite lockout that would be observed by Pemex retailers statewide— most of whom, he claimed, were abiding similar coercive tactics from the FTNL.[37] In contrast, the FTNL adopted a position of compromise, accepting the mechanics of collaborationism and understanding full well that the potential negative economic impact of a large-scale gas station shutdown was a risk that federal authorities were not willing to take. As such, federation leaders acceded to additional negotiations. The strike was rescheduled for June 13, giving state labor authorities an additional forty-eight hours to broker an agreement and avert crisis.

Accusations and insults continued to fly between gas station owners and unionists in the days that followed. In tripartite talks organized by the Local Conciliation and Arbitration Board, gasolineros held fast to the position that the FTNL was inciting their unionized employees to strike with false allegations of contractual violations and was intimidating their nonunionized employees into joining its ranks. Station owners claimed to harbor no bias against their workers unionizing but questioned the veracity of FTNL assertions about their workers' desire to organize. In the event of a strike they promised to poll their employees to see who among them wished to be part of the union. As elsewhere in Mexico at the time, the matter of worker choice was a pivotal issue that complicated labor-capital relations in Monterrey.[38]

June 13 arrived and still no resolution had been reached. The situation, though, took an unexpected turn when FTNL officials failed to appear at a mandatory conciliation and arbitration board hearing scheduled to precede the outbreak of the strike. In response, Homero Martínez, president of the local board, declared forty-four of the FTNL's strike petitions invalid, leaving only three files active among those for which it had earlier filed extensions. Owners interpreted this development suspiciously. García spoke on their behalf and remarked that the nonappearance was characteristic of the organization's penchant for chicanery. Moreover, the gasolineros remained firm in their intolerance, and he repeated the warning that they would lock out their employees and deprive the entire city of gasoline for an indefinite period should even one bandera rojinegra be waved over their stations on June 17, the new strike date.[39]

The small businessmen who owned gas stations and confronted organized labor in Monterrey had powerful allies around the state. The zero-tolerance position iterated by Manuel García had great appeal to the business elites who gathered in Monterrey on June 14 to discuss the situation. There members of the Monterrey chapter of the National Chamber of Commerce expressed their mutual disgust over the "gangster-like syndical practices that utilize the right to strike in an abusive way that has fostered phantom unions to blackmail the merchant," as the chapter's director general Eduardo Hovelman described them.[40] He elaborated. The FTNL's illegal tactics had brought to the area a state of "undoing" that required strong measures to combat. Resolved to counter union intransigence, the 150 voting members of the chamber unanimously approved a resolution to conduct a general lockout by the organization's nearly six thousand members on Tuesday, June 18. The tactic, they hoped, would demonstrate the collective disgust, power, and unity of the area's commercial forces, as well as pressure local and federal authorities to sponsor a better climate of business investment in the state. In the event that the lockout did not achieve these goals, merchants of the city were resolved to stop paying taxes in order to force proper government collaboration with business.

The massive lockout and resulting commercial shutdown planned by Monterrey business owners for June 18 garnered wide attention. On June 15 commercial leaders addressed the public and summarized business's desired goals. José Luis Coindreau, president of the Monterrey chapter of the National Chamber of Commerce, voiced the familiar position that the lockout would essentially "protest the undoing in which [the businessman] lives, because he has seen the principle of law constantly corroded, creating a situation of chaos and instability."[41] Corruption and criminality inside organized labor was also cited as forcing the hand of businessmen, who freely used the epithet "gangsters" to describe the state's union leaders.

Nervous tension abounded in Monterrey on the eve of the shutdown, June 17. Consumers rushed local stores in preparation for impending shortages. Stores met customer needs by staying open late into the night.[42] That afternoon, José Campillo Sáinz, secretary of industry and commerce, arrived in Monterrey to persuade merchants to reconsider the action they had scheduled for the following day. He delivered members of the Monterrey Chamber of Commerce a petition from Echeverría asking that the body work diligently to find a resolution. The gasoline workers strike scheduled to ignite at two that afternoon was also on the secretary's itinerary. Worker activism in this instance, however, was delayed again as the state's conciliation and arbitration board granted the FTNL another two-day extension that pushed back the planned strike until midday June 19. That evening Campillo sat down with Coindreau and Zorrilla, who chronicled for him a litany of acts that they felt were perpetrated in "gangster-like" fashion by the FTNL to promote chaos and instability in local commerce.[43] By day's end it had become clear to the secretary that the position of local owners was unyielding. The president's petition was unpersuasive; the lockout could not be averted.

The atmosphere in downtown Monterrey on June 18 was described by local observers as resembling a "midweek Sunday" in that it was calm and quiet and the principal arteries of the city were deserted. On that day upwards of 10,000 establishments—many more than the 5,846 officially registered with the Monterrey chamber—refused to open in solidarity with local businessmen. Owners agreed to pay their employees though their doors were locked and their lights were off. The solidarity that bound merchants together in the face of a common threat was no more evident than in the image of the Frutería La Victoria, a produce market that had been open for business consistently—twenty-four hours a day, seven days a week—for the past thirty years. Passersby saw a giant tarpaulin draped over the famous fruit market's booths, thus symbolically "closing its doors" for the first time in a generation. Visitors to Monterrey were also greatly inconvenienced by the display of commercial unity. Hotels were shuttered, causing over two thousand tourists who arrived in Monterrey to leave the city and move on to nearby locations in search of lodging.[44]

Observing the situation early that morning, city business leaders declared the commercial shutdown of June 18 a success. They estimated that commercial interests in Monterrey would lose in the area of 35 million pesos as a result of the massive action.[45] Economic loss was never an attractive prospect, yet commerce leaders judged the hit taken by the local economy as a necessary evil that would force the government to curb the excesses of organized labor in the region.

Fidel Velázquez evaluated the day's events quite differently. He spoke to the press in Mexico City the following day, calling the merchants who closed their doors "delinquents" and promising to counter their illegal work stoppages with a great demonstration in Monterrey and a new wave of strikes against gas stations, restaurants, and hotels in the city. This was a course of action he felt was obligatory to combat the patrones of Monterrey, who continued to try to live "in an environment of privilege at the cost of the working classes."[46] Velázquez's typical hyperbole and classist interpretation of events in Monterrey was even more concisely articulated in the pages of his personal mouthpiece, *Ceteme*. The weekly reported on June 22 that the various struggles waged by *cetemistas* in Monterrey gas stations, hotels, and restaurants over matters of collective contracts were historic clashes, undertaken to protest "the eternal reactionary and antinational policies of the Grupo Monterrey."[47]

In the same edition, Raúl Caballero Escamilla, secretary general of the FTNL, wrote to remind readers about the historical antiworker attitude of the commercial elite based in his city. None of the businesses cited in strike petitions, he wrote, paid their workers the federal minimum wage, nor did they pay them overtime pay as was afforded to them by law. Neither did they grant their employees social security, workers' housing, vacation, profit-sharing, and retirement benefits—all of which the NLFT legally mandated. Finally, many of them, Caballero alleged, had created sindicatos blancos that undercut their employees' abilities to procure basic rights granted them by law—constituting yet another abuse that the FTNL promised to challenge with "unending strikes" to force them to alter their defiant stances.[48]

The lockout of June 18 necessitated more than just a rhetorical response. At 10:00 a.m. the next day, June 19, the often threatened and just as often delayed strike was finally carried out at four Monterrey gas stations. Banderas rojinegras were hung and labor activities ceased. Later that day members of the National Union of Pemex Distributors gathered and sought to make good on their promise of intolerance. They conferred with other gas station owners and scheduled another citywide closure of gas stations, to be carried out on Saturday, June 22, if the Monterrey conciliation and arbitration board had not by that date declared the current strikes nonexistent. Their request elicited skepticism from the board's president, Homero Martínez, who stated that it was not possible to produce such a ruling in just seventy-two hours.[49] Gas station owners objected and in doing so, ironically, voiced a complaint commonly lodged by union officials about the sluggish pace of the board's decision-making process. The workers' strike proceeded in the coming days, free from government censure, and the prospect of the citywide lockout threatened by gasolineros loomed on the horizon.

On June 21, a typically scorching early summer day in Monterrey, local station owners reaffirmed their intention to shut off pumps the next day to protest worker strikes they deemed illegal. Local labor authorities worked furiously to determine the legality of the strikes and avert another costly gas station shutdown. Pemex officials again intervened. The company issued a public statement confirming that it was nonaligned in the local conflict between workers and owners, though it reminded leaders of the National Union of Pemex Distributors in a phone call that any unsolicited lockout they might conduct would incur penalties up to and including the retraction of fiscal concessions and the loss of operating licenses.[50]

Monterrey owners withstood government pressure better than most; a long history of state and business animosity in the region had made their skins resistant to the jabs of government officials. Threats from Pemex officials, therefore, were not enough to convince gasolineros to reconsider their positions. Relenting in this instance would mean that local business owners retreated on a major question that had historically driven labor-capital battles in the region: worker choice. On the eve of the promised lockout, gas station owners determined to settle the question of worker choice in a very logical manner: by simply asking their employees what they wanted to do and who they were affiliated with.

Pedro Treviño, owner of Central Gasolinera, one of the four gas stations closed by strike activities, assembled his employees at 5:00 p.m. to vote in the presence of local labor authorities. The questions posed to them were: "Are you in accordance with the strike conducted here?" and "Do you desire to join the FTNL/CTM in the future?" Treviño reported that he had twenty employees. Forty-three registered a vote that afternoon. Each of the twenty employees that Treviño listed voted no on both questions, thus unanimously rejecting the strike and refusing to join the ranks of the CTM. Of the other twenty-three who voted, Treviño claimed he did not recognize a single one. When interviewed by labor authorities the twenty-three claimed diverse professions at the store, including pumpers, greasers, car washers, and drivers. But when asked to corroborate their votes, not a single one provided a name, reported a domicile, or consented to have a fingerprint taken.[51] Not surprisingly, the votes of these "supposed employees" went counter to the votes of those on the store's official payroll; they voted unanimously in favor of the strike and in favor of CTM inscription.

The facts of the bizarre situation came to light in due time. *El Norte* reported the following day that a registered worker at the station claimed to have seen the same group of men assembled together that morning at a restaurant where employees were being polled on similar questions of worker choice and union affiliation. Another confirmed that a city bus had been used to ship in the nearly two dozen individuals to deceive labor officials and steal the election. The false employees were hence not only revealed as *acarreados* "carried-in" by the union to inflate perception of its strength and numbers but also slandered as *cachirules*, a term used to mean "scabs" but one that more literally translated to "illegitimate children" or, more crudely, "bastard sons."[52] The CTM's tactics fooled no one. One employee claimed that the "cetemista theater" was the worst pantomime he had ever seen.[53]

June 21 concluded with the CTM fully exposed, but worker strikes continued in earnest. Gas station owners went on record the following day, June 22, and held fast to their promise of a city-wide lockout—now scheduled to go into effect at two that afternoon—should local labor authorities fail to declare the strikes nonexistent before then. Monterrey's top commerce figure, Eduardo Hovelman, raised the ante. Nuevo León's patrones, he informed the press, were now considering a total commercial and industrial shutdown to protest the state's passivity toward syndical corruption and the slowness of labor authorities in resolving labor-capital disputes. The episode witnessed at Central Gasolinera the evening before, however, laid the groundwork for eventual resolution and averted the need for such action. Gas station owners at the three picketed stations replicated the scene witnessed at Central Gasolinera and polled their workers on the morning of June 22 under the supervision of the state's labor authorities. The results they received confirmed what they already suspected to be true: that their stations had been seized by cachirules who were not real employees but CTM stooges brought in to tip the balance of power in its favor. The next day *El Norte* trumpeted the results. The "final tally" was published in a front-page table:

Table 1. The final tally

Gasoline stations on strike	Gas station workers	CTM members	Cachirules
Central Gasolinera	20	0	23
Mercado de Abastos	18	0	25
S. Bernardo Reyes	14	0	21
Servicio Monterrey	11	0	13
Total	**63**	**0**	**82**

Source: "Marcador global," *El Norte*, June 23, 1974, 1.

As could be inferred from the results, the four gas stations shut down by the strike on June 19 employed a total of sixty-three workers. Curiously, 145 votes were cast—a fact that led observers to conclude that eighty-two votes were cast by CTM plants. The strikes themselves were hence understood to be the product of CTM shenanigans, a fact that infuriated not just the owners of the paralyzed stations but the region's entire business community. Quantitative evidence, it appeared, now corroborated ownership's claims that the labor movement led by the CTM had acted in a "gangster-like" fashion to influence the terms of labor-capital relations in the region.

Monterrey business owners were right to accuse the CTM of manipulating the business climate with strikes or planned strikes that were illegally waged. They were right to denounce the maneuvers of "phantom unions" that used monkey business and aggression to clog the docket of the state's labor board and to strong-arm business in the state.[54] On the hot pavements of city gas stations, therefore, one saw a microcosm of a larger battle fought in thousands of settings nationwide between the CTM and patrones. This was a battle that Mexico's most powerful unionist movement had fought hard (and won) in Monterrey before. Its efforts this time, although they included tactics that were far from admirable, would again pay off.

After tallying the votes cast by gas station workers, representatives of owners and unions reached a resolution. Tripartite authorities gathered in the offices of the state headquarters of the PRI on June 22 and worked late into the night. At 11:30 p.m. a deal was finally brokered that ended the Monterrey gasolinera strike and averted the massive lockout promised by merchants and industrialists.[55] Raúl Caballero of the FTNL committed his charges to lower the banderas rojinegras and permit operations to resume at the four gas stations closed by strikes. In exchange, the FTNL/ CTM received much. National Union of Pemex Distributors representative Filiberto Jiménez Orozco granted permission to gas station employees to form an industrial union, being that they worked in the same industry but performed different jobs, and he pledged that the distributors' union would recognize the validity of gas station workers' demands for collective contracts.[56] Immediately the glaring inequity of the accord astonished observers. An editorialist expressed his open amazement in a column published the next day. How could it be, he inquired, that despite losing votes at four gas stations by a combined count of sixty-three to zero, the CTM still obtained an agreement that committed all employees to become affiliated with its state organization, the FTNL? How could it be that, despite presenting "fakers" that fooled no one in the voting process, the CTM still won mandatory union inscription? These questions puzzled the writer. He concluded, "By losing, the CTM wins."[57]

Gas station workers interviewed in the coming days were also incredulous at the outcome of the negotiations. Employees repudiated the agreement reached by their employers' representatives and some lamented being sold to the CTM. Others cited their right to free association and pointed out that they had no desire to join the ranks of the CTM due to the good conditions, benefits, and salaries their employers already granted them. Rubén Martínez, an employee at one of the recently reopened stations, summarized a position many workers shared toward the organization: "The CTM's activities waste time and don't produce anything," he felt. Martínez was also indignant that an agreement was signed without worker input. The perception that worker choice had been violated was widespread, and not just among gas station employees.

A spokesperson for the PAN in Nuevo León condemned the agreement, calling it a complete refutation of authentic syndicalism. "In no way," he declared, "can owners and labor leaders make a pact with respect to the interests and rights that are exclusive to the worker."[58]

Negative reactions to the agreement continued to pour in over the coming days. *El Norte* related on June 27 that owners whose stations faced future strikes promised to sell their businesses if worker affiliation with the CTM was enforced. José Gracida, owner of the station S. Bernardo Reyes, explained that he and his colleagues were resolved to sell their businesses before permitting a CTM "intervention that no one asked for."[59] Workers too promised action. Some vowed to quit if the distributors' union insisted on affiliating them with the FTNL. Others discussed the possibility of forming their own union to offer workers an independent and autonomous alternative.

Partisans of business similarly loathed the agreement and saw politics behind it. Ernesto Leal Flores, editor of the staunchly probusiness *¡Óigame!*, wrote on June 25 to cast blame at all parts of the process, seeing the accord as demonstrating organized labor's as much as ownership's disregard for the free will of the worker. What it also revealed, he believed, was the keen sense of political survival harbored by its creators. As he saw it, the CTM was "naturally" part of the PRI. Any agreement, therefore, that expanded union ranks also promised to benefit the official party of the nation. It was no wonder, therefore, in a setting like Nuevo León where an antistate, probusiness ethic had long been nurtured by political opponents in the PAN, that an agreement so antidemocratic in nature would be ratified by the state's political and labor authorities, virtually all of whom were members of the PRI. "And what to say about the political party that sanctioned such an anti-revolutionary and non-democratic agreement in its own offices and before its maximum state authority?" Leal Flores asked with biting invective. "What does it say as well about the bureaucrats and high-level authorities, including our own governor, that sanctioned a pact that contains so many legal incongruities?"[60]

The curious way that the conflict was resolved revealed all of the inherent flaws of the system at work. Editors of *El Norte* termed the resolution process a "joke" and wrote that although Article 358 of the NLFT states clearly that no person can oblige another to join or not join a union, it was precisely unionization that was forced upon gas station workers by employer and union representatives. The accord was hence illegal. Worse than that, it was an insult to all of those it feigned to benefit. "The comedy that cetemistas and gas station owners presented," they concluded, was "a mockery of the rights of the worker and of all the citizens of the state that deserve more respect."[61]

What Monterrey patrones and partisans saw as a "mockery" of justice, those in organized labor's upper echelons saw as validation. To CTM opinion makers the gasolinera conflict was more than a local dispute, it was part of a century-long struggle waged by the Mexican worker against the employer class encrusted in Monterrey. The episode showed that the insolence of the Grupo Monterrey had not abated since it was so famously curbed by Cárdenas four decades earlier. Unfortunately, *Ceteme* editors advised, the Grupo Monterrey still relied on false accusations and threats to halt the upward ascension of the revolutionary Mexican worker. It harbored the same ancestral hatred of organized labor in 1974 as it did in 1936, they claimed, and it continued to accept the validity of only those unions it called "independent" and exercised control over. That business owners of the area continued to cling to their historical airs of privilege only served to strengthen the resolve of the CTM—"an organization of firm and permanent struggle, of a revolutionary and invincible force."[62]

The Monterrey gasolinera conflict of 1974, although a relatively minor incident that involved a mere one hundred or so workers and only four city gas stations, was a microcosm of the issues that defined that era of heightened labor agitation. On its surface, the conflict's resolution seemed lopsided and favorable only to state and organized labor interests. A deeper assessment, however, suggests how all parties stood to benefit from the accord. Owners, the perceived losers in the affair, could actually come out winners if the concessions they made succeeded in averting costly strikes and restoring a more profitable state of harmony to the workplace.

The CTM expected to (and actually did) reap benefits by emerging from negotiations with a well-publicized victory that gave it the countenance of strength and prestige: two of the most important weapons it could wield in its dealings with patrones. And the Echeverría state, finally, profited from a process in which labor authorities in Monterrey mediated a resolution that publicly favored organized labor while averting a crisis that stood to diminish its already questionable legitimacy in a pivotal economic region.

To the great dismay of many, however, the conciliatory spirit that settled the gas station conflict did not extinguish the intense union activism that then burned in Nuevo León and in other parts of the country. Barely two weeks after forcing the hand of gasolineros, the FTNL dangled the threat of the general strike before local patrones and induced them to revise the collective contracts of over five hundred culinary industry workers employed in the state's hotels, restaurants, cafeterias, and bars.[63] Seeking to put its new political capital to good use nationwide, the CTM issued demands for workers in diverse sectors. When negotiations stalled, as they did between the leaders of the Union of Mexican Textile Industry Workers, a CTM affiliate, and representatives of the national textile consortium, the CTM acted. A nationwide strike that exploded at 12:01 a.m. on June 26, 1974, saw forty-three thousand textile workers employed at over four hundred companies leave their posts in solidarity.[64] Banderas rojinegras were hung all over Mexico and were particularly visible in Nuevo León, where four thousand workers at multiple factories picketed while clamoring for provisions including the forty-hour workweek, higher wages, better vacation and retirement packages, paid technical training for employees, and scholarships for children of workers to be written into the legal contract that governed their industry.[65]

In their demands could be seen the full gamut of organized labor's operational objectives during the "Strike Years" of 1973–74. Conversely, one heard in the responses of patrones many of the talking points that grounded their arguments of the day. Increasing workers' salaries, some contended, would cause the cost of producing fabric to rise, thus creating a burden that would fall inordinately on the shoulders of the Mexican consumer. In this way textile producers echoed their counterparts in other industries by slandering the character of their striking workers. Union bosses, they deemed, were *charros*, gangsters, or criminals. Their footmen, the unionists, were privileged, unrealistic, and selfish. None of these were qualities typically understood as revolutionary.

1. Aerial view of Mexico City's Plaza de la Constitución, better known as the Zócalo, in 1970. After October 2, 1968, this symbolic and not easily filled public space was the primary venue for state-allied trade unions to demonstrate support for the regime. AGN Fototeca, Archivo Fotográfico Presidencia de la República, Luis Echeverría Alvarez, Expediente 110/1.

2. The *bandera rojinegra*, the red-and-black flag of worker militancy, is hoisted by student protestors and flies over a largely vacated Zócalo on the morning of August 28, 1968. IISUE/AHUNAM/Colección Manuel Gutiérrez Paredes "Mariachito"/Expediente 52/2525.

3. *Electricistas* march in solidarity with students and show their support for independent unionism in September 1968. IISUE/AHUNAM/Colección Manuel Gutiérrez Paredes "Mariachito"/Expediente 58/2897.

A pesar de todas las maniobras patronales,
los trabajadores venceremos

4. "In spite of all the patronal maneuvers, the workers will defeat them." The Confederation of Mexican Workers expresses its support for the creation of a new federal labor law in its weekly journal. *Ceteme*, no. 900 (January 11, 1969): 2. Courtesy of Hemeroteca Nacional.

5. Gustavo Díaz Ordaz (*center, waving*), Edgar Robledo Santiago (*left of the president*), Fidel Velázquez (*right*), and other principals of the labor establishment view the First of May festivities from the balcony of the National Palace on May 1, 1968. AGN Fototeca, Archivo Fotográfico Presidencia de la República, Gustavo Díaz Ordaz, Expediente 125/2.

6. "El Destape" of presidential candidate Luis Echeverría is cause for confetti, streamers, and mass celebration in the Zócalo, October 21, 1969. AGN Fototeca, Archivo Fotográfico Presidencia de la República, Luis Echeverría Alvarez, Expediente 146/1.

7. Velázquez congratulates Echeverría and gives official labor's blessing for his candidacy on October 22, 1969. AGN Fototeca, Archivo Fotográfico Hermanos Mayo, Luis Echeverría Alvarez, Expediente 061-A/28.

8. Echeverría accepts his party's nomination for president at PRI headquarters, November 15, 1969. AGN Fototeca, Archivo Fotográfico Presidencia de la República, Luis Echeverría Alvarez, Expediente 85/3.

9. The "preacher" and the "compañera" dance a traditional *baile* while donning popular Mexican garb, n.d. AGN Fototeca, Archivo Fotográfico Hermanos Mayo, Luis Echeverría Alvarez, Expediente 067-1/s.n.

10. "SME: private initiative is reactionary and fascist." Members of the Mexican Electricians' Union, the SME, demonstrate on May 1, 1976, and hoist banners endorsing their vision of the revolutionary economy. AGN Fototeca, Archivo Fotográfico Hermanos Mayo, Luis Echeverría Alvarez, Expediente 063-TIT 4/15.

11. Echeverría (*second from left*) stands in the cortege at the funeral of a *constituyente*, a signer of the Constitution of 1917, whose remains are displayed at the Casa de Carranza, Mexico City, n.d. As he did as president-elect at the funeral of Cárdenas in 1970, the Mexican president's flanking of the casket symbolically expressed his desire to be seen as the natural inheritor to a political legacy—in this case, the one outlined by the nation's seminal document. AGN Fototeca, Archivo Fotográfico Hermanos Mayo, Luis Echeverría Alvarez, Expediente 46/7.

Grabado de MEXIAC

¡DURO Y MACIZO!
Sólo los Obreros Acabarán con la Explotación y el Sindicalismo Blanco

12. "HARD AND SOLID! Only Workers Will Put an End to Exploitation and White Unionism." The CTM coaxes workers to combat company unionism. *Ceteme*, no. 975 (June 27, 1970): 3. Courtesy of Hemeroteca Nacional.

CHAPTER 6

"The False Redemption of May 1"

Testing the State's Alleged Preference for Organized Labor

Newspapers went to press in Monterrey on May 1, 1970, the International Day of Labor and a national holiday. This differentiated them from *El Universal*, *Excélsior*, *El Día*, and other Mexico City dailies, which did not produce editions for that day. Monterrey's largest newspaper, *El Norte*, of course, did, and in the reports, op-eds, and humor pieces it ran was evident an editorial hostility toward Labor Day and its significance. A cartoon run to commemorate the holiday was particularly evocative. Titled "Deservedly . . . ," the image depicted two slobs, more or less, lounging on a city sidewalk. They were both unshaven with wild, unkempt hair. One was missing teeth and the other had his shirt undone. He with the checkerboard smile was turned toward his partner, questioning. The response he received was brief but spoke volumes. The caption read, "Well, I'm just here bro . . . celebrating Labor Day."[1]

El Norte readers needed little additional information to infer the meaning of the illustration. The characters depicted in the image were to be understood not as vagrants, despite their sloppy appearances, but workers. And, one could reasonably infer, they were unionized, thus giving them the luxury of abstaining from productive activities on that day and lying about in the streets. A clear message was conveyed: the typical unionist was lazy. Even more so, he was entitled. An insert included in the same edition of *El Norte* continued the assault, this time condemning the New Federal Labor Law, which went into effect that day. It announced, "The False Redemption of May 1st—Tragic Agony of the Small Industrialist!" The byline elaborated: "The Labor Aristocracy and the Consortiums Finish Off the Medium Industrialist," a depressing reality, it posited, made possible by the "growing conquests of the nation's unionized workers." All of this threatened the spirit of entrepreneurialism, the message concluded, and businessmen in the nation were threatened by yet another institutional force—the federal government and the PRI, that which, "Without Fixing a Goal," arbitrarily "Accelerates or Halts Our Development."[2]

In a city like Monterrey where notions of entrepreneurialism, hard work, and industriousness formed integral parts of the collective identity, such perceived mediocrity and government meddling in business were particularly distasteful. Editorials printed in *El Norte* and elsewhere encapsulated a view shared by many across the nation that May 1 was not a day of redemption for the Mexican worker but a day that epitomized the privileges afforded a specific and relatively narrow segment of the working class. This chapter tests the validity of accusations heard so often in the post-Tlatelolco period alleging that unionists composed a sort of "labor aristocracy" that pursued its ends at the expense of the nation. First, it reviews the language and stipulations of the New Federal Labor Law of 1970 to gauge the ways that the law did or did not privilege the rights of employees (and unionized employees, in particular) over those of employers. Then it probes individual labor suits and collective actions for evidence of an institutional bias in the labor arbitration process.

Looking for Bias in the New Federal Labor Law of 1970

Social Justice and the Right to Strike

The notion that labor law in Mexico was historically prejudicial toward business was widely held but should not have been accepted wholesale.

Paragraph 19 of Article 123 of the Constitution of 1917 recognized the rights of employers to call a lockout when they had determined that the economic conditions of the market necessitated a temporary suspension of activities, thus giving owners a legal instrument equivalent to the workers' strike (*huelga*).[3] Furthermore, the 1931 Federal Labor Law established the rights to negotiate collective labor contracts and to halt labor activities, but these were not rights that pertained only to, nor exclusively bene-fited, workers. Collective contracts protected the interests of employers as much as they guaranteed the terms of employment for workers. Even the language of the Federal Labor Law as it stood on the eve of reform in 1969 belied the notion that employees were categorically favored over employers. After having undergone sixty-three revisions since its intro-duction in 1931, Article 6 of the code still subjected the workers' strike to a "nonexistent" (i.e., invalid) ruling by state authorities if said action "attacked the rights of third parties or injured society."[4] In all, there was very little legal basis to slander federal labor law as excessively proworker or anticapital prior to 1970.

Undeniably, some basic expressions of workers' and owners' rights gave way to more ideologically charged concepts in the succeeding labor code. Injected into the opening section of the NLFT was a concept that had not been prominent in federal labor law to that point: social justice. The tone of the text of Articles 2 and 3 was notable. Article 2 read, "Labor regulations tend toward the achievement of equilibrium and social justice in worker and employer relations." Article 3 further announced, "Labor is a right and a social duty. It is not an article of commerce; liberty and dignity is demanded by those who loan it and it must be effectuated in conditions that assure life, health, and a decorous economic level for the worker and his or her family. Distinctions between workers based on race, sex, age, religious creed, political doctrine or social condition will not be able to be established."[5]

Article 450 confirmed that the worker's right to strike first established in Article 123 remained a central precept in Mexican labor law. The definition of what a strike was did not change. Article 440 of the NLFT, much like Article 259 of the 1931 Federal Labor Law, defined the strike as a legal, temporary suspension of labor brought about by a coalition of workers. The most significant change between the two laws was seen in the definition of the acceptable parameters of a strike. Subsection I, Article 450, of the NLFT sanctioned any strike actions carried out to: (a) achieve balance between the diverse parts of production, harmonizing the rights of labor with those of capital; (b) obtain from an owner the fulfillment of a collective contract or demand the revision of its validity period; (c) obtain from an owner the fulfillment of a legal contract; and (d) wage a "solidarity strike" in support of an outside movement pursued to achieve one of the goals denoted above.

Except for some minor textual differences, these stated objectives largely mirrored those in Article 260 of the 1931 code, save for an important difference: Clause V, Article 450, of the NLFT sanctioned strikes waged to "demand the fulfillment of legal dispositions regarding the sharing of profits."[6] Being given legal sanction for strikes waged in pursuit of profit sharing buoyed one of organized labor's most important campaigns of the time. Changes to other parts of the law similarly gave workers a wider berth to strike. Importantly, the NLFT removed a central provision found in Article 269 of the 1931 Federal Labor Law stipulating that a workers' strike could be ruled nonexistent and struck down by labor authorities if it could be declared to contravene terms established in a collective labor contract. The NLFT included no similar mechanism for employers to challenge the validity of workers' actions—a fundamental omission that shows that by 1970 labor authorities accepted that workers could strike to demand revisions even to collective contracts whose terms of validity (*vigencia*) had not yet expired. With the NLFT, workers could hence construe that their eternal quest for equilibrium was perpetual and not limited, not even by contractual terms that they had previously agreed to.

Owners who suspected that the post-1970 labor climate had shifted against them may have found evidence of bias in other sections of the NLFT as well. Article 451 stipulated that a strike required a simple majority of workers (half plus one) to force contractual talks but did not specify the composition of the striking force. Unionized workers, wrote Baltasar Cavazos Flores, a law professor and the lead attorney for the Mexican Employers' Confederation, could therefore recruit the assistance of "free" (i.e., nonunionized) workers in their campaigns. This was a curious situation, being that free workers who were not technically covered by collective contracts stood to gain nothing from the creation of a contract between ownership and the union. Why, he wondered, would nonunionized workers go on strike and risk losing their jobs to participate in a cause that did not benefit them? Regardless of what their potential motivation may have been, this provision, like others in the NLFT, seemed to Cavazos to encourage labor agitation that needlessly disrupted the production process, hurt the economy, and nourished the tissue of syndical privilege—all to the detriment of Mexico.[7]

The NLFT limited employers' powers to challenge the validity of strikes and gave workers a wider berth to strike but did not deprive owners of all legal weapons. The NLFT maintained the state's prerogative to curtail the workers' strike in the event that it had adverse social effects. According to Article 466 the right to strike was limited for workers in the transportation and public health sectors.[8] Moreover, Article 467 gave federal authorities the power to require that a number of workers remain on the job so that the suspension of labors did not harm the general population, and Article 468 stipulated that workers who persisted in striking against federal orders could be replaced with temporary personnel whose installment would be guaranteed by public force if necessary. In this regard, at least, the NLFT, like the code it replaced, conveyed a familiar vibe of "conservative nationalism" that belied business's accusations that it was irresponsibly proworker.

The Collective Contract

Organized labor's post-Tlatelolco desire to drape labor-capital relations with a banner of social justice is most evident in the language of the collective contracts established in the period. Collective labor contracts were legal agreements reached between a designated group of workers organized into a union and the ownership of a single company or multiple companies that employed said workers. The document was produced via negotiations held between labor and corporate representatives and was organized into three distinct sections: (a) the cover (*envoltura*)—which related the conditions that spawned the birth of the contract and outlined clauses relative to the its duration, modification, and termination; (b) the regulator (*normativo*)—which listed the names and residences of all *titulares* (designated representatives of the contractual entities) and specified the conditions of work, including salaries, work schedules, holidays and vacations, required safety measures, and terms of social programs, among many other items; and (c) the obligatory element (*elemento obligatorio*)—which stated the measures available to enforce compliance of the terms fixed in the regulator.[9] Union representatives and management drafted the terms of the contract, but it was subjected to scrutiny by state and federal labor authorities before enactment. With government certification the contract acquired full legal authority to dictate labor-capital relations between the listed contractees for a period established in the document, typically two years.

Very little in the NLFT's language that established the collective contract, however, indicated a bias for workers over owners. The rights to modify, suspend, and terminate collective labor relations were guaranteed to owners and workers alike in Chapters VI, VII, and VIII, respectively. The collective contract was defined similarly in the 1970 and 1931 codes, yet there were some important differences. Article 42 of the 1931 Federal Labor Law and Article 386 of the NLFT mutually defined the collective contract as an "agreement reached between one or several trade unions and one or several employers, or one or several unions of employers, toward the end of establishing the conditions by which labor must be lent," though the latter code clarified that it would regulate relations "in one or more businesses or establishments."[10] Follow-up articles showed variations that were more interesting. Article 43 in the 1931 code explained that "any employer that employs workers belonging to a union will have the obligation of reaching a collective contract with that union when it solicits it."[11] Article 387 of the NLFT reproduced the language but included an addendum giving workers near carte blanche to exercise the right to strike as consigned in Article 450 of the current law.

Clearly significant, the additional language suggested that labor law in the post-1970 period would have an action-friendly bent. Article 426 of the NLFT specified that unions and owners would henceforth be able to solicit conciliation and arbitration boards to modify labor terms set in collective contracts when either (a) economic conditions existed that justified it or (b) an increase in the cost of living provoked an imbalance between capital and labor.[12] No similar language was found in the guidelines set for modifying collective contracts in the 1931 statute.[13] Even so, this did not signify a bias in favor of one side or the other. The new code guaranteed employees and owners similar access to federal arbitration, and it was only under the assumption that an "imbalance" in the distribution of profits between labor and capital benefited only owners that one could read an inherent bias for workers in the language of the law.

Other aspects of the new law, however, gave critics grounds for legitimate concern. In particular, an owner's rights to modify, suspend, or terminate a collective contract were curtailed in the NLFT. Article 427 of the NLFT reaffirmed the rights of owners to legally suspend collective labor contracts for reasons including the lack of primary materials, the lack of necessary funds to continue operation, an excess of their product in the marketplace, and other reasons previously outlined in Article 116 of the 1931 Federal Labor Law.[14] What the NLFT did not list, however, worried employers, as they were hence deprived of the right to suspend a collective contract with workers who contracted a contagious illness or failed to fulfill the terms of the labor agreement due to arrest or imprisonment, powers granted to them in the 1931 law.[15] The pain of this injury was compounded by the fact that Article 430 of the NLFT made all employers' suspension decisions subject to review by the Federal Conciliation and Arbitration Board, which could then overturn the decision, dictate compensation terms, or reinstate workers after considering factors such as the probable period of the suspension and the possibility of the suspended workers finding new jobs.[16]

The legal methods by which collective contracts could be created were also amended after 1970. The NLFT established that collective contracts could be born of two processes: first, by means of a company granting the request of a union or unions whose members constituted less than half of the total workforce; and second, by way of a strike undertaken lawfully when union workers represented more than half of company employees. In the first instance, the realization of the contract was not guaranteed by law. Owners who employed a majority nonunionized workforce had no legal obligation to negotiate terms of employment with unions in their employ. Collective contracts were sometimes in place to regulate relations with unionists who performed tasks central to the company's operations, but more likely collective contracts were born from strikes waged to pressure ownership to sit down at the negotiating table. Article 387 of the NLFT confirmed the strike as the primary negotiating tactic for unions, as it read, "The employer who employs workers belonging to a union will have the obligation of reaching a collective contract with the union when it solicits it. If the employer refuses to sign the contract, the workers will be able to exercise the right to strike as consigned to them in Article 450."[17]

Thus the NLFT, overall, reduced employers' ability to suspend and fire employees who labored under the rubrics of collective contract (while putting those decisions in the hands of governmental authorities) and legitimated the workers' strike as a standard tactic for unions to use in their ongoing quest to achieve equilibrium in the workplace. Undoubtedly, the NLFT bolstered the presence of the collective contract in workplace relations and made that instrument appear to be the vehicle by which unionists could revive the quest for social justice that they felt had lagged in the four decades since the 1931 Federal Labor Law first articulated it.

This spirit is ubiquitous in the language of post-1970 labor agreements. An example can be found in the collective contract reached between members of the union Librado Rivera and the executives of the Veracruz-based companies Aluminio and Inmobiliaria Aluminio to govern workplace relations from March 1973 to March 1975. Page 1, Article 3, of the contract included the following language, lifted in part directly from the introductory language of the New Federal Labor Law: "The rules of work are designed toward achieving balance and social justice in worker-business relations. Labor is a right and a social duty. It is not an article of commerce, it demands respect for the liberties and dignity of those who conduct it and it must be undertaken under conditions that assure life, health, and a decent economic level for the worker and his family." The twenty-eight-page document included no similar language affirming the social rights of owners. The companies' owners were contractually granted the right to demand respect from their employees—Article 51, Clause B, obligated workers to "lend their services to the companies subordinately"—yet the contract made no reference of the right of owners to secure their and their families' economic and physical well-being as it had done for workers.[18]

Many collective contracts featured proworker rhetoric but were not partisan script. Collective contracts were the products of labor-capital negotiations and were subjected to the rigors of approval and certification by labor authorities. They were, as such, bilateral documents that were designed to represent the will of the worker as much as the will of the owner. Still, owners alleged that they operated at a distinct disadvantage to workers in the negotiating process. Baltasar Cavazos Flores, a business advocate, alluded to this injustice in a 1971 manual he produced to interpret the legal and practical ramifications of the new labor code for businesses. As he saw it, the collective contract was "inadequate" because it was less a testament of the wills of owners and more an expression of the supremacy of workers' priorities.[19] He judged the collective contract in contemporary Mexico such an imbalanced instrument that it had even invalidated its name. The title "collective" was no longer applicable, he felt, and "Professional Labor Pact" was a more appropriate moniker, being that the instrument was artificially weighted to benefit the "professional" core of workers, that is, unionists, and offered very little for nonunionized employees.[20]

Organized labor partisans confronted cynics and allegations with statistics. Writing in *Revista Mexicana del Trabajo*, the Secretariat of Labor and Social Welfare's quarterly publication, in 1975, Miguel Barona de la O. and José Luis Huerta Cruz admitted that syndical groups, "because of their force, unity, and organization . . . obtain better benefits." Yet the authors defied those who asserted that legislative advancements in the labor sector had benefited only a minority of unionized workers. They reported that salaried workers represented 62 percent of the nation's workforce, and of that number nearly ten million (39 percent) were organized under collective contracts. Taking into account that the salaries of those workers supported an average of 2.8 people, Barona and Huerta calculated that there were at least thirty-eight million Mexicans who based their subsistence on company wages. And of this mass, they added, the majority benefited from social programs such as social security and the National Workers' Housing Institute created to improve the living conditions of the working class.[21] With these considerations in mind, the authors argued that the nation was in need of more, not less, unionization efforts to permit a larger nucleus of workers and their dependents to enjoy its advantages. More, not less, collective contracts were hence required if the nation wished to pursue social justice and eliminate industrial practices that objectified workers by turning them into dispensable commodities.

Worker Safety and Hygiene Provisions

Laws protecting workers' health had been on the books since before 1931, but their enforcement was irregular. The NLFT strove to reverse this situation by ramping up federal oversight and forcing owners to comply with safety and hygiene provisions outlined in the new law. The NLFT also required companies to install new, safer equipment at their own expense and create education programs to train workers about new safety and hygiene provisions. Additionally, the NLFT vastly expanded the range of ailments that workers could claim were job related, from 50 in the 1931 Federal Labor Law to 161 in the NLFT of 1970, demonstrating an acceptance on the part of legislators that industrial labor inflicted psychological as well as physical harm on workers. Owners objected to the new requirements because of the costly technical changes they imposed upon them and saw in them onerous mandates that were prejudicial to their interests.

Safety inspection reports filed by federal labor officials in the post-1970 period scarcely resembled the skeletal, largely pro forma evaluations submitted in earlier times. Using an enhanced form, post-1970 inspectors submitted reports that meticulously listed the names of the worker and company representatives to the safety and hygiene commissions, company-level bodies charged with monitoring safety conditions on the shop floor, and verified the owner's registration status with the Mexican Social Security Institute. The reports listed the company's affiliated union, if any, and detailed the number, names, sexes, and positions of unionized and nonunionized workers. Post-1970 reports also complied better with federal law mandating the identification of foreign workers, and they were more thorough in detailing the types of floorings, ceilings, and equipment and machinery used. Finally, inspectors more carefully reported the number and nature of industrial accidents suffered in the past year and they submitted reports that detailed the types of safety apparatus present on shop floors—antifire shields, insulated wiring, safety goggles, boots, and so on—while giving specific orders to employers to ensure their compliance with federal law, ranging from the installation of motor guards on equipment to the hanging of No Smoking signs.[22]

Not surprisingly, although the de jure regulations had been altered the de facto reality still lagged behind. Safety inspection reports from as late as 1975 reveal that many companies had yet to comply with NLFT regulations that had by then been on the books for five years. An inspection report from the Puebla-based company Productos Alimenticios la Morena submitted to Federal Labor Delegation No. 7 on November 3, 1975, was exemplary in this regard and told much about company life beyond mere matters of industrial safety. Morena, it reported, was a cannery that packed mainly serrano and jalapeño peppers in addition to some tomato, onion, carrot, pineapple, and vegetable and vinegar oil products. The cannery was a medium-sized and private enterprise that had eighteen production workers (fourteen men, four women) in addition to thirty-one other employees (twenty-five men, six women) involved in office and management roles. The report specified that the production workers were organized into the General Packing Industry and Affiliated Workers' Union of Puebla, an affiliate of the CTM, and that a collective contract governed workplace relations. The office workers were classified as "free employees," indicating that they were not unionized and did not have a collective contract.[23]

As for Morena's compliance with safety terms established in the NLFT, the report conveyed a spotty record. The company operated with old machinery and had failed to create a worker-training program to instruct new and existing employees about modern safety practices. Company executives were also cited for their failure to install fire and smoke detection equipment as required by law. They were ordered to immediately remit to state labor authorities a plan for compliance as well as show evidence that they had installed metallic protection to shield workers from chemical dust. Finally, Morena management was instructed to hang signage to remind employees of the company's antismoking policy and of the obligatory use of safety equipment, including boots, gloves, and aprons.

The Morena report resembled the great majority of others conducted in that period. Post-1970 workplace inspections were intensive, typically lasting two to three days, and virtually all reported some degree of noncompliance on the part of ownership. In many cases the reported violations were minor; Empacadora Regiomontana, a Monterrey-based cannery that employed just two floor workers (*operarios*) and one office worker (*empleado*), was cited in December 1975 for not having a map that showed the location of fire extinguishers.[24] In other cases the reported violations were more serious; Productora de Papel, a paper company located in San Nicolás de los Garza, Nuevo León, was cited in 1975 for lacking a sprinkler system and for employing four persons as cauldron blowers without being licensed to do so.[25]

It was at small companies like Empacadora Regiomontana, typically, that onerous and expensive requirements were least likely to be met. One can imagine that it was exactly this kind of demand on employers, so frequently imposed in the NLFT, that small, family-run companies loathed as an unproductive form of government intervention in their business. Many *patrones*, big and small, refused to comply with government mandates they deemed burdensome. Based on the inspection reports described above, management at Morena, Productora de Papel and Empacadora Regiomontana were negligent in meeting their responsibilities to their workers in several regards. But did this mean that these owners were unpatriotic? Perhaps not. A scan of labor inspection reports from 1975 suggests that few companies executed perfect worker safety practices and complied with each safety provision required in the NLFT. Very likely these employers mirrored their counterparts at other companies in the gradual pace with which they implemented newly mandated safety reforms.

Assessing the Unionist Privilege in Labor Arbitration

Previous chapters have demonstrated that post-Tlatelolco officials showed a real rhetorical bias for the interests of labor over capital. Did this verbal posturing, however, produce real gains for workers in their individual battles with employers? This chapter now examines instances of individual activism via the filing of *pleitos*, which were labor suits or grievances raised by workers or owners and decided by a tripartite board composed of labor, capital, and government representatives to assess the arbitration process and further challenge the assertion that labor relations had a distinct proworker bent in the post-Tlatelolco period.

Personal Indemnification Suits

Trinidad Cruz Rodríguez was not a member of a union when he signed an individual contract for temporary employment with the Federal Electric Commission to work on a crew clearing weeds about ten kilometers outside of the city of Villahermosa, Tabasco. The job turned bloody on the afternoon of October 25, 1973, when a blow from a coworker's machete struck Cruz and nearly severed the pinky finger from his right hand. He was rushed to a hospital in Villahermosa where the unsalvageable finger was amputated and the wound sutured. Incapacitated, Cruz was granted six weeks of recuperation time. When he returned to work on December 6 he noted that he carried out his labors painfully and with diminished strength. A subsequent examination by the CFE's Medical Services Department determined that the injury he suffered left him permanently disabled but was not serious enough to prevent him from resuming habitual life activities and continuing his labors. Company officials determined that the injury, being a result of work activities, entitled Cruz to indemnification, though the extent of the injury, they felt, was minimal. The accident was deemed to hinder Cruz's performance by only 10 percent—a logical but somewhat Faustian conclusion given that he had lost exactly one-tenth of his manual digits. The company then resolved to indemnify him at a rate established in Clause 27 of the NLFT's Permanent Injury Table of Valuations—a total that would award him 4,013.17 pesos, representing 10 percent of 1,095 days of his salary of 36.65 pesos per day.

Cruz took issue with the judgment. He rejected the company's settlement offer and filed a pleito with federal labor authorities to force the CFE to compensate him at a level he deemed fair and appropriate. For Cruz, a free worker, the wheels of justice moved especially slowly. Twenty-one months after he suffered the injury and more than a year and half after he disputed the medical evaluation his case was finally concluded by federal labor authorities. A July 21, 1975, letter from Federal Labor Delegate Ignacio Olvera Quintero to José María Esquivel Torres, CFE Southeast Division manager, upheld the company's decision. Olvera agreed that the injuries sustained by the worker while on the job constituted a 10 percent disability. In accordance with terms set by the law, this entitled him to a compensation package equal to 10 percent of 1,095 days of salary, or 4,013.17 pesos, as previously determined by the company.[26]

Cruz's labor suit was unsuccessful. His attempt to force his employer to better compensate him for his injuries was denied. Labor authorities saw fit to enforce the minimum terms established by law and award him for injuries sustained while on the job, but the amount was a pittance in the opinion of the aggrieved worker. What may account for this injustice? The labor status of the worker in this instance was crucial for Cruz, although he labored for the CFE with an individual contract in place, was a free worker, and was not unionized. This differentiated him from the great majority of CFE employees, who were *sutermistas*—electrical workers grouped into the SUTERM, the nation's largest electrical workers' union. Constituting the vast majority of CFE employees, sutermistas exerted a collective sway over the company that enabled them to write generous terms into the collective contract that governed workplace relations.

Certainly, the indemnification package given to Cruz in accordance with the NLFT would have been unacceptable to the typical sutermista.

Clause 61 of the CFE-SUTERM labor agreement put in place for 1974–76 stipulated that a worker who suffered partial and permanent incapacitation was entitled to receive an indemnification payment equal to 1,450 days of salary. The worker could then choose to retire with a pension according to his or her employment history or return to work if he or she desired so and was capable.[27] Hypothetically, therefore, had Cruz been a member of the SUTERM, his lost finger would have fetched him a compensation check in the amount of 53,142.5 pesos—substantially more than the 4,013.17 pesos he received—and even more, were he to earn a salary commensurate with that of the typical sutermista. Other pension terms established in the CFE-SUTERM collective contract, particularly in the area of death compensation, were similarly munificent, though widows of deceased union members were frequently required to raise labor suits to enforce company compliance with them.[28]

Justo Pérez Romero was alive and well when he pondered retiring from the CFE in 1975 after twenty-five years of service to the company. Seeking to put his ducks in a row, he inquired about the size of his pension and was shocked to learn that it was significantly less than he expected. Fortunately for Pérez, he was a member of the SUTERM and the terms of his retirement were clearly demarcated in the existing collective contract. Aware of his rights, he went to his union representative and asked that he raise a case with federal authorities to force the company to fulfill its contractual obligations to him. His union representative filed a petition on November 6, 1975, with the Federal Permanent Conciliation Board No. 14 located in Mérida, Yucatán. In it, the SUTERM demanded that the CFE honor terms established in Clause 69 of the collective contract and issue Pérez a check for 77,118 pesos—a sum corresponding to twelve days of wages for each of the twenty-five years he had been on the job. The demand was granted and the CFE was ordered to pay Pérez the amount he was contractually owed. Upon receipt of his pension, we can assume, Pérez received what would have been a small fortune to the average worker in his area. On the other hand, Pérez was not an average worker. He was a member of one of the nation's premier unions and as such enjoyed a salary of 257.06 pesos per day, which distanced him from the typical Yucateco, who was guaranteed by federal law a minimum daily salary ranging only from 55.40 to 73.20 pesos depending on the location of employment and the nature of the work performed.[29]

Unlawful Termination Suits

Another major field of individual action was labor suits raised by workers to protest what they deemed was unlawful termination (*despido injustificado*) of their employment. In this regard one's labor status again played a role in the resolution of one's case. Unionists frequently benefited from the presence of a collective contract that gave them job security. Free workers, on the other hand, often went to work unaware of even the minimum rights guaranteed them by the law. Still, free workers, like unionists, filed labor suits by the thousands with labor authorities claiming that they had been wrongly dismissed from their jobs and seeking proper redress. Cayetano Cárdenas Estrada, a construction worker and member of Local 74 of the Industrial Union of Mexican Cement, Lime, Plaster, and Affiliated Industries in Chihuahua City, Chihuahua, was fired by his employer, Empresa Materiales, on October 19, 1974, for demanding an increase in his salary to reflect changes in his job duties. According to labor authority records, Cárdenas was fired after an altercation he had with his supervisor, Pedro Peña, who told him, "If you don't want to work, get the hell out of here!"[30] Peña then dismissed Cárdenas from the job site and promised to see him fired. Cárdenas informed his union of the situation and filed a complaint with Federal Labor Delegation No. 3 claiming that his firing was unlawful and in violation of terms established in the contract between the company and his union. A conciliatory meeting that brought together company, labor, and government representatives was convened on November 4. The meeting concluded with Cárdenas having his job returned to him and the union rescinding its complaint against the company.

Jorge Aviles Nava worked as assistant office manager at the San Luis, Sonora, branch of the CFE. On July 22, 1975, he was accused of stealing from the cash drawer where customer payments were collected. When questioned further, Aviles produced a large quantity of money and returned it to company officials. He was promptly fired. Aviles, a member of the SUTERM, contacted his union liaison, who then approached management and admitted that although Aviles was in possession of a large amount of funds, the shortage resulted from an accounting error and was not evidence of criminal activity. This was a risk, apparently, that had long worried the union, and it had requested on numerous occasions that the CFE create an overage fund to prevent workers from having to cover shortages out of their own pockets and to protect them from accusations of theft.[31] Aviles stayed fired, however, forcing the union to file an unlawful termination petition with state labor authorities. In testimony given to Federal Labor Delegation No. 1 in September, local union leader Ramon Juárez Beltrán spoke on behalf of Aviles and expressed the SUTERM's belief that the worker had been dismissed for political reasons. Moreover, he felt that the firing had violated Clause 39 of the valid CFE-SUTERM collective contract that required the company to inform the union in writing of its intention prior to dismissing a worker. Therefore, the union did not consider Aviles fired and did not replace him.

Following the testimony of Juárez, José Vidrio Casillas, superintendent of the San Luis zone, spoke on behalf of the CFE. He explained that he fired Aviles after it became apparent that he had used his position to embezzle funds from the company. This was a legitimate and lawful course of action, he maintained, and he cited Article 47 of the NLFT, which afforded employers the power to fire employees who violated basic workplace conditions. Federal Labor Inspector Raul Marmolejo Lozano considered the merits of the contrasting positions and emitted a ruling. In his opinion, the facts of the case revealed that crucial aspects of the valid collective contract had been violated. Specifically, he pointed to Clause 39 of the contract, which gave the SUTERM power to fill open positions in the company and made the CFE's firing decisions subject to union review. Based on a strict interpretation of this language, Marmolejo had no choice but to endorse the union position. The union did not sanction the Juárez dismissal. As such the firing violated contractual language and was thus illegal.

The cases described above shed light on a larger trend in tripartite labor arbitration of the period. In the first case, the worker Cárdenas was dismissed from his job for purportedly refusing to work. In the second case, the worker Aviles was dismissed for allegedly stealing. In both instances the process of labor arbitration ran its course and concluded with the reinstatement of the fired employees. Cárdenas and Aviles returned to work in the following weeks. Employers who ended up on the wrong side of the judgments had cause for concern. To them, the trend in labor-capital relations tending toward the interests of workers over those of owners seemed ever more real—but with an important qualifier. In the post-1970 era of social justice and workers' vindication, an employee's transgressions appeared irrelevant only if a collective contract was in place and the worker was enrolled in a union. In a real sense, owners lacked even the power to decide who worked for them and who they could remove. The employees in question were unionists. They were, one could surmise, entitled to their jobs.

This perception, as real as it may have seemed to patrones, is not provable—at least not empirically. Tripartite boards of the period did not rule unanimously in favor of employees when hearing unlawful termination suits. Company policies varied, but Article 47 of the NLFT gave employers the right to fire employees for thirteen separate reasons, including "immoral acts" in the workplace—for example, stealing (Clause 7)—and absenteeism without authorization (Clause 10).[32] Complete data at the national or even state levels does not exist, but dozens of cases I have examined show that employers' decisions to fire workers for these reasons were largely upheld by labor boards. In the overwhelming majority of cases employers testified and cited Article 47 to justify their firing decisions. In most cases their actions were endorsed; their decisions to fire workers were seldom overturned. Employers hence based their claims of bias on the difficulty of firing unionized workers. Clearly unionists wielded power in the tripartite arbitration process, and at no time more so than when they engaged the system collectively.

The Power of the Union in Collective Labor Negotiation

On the morning of August 27, 1973, three men who had recently lost their jobs as temporary workers on a federal highway project appeared in the offices of Federal Labor Delegation No. 3 in the city of Torreón,

Coahuila. There the men, Angel Jacquez, Claro Frayre, and Roberto Cruz Martínez, lodged a complaint against Roberto Santos, the foreman of the road crew they had labored on near their homes in Cuencamé, Durango. As the men told Salvador Castillo Rivera, the federal labor delegate, Santos gave them "very difficult tasks" and did not pay them the minimum salary nor the seventh-day pay they were entitled to.[33] They called his assignments "inhumane," and they vowed not to accept them as they were (only) *trabajadores de raya*, or line workers.[34] They demanded that Santos be ordered before labor authorities to answer for his actions and that he testify at a hearing convened closer to where they lived. Castillo granted the men's requests. Santos was ordered to appear before labor authorities in Cuencamé on September 5.

Before Santos made his appearance to discuss conditions at the job site, he took matters into his own hands. On August 29 Santos informed the seventeen men who formed the crew that worked at kilometer eight of the highway being built to span the villages of Santa Clara and El Naranjo (both in Durango) that all labors on the road had been suspended. He collected their tools and equipment and dismissed them, in effect leaving them unemployed. Three days later, Castillo received many of the recently fired road workers in his Torreón office. They requested that he investigate the illegal conditions under which they toiled and asked him to reinstate their jobs and compensate them for lost wages.[35]

These and other issues were on the agenda at the September 5 meeting held in Cuencamé. The site of the meeting was not neutral ground (it was held in Santos's office), yet employees and management were given equal opportunity to state their cases before José Santos Reyes Gaytán, an inspector dispatched by Castillo. Workers reiterated their discontent over conditions imposed upon them by Santos. In his defense Santos argued that the job performance of the workers was poor and that it did not meet the standards required by the Secretariat of Communication and Public Works—the government ministry that sponsored the project. Santos testified that he instructed workers only to make holes of four cubic meters, a minimum task he claimed they failed to accomplish. With regard to their pay he explained that he adjusted wages according to the minimum salary established in the region in which they worked and that the seventh-day pay was included as part of a 3-peso-per-day bonus given to workers upon the completion of each shift. After six shifts, therefore, workers accrued 126 pesos—a total that, divided by seven, was 18 pesos per day, satisfying the minimum wage threshold in the region. Finally, Santos spoke to the issue of the lockout and the dismissed workers. He admitted that he shut down the site on August 29 but said that he did so because of problems that were festering. He blamed Cruz Martínez for agitating workers with distorted truths and riling them up with excessive demands. As for the other fired workers, Frayre and Jacquez, he explained that Frayre was terminated weeks earlier after he left the job site without permission and Jacquez and Cruz Martínez were let go for insubordination, though they continued to report to work thereafter.

Reyes Gaytán heard the parties' arguments, then offered a deal. Santos, he proposed, would resume construction under the conditions presented by the petitioners to the Federal Labor Delegation and the workers, in exchange, would submit to the orders they received from the public works ministry (via Santos). On this topic, Reyes Gaytán impressed upon both sides that they were mutually employees of the federal government and it was the secretariat, not Santos, that was the employer on the project. As such, they were encouraged to put aside personal animosities in favor of compromise and, perhaps, even patriotism. Both sides acceded to the inspector's terms and resolved to resume working on September 11, the start of the next two-week pay period.[36]

The following day, September 6, Reyes Gaytán sent his official report to Castillo. He detailed the resolution, the crux of which was an agreement that the dismissed workers be rehired under the condition that they obey the directives Santos issued them and that Santos implement working conditions as determined by the public works ministry. The deal was agreeable to both sides. Workers approved of it because it gave them their jobs back and it allowed federal labor authorities to intervene to correct violations they perceived to be present. The deal placated Santos as well because it guaranteed him the subordination of his employees and permitted him to complete the project without further worker agitation.[37]

The matter, however, although resolved by the government's standards, had not yet concluded for the aggrieved workers. Days after reaching the accord with Santos, members of the road crew petitioned labor authorities again, this time to recover wages lost during the three-day period when work at the site was suspended. Another letter was addressed to Reyes Gaytán, signed by several members of the road crew, including Diego Beltrán Rodríguez, Zeferino Beltrán Rodríguez, and Margarito Beltrán Rodríguez—all residents of Santa Clara and very likely brothers.[38] Certainly these men considered their lost pay significant. Reyes Gaytán, however, although he had previously written that he believed their wages were too low, rejected their claim on the grounds that the dispute had been settled. He instructed them to take up any future salary disputes directly with their employer, the Secretariat of Communications and Public Works. This kind of bureaucratic maneuvering did not deter the workers. In a September 15 letter to Reyes Gaytán they confirmed their intention to pursue the matter of lost wages with the public works ministry.[39]

The case of the Durango road workers, though small in scope, yields a broader understanding of contemporaneous workplace relations. The case's details are illustrative primarily for the ways they reveal the intense disparity in benefits and privileges enjoyed by unionized and free workers. The men who toiled on the road crew described above were, quite obviously, not unionized. Classified officially by authorities as temporary workers (*eventuales*), the men in fact held an even lower position on the labor pecking order, as they were line workers who had been awarded temporary employment simply for being at the top of a list of available workers. Working for the government, however, afforded men like the Beltrán Rodríguez brothers some benefits and protections. They were not mere day laborers or peons—they had a fixed salary and did not arrive at work each morning expecting their wages to fluctuate in accordance with the size of the available labor supply. Nonetheless, their employment was dangerous, unstable, and poorly paid.

Our road workers complained of conditions that were "inhumane" but did not specify exactly how the conditions imposed upon them were unlawful. Had they been unionized, they could have benefited from a union representative or lawyer who could cite each of the safety violations present at the worksite. They pursued legal action and achieved a semifavorable resolution, yet labor authorities did not mandate the creation of workers' safety, hygiene, or training programs, as was commonly done in the resolution of union-company disputes. Moreover, actions taken by Santos showed that the nature of their work was precarious; they could be summarily dismissed at the whim of a foreman without any immediate legal recourse. Finally, the wage question demonstrated the disadvantaged status of the free worker. The federal labor inspector deemed the wages that they received insufficient—a logical conclusion when considering the paucity of their twenty-one-peso-a-day salary against the demands of doing construction on sun-baked roads in Durango—yet he was unwilling to assist them in recovering what they had lost due to the lockout.

The resolution achieved by the Durango workers would have been a pill impossible to swallow for the typical post-Tlatelolco unionist. Certainly the members of the aluminum workers' union Librado Rivera pursued loftier goals when they threatened to strike against their Veracruz-based employers in early 1973. The brazenness of their position corresponded to the strength of their bargaining position. Staffing two local companies, including Aluminio, which had over 1,500 employees and produced over eighty thousand tons of aluminum a year, Librado Rivera members threatened to shut down operations at a company that was one of the most important manufacturers of that metal in Latin America.[40] Formed into the CROC, a national labor organization with clout surpassed only perhaps by the CTM, members of Librado Rivera were also found at work in nearby shipyards, where they constructed ships in Veracruz harbor. Clearly their labors were highly valued, and they demanded commensurate compensation.

On February 6, 1973, leaders of the union filed a strike petition with Federal Conciliation Board No. 12 in Veracruz resolving their members to strike at 11:00 p.m. on March 1 if certain terms they desired were not included in the collective contract they were negotiating with management.[41] On February 8, two days after the union filed its strike petition, the companies' managers stated their case to federal labor authorities by responding to the claims filed against them. Gustavo Ortega O., attorney for the companies, explained to officials that negotiations between labor and management had stalled due the union's intransigence. The petitioners, he believed, were not truly committed to finding "equilibrium" but instead were making demands that were "in every way exorbitant and unrealistic." Ortega assured officials that the companies remained committed to continuing talks with the union, but only if talks were based on "just and equitable bases" and moved toward the end of "harmonizing" the rights of labor with those of capital.[42]

Ortega's assessment of the state of negotiations was revealing. He assailed the union's demands, yet he accepted the workers' fundamental right to pursue balance in the production process. That Ortega, a company representative, incorporated the watchwords of *equilibrium*, *just and equitable*, and *harmony* into his testimony proved that such concepts were impossible to exclude in tripartite discourse of the era. Owners could not promote a strict capitalist line and reasonably expect a positive outcome from state officials. Social justice, it appeared, had become a rubric within which all elements were required to operate. Ortega followed this dictate and argued ownership's case by deriding the ways that workers' demands contravened concepts so ubiquitous and so often lauded as noble and revolutionary.

Why, exactly, did Ortega view union demands as exorbitant or unrealistic? How, for instance, could employers view workers' priorities as adverse to the social goals of balance, justice, and harmony? For potential clues let us consider the terms proposed in the hotly disputed contract draft presented to the companies by the union in December 1972. The twenty-eight-page document included a three-page pay scale setting wages for each job conducted by members of Librado Rivera. Employees were classified in several ways. Article 4 stated that technical experts the company hired (*personal de confianza*) need not be members of the union. Their numbers, however, could never exceed 2.5 percent of the number of union members at work in the company (Article 10). Provisions were made for the hiring of temporary and part-time workers brought on in various capacities for the completion of determined jobs (Article 9), though the contract stipulated that the hiring of these nonunionized employees required written approval of the union prior to their arrival (Article 14). The company was also required to make the union aware in writing of all vacancies so that it could furnish the company with a replacement within seventy-two hours. In the event that the union could not fill the position within that time frame, the company was free to hire an employee, though he or she was to be paid a salary that corresponded to the union rate afforded for that post (Article 8).[43]

The union's demand to oversee the hiring and compensation processes demonstrated its desire to solidify its status as an indispensible component of company operations. Requiring the company to solicit its approval prior to contracting with a new worker and mandating that the company pay a nonunionized worker union wages were both important safeguards against the company's hiring of low-wage replacement (scab) workers. The contract then turned its attention to regulating the terms of the workweek, yearly calendar, vacation structure, annual bonus, and severance pay for workers. The workweek was to have a duration of forty hours for day workers, thirty-seven hours, twenty minutes for those who worked mixed (night/day) shifts, and thirty-five hours for those who worked exclusively at night. Unionized employees were to work a five-day, forty-hour workweek and rest on Saturday and Sunday, though Article 31 called for the company to compensate unionized employees for a full seven days of work (fifty-six hours). Article 39 stipulated that if a worker chose to work on Saturday or Sunday he or she was to receive triple-time pay. The worker would then also be entitled to a paid day off the following week. These were extraordinary demands, out of line with even the CTM's and Fidel Velázquez's campaign to institute the maximum five-day, forty-hour workweek for unionists with pay for six days, or forty-eight hours.

Article 40 listed the obligatory days of rest. Twelve dates, all days of patriotic importance, were listed, and there were three other Catholic observances that the union requested as holidays as well. Article 41 outlined the vacation policy. Employees with more than one year of service were entitled to nine paid vacation days; those with more than two years of service, eleven; more than three years, thirteen; and more than four years, sixteen.[44] Year-end bonuses (*aguinaldo*) were also cemented as a right of the unionist. Article 48 called for members of Librado Rivera to receive an annual bonus to be delivered on December 15 so as to properly anticipate Christmas expenses and in an amount equivalent to forty-five days of salary. Finally, the contract draft set the terms for severance pay for retiring workers. Article 79 specified that in the case of voluntary termination of employment, the company was to pay the worker fifteen days of salary for each year he had worked up to five years. If he had worked more than five years, he was to receive twenty-five days of salary for each year served.[45]

Further analysis of the collective contract draft proved that, very often, it paid to be unionized. Members of Librado Rivera expected to go to work each day enjoying benefits that free workers could only dream of. Based just on the pension clause described above, it was apparent that they left work as well with a security blanket that further distanced them from their nonunionized brethren. An aluminum worker who joined the ranks of Librado Rivera and was employed building ships in Veracruz harbor was guaranteed a daily wage of 80 pesos. Hypothetically, therefore, according to Article 79, the aluminum worker could retire after twenty years of service with a severance package of 40,000 pesos (80 pesos in daily salary × 20 years of service × 25 days of salary for each year served).

Article 49 imposed other requirements on ownership. Employers were mandated to meet all labor regulations, pay salaries that met standards established in labor law, and provide employees with tools, instruments, and materials needed to fulfill their job functions, a place to store their equipment, and sufficient chairs. Employers were also obligated to refrain from using abusive speech toward their workers, produce a biweekly pay stub that specified days worked and salary earned, provide their workers with medical assistance and periodic checkups, and ensure that nonunionized employees treated union members respectfully by suspending those who violated said stipulations. Several other provisions in the contract prescribed the companies' specific duties as they pertained to union relations. Owners were obliged to provide the union a comfortable and hygienic place "where refreshments and foodstuffs are sold" (Article 49), make deductions from workers' salaries and deliver monies immediately to the union (Article 46), cover the salaries of the members of the union's executive committee (Article 61), and grant employees paid leave to conduct union business (Article 84, Clause B). One provision even attempted to enforce corporate reverence for the public status of the Mexican worker. Article 81 called for the company to dispense 70,000 pesos annually toward the purchase of uniforms to be worn by workers in civic parades.[46]

Also visible in the collective contract draft was the era's renewed focus on assuring the physical and psychological health of the worker. Clauses written into the document were meant to ensure that the companies met each of the exigencies legislated by the New Federal Labor Law in the areas of worker safety and hygiene, professional and social development, housing, and transportation. Article 55 listed several long-term ailments that workers ran the risk of contracting due to the nature of the work they performed. Aluminosis, anthracnose, heat dermatitis, rheumatism, hemorrhoids, gas inhalation intoxication, dust asphyxiation, and fungal infection were identified as professional hazards. To offset the dangers incurred at the workplace, employers were asked to make on-site medical attention permanently available. Because of the dangerous and unhealthy nature of the work performed at the worksites, employers were also instructed to observe the rules and agreements dictated by the Permanent Safety and Hygiene Commission—to be composed of company and union representatives and to be funded with company resources and housed on company property. Dangers abounded at the workplace, the draft pointed out, and workers were to be compensated for time lost due to injury. Moreover, workers who avoided injury were to be rewarded. Article 77 proposed that any worker who did not suffer an injury during the course of the year should receive a bonus of 1,200 pesos in addition to the annual bonus workers received in December.[47]

Other provisions in the document further affirmed the unionists' quest for social justice. Members of Librado Rivera assigned management a "high responsibility" to stimulate the social advancement of the worker's family. In pursuit of this mission employers were asked to provide all children of workers with books and school materials (Article 82) as well as award a minimum of twenty education scholarships a year to cover other costs of inscription, uniforms, and school materials. In addition, four scholarships were to be made available to employees who wished to return to school and "better themselves" (Article 63). Companies were also charged to spend 20,000 pesos biannually to sponsor the development of sport programs for workers. The social value of athletics to the worker was understood as paramount, and any worker injured while participating in sports was to receive full pay while he or she recovered (Article 64). Housing allowance provisions were included in the contract in a similar effort to bolster the worker's home life. Salaries were to be augmented with an additional stipend of 400 pesos a month, to be put by the worker toward rent or a mortgage (Article 65). Workers with more than one year of tenure on the job were to have access to company housing (Article 66). Article 68 reminded employers of their federal obligation to provide worker housing and recommended they fulfill their duty by creating a rotating fund to issue loans of 80,000 pesos to workers to purchase a home in or near the city of Veracruz. Employees who did not wish to purchase homes would still have access to the funds, it stipulated, though they were to use them toward the purchase of land. Finally, the worker's home was not to be unduly disrupted by the burden of commuting. Article 87 of the contract draft obliged the company to provide employees bus service to and from central points in the city at the beginning and end of each of the day's three shifts.[48]

The generous social perks that members of Librado Rivera sought to write into their collective contract was accompanied by a substantial wage demand. A pay scale (*tabulador*) listed each job performed by union members in the companies and assigned it a daily wage. The salary range was broad across the diverse professions, yet even the lowest-compensated tasks were rewarded relatively well. The professions listed in the pay scale worthy of upper-level compensation in each section of industry (with their daily salaries, in pesos) included: group supervisor (80.70), operator supervisor (76.42), and siphoner (74.25) in the electrolysis department; first material discharge operator (76.42), first coal discharge operator

(76.42), and manifold worker (66.80) in the area of ship/cabin services; master mechanic (94.12), lathe operator (87.28), mechanic (80.45), and welder, blacksmith, plumber, master painter, and mason (80.00) in the mechanical shop; master automotive mechanic (94.12), second automotive mechanic (80.45), and electrical automotive mechanic (77.84) in the automotive shop; casting-group supervisor (80.07), D.C. casting molder (71.35), and saw worker (71.15) in the casting department; master electrician (94.12), electrical welder (87.28), and second electrician (87.15) in the electrical shop; and warehouse administrator (75.00) and tool shop supervisor (73.62) in the warehouse.[49]

In those same departments, the following professions were tagged for middle- and lower-level compensation: production operator (69.82) and second-line sealer (44.99) in the electrolysis department; operator (58.40), burner cleaner (55.05), and duct cleaner (51.15) in the area of ship/cabin services; painter (59.98), repairer (59.78), assistant welder, assistant mechanic, assistant iron worker, and assistant mason (51.23), and greaser (51.05) in the mechanical shop; automotive assistant (51.23) in the automotive shop; shipment operator (69.05) and assistant caster (49.08) in the casting department; type-B electrician (73.63) and assistant electrician (51.23) in the electrical shop; and freight yard warehouse administrator (66.14) and warehouse assistant (58.69) in the warehouse.

Other union members involved in nonindustrial tasks were assigned the following wages: cleaning-crew supervisor (51.23), onsite nurse (61.16), general operator (58.69), and gardener (51.23). Finally, each department employed a cleaning person (*mozo*). Regardless of the department in which they labored, these workers were assigned salaries of 44.99 pesos per day—the minimum to be received by members of the union Librado Rivera.[50]

Librado Rivera's leaders demanded much, but unionists were not simply recipients of employer beneficence; a collective contract was, after all, a reciprocal agreement that balanced the interests of labor and capital by imposing obligations on both sides of the production line. This contract was no different. Article 51 of the draft mandated that union members observe good conduct and successfully meet the job requirements, loan their services to the companies subordinately, execute the job in the agreed-upon manner and with sufficient care and neatness, keep all tools in a good condition and return them to the company upon termination of each shift, communicate to the company any deficiencies that existed, and scrupulously guard any technical and commercial secrets whose divulgation could cause damage to the company, among other requirements. Article 52 barred members from reporting to work drunk or under the influence of any drug save medications prescribed by a doctor. Members were similarly barred from bringing arms into the workplace.[51] Yet even with these requirements and proscriptions in place the collective contract draft that was to govern relations between Librado Rivera and the companies Aluminio and Inmobiliaria Aluminio gave substantially more attention to the obligations employers owed to employees than vice versa.

The wages and benefits that Librado Rivera demanded from its employers were lofty by the standards of the day, especially when considered against those typically afforded nonunionized workers in Veracruz and elsewhere. Granted, minimum wage figures of the period varied greatly from state to state, and differentiations were even made inside states between urban and rural areas, but the fact that even the lowest-paid member of Librado Rivera, employed in the shipbuilding industry of Veracruz cleaning offices and workshops, was to receive nearly forty-five pesos a day for his or her work was revealing. Though not a king's ransom, forty-five pesos was still more than twice the daily salary awarded to the temporary, nonunionized worker in Durango who would toil on a scorching-hot road later that summer. This is to say nothing of the other vacation, social, housing, and wage-related benefits that the unionist received and the free worker did not receive. These were disparities that Aluminio and other employers of the era cited when they complained that the modern unionist was privileged, unrealistic, and entitled.

The initial failure of the collective bargaining process hardened Librado Rivera's resolve. The strike it promised was not an empty threat. Although postponed one day, the strike exploded on the evening of March 2, 1973. Local news coverage understood the action as waged primarily over the issue of employee pay. The strike, it was reported, was due to the unwillingness of the company to grant the union the 18 percent salary increase it had requested; the companies offered only 15 percent. This point was non-negotiable, according to union leader Moisés Rodríguez Mendoza, who directed operations from Mexico City while in negotiation with company leaders and labor ministry officials. Via telephone, Rodríguez instructed strike committee members to solicit the CROC for assistance, and he warned local observers that the strike would continue indefinitely until an agreement was reached. Activities at the company halted. Only striking workers who picketed and "kept guard in front of the factory" to prevent the entrance of scab replacements were in motion, news coverage reported.[52]

Clearly the position of the workers overwhelmed company resistance; the strike that closed Aluminio and threatened to halt production at one of Latin's America's most important aluminum plants indefinitely lasted just one day. On March 3, barely twenty-four hours after the strike exploded, company officials conceded to Librado Rivera workers an across-the-board salary increase of 18 percent as well as a series of the other benefits demanded by the union. Official sources reported that along with the wage increase, union workers were given life insurance benefits up to 80,000 pesos, annual bonuses equivalent to thirty days of salary, loans for 1,000 pesos, and houses for workers varying in price from 50,000 to 60,000 pesos depending on the salary of the worker. Other benefits included scholarships for children.[53] Content with the negotiations, union leaders lifted the strike. By the morning of March 4, life at Aluminio had returned to normal and a potentially long and costly workers' strike had been averted.

In mid-April company and union representatives signed a collective contract that appeased both sides. The terms of the settlement revealed a give and take between workers and owners that is instructive. By signing the contract, union representatives pledged that employees would observe the instructions of their supervisors and work faithfully under their direction. The contract also gave attention to subordinating certain of the union's technical workers to management, a fact that leads us to presume that previously some technicians' relations with the companies were particularly hostile. In addition, the new contract included language that stipulated that no area would be expanded while the contract was in place. The signatories agreed that no new jobs would be created during the two-year term of the agreement.[54]

Union concessions on the matters of subordination and hiring, though, were likely offset by gains made in the arena of wages. In general, the pay scale created in the April 16 agreement granted workers the daily wages demanded by their union in its December 12 contract draft, with some exceptions. Certain positions were afforded less by the company than initially requested. These included the production operator, master automotive mechanic, and shipment operator. In other cases, negotiations produced wages higher than were initially demanded by the union. This was the case for the master electrician and the repairer. Yet the contract's new pay scale pleased workers as it granted them increased salaries to combat rising costs of living. The collective contract reached between the union Librado Rivera and executives of Aluminio and Inmobiliaria Aluminio was officially filed in the offices of Federal Conciliation Board No. 12 in Veracruz on May 2, 1973.[55] When considered against the initial demands presented by the union in its December 1972 contract draft, the terms of the new collective contract showed that compromises were made between company and union officials on crucial issues. Still, the union's inflexibility and ultimate victory on the wage increase issue demonstrated its collective clout.

Mexican patrones of the 1970s echoed their counterparts of the 1930s when they complained about a labor aristocracy that exerted an inordinate influence over labor-capital relations in the country. A privileged clique of unionists, they contended, acted selfishly and whimsically, opting on occasion to hold local economies hostage while it pursued antinational ends. It maliciously pursued its ends to the detriment of free workers, others alleged, going so far as to use its influence over state entities like the National Workers' Housing Institute to deny nonunionized workers housing and other benefits rightfully owed them.[56] All of this while it received encouragement—symbolically in the form of words and practically in the form of laws—from an ideologically suspect, even socialist, Mexican state! Aggregate numbers gave business partisans reason to grumble. A marked increase in the number of strikes carried out was seen from 1972, when there were thirty-three, to 1973, when there were fifty-seven. This heightened level of strike activity stayed relatively the same in 1974, when fifty-five strikes were carried out at the federal jurisdiction level. Yet trends within the statistics undermined accusations about a bias for labor on the part of the state. Although 5,557 and 5,182 strike petitions were filed in the years 1973 and 1974, respectively, workers enjoyed the lowest percentage of strike petitions ever approved by the Federal Conciliation and Arbitration Board during these "Strike Years," reaching a nadir of just 1.02 percent in 1973 and improving only slightly to 1.06 percent the following year.[57]

Although a mere sliver of the total pie of labor activism in the period, the cases profiled herein reveal that workers raised labor suits with authorities and went to battle with their employers wielding weapons of different calibers. Undoubtedly the employee of the Federal Electric Commission who filed a grievance against his employer operated at a distinct disadvantage if not organized into the powerful SUTERM. Similarly, the unionized dockworker was better equipped for battle against his company than was a road-crew member who tangled in arbitration with his employer, lacking a basic knowledge of labor law. In both instances, questions of union status, collective strength, and bargaining position were the decisive factors in producing the vastly different outcomes. Be they members of big or small unions, or unionized or free workers, employees engaged the labor arbitration process in record numbers after 1970 to force employers to abide by terms established in collective contracts and to protest violations of workplace conditions mandated in the NLFT. And in the majority of cases, they were successful. Most labor suits, in fact, were settled privately, suggesting that employers were prone to grant their disgruntled employees something and feared the alternative of what a *laudo*, or formal board ruling, would produce.

But does the fact that most labor suits produced favorable judgments for workers signify that the arbitration process was weighted in favor of employees and against employers? Probably the language of social justice in the NLFT and the saturation of the era's air with talk of revolutionary redemption did impact labor arbitration; it certainly affected the tone and actions taken by employers who feared weakening their positions with government representatives in impending arbitration. But what is more likely is that the majority of officials on tripartite labor boards made decisions that merely met the standards of the new law—however proworker or antibusiness one determined it to be. Critiques constantly made by unionists of the era further undermined the claims of systemic bias in their favor. In some workers' views, the Mexican state after Tlatelolco remained as firmly as ever in the clutches of patrones—a belief endorsed by the regime's actions and inactions on maquiladoras, sindicatos blancos, and the frequent repression of unions that operated independent of the labor establishment, the subject of chapter 8. To the more "revolutionary" segments of the organized labor movement, therefore, the so-called redemption of May 1 and the perceived state bias for labor were fraudulent and self-serving constructs that were more rhetorical than real.

CHAPTER 7

"Beautiful Little *Compañeras*" and "Shameful Spectacles"

Gender Complementarity in the Workers' Movement

The fact that workers of the 1970s threatened to strike at record rates despite facing historically long odds for success is telling. Clearly the New Federal Labor Law of 1970 gave them new guarantees that they believed could be won via collective action. The nation's difficult economic situation also clarified for them the need to bring legally guaranteed rights to bear. Examining strike petitions reveals that the great majority of worker activism in the period was waged over basic meat-and-potatoes issues, for example, a forty-hour workweek, alleged contractual violations, and demands for higher wages, and not toward ideological ends. Unions that took action to procure contractually guaranteed wages or federally mandated safety provisions, for instance, were sometimes successful. Workers who were inspired to strike by their president's lofty language on *tercermundismo*, on the other hand, typically failed. Nevertheless, presidential rhetoric on class solidarity, gender equality, and union democracy was heard by more than just the *charros* who controlled the large labor confederations that received federal subsidies. Workers of all stripes moved to hold the regime to its word, and in their militancy they exposed the gaping chasm that existed between the rhetoric and reality of labor relations in the period. It was female unionists who bucked the traditional norms of male unionism and electrical workers who swam against the tide of the labor bureaucracy, most importantly, who would bring this paradox to light and most seriously test the discourse of revolutionary redemption in post-Tlatelolco Mexico.

The Diminishment of Women's Labor in the Revolutionary Narrative

Judging from official statistics, Mexican women in 1970 worked less than their counterparts in other Latin American countries. That year's federal census reported that only 16.4 percent of women in Mexico were "economically active" (meaning that they conducted activities in the formal labor market) and thus that a lower percentage of them worked than did women in Nicaragua (17.0 percent), Chile (18.2 percent), and Brazil (18.5 percent), and far lower than women in Venezuela (22.6 percent), Argentina (24.5 percent), and Panama (25.7 percent).[1] Official statistics, then, intimated that Mexican women were confined to the home in a greater proportion than their counterparts in other Latin American settings, a point of pride when considered within the context of an official narrative of state paternalism and the protection of women and children.

The contribution of female workers had been diminished in speech and in print even before the Revolution supposedly redeemed them from exploitation by removing them from the workforce. As the twentieth century progressed, however, women were "re-inserted" in the workforce in a way that challenged the veracity of this narrative. After 1940 Mexico witnessed rapid industrial growth in both the heavy and light sectors, with the expansion of the latter concentrated in cities near or bordering the United States. The explosion of assembly plants called maquiladoras in the 1960s and 1970s provided women wage-earning jobs in record numbers, bringing the rate of economically active women to 28 percent in 1980.[2] The flood of women into the formal workforce challenged the presumption that a Mexican "Miracle" was underway, as women who toiled in assembly or food-processing plants were as unlikely as their male coworkers to be able to use their wages to overcome rising costs of living and inflation.

Female workers challenged official narratives in other ways as well. Postrevolutionary regimes heaped praise, honor, and financial reward on the overwhelmingly male ranks of miners, electrical workers, petroleum workers, and railway workers in recognition of their role in inciting and fighting the Mexican Revolution. The contribution of female workers in fomenting revolution and carrying out its goals afterward, on the other hand, was largely ignored. This, explains Jocelyn Olcott, in spite of the fact that textile and other women workers organized constantly for political rights in the early stages of regime consolidation, in the process rebutting the image of Mexican women as conservative and antinational and challenging prevailing beliefs about the masculine foundations of citizenship.[3]

Conceptualizing the postrevolutionary state as essentially masculine, says Jean Franco, fit the goals of a regime intent upon projecting strength and unity. "The Revolution," she explains, "with its promise of social transformation encouraged a Messianic spirit that transformed mere human beings into supermen and constituted a discourse that associated virility with social transformation in a way that marginalized women at the very moment that they were supposedly liberated." The realization of the new society envisioned by the state, therefore, required that the architects of the regime construct a national identity "posited on male domination."[4] Female workers, and female unionists even less so, were not to form the basis of the Mexican proletariat. Their labors in constructing the postrevolutionary society were to be auxiliary to men's, if required at all.

The prevalence of economically active women also confounded the goals of organized labor, as it challenged a gendered ethic that had since the Revolution conflated trade unionism with masculinity. Unionists internalized this ethic into their organizations wholeheartedly. The workers' movement, which owed so much to the contributions of women's wage work before the Revolution, began afterward to assume an ever-increasing quality of manliness that linked unionism with a man's right to provide for his family. This was the dominant message espoused after 1918 as the CROM courted unskilled female workers while excluding them from skilled positions. Women were virtually absent from leadership positions inside Mexico's major postrevolutionary labor organizations, and as the power of the CROM and later the CTM rose, women's rate of participation in the formal labor force dropped precipitously, shrinking from about one-quarter of industrial workers in Mexico City in 1930 to about one-sixth in 1970.[5] State and labor officials celebrated this drop-off and attributed it to a twofold process that (a) increased the rights and salaries provided to female workers under the Constitution of 1917, affording them savings that they could bring to a family after they inevitably married, bore children, and left the workforce; and (b) paid men (i.e., their husbands) a "breadwinner" wage that permitted women (their wives) to leave the workforce and tend to the home.

By the late 1960s, however, even the most ardently revolutionary and paternalistic male unionist no longer believed the fiction that a man's salary enabled him to maintain his household on his own. Very likely his wife or his children contributed to the family's income, and their contributions were vital. The claim that a mere 16.4 percent of Mexican women were "economically active" in 1970, although it buttressed state and union rhetoric about the power of the Revolution to save women and children from exploitation, hence rung hollow to most working-class families, who saw their members—male and female alike—labor side by side in wage-earning settings.

Official statistics also belied reality by ignoring the legions of women who worked in the informal "homework" sector, carrying out piecework or contract labor at home, beyond the protections of labor laws. Moreover, many more women than were reported also worked in industrial settings, concentrated in low-paid and physically dangerous jobs. Nearly one-fifth of economically active women in 1970 worked in light industry, and women employed in this sector were grouped into five principal areas (in decreasing order of numerical importance): clothing, processed foods, machinery assembly, electronics assembly, and footwear. Of these groupings, the clothing industry represented the great locus for women workers, employing 29.1 percent of the entire female workforce employed in light industry. Furthermore, clothing represented the only area in the sector wherein female workers outnumbered males by a significant margin: of the 206,401 total workers, 130,129 (63 percent) were women.

Additionally, there was a plurality of young (aged twenty-four and under) and single women involved in economic activities. This trend separated Mexican female workers from their counterparts in developed nations like France, Denmark, and West Germany, where older and married women made up nearly two-thirds of the female workforce.[6] Numbers—even these artificially low ones—hence confirmed what government and union leaders liked to deny: women in 1970 were omnipresent in the Mexican workforce and were greatly exposed within it.

Redeeming the Women's Revolution in Print and in Speech

Female workers hence factored into the post-Tlatelolco state's calculus of redemption. Their continued allegiance was determined to be a necessity, and they were believed to be in need of a refresher course on the redemptive qualities of the nation's formative event. Mexican women of all kinds received a lesson on this subject via *Derechos de la mujer mexicana*, a book published by the government and freely distributed to the public in 1969. The volume's twenty credited contributors were all women, consisting of nine federal deputies, five lawyers, and various other professional women. The editorial committee, in contrast, consisted entirely of men, and five of the six members were federal deputies. The propagandistic history dismissed women's participation in the Mexican workforce prior to and during the Revolution as minimal and instructed its readers that the "rise of the female worker" was made possible only with the success of the armed movement in 1917. Women thereafter, so told the narrative, entered the salaried workforce in greater numbers, and their commendable performance helped them gain consideration as subjects worthy of rights equal to men's. This process, the authors claimed, helped affirm the validity of women's work and necessitated its protection in the 1931 Federal Labor Law.

It is true that the Revolution and its ensuing regimes attended to female-specific issues. Article 123 gave women and children benefits and protections that were extraordinary for their time. Sections 2, 3, and 5 provided safeguards for female workers under the age of sixteen and banned children under fourteen from work altogether. Article 123 also advanced maternalist priorities, but it took the creation of legal contracts (blanket regulations for entire industries) in 1925 to provide female workers maternity leave, nursing stations, and daycare centers in the cotton, sugar, and other agricultural industries. Finally, the creation of the national social security system in 1942 obliged employers to provide health care coverage to their workers, a development described in *Derechos de la mujer mexicana* as a "godsend" for the "working man and his family" and one of the most generous gifts of the Revolution to workers.[7]

Authors writing in *Derechos de la mujer mexicana* were aware of the widespread disenchantment that simmered within women who participated in the unprecedented student, peasant, and worker activism of the period. Their essays, we can conclude, represented efforts at political outreach in the wake of the realization that modern women were political beings in spite of historical proscriptions imposed upon them. Women of all classes and professional statuses marched in large numbers in Mexico City in the weeks following October 2, 1968, thus belying entrenched beliefs in the passivity of women in the face of state oppression. Marching in some cases with babies in their arms and assembling in front of the Monument to the Mother, capital city women joined the discontented fray by voicing their opposition to the regime. Messages on large placards did not mince words when they announced, "The Mothers Are in Mourning! The Soldiers 'Covered in Glory'"; "Mr. President: We Ask the Freedom of Our Children"; and "A Jail Cell for Each Child Killed."[8] Perhaps women militating in the National Union of Mexican Women best expressed the crowd's sentiments on that day with large a banner that read, "Dialogue Is the Vehicle of Intelligence—No More Bayonets."[9]

As he did with other important interest groups, Luis Echeverría pursued the nation's highest office in 1969–70 with an interest in appeasing disgruntled groups of women. Before the PRI's Female Assembly in Monterrey on April 12, 1970, Echeverría thanked the loyal *priísta* women for their participation in the nation's modern political life. He cited their efforts as vote counters in past elections and informed them that their contributions placed them at the heart of the party. He described such acts as constituting a great sacrifice, "an intense activity that helps raise a new Mexico together with the traditional activities of men."[10]

During one campaign stop Echeverría met Alicia Sánchez Jara, who had been one of the primary protagonists in winning the vote for women in 1953 and who was then a point person for the PRI in mobilizing the female vote in national elections. Shortly thereafter Sánchez Jara published a children's book, *La maquinita*, that described in short vignettes twenty-four facets of Mexican life, ranging from cultural features (folkloric dance, sweet breads, the National Anthropology Museum) to social relationships (friendship, childhood) to national symbols and political rituals (the national shield, Mother's Day, elections, etc.). The highly idyllic accounts in *La maquinita* had the same propagandistic tone of *Derechos de la mujer mexicana*, and nowhere more so than in the chapter entitled "The Olympiad 'Mexico 68.'" Describing the thoughts of a Mexican female athlete who bonded with her Japanese roommate in their Olympic village dormitory, the story celebrated the cultural diversity and camaraderie of the international sporting experience. Not surprisingly, it ignored the social strife and bloodshed that surrounded the infamous 1968 games, gushing patriotically about the "emotional goodbye"—the moment when all visiting athletes "who had come to identify with our customs" cried together and embraced one another in Olympic Stadium while doves of peace filled the sky to the tune of mariachi music.[11]

Sánchez Jara, whom I discuss in some detail in the epilogue, did not express high esteem for Echeverría when I spoke with her in 2013. The language of her book, however, suggests that as a younger woman she was neither critical of his regime nor opposed to the gendered and sexually divided world of politics he then presided over. Like his predecessors Echeverría conveyed a message to politically active women that their roles in society were important albeit different from those carried out by men. This concept of complementarity had by the 1970s become a near truism, ingrained in all aspects of Mexican life and consistently proclaimed in official messages and the workers' press. State and organized labor missives mutually conveyed this message, describing the home as a microcosm of society where the man (a unionized industrial worker, ideally) replaced the state as the practical and symbolic head of the family. Fidel Velázquez frequently reminded his underlings about women's important, albeit secondary, status in the fight for workers' rights. Addressing the CTM Congress in June 1964, Velázquez declared, "In women, men have their best allies in the present and future permanent struggle for enforcement of rights acquired and bestowed by law." He proceeded to call on all female *cetemistas* "to act decisively, side by side with the men of the CTM, to fortify the ranks of the organization and to achieve just economic and social reforms."[12]

Gender complementarity, interestingly, was a message challenged by the Mexican First Lady, María Esther Zuno, whose strong personality afforded her an independent voice in her husband's administration. Zuno's longtime advocacy of women's rights was given a platform when in 1975 Mexico City was tapped by the United Nations to host the International Women's Year conference. Mexico City's selection as host city infuriated some government opponents, who feared that Echeverría's "demagoguery" and "false" promotion of a progressive Mexico was gaining traction with international observers.[13] Zuno convened the conference, speaking to feminists from around the world as she described how women everywhere confronted a "depressing alternative": to become merely reproductive beings and renounce their social creativity or to sacrifice their maternity and abandon their family. Such a "crippling disjunction," warned the mother of eight, had to be overcome if women were to realize their full potential. Zuno granted that "oppressed men" still formed the majority of the world's population, but women, she noted, also felt the weight of oppression inside the family. Zuno applauded Mexico for passing laws meant to combat discrimination, but women's true integration, she contended, required more than mere legislation. "The translation of equality before the law into reality," she felt, required "the establishment of equal social conditions, equal opportunities in education and employment, and . . . a true transformation in the economic and social structure of a world configured by men." She did see a leading role for the government in this process, however, as it could "enact the measures to orient public opinion toward the elimination of prejudices that suggest female inferiority." The media, too, required reforming, and she called upon newspapers and other outlets to end the "anachronistic sentimentality that presents woman as the paradigm of abnegation, as the sum of all anguishes and suffering," sparking hearty applause from her listeners.[14]

Zuno's message was by no means radical; she asked women to pursue equality inside legally established frameworks and called upon the regime to pursue gender equality in a way that complemented its interventionist agenda. Still, she advanced an understanding of gender roles that demanded strict equality in the workplace, not the acceptance of fundamental difference as had been previously advocated.

Such demands for equality among the sexes probably had more appeal to working women than did their political and labor leaders' calls for submission and partnership. Nevertheless, the line of gender complementarity remained dominant in workers' discourses of the era. Unions were praised by unionists of both sexes for the ways they afforded female workers the same opportunity and respect accorded to men as militants. Issues of *Ceteme* in 1975 were filled with stories celebrating organized labor's "historical defense of female workers' rights" and women's integral contributions to the organized labor movement.[15] The climate of female vindication even influenced the organizing strategies of the CTM, which made efforts to recruit previously ignored women into its ranks from the overwhelmingly nonunionized clothing and food service industries.[16]

The spirit of International Women's Year seemed contagious. Later that year the recently established Center for Historical Studies of the Mexican Workers' Movement joined the festivities praising women by producing an anthology of articles that cited the difficulties faced by yesterday's *obrera* in her efforts to juggle the tasks of worker and mother/ wife, deal with a low salary, overcome exploitation and discrimination at the workplace, and gain entrance into workers' associations. Officially this gloomy historical portrait was painted to instill in the reader an appreciation for the challenges overcome by women in procuring their right to work.[17] A less overt but equally important goal of the volume, it appeared, was to juxtapose the wretched condition of female workers in Porfirian Mexico against the legally established and protected status of working women made possible by the Mexican Revolution and its succeeding regimes.

Hegemonic Female Unionism

The great majority of unionized women in post-Tlatelolco Mexico behaved according to the dictates of the large state-allied labor confederations and the government. Oftentimes, collective contracts placed formal limitations upon women's work that restricted them to certain tasks and limited their compensation. A 1976 contract that governed relations between the Compañia Constructora Canales and the National Union of Mexican Construction Workers, Plumbers, and Affiliates was typical, restricting the union's female members to secretarial or office work.[18] This restriction advanced two major trade unionist goals: it confirmed the presence of a gendered ideology about construction work (it was no place for women, essentially) and it assigned women lower-paying jobs than those held by men. The pursuit of these goals may be viewed as at least partially successful if we consider the low proportion of unionized women in industry and the paucity of women in leadership positions in Mexican unions.

Restricting women's access to top-tier jobs and leadership positions inside unions was nothing new; it had occurred at least since the formation of the CROM in 1918. Yet the motivations that drove men's efforts to subordinate unionized women in the 1970s had changed in the intervening period. Recent events revealed to contemporaneous unionists that organized labor had lost much of the clout it once possessed. The heightened levels of union agitation in the late 1950s and 1960s showed that the labor movement's decline in corporate status was widely recognized by workers. In this context the increasing presence of women—unionized or otherwise—in industry was a phenomenon that threatened the vision of the male worker as integral to the nation's production process. In the post-Tlatelolco world, therefore, organized labor committed itself to reviving the belief in the working (that is, the unionized) man's indispensability to the nation's industrial advancement.

One could construe just from reading *Ceteme* in the 1970s that female worker activism was rare. Major strikes led by women during the period were frequently ignored. Neither the female-led strike waged at Rivetex, a clothing factory in Cuernavaca, nor that at Luxor, a rug factory in Texcoco, was mentioned in *Ceteme*—two not surprising omissions, given that Rivetex was carried out without CTM authorization and Luxor workers belonged to the rival Revolutionary Workers' Confederation. *Ceteme* editors, however, made a rare reference to women's activism on February 15, 1975, when they could not help but mention the ongoing strike waged by 1,200 female cetemista employees at the Teleindustria Ericsson telephone plant outside of Mexico City. To their "female companions in struggle" CTM principals sent their warmest congratulations for "their combative spirit and the decided defense they make of their rights as union members and [members of] the working class."[19]

Frequently, though, when female labor activism was reported upon in the workers' press it was filtered through a gendered lens that stressed the female-specific aspects of the workers' actions. A report from June 8, 1974, described a massive demonstration launched by the women's branch of the FSTDF to inform women about the ways they helped combat the nation's economic ills. Inviting women of the capital to join in solidarity with the cause of the worker, the organization endeavored to fight the current food and basic goods shortages by integrating urban housewives into the CTM. Women's participation in the movement, the writer concluded, would in turn instill in new converts the realization that women, as keepers of the home and as "merchants, industrialists, and businesswomen," had the economy of the nation in their hands.[20]

Clearly, to advance the cause of unionized workers in Mexico strong women were sometimes deemed necessary. And in this process female-specific qualities like sexuality were deemed useful. We turn to a major union's coverage of the events of May 1, 1973, for an example of this. *SUTERM*, the monthly publication of the United Electric Workers' Union, covered the newly minted union's first participation in the traditional First of May parade extensively. It reported that over fifteen thousand union members employed at the companies of General Electric, Kelvinator, and Eveready took part in the festivities to salute President Echeverría and demonstrate the solidarity of the electrical workers' cause. Many participants also represented the Federal Electric Commission, the primary employer of SUTERM members, and among this contingent were hundreds of female employees who worked in office positions. Union women formed the "Float Brigade" and led the impressive procession that the union presented. A photograph accompanied the article and depicted female *sutermistas* marching in unison, waving the Mexican flag and wearing matching outfits of glittery miniskirts and sleeveless tops. The photograph's caption read, "The flashy spectacle of our beautiful little *compañeras* of the national offices, impeccably dressed, waving flags that together form the colors of our nation's standard, of our war stripes . . . gave a distinctive note to the parade."[21]

Complementarity among the sexes was on display again at a subsequent First of May parade organized in Mexico City and involving a large contingent of members of the FSTSE, a nationwide federation of public sector workers' unions. Photographs from the march show stern men and boys arm-in-arm, presenting a unified front of syndicalism that forms a symbolic and (if necessary) literal cordon against employer abuses. Replicas of the federation's shield hang from street poles, some with the silhouetted face of Echeverría printed on them. Large placards declare the federation's loyalty quite clearly: "With Echeverría." A single photograph in the file suggests the role of women in the parade. Dressed in matching uniforms with white long-sleeved tops, bell-bottom pants, and straw hats and carrying snare drums, twenty women form a drum corps meant to announce the federation's presence. Stationed behind them is a matching bugle corps formed by men, whose instruments, uniforms, and hats neatly complement those of their compañeras in the procession.[22]

Looking more like majorettes than militants, unionized women who marched in First of May parades expressed a unique image of strength that fit the model of gender complementarity practiced within the labor bureaucracy. They were unionists, yes, but their strength was derived not so much from their status as workers as from their abilities to support their male compañeros. Their sexy appearances and proud countenances were also useful assets. Placed at the front of the parade line, women symbolically led the cause of the industrial workers in Mexico. Although their efforts were described as auxiliary, and with more than a hint of condescension, the nature of their performance in the parade defied many of the commonly held assumptions about women in Mexico. In their sexuality they conveyed strength, not submission; in their confidence one saw power, not weakness. Sutermista women who led their union's processions were far from the "paradigm of abnegation, and the sum of all anguishes and suffering" that the First Lady criticized. And although they were not the militant women of Rivetex and Luxor who demanded sexual equality in the Mexican workplace, they nonetheless contrasted with the self-sacrificing and submissive qualities so often ascribed to women in Mexico.

Counterhegemonic Female Unionism

Contrary to reports in the workers' press, unionized women made waves in the post-Tlatelolco period. High-profile strikes carried out by workers in female-dominated industries showed that women were willing to militate and confront management to improve working conditions. Just as they had prior to the Revolution, workers in the female-dominated clothing industry in the 1970s struck often because of the poor wages and benefits they received. Nearly half (46.1 percent) of women involved in the industry earned less than 500 pesos biweekly and 84.2 percent earned less than 1,000 pesos. These percentages stood in contrast to only 27.8 percent of male workers who earned less than 500 pesos in a fortnight and 64.1 percent less than 1,000 pesos.[23] One notable textile strike was carried out by workers at the Inter-American Industrial Group (commonly called Rivetex) on the morning of August 11, 1972, in Morelos. There, 310 workers in the company's business suit department ceased labors and picketed outside the factory demanding changes to the existing collective contract. Some strikers, of whom four-fifths were women, drove about the city soliciting help over loudspeakers and lobbied the nearly seven hundred employees in other departments to shut down operations. Together their actions threatened to expand the strike to well over one thousand workers and to paralyze the company's profitable production of cashmere clothing.

La Voz, a Cuernavaca daily that covered the event, summarized the chronology of the event in the following way. In February of that year, the workers, organized into the Unified Union of Suit, Dress, and Tailoring Industry Workers, signed a two-year collective contract with the company. On August 3 the union, which was affiliated with the CTM but was acting independently, filed a strike petition with the state's conciliation and arbitration board that listed twenty-three ways the company had purportedly violated the contract and expressed the union's intention to strike if the contract was not modified. Rivetex executives answered, claiming the company had fulfilled its obligations to workers and would not accept amendments to the existing contract. Talks were held on August 8, 9, and 10 under the aegis of the Local Conciliation and Arbitration Board but the sides were unable to reach an agreement. The strike commenced as promised on August 11. Company and worker representatives met on August 19 in a meeting that again produced no resolution. According to *La Voz*, the company addressed the twenty-three complaints one by one, each to varying degrees of satisfaction, yet a settlement was not reached due to the "frankly intransigent attitude" demonstrated by union leaders acting under the counsel of Jorge Viveros Reyes, not an employee of the company but a law student at the Autonomous University of Morelos. In the absence of a settlement, the conciliation and arbitration board intervened on August 22 and declared the strike nonexistent, in essence ruling in favor of the company. Reacting to the ruling, *La Voz* editors reported that "the resolution of the board was founded in the strictest juridical reasoning." The ruling also had public safety merit, in that it "put a stop to, once and for all, the agitation and uncertainty that subversive elements" tried to create in Morelos.[24]

Labor authorities could declare a strike nonexistent for a number of reasons. Once so declared, a strike was deemed illegitimate and in violation of federal labor law. In the case of Rivetex union members were castigated specifically for their failure to announce the strike to company officials twenty-four hours before its scheduled outbreak. The Local

Conciliation and Arbitration Board ordered workers to return to work on August 23. Few did. Most chose instead to assemble in front of the Government Palace in Cuernavaca to voice their demands before Morelos governor Felipe Rivera Crespo, a perceived ally. *La Voz* editors mocked the demonstrating workers, "the majority women," who continued to try to force changes to their contract under the guidance of "little leaders" who deceived them. The next day the newspaper's pity for Rivetex workers grew. It told that a small group of self-proclaimed communists had taken advantage of the good faith of female workers and were destined to hurt them. Editors commanded the women to return to their jobs, to reflect on their situation, and to stop being "managed like puppets" and incited into lawlessness by "little leaders who think they are geniuses."[25]

After the company announced on August 29 that it had fired all 310 striking employees, newspaper editors derided them for their immaturity and for the ways they had failed their families. To them, it was painful to think that 70 men and 240 women had lost their jobs because of the vanity of green leaders who dragged them into an unjustified strike and continued the conflict even after having won a resolution of the major points of contention. Speaking of the now-unemployed workers, the editors asked, "What will those parents do that now confront the reality of the lack of a secure income? What will those young mothers do without the economic support of a job that was lost because they let themselves be taken in by a negative bunch of show-offs? What will they answer when they solicit another job and have to tell where they worked before?"[26] Such commentaries criticized men and women equally, indicting both sexes for letting poor judgment deprive them of the ability to provide for their families. Arguably, however, the fired female employees of Rivetex were scolded on a more personal level, for their activism was not deemed as valid as men's. Their actions, in contrast to those of their male counterparts, were understood to be driven more by ignorance than by politics. Such was the rationale to explain a gathering of fired Rivetex workers in Cuernavaca's main plaza on September 9. According to *La Voz* staff writer Fermin Gutiérrez, tourists and other passersby were disgusted by the scene that played out in the city's most public area. There onlookers saw a small group of "señoritas" being bamboozled into thinking that their actions would influence the government. At the head of this "shameful spectacle," which saw women waving banners, banging pots, and donning raggedy clothing, was Jorge Viveros, the "good-for-nothing" rabble-rouser who had tricked "his women" into believing false ideas.[27]

Almost incredibly, the tactics Viveros and the Rivetex women used in front of the Government Palace were effective. Governor Rivera Crespo intervened to broker a deal between the company and the union on September 15. In the negotiations the company, clearly considering the costs involved in training a new workforce, acceded to many of the union's major demands, including the reinstatement of all fired workers (including strike leaders), payment of 45 percent of wages lost during the strike, a restructuring of the seniority system, and reinscription of all fired workers in the social security system. On the whole, the Rivetex strike, although widely derided in the press, not supported by the CTM, and deemed illegitimate by the state's labor authority, ended in a draw. Workers were unsuccessful in restoring wages reduced by the company to offset maintenance and renovation costs but succeeded in renegotiating the most polemical parts of the collective contract. The strike also proved Morelos to be a hotspot of counterhegemonic unionism and encouraged other nonaffiliated and disgruntled CTM-affiliated unions there to conduct actions independent of the labor monolith. Perhaps most importantly, the conflict at Rivetex showed that a largely female and unionized workforce could successfully mobilize and pressure management to grant it better working conditions.

The female workers of Rivetex organized and defeated their adversaries in the workplace but could not overcome ingrained stereotypes about labor activism and women. Media perceptions of female strikers were often sexualized—and not just by those who opposed them. *Presente!*, a progressive weekly based in Cuernavaca, celebrated the contractual revisions won by strikers with a cartoon entitled "David versus Goliath Once Again, Rivetex versus Women Workers."[28] The image conveyed a message of workers' strength that was problematized, arguably, by the qualities ascribed to the protagonists. In the image, "Goliath," who represented the vanquished executives of Rivetex, lay on his back. He had a long, dark beard, wore a short-sleeved shirt, and hair covered his exposed limbs. "David" stood quite obviously for the female workers of the company. She trampled on the body of her fallen rival. She held a slingshot in the air but was dressed in a sleek dress so short that the upward motion exposed her slip. She wore lipstick and had a bob cut that made her resemble an upper-class flapper more than a working-class laborer. Certainly the David in this image resembled the women of Rivetex even less than the Philistine-like Goliath did the company's owners. And although she was sexy and certainly strong, she hardly resembled the typical female factory worker. What she did beautifully, on the other hand, was capture the contradictory understandings of unionized women and their place in the post-Tlatelolco organized workers' movement.

CHAPTER 8

"Yes This Fist Is Felt!"

The *Independentista* Challenge and Repression

The women of Rivetex belonged to a union affiliated with the CTM but defied their patron by striking without its consent. Posing an even greater threat to the state's hegemony over workers were the hundreds of unions that functioned entirely outside of the tutelage of the labor bureaucracy. Some of these unions opted to go it alone in their battles with employers, though the majority affiliated themselves with one of a handful of organizations that emerged in the period to build a self-governing movement free from state control. Member unions of the Authentic Workers' Front (FAT), for example, vociferously criticized the labor bureaucracy that kept the majority of organized workers under the thumb of the nation's political elite. Specifically, the *independentistas*, or those who advocated for an independent unionism in Mexico, criticized the power of the federal and local conciliation and arbitration boards to determine the legality of strikes and assailed the processes by which political and financial subsidies were awarded to favored organizations.[1] Members of the socialist FAT surely expected little government help in their efforts to organize, and they received little.

Other legal aspects further obstructed the cause of independent unionism in post-Tlatelolco Mexico. Article 365 of the NLFT outlined the process of registering a union with the Secretariat of Labor and Social Welfare, specifying that aspiring unions must present an act of constituent assembly listing the prospective union members' names and residences, as well as the names and residences of the employers to which they were to lend their services; an authorized copy of the union's statutes; and an authorized copy of the act by which union officers were elected. Subsequent language guaranteed that "no corresponding authority will be able to deny registration to unions in compliance with these requirements."[2] The process of satisfying these theoretically simple requirements, however, became a bureaucratic minefield upon which aspiring unions could see their quest to unionize blown apart by bureaucratic chicanery. Very often when an application was submitted to the General Office of Association Registry by an independent organization it fell into the hands of a tripartite board on which one or more members might be predisposed to oppose it on political grounds. These officials might reject the application outright or cite some sort of technical flaw meant to delay certification indefinitely and, ideally, exhaust the will of the applicants to unionize.[3] Thus, although the de jure requirements seemed clear, the de facto reality of registration was often quite different for independent unions. Their efforts to register were complicated by pretexts for denial that were, in the words of one labor lawyer, "as vast as one's imagination."[4]

Workers' hatred of the vertical and undemocratic nature of their organizations was another raison d'être of the independent unionist movement. Union democratization was the engine that drove railway workers to contest their union with massive strikes and other labor actions in the late 1950s. The cause of democratization helped spur the student movement of 1968 and became a cause that many politicians endorsed after Tlatelolco. The embrace of democratization, however, was a trend bucked by most leaders of the labor bureaucracy, who argued for the necessity of hierarchy and submission within union ranks. Virgilio Cárdenas García, a high-ranking official in the United Electric Workers'

Union, stressed this point in his union's newsletter in July 1973. Vertical organization, he contended, which was characterized by a centralized decision-making power that governed workers in the same industry, was preferable to a horizontal organization in which unions representing workers of the same profession maintained a degree of decision-making autonomy. The latter form of organization had "certain advantages derived from independence and liberty of syndical actions," yet it could not, he felt, match the type of cohesion and bargaining power that vertical organization offered. Cárdenas alluded to the presence of electioneering and corruption in many state-allied unions but did not believe it a flaw serious enough to make the horizontal alternative preferable for workers. The horizontal option was, in fact, a nonoption; it was an "organizational form that belonged to the past" and was "obsolete." Vertical organization, on the other hand, was a "concrete need of the workers' struggle" and the only "answer to business's gigantism; to the increase of ownership's power."[5]

Independents also lambasted the status quo for the ways it had nurtured *charrismo*, the system overseen by co-opted union bosses who served the interests of company and/or state officials. Although the details are best left to another discussion, it is important to note that corruption within the labor bureaucracy was a primary impetus for the emergence of the independent unionist movement in the era. Unionists spoke openly about their leaders' corrupt practices, often griping about how they embezzled money from union funds to augment their incomes, which were modest on paper. Many *charros* had access to pots that were not negligible; recall that SUTERM members paid 2 percent of their wages to the union, and as employees of the Federal Electric Commission they were paid very well. Demetrio Vallejo claimed that some CTM leaders of the period rewarded themselves to the tune of over USD 600,000 a year.[6] Upper-echelon unions also expanded their coffers with federal subsidies—sometimes in amounts that exceeded millions of pesos. Skimming off the top of union funds, however, was just one way union bosses earned extra money, critics alleged. Unsavory charros could also fatten their wallets by:

a. bribery—taking payment from an employer or another individual or entity in exchange for actions to defuse worker activism and/or prevent a strike;

b. kickbacks—taking payment for the transfer of a labor contract (typically from a national union leader to a local leader);

c. manipulation—colluding with ownership to agitate workers into unlawful labor activity and receiving payment following their legal dismissal; and

d. trafficking—using the workers or vehicles one has at one's disposal to conduct criminal activities, such as transporting drugs or weapons, as Fidel Velázquez was accused of doing by his most ardent opponents.[7]

On the topic of bribery, some speculated that the top brass of Mexican organized labor took large sums of money from the Regional Inter-American Organization of Workers, a pan-hemispheric labor confederation started in 1951 with U.S. government funding and committed to preventing the spread of communism inside Latin American workers' organizations. For its part the CTM was adamant about refuting any allegations that Velázquez had ties with the United States and especially denied any with the Central Intelligence Agency. A cartoon run in *Ceteme* on January 11, 1975, showed a serpent-like creature with a man's face, bearded and wearing dark shades and a CIA cap, leading a group of foreign soldiers to seize Mexican oil derricks. The caption read, "Mexico and All the Third World, You Must be More Alert Than Ever."

The critique of charrismo crescendoed in late 1971, fueled by the CTM's violent repression of yet another railway workers' movement in Oaxaca.[8] Feeling himself mercilessly attacked, Fidel Velázquez, the *charro de todos charros* (boss of all bosses), as he was viewed in the eyes of admirers and detractors alike, responded rather recklessly. He spoke in Tepeji del Río, Hidalgo, in January 1972, stating that the CTM would fight all potential enemies inside or outside of the constitution, if necessary. The CTM, he further warned, had an army of workers ready to combat "subversives" or anyone, who, in his view was not allied with the union.

Quickly Velázquez's comments incited a firestorm of criticism, and for obvious reasons; rumors still circulated at that time about the CTM's links to the Halcones—the mysterious paramilitary group that clashed with student protesters on June 10, 1971, and left scores dead. Among those repulsed by the statement was José Guadalupe Zuno, father of the Mexican First Lady. Zuno went on record to express his distaste for Velázquez and organized labor in general. As he saw it Velázquez was the "shame of Mexican unionism"; union elections were "embarrassing." To correct these "defects" Zuno advised workers to "overthrow" Velázquez, although he doubted that Mexico's "syndical body," lacking vigor, had the stomach to do so. It was hence incumbent upon the president, his son-in-law, to do away with don Fidel. Zuno assured that such a show of executive authority would be welcomed despite Echeverría's pledge not to intervene in union matters.[9]

Still reeling from the fallout of the Corpus Christi massacre and seriously weakened by public knowledge of the CTM's frequent reliance on *esquiroles* (paid unionists or other recipients of patronage brought in to counter workers' actions), Velázquez began 1972 confronting the most serious challenges he would face during his long stay at the pinnacle of Mexican unionism. *Cetemistas* came out strongly in defense of their embattled leader on January 20 when one hundred prominent officials assembled outside the tomb of Fernando Amilpa and swore an oath to keep him in power.[10] But even with this show of loyalty Velázquez's position was precarious. It was not only Zuno who implored the president to remove Velázquez but also employers who detested the extortive techniques they claimed he employed and independentistas who demanded an end to charrismo and the democratization of union practices.

Critics of Velázquez had reason to believe Echeverría was sympathetic to their pleas, at least initially. In 1970, while on the campaign trail as a candidate, he asked, "How can we speak of democracy in Mexico if in electing union leaders there is no democratic process?"[11] On August 13, 1970, while still just president-elect, he procured the release of Demetrio Vallejo and Valentín Campa from prison, in the process helping foment a new wave of independent unionism. After taking the presidential reins officially, he worked quickly to implement changes that one former critic praised for causing "disgust in the revolutionary family that has stayed in power without doing anything" for thirty-five years, citing specifically the case of Fidel Velázquez.[12] Later, in mid-1972, he invited a group of six hundred youths who had participated in the events of 1968 to the presidential residence to demonstrate the "clear and definitive" differences between his and his predecessors' governments.[13] These gestures and others formed part of Echeverría's "democratic opening," a presidential promise that some workers, students, peasants, and others interpreted literally and used as their basis to challenge the grasp on power that select groups had maintained since the Revolution.

But as was so often the case in Echeverría's Mexico, government action belied idealistic rhetoric and snuffed out any optimism that skeptics might have harbored toward the new president. The early years of the sexenio saw independent union activity intensely surveilled by government agents, the majority of whom tended to lump independentistas together with members of more radical groups that the state was then repressing with extraordinary vigor and brutality. DGIPS reports documenting various May 1972 demonstrations in Chihuahua City and Ciudad Juárez emphasized the solidarity between diverse groups of marchers, noting the presence of placards that conflated the priorities of local shantytown residents and university students with those of electrical workers and members of the Authentic Workers' Front.[14] The fairly blasé language expressed on placards and cited in the reports, however, seemed greatly overshadowed in importance by the inflammatory rhetoric agents heard from within the crowd and voiced in postmarch speeches. In Chihuahua City FAT leaders incited the Labor Day crowd to hurl shouts of "death" at Fidel Velázquez, whom they called a "Halcón" and a "servant of power."[15] On May 16 a demonstration monitored by the government and featuring many of the same players from the May 1 event saw students and teachers from a local teaching college march alongside electrical workers in a unified protest against the kind of charrismo that predominated in the state's electrical power industry—a topic discussed later in this chapter.[16]

Ramped-up surveillance of independentistas during the Echeverría regime and frequent repression of it assured that despite the presidential promises of democratic reform and the intense criticism that surrounded Velázquez no "crumbling" afflicted the union leader like that which had victimized CROM strongman Luis Morones in 1928. No rift, in fact, ever publicly surfaced between Echeverría and Velázquez beyond what was speculated about in elite political and leftist circles. Even during the peak of Velázquez's travails in 1971–72 the workers' press maintained that workers could not have asked for a better, more tireless, and more sincere advocate for their cause than the Mexican president. The message was consistently stressed in the workers' press that unconditional bonds tied the workers' movement with the regime, and during the Echeverría sexenio unionists read journals chock full of imagery showing their leaders side by side with the Mexican president as they, conceivably united in their vision for the Mexican working classes, finalized a legal contract or inaugurated a housing development.[17] In this regard the nation's most powerful labor organization, the CTM, was exemplary as it denied any rift in the revolutionary family and conveyed a singularity of mind and purpose between its leader, Velázquez, and Mexico's other great patriarch, Echeverría. A cetemista reading his or her union journal in the period routinely saw photos showing the two men embracing or "chatting amicably" while they collaborated to find a solution to the problems that union members faced.[18]

The *Electricista* Rebellion

Presidential promises of a democratic opening inspired unionists to buck the collaboration-through-submission ethic imposed upon them and tested the fabric of collaborationism in real ways, despite editorial claims to the contrary. *Electricistas* led the charge for union democratization and against charrismo in the post-Tlatelolco period—a fact not surprising given the tumultuous history of organized labor in the electrical power sector. Electricistas, in some ways, had fought to preserve their independence from state control since the establishment of the SME in 1914. And although the SME formed part of the labor establishment through its affiliation with the CROM and then the CTM, it never abandoned a horizontal structure that permitted locals to elect their own leaders and negotiate collective contracts without central union oversight. A democratic structure was a point of pride within the SME, but it pitted the union against the other major unions of electrical workers in a way that disadvantaged it in its contest to win government contracts.

The SME's organizational qualities gained additional credence in a post-Tlatelolco orbit in which the quest for democracy was paramount. Fortunately, SME members were not the only ones to militate for the cause in the period. Led by Rafael Galván Maldonado, the democratically organized Mexican Electrical Workers' Union (STERM) maintained a running critique of charrismo that pitted it against the CTM and its primary electrical affiliate, the National Electrical Industry Workers' Union (National). Conflict in the sector boiled over in 1970 when the Congress of Labor, pressured by the CTM, expelled the STERM in direct contravention of its statutes. The STERM's expulsion from the Congress of Labor opened the door for the Federal Electric Commission to make the equally dubious move of invalidating the contracts it held with the union and transferring them to National, a more reliable labor partner, in its opinion. The STERM responded by raising a labor suit with the Federal Conciliation and Arbitration Board. The board's subsequent ruling in favor of National and against the STERM demonstrated the dangers of defying the labor establishment but did not deter Galván and his supporters. Inspired by the injustices suffered by the STERM, workers in 1971 ushered in the revival of the independent unionist cause in Mexico, with Galván's electricistas and Demetrio Vallejo's railway workers carrying the banner for union reform.

The years 1971 and 1972 saw substantial electricista activity in cities across the country in support of independent unionism and unification of the electrical sector. In this fight Local 39 of the STERM, based in Torreón, Coahuila, was particularly noticeable on the government's intelligence radar. DGIPS agents vigorously monitored its internal discussions, public demonstrations, and contract negotiations with the CFE during that period. Several intelligence reports from February 1971 described the movements and language of union leader Galván, whom one newspaper concluded had acted only to "foment division" between the union and the company.[19] In a related episode that came to a head in April of the following year, Section 25 of the STERM out of Chihuahua City demonstrated demanding that titular contractual status, which had recently been revoked by the Local Conciliation and Arbitration Board, be returned to the local and calling for all "democratic" workers in the sector to unite. Hoisting a banner that read "Combative Worker Unity against Charrismo" and carrying a casket labeled with the names Fidel Velázquez, Francisco Pérez Ríos, and JLCA, some 250 electrical workers and 20 students marched along the city's central boulevards, ultimately accusing the CTM of strong-arming the JLCA to pry away the collective contract from the CFE.[20]

Such movements, inspired by similar antecedents and in pursuit of similar goals, coalesced in July 1972 with the formation of the National Union of Workers, which brought together many of the strands of the workers' insurgency—for example, the STERM, FAT, and the Unionized Railway Workers' Movement—into a single organization sizeable enough to challenge any potential rival.[21] Worker discontent and division in the electrical power sector thus posed a real threat to the redemptionist goals of the state. Echeverría felt obliged to intervene in spite of his pledges to steer clear of union matters. Pressuring all involved parties, he pushed through the creation of a Unity Pact on October 26, 1972, which merged the STERM, the National, and several other electrical worker unions into a single organization, the SUTERM.

With this the long-demanded unification of the sector was nearly achieved, but with two major qualifications: the SME, we recall, remained independent, and anger stewed inside those who had before operated outside the tutelage of official labor but were now forced into a "charro" union by presidential edict. Immediately Galván's name was cursed in leftist circles for his apparent capitulation to the labor establishment. By acceding to unification and accepting an executive position inside the new union he reinserted himself back into the labor bureaucracy that many of his allies blamed for the current problems of Mexican workers. Still, the capitulation of Galván and the forced creation of the SUTERM did not end division in the electrical sector as state and labor officials had hoped. Initially the new union represented only a tenuous alliance of former enemies that was held together at times by nothing more than a common enmity toward the SME. In short, the SUTERM's formation did not stamp out the desire for democracy and self-determination so prevalent among electrical workers. The SME forged ahead, and its independent streak still ran strong in the breasts of workers who had once formed part of the STERM. To combat this, current SUTERM leaders instructed electricistas on the benefits of unity—a condition that was, ostensibly, unobtainable without vertical union organization.[22]

Despite their best efforts SUTERM leaders were not successful in convincing everyone in their ranks that blind submission was in their best interests. A strike carried out by workers at General Electric's Cerro Gordo plant in Ecatepec (State of Mexico) pushed the envelope on the question of union democracy and self-determination within the SUTERM. There, an estimated three thousand workers belonging to SUTERM Local 49 ceased operations on June 13, 1974, and hung the *bandera rojinegra* from company walls. Men and women connected by chains marched around the perimeter and blocked access to the plant's nine entrances. Violence erupted as marchers were forced to defend themselves on June 14 from three hundred "*esquiroles* and Halcón-like types" brought in by the union as a strike-breaking force.[23] Blows were exchanged and a worker was gravely injured. The movement withstood this initial onslaught and a second round of violence on July 1. Solidarity committees that formed in nearby schools provided the now-fired workers with food, money, and other logistical support, though most strikers crossed the picket line and returned to work within a few weeks.[24] By September a group of 550 painstakingly maintained the strike while their prospects for success grew dimmer by the day. On September 26 an accord was reached with management that reinstated all fired employees except strike organizers and ended the action. Workers put down their banners of militancy and returned to work having made no substantial gains.[25]

What was at the heart of the Cerro Gordo conflict? Workers at Cerro Gordo were driven to strike largely by their refusal to accept contractual terms won by national SUTERM officials in their negotiations with company officials. The 19 percent salary increase and the two hundred new jobs written into the new contract were merely "crumbs," in the opinion of strike leaders. Discontented *sutermistas* formed an impromptu assembly and elected a representative committee to negotiate with the company directly. The committee, which did not have formal union recognition, published a manifesto days after launching the strike that listed its demands, which included (a) worker control; (b) nationalization of the company; (c) an authentic worker democracy; (d) an opening of company books; and (e) solidarity with other workers "in struggle" (i.e., currently on strike).[26] Union leadership in Mexico City received the document disdainfully. SUTERM officials, always ready to speculate on the communist affiliations of rogue strikers, alleged that "strange" elements had seized control of Local 49 and had deceived it into making "ridiculous" demands. An August 1 circular distributed to all SUTERM locals declared that the strike was devised by "enemies of the Mexican working class" who sought only to break the unity of electrical workers.[27]

In reality, official union hostility to the demands of the striking workers was hypocritical. Three of the stated demands repeated well-articulated goals of official labor almost verbatim. The SUTERM, like the strikers at Cerro Gordo, had called for the nationalization of all electrical power resources in Mexico and considered the "opening of company books" a requisite step in the process of writing profit-sharing clauses into the NLFT. Moreover, the union had voiced support for solidarity strikes, a right of workers guaranteed by the NLFT. Hence it was the right of Local 49 to elect its own leaders and to directly negotiate with employers that formed the crux of the matter. The SUTERM offered support for the right of self-determination in print but with great qualifications. Yes, one SUTERM editorialist conceded, workers had the right to strike in defense of salaries, benefits and union structure and to protest the hiring of nonunionized workers at a plant, as they had done at Cerro Gordo. But when it came to negotiating with management, the workers' interests were best pursued by their superiors. The "favorable" terms granted to GE workers at Cerro Gordo, which included a salary increase of 19 percent, an additional 8 percent housing subsidy, and a 700-peso maternity leave bonus, among other items, he felt, were proof of this, and only with unity and vertical organization could workers' goals be brought to fruition.[28]

The GE workers' strike at Cerro Gordo proved to be the grain of sand that tipped the fragile balance of peace inside the SUTERM. Galván openly supported the strike. He kept up extraofficial communications with the strikers and even offered them terms of settlement that differed from those won by the SUTERM central committee.[29] Moreover, he did not sign the August 1, 1974, circular condemning the movement. Galván's intransigence on the Cerro Gordo matter pitted him against Francisco Pérez Rios, secretary general of the union, whom he slandered publicly as a charro. Clearly this sort of division inside a union of such central importance to the Mexican labor establishment could not be tolerated.

A special congress was called by the SUTERM on March 21, 1975, to debate the Galván issue. Sutermistas heard first from Fidel Velázquez, who railed against Galván in an unusually impassioned way. It was high time, Velázquez felt, for electricistas to "grab a 'flit' bomb and finish off the insects that are gnawing away at the unity of this organization." Grab a broom, he commanded them, and "take out the garbage from this great house of workers." Velázquez promised CTM support for the expulsion of Galván and his partners, who, "for the nth time have betrayed the Mexican workers' movement and have encrusted themselves . . . in the ranks of this great union." News reports confirmed that listeners responded positively to Velázquez's call to arms. "¡Fuera! ¡Fuera!" (Get out! Get out!), they chanted in unison. A parade of speakers followed Velázquez and echoed his aggressive message. Their speeches, however, were superfluous. Galván's fate inside the SUTERM had already been sealed. A vote was cast and he was expelled from the union.[30]

Thus Galván was shunned for a second time by a labor bureaucracy that he had attempted to reform from the inside. Future actions on his part to force reform would eschew any effort to work within the superstructure of organized labor. The expulsion of Galván opened a vein that flowed through the SUTERM's ranks. Some workers who supported Galván defected from the union; others kept their union cards but voiced their support for his cause. Exact numbers are difficult to ascertain, but the pro-Galván faction has been estimated to represent about one-sixth of the union's thirty-five thousand members. Suffice it to say a large number of defectors and supporters met on April 5 in Guadalajara and celebrated the first public meeting of a group calling itself the Democratic Tendency (TD). There the group united under the slogan of "Yes this fist is seen!" in reference to the closed fist that was the shield of the SUTERM, and articulated an ambitious agenda that pursued (a) union independence; (b) a general reorganization of the workers' movement; (c) the unionization of all salaried workers; (d) across-the-board salary increases; (e) the creation of an adjustable salary scale; (f) an expanded system providing for workers' housing, rent freezes, and the municipal control of public transportation; and (g) complete worker control over an expanded parastate sector.[31] Other parts of the TD platform, including revolutionary education, agrarian collectivization, and the expropriation of "imperialist" businesses, iterated broader social goals that were in line with those of kindred groups like the FAT, the Unionized Railway Workers' Movement, and the Revolutionary Unionist Movement.

In the following months the TD grew to include approximately six thousand electrical workers, and it organized dozens of demonstrations and meetings across the country (each meticulously described in DGIPS reports) to criticize the CFE for interfering in union matters and to protest harassment that its members suffered at the hands of esquiroles or other hired thugs.[32] On November 15 the TD brought together an estimated 150,000 demonstrators, who marched in support of independent unionism, waved red and black flags, and chanted and carried placards with slogans such as "Jail the Charros!," "Death to Fidel!," and "Porfirio, Pinochet, Franco, and Fidel—symbols of fascism."[33] The march was orderly and moved along Mexico City's primary boulevards, down Paseo de la Reforma, Avenida Juárez, and Avenida Hidalgo. It culminated in the Plaza de la República at the base of the Monument to the Revolution, just meters from CTM headquarters, and there a train of speakers, including Galván; Cuauhtémoc Cárdenas, son of the legendary president; and Demetrio Vallejo, rose to a makeshift podium to call for a new unionism in Mexico free from charro control. Immediately the importance of the massive demonstration impressed observers. The Mexico City daily *Excélsior*, which was relatively sympathetic to the independent cause, termed it "the first demonstration of free and independent unionism since the tragic repression of 1959," and the leftist periodical *Bandera Roja* judged it to be, "without a doubt," the most important march seen in the Federal District since 1968.[34]

Not to be outdone, the PRI held a simultaneous demonstration in the Zócalo under the pretense of rallying support for José López Portillo, who had recently accepted the party's nomination to run for president in the coming year's election. Estimates put the size of the rally at between one hundred thousand and two hundred thousand participants. Composed largely of sectoral elements from the CTM, the National Peasants' Confederation, and the National Confederation of Popular Organizations, the crowd was augmented with (we can assume) a healthy dose of *acarreados* brought in to inflate the size of the supporting mass. López Portillo addressed the crowd and never mentioned the massive demonstration that had convened just a few kilometers away. He celebrated the status quo in Mexico and praised the party of Cárdenas and Echeverría, who, curiously, was not present at his childhood friend's political unveiling. He expressed his deep pride in taking the mantle of a party that had always fought for the "causes of the majorities organized around our Constitution that prevail in this country."[35] With this pledge, López Portillo took a subtle swipe at the independentistas, who pursued ends that he and other loyal *priístas* saw as marginal, counterhegemonic, and as such, anti-Mexican.

Amazingly, considering their proximity to one another, no scuffles broke out between participants of the November 15 events. Violence, however, would not always be averted when competing events were held by state-allied and independent labor groups. A series of demonstrations organized in 1976 by the TD in San Luis Potosí (January 24), Zacatecas (February 21), and in Mexico City (March 20) incited counter actions by a group calling itself the Nationalist Tendency, and with bloody outcomes. Most notably, nine demonstrators were injured by esquiroles aligned with the Nationalist Tendency during the San Luis Potosí event on January 24. November 15, 1975, thus was just the first episode in a cat-and-mouse story of mass politics that unfolded over the course of a year, with the Mexico City event of March 20 being the most substantial.

March 20, 1976, was an extraordinarily busy day in Mexico City, even by that city's frenetic standards. Denied a permit from the city for its planned February 28 event, the TD and its allies had additional time to plan for a rescheduled event that was to be the largest show of mass politics ever waged in support of union democratization in Mexico. Again, as had happened the past November, establishment forces held a counter event, this time under the pretense of honoring the 170th anniversary of the birth of Benito Juárez. The adversaries staked out their regular spots, the independentistas holding ground in the Plaza de la República and the pro-state alliance occupying the Zócalo. Once again the turnouts were massive, with each side assembling crowds in excess of one hundred thousand. Police helicopters flew overhead. Already bustling city thoroughfares were further crowded with the presence of more than twenty-three thousand police officers, who did not carry rifles but were well armed with batons and antiriot gear, including tear-gas launchers and urban tanks.[36] The militarized state of the city created an atmosphere reminiscent of 1968.

Heated rhetoric was slung from both podiums, though the most pointed jabs came from TD sympathizers, who had the most to gain from explicit attacks on the regime. Their adversaries at the top of the labor establishment, in contrast, continued a line of minimizing the independent unionist cause. In speeches, the cause of Gálvan and Vallejo was not mentioned explicitly, although PRI president Porfirio Muñoz Ledo alluded to its when he repeated the popular maxim that "a revolution that does not have enemies ceases to be one." Muñoz Ledo's inference that the independentista movement was an enemy was, in fact, an upgrade from the line more commonly expressed by officials, who mocked it as mere minor nuisance on the political and labor scenes.[37]

Fortunately, as had happened on November 15 of the prior year, violence was averted on the capital's streets that March day; the massive police presence in the city saw to that. Subsequent brushups between the combatants, however, did not proceed as peacefully. On June 12, believing all negotiating avenues with the CFE and its union to be blocked, the TD called upon its members to strike, an action to begin on June 30. A strike petition was filed with the JFCA wherein the goals of the action were listed. They included (a) the reinstallation of all workers dismissed for political reasons; (b) a CFE guarantee of future noninterference in internal union matters; (c) the implementation of direct elections inside the SUTERM, with universal voting and secret balloting; and (d) the immediate nationalization of all the nation's electrical power–generating resources.[38] The JFCA acted quickly and decisively. It ruled on June 14 that the strike petition filed against the CFE for alleged violations to the collective contract was unlawful, being that the "coalition" lacked titular status to contest terms of a collective contract.[39] TD leaders took the news in stride; they had expected nothing less than complete government opposition to their cause. They proceeded with planning for extralegal action.

The TD's plans rankled SUTERM leaders but did not dissuade them. Union boss Leonardo Rodríguez Alcaine (who took over following the death of Pérez Rios) assessed the prospects of the TD's strike petition accurately when he predicted that the "so-called Democratic Tendency," lacking legal standing, had little chance of success.[40] The threatened action, he believed, was merely the machinations of a demagogue who was driven to break electrical worker unity and who acted without regard for the nation's stability and prosperity.[41]

Straw polls were administered and workers were forced to denounce the TD and swear loyalty oaths in the run-up to the strike date. According to SUTERM officials the count demonstrated that the TD was greatly outnumbered by loyalists inside the union, by a rate of five to one.[42] TD spokesman Héctor Barba, in contrast, later told the press that over seven thousand sutermistas were suspended for their refusal to take the loyalty oath, a number that the SUTERM claimed was greatly exaggerated.[43] Several large rallies jointly organized by the SUTERM and the CTM were held in hopes of diffusing TD support for the action planned for July

16.[44] SUTERM-CTM opposition had little effect. The first strikes began as scheduled at 6:00 a.m. on July 16, and others appeared intermittently throughout the day.

Overall the early results of the strike were dismal. Electrical service was suspended in some locations when workers chose the no-show or walkout routes to support the TD position, but others who attempted to take control of CFE installations largely failed; in one instance (in Monterrey) they were confronted by forces of upwards of one thousand men called in to oppose them.[45] In Querétaro army soldiers assisted by two hundred CFE employees brought in from the nearby city of Tula wore the yellow bracelet of SUTERM unity and kept guard at a company to prevent the entry of TD members. Operations proceeded normally, and customers paid their monthly bills without incident. In Puebla TD supporters met in front of University Hospital at 5:30 p.m. to discuss the failed strike efforts elsewhere and to plot strategy for their own action, scheduled to begin at six. Their discussions were interrupted by CTM members of various professions who, given the day off, had license to heckle TD sympathizers and prevent their entry onto CFE grounds. Similar opposition to the TD cause was witnessed in Guadalajara that afternoon when potential strikers were denied access to company facilities by large crowds composed mainly of esquiroles.[46] These initial setbacks were not reversed in the coming days. Hundreds who abstained from work in the first days were fired. The TD's core saw its plan to shut down CFE headquarters in Mexico City derailed by an army battalion that was posted outside the building's gates. Soldiers prevented protestors from hoisting the bandera rojinegra on company grounds.

The setbacks suffered by the TD were chronicled and the roots of its failure assessed in the pages of the workers' press. Articles run in the July 24 edition of *Ceteme* celebrated the fact that the CFE had resumed normal administration of electrical service throughout the nation. Reports of the strike's dwindling ranks and promises of amnesty were made to all remaining TD supporters who "laid down their arms" and returned to the union and their jobs. SUTERM officials emphasized that the union had not entertained any talks of a truce with leaders of the TD, whom they viewed as mere "pirates of unionism," and that the action was carried out without legal authorization and for political ends.[47] The SUTERM's position had full governmental support. Secretary of Labor Carlos Gálvez Betancourt expressed his opposition to the TD's actions. The June 14 ruling of the JFCA, he told the press, was correct, for the government respected the workers' right to strike but only when it was exercised lawfully, never by means of "crazy work stoppages." Gálvez thus, although sympathetic to the cause of the TD, whose leaders he had spoken to on several occasions, was required by the rules of the labor establishment to reject it.[48]

The tense situation between supporters of the TD and the SUTERM turned violent on the morning of July 26, when the two sides clashed outside CFE offices in Puebla. Reports vary, but shots exchanged between the two sides resulted in at least thirteen injuries and the death of Juan Guevara Botello, a local police officer.[49] *Ceteme* editors saw the gunfight as evidence of the TD's "moral bankruptcy" and as a harbinger of its imminent fall. The so-called Democratic Tendency, they wrote, had now earned the moniker "Terrorist Tendency" by resorting to violence in its quest to break the unity of the workers' movement in Mexico.[50] In its defense the TD claimed that it was the CTM that had sent *pistoleros* (gunfighters) to heighten tension and that was responsible for the bloodshed.[51] Blame in this instance ultimately could not be established. In any event the Puebla incident helped damn the TD cause, as it gave fuel to the arguments of its opponents, who now assailed the TD for waging not only an unlawful strike but a murderous one as well.

Lacking legal validity and facing growing opposition from the public, the TD strike faced a quick end. TD unity wilted under the combined forces of public opposition and the financial strain of unemployment, which compelled workers to accept bribes offered them by employers and union leaders. On the morning of July 31, barely two weeks after the Puebla incident, Mexican attorney general Pedro Ojeda Paullada visited TD headquarters in Mexico City's Roma neighborhood to broker peace terms that would enable union supporters to resume their labors at the CFE. Ojeda emerged from the meeting visibly satisfied. He told reporters that the union's offer to let striking workers resume their jobs unmolested was still on the table, provided that the followers of Galván denounced the TD and recognized the executive committee of the SUTERM. Another condition of the deal was that Galván and seven other TD leaders who had been expelled from the union would not be permitted to return to it. When interviewed shortly thereafter, Galván announced that ten thousand electrical workers from forty-eight sections of the SUTERM would return to work the next day via an agreement that, although not one that produced "vanquished or victors," was an important step toward the regularization of union activities in the electrical power industry.[52]

Galván's first impression of the deal that ended the electricistas' strike of July 1976 was overly optimistic. Likely Galván sugar-coated the terms of a deal that he hardly viewed as satisfactory. To those on the other side the deal was a resounding victory and represented the defeat of the TD challenge. Opinion makers in the workers' press gloated over their success in word and image. A cartoon printed in *Ceteme* on August 14, 1976, depicted Fidel Velázquez bedecked in his typical dark suit, white shirt, dark tie, and dark glasses standing next to a TD member (presumably Galván) wearing a t-shirt labeled "Democratic Tendency." The TD supporter stood with his left fist raised, though he appeared dazed after having just received a vicious right cross from the labor leader. "Yes this fist is seen . . . !" he must have whimpered. "Yes this fist is felt!" Velázquez answered, triumphantly.[53] Surely the July 31 agreement was a SUTERM win, although relations between the CFE, the SUTERM, and the pro-TD minority in the union remained hostile. Union-organized pistoleros confronted workers on October 25 and prevented their entrance into a CFE building in Torreón for refusing to denounce the TD. Many who remained loyal to the TD cause found themselves fired for "unrelated" reasons.

Organizational changes made inside the SUTERM in subsequent months further hindered the cause of independent unionism inside the electrical power sector. Bylaw changes enacted at the union's Fourth Congress held later that year annulled the legality of sectional autonomy inside the SUTERM and reduced the decision-making power of locals by placing even membership questions in the hands of the national committee. Additionally, the congress reelected Leonardo Rodríguez Alcaine to another term at the head of the union and voted to alter the union shield by replacing the closed fist, which by then had become closely associated with the TD insurgency, with the toothed wheel of the CTM—a more appropriate symbol of the union's strength.[54]

The causes of the TD's failure to force reform inside the SUTERM were many, although some factors bear specific mention. The strike failed partly because it was not successful in inspiring the kind of widespread solidarity witnessed in the past and so vital to the success of other student and worker movements. The great majority of sutermistas remained loyal to the union, and few halted their labors in solidarity with their fellow electrical workers. Only the Academic Personnel Union of UNAM, who called for a work stoppage on July 29, and the Federation of University Unions, who stopped work for two hours the following day, rose in support of the cause of the TD. The government's position toward the strike was another factor that doomed it. As a "nonexistent" and hence unlawful worker action, the TD strike caused the government to dispatch the army to disband crowds of strikers and protect government-owned installations. Military intervention at CFE headquarters in Mexico City and elsewhere marked the beginning of the end of the Echeverría state's supposed noninterference in union matters and publicly aligned the regime with the SUTERM and CTM leadership. Finally, the involvement of the Mexican attorney general (which eclipsed that of the labor minister) indicated that the federal government was actively against the strike and was intervening in a series of events that, although of a purely labor nature, were being treated as political matters. All of these factors helped subvert the campaign waged by Galván and the TD in the mid-1970s.

The defeat of the TD in 1976 damaged the independentista cause in Mexico but did not bring its immediate end. Other groups of workers made limited gains in their efforts to contest the labor bureaucracy. Members of some of the nation's most important unions mimicked their *compañeros* in the railroad sector by pressuring entrenched leaders to step down and instill democracy in union practices. Steelworkers of the 1970s successfully democratized their locals, though they failed to remove their union's powerful leader, Napoleón Gómez Sada.[55] Overall, the challenge that steelworkers posed to union bosses and employers paid off handsomely, as their real wages reached their twentieth-century peak in 1976.[56] Automotive industry workers also led the charge for union reform by seceding from the CTM on several occasions and rewriting internal statutes in ways that increased members' participation in union affairs and enhanced their bargaining efficacy with management.[57] All of this counterhegemonic activity, in conjunction with actions led by the Railway Workers' Union Movement, the Authentic Workers' Front, and the Democratic Tendency contributed to a climate that saw strike activity in 1970s Mexico reach its highest level in forty years.

Battles won by workers in independent unions caused some to conclude that the lines of the playing field upon which tripartite relations had been contested in Mexico since the Revolution had been redrawn. In late 1975, during the peak of the workers' insurgency, a writer for the Cuernavaca-based weekly *Presente!* judged that the weight of counterhegemonic worker activity was causing the nation's very political corpus to crumble. A cartoon run on December 17 depicted a huge Frankenstein-looking statue in need of repair. The decrepit monster's body parts were labeled, with its head representing the CTM, his torso the SUTERM, his right thigh the Popular Socialist Party, and his left thigh the National Peasants' Confederation. One of the workers, Luis Echeverría, clutched tools while he hung from the statue's head, trying to remedy its ills with a simple turn of the screwdriver. "If this botched statue fails us," the president in coveralls warned, "there won't be anyone later to disarm the force that it will acquire." Echeverría's efforts seemed foolhardy, though, to an observer who watched from afar and made the analogy that "like the scarecrows that later scare their own creators, this Frankenstein is ever more dangerous, [and] when it begins to move with the rope that they've given it, we'll see who'll [be able to] stop it."[58]

The image featured in *Presente!* referenced two commonly held notions: first, that despite having given the independent unionist movement the "rope" it needed to exist via his democratic opening, Echeverría was unwilling to permit real reform that could alter the labor status quo; and second, that the independentista challenge had rocked the labor establishment to the point of collapse. On the one hand, critics of the regime were justified in citing the hypocrisy of state rhetoric on democratization and the hollowness of government pledges for reform. On the other hand, they greatly overestimated the damage that their rebellion had done to the prevailing political system. The combined pressure of independent challenges waged across many industrial sectors had shaken the foundations of the labor establishment, but the collaborationist framework remained intact. After nearly five years of battle, traditional union hierarchies like that of the SUTERM were forced to concede their adversaries very little: neither union democracy, nor the removal of charros, nor even the reinstatement of workers who had led opposition movements. Overall the worker insurgency that emerged during the Echeverría presidency had only a minimal effect on altering the modus operandi of state-organized labor relations.

Scholars have shown that the democratic opening as promised by Echeverría encouraged the emergence of reformist groups inside the tightly regulated organized labor movement, yet this study demonstrates that state goals were multifaceted and not mutually exclusive.[59] While policy makers were willing to permit rank-and-file dissent among male and female workers, they also coveted the opportunity to revive a relationship dynamic with top union brass reminiscent of an earlier time. Velázquez and other major union leaders of the era may have resented officials' anticorruption and prodemocracy diatribes, but they were not ready to wage public war against a one-party system that guaranteed their positions and, ultimately, buttered their bread. Critics of the regime may have assessed things differently, but from the general public's perspective the historical state-organized labor alliance appeared as strong as ever as the Echeverría presidency drew to a close. And thankfully so from the government's perspective, as profound challenges and new battles lay ahead.

CHAPTER 9

"The Mexican [Redeemer] Never Asks for Forgiveness!"

Sectoral Friction in the Late Echeverría Presidency

Mexico in 1975 was a nation that had undergone sharp and rapid economic decline. Gross domestic product showed almost no growth that year, real wages had fallen below 1972 levels, private investment had shrunk for the first time in five years, the balance of payments deficit had quadrupled since 1971 and the public sector deficit was seven times greater, and underemployment affected 45 percent of the economically active population.[1] This fiscal downturn drastically contrasted with the economic mood of the country in the late 1960s, when GDP growth still hummed along at an average annual rate of 6 percent. The "five bad years" since 1970 combined with the trend toward "mexicanization" and the acrimony that cloaked most of the business sector's dealings with the Echeverría administration deterred capitalists from investing in the country and provoked a capital flight that economists calculated in the area of USD 10 billion.[2]

A position taken by the president on the question of Israel and its occupation of Palestine actually exacerbated the situation and caused additional capital to flee. Toward the end of 1975, Echeverría, who had faced accusations of anti-Semitism before, took charge of a United Nations effort to pass a resolution that condemned Zionism and declared it "a form of racial discrimination." Infuriated Jewish groups and the Israeli government responded by organizing a massive boycott that instructed Jews not to visit the country and not to conduct commerce there. Immediate economic pressure forced the Mexican government to amend its stance, and the resolution was not advanced. Emilio Rabasa, secretary of foreign relations, was tasked with giving the mea culpa and affirming that Mexico's government did not believe that Zionism was racism. Echeverría, for his part, was unapologetic and refused to retract his previous statement. "The Mexican never asks for forgiveness!" declared the president, thus closing the incident in famous fashion.[3]

Echeverría's pithy maxim in the Zionism incident encapsulated the stubbornness that characterized his final two years in office, when he adopted a stance suggesting that the "Redeemer" (i.e., Echeverría) need not ask for forgiveness for the failed policies of present or past regimes. During this period the so-called preacher routinely eschewed the example of forgiveness and compassion offered by Christ in favor of heightened repression of peasant, student, and other militant groups and increased friction with business adversaries who opposed his policies. Political troubles further confounded Echeverría's goals as discord surfaced within the revolutionary family over which he presided.

Economic Malaise, Political Discord, and Continued State-Business Friction

Beginning in 1975 and continuing until his last days in office Echeverría's relations with the business community were more polemical than at any other time during his presidency. Feeling their priorities undervalued by the federal government, a group of leading employers coalesced into a national coalition called the Business Coordinating Council (CCE) in early 1975 to better advocate for their interests. The CCE henceforth would be the private sector's foremost interest group and would exert real political and economic pressure on all subsequent regimes in Mexico.

A petition sent to Echeverría in May 1975 articulated the CCE's top priority: the privatization of parts of Mexico's parastate sector.[4] Echeverría rejected this demand while attending the Exposition of Mexican Industrialists in Monterrey on May 8. "The economic policy of the regime of the Revolution will not vary," he explained, as it had "its origin in the history and in the interests of [the] nation's majorities."[5] Secretary of Internal Affairs Mario Moya Palencia spoke the following day and affirmed the president's position while casting a new round of aspersions on the patriotism of the employer class. As he saw it, the CCE's petition reflected a "retrograde attitude against the advances of the mixed national economy" on the part of *patrones*. Their words, he judged, made it seem that Articles 27 and 123 of the Constitution, "those that assured the participation of the great masses of peasants and workers, not only in the productive aspect but in the distributive aspect of the economy as well," did not exist for them.[6]

Employers shot back quickly in their defense. Monterrey *patrones* denied that the CCE was a force that resisted change.[7] Andrés Marcelo Sada Zambrano, the director general of Grupo CYDSA, Latin America's largest producer of PVC piping, addressed the XIII Pan-American Congress of Sales and Marketing Executives in Mexico City on May 13 and implored the some three hundred people in attendance to defend the business sector—"the most harassed of the institutions in contemporary society"—by taking to the airwaves, to the classrooms, and to the streets in its defense.[8] Their continued silence, he warned, could have dire consequences. Their activism, on the other hand, could stop Mexico's advance toward "totalitarian collectivism."[9]

Sada Zambrano's fears were widely shared but were largely overblown; economic indicators proved decisively that the nation was not creeping toward socialism. But devout capitalists' anxieties seemed reasonable in the contemporaneous climate of *tercermundismo*. Shortly following his visit to Monterrey Echeverría, along with the First Lady, embarked on what would be the most extensive foreign mission of his presidency, visiting fourteen countries on three continents during the course of a month and a half.[10] Dining, dancing, and sermonizing with premiers, sovereigns, and presidents of the world's most prominent developing nations (notably, China and India), the preacher and the *compañera* used the tour to further their ongoing quest to position Mexico at the vanguard of a rhetorical struggle between "imperialism" and the "Third World." Seen in another light, a U.S. intelligence officer cabled state department officials on August 1 that with the tour Echeverría was "clearly campaigning for [the] post of Secretary General of the United Nations to succeed Secretary General [Kurt] Waldheim in 1976," a candidacy, the agent added, that was "all but an accepted fact in Mexico."[11] The Echeverrías concluded their jaunt around the world on August 17, 1975, with a visit to Cuba and its president, Fidel Castro, the undisputed first chief of Latin American redeemers. In Havana the Mexican president received a parade in his honor that mobilized Cuba's machinery of mass politics and featured music, speeches, and placards celebrating Latin American solidarity.[12] Most importantly, the Cuba visit produced a joint communiqué in which the presidents condemned apartheid in South Africa, supported Panamanian sovereignty over the Panama Canal, and criticized Augusto Pinochet's dictatorial regime in Chile.[13]

Ultimately the Echeverrías' self-serving and expensive foreign junket produced nominal returns, as it solidified support only from a small minority of labor groups and typically those with established leftist tendencies. In the mid-1970s, as this book has emphasized, the labor bureaucracy harbored little sentimental or practical regard for socialism, and only unionists on the extreme of the political spectrum (some teachers and members of the SME, among others) praised Echeverría's purported tercermundismo. Nor was the general public particularly receptive to the socialist alternative in Mexico, as was revealed by an opinion poll that questioned some four thousand people in Guadalajara in May 1975. Asked if Mexicans would have a better opportunity to achieve their objectives under a socialist form of government, 23 percent of Tapatíos either strongly agreed or agreed with the contention—a percentage that signified some openness to socialism but less, in fact, than had existed at earlier points during Echeverría's presidency.[14]

On the right, the voyage (and the Castro visit in particular) sharpened the tongues of opponents who were already prone to criticize the first couple for their demagoguery, socialist dalliances, and practice of a false and destructive populism. The rhetorical attacks from business partisans continued throughout the summer of 1975 but subsided somewhat after it was announced on October 5 that José López Portillo, who was then serving as secretary of the treasury, had received the PRI's nomination for president in the next year's election. Some in the private sector were leery of the close personal bond between the sitting president and López Portillo, although others praised the pick because of López Portillo's frequent assertions that he was "neither of the right nor the left."[15] Ideological centrism thus distinguished him from the incumbent as well as from Jesús Reyes Heroles, the current president of the PRI and someone whom many believed was the likely pick for the nomination.

Employers' worries about a potential Reyes Heroles candidacy were largely unwarranted. His selection was never a realistic prospect due to the serious friction in his relationship with Echeverría. Since taking the reins of the PRI in 1972 Reyes Heroles had frequently criticized the president for a kind of demagoguery he believed was hindering the political process and preventing cross-class compromise. He famously stated, confusing nobody about the subject of his critique, that

> We must not uselessly frighten by verbal insults, by linguistic radicalisms, by ideological pyrotechnics. . . . Do not plant false hopes nor produce unnecessary fears. The verbal indiscretion is very expensive. It charges what is said and not what is done, when, revolutionarily, what is done is more important than what is said. . . . Yes, the old [kind of] politics was bad, but it knew how to coordinate antithetical interests, it could overcome seemingly insurmountable conditions, it safeguarded several times the national survival, it permitted us advance and thanks to it today a new kind of politics may be had.[16]

Moreover, to restore the credibility of the party that he led Reyes Heroles was intent upon disassociating the PRI from the state in the structure of government and in the minds of the Mexican public. He was highly critical of the kind of undemocratic procedures inside the party that placed the selection of the presidential nominee, for instance, under the sole purview of the sitting president.[17] Echeverría, writes José Augustín, knew neither what to say nor what do against this "frank transgression of the unwritten rules of the system, those which stipulated that the president was untouchable."[18]

The rift between Echeverría and Reyes Heroles became fodder for gossip and media speculation early in 1975 when rumors began to circulate that Echeverría was considering amending the Constitution in order to seek another term. Reyes Heroles broached the topic in a February 5 speech that commemorated the signing of the Constitution of 1917—which limits politicians to a single term. Then Reyes Heroles quipped, shrewdly, "Those dopes that want reelection hurt the Revolution, they deny our institutions and offend the revolutionary Luis Echeverría."[19] Very likely this seemingly incredulous remark that reminded the public about the inviolability of the no reelection principle helped dissuade any notions that Echeverría may have had about another term. Shamed into respecting the institutions of the Revolution, Echeverría then resigned himself to molding his successor, López Portillo (who had been his close friend since boyhood and stood as witness at his wedding), in order to install his own Maximato à la the one Calles presided over after 1928. Reyes Heroles, it thus appeared, had once again checked the excesses of the Mexican president. Not surprisingly, Reyes Heroles tendered his resignation as PRI president later that year, although by no means was his political career ended. He continued his odyssey through the upper echelons of the government, being named director general of the Mexican Social Security Institute in September.

Although neither party had publicly slandered the other, the rivalry between the president and the head of the official party demonstrated even more definitively than the rumored Echeverría-Velázquez feud that serious cracks had emerged in the political substratum. Few, moreover, believed that their assigned leader (a famously arrogant and pliable politician) was capable of mending them. The López Portillo nomination produced the customary affirmative responses from organized labor's leadership, but not because of any particular fondness for the candidate.

Congress of Labor and CTM support for López Portillo came because he, as former director of the Federal Electric Commission, had spoken critically of Rafael Galván and maintained warm relations with SUTERM leadership. This posture contrasted him with Echeverría, who had upset the status quo by giving lip service to the democratic pretensions of non-state-allied unions.

For all intents and purposes, López Portillo became the nation's president-in-waiting as early as October 1975, when he received the nomination, because division in the National Action Party prevented it from fielding a presidential candidate in the 1976 contest. López Portillo campaigned energetically in 1976, nevertheless, sprinkling into his so-called Campaign Against the Wind events that celebrated his athletic, musical, and intellectual proclivities. Mimicking his predecessor, he stressed the importance of continuity and outlined the PRI's plan "to continue the Revolution by way of the institutions."[20] And again like Echeverría, he adopted a self-critical stance, advocating a reformist message that cited extant problems in the system. "We are all the solution" he repeated ad nauseam as he encouraged the electorate to get involved in the preservation of the one-party system.

The lack of any political opposition to López Portillo placed Echeverría in a more prolonged state of diminishment than was normal for outgoing presidents, although he refused to wear the lame-duck suit fitted for him. The perpetual war of words waged between Echeverría and the business community escalated sharply after the election of López Portillo on July 4, 1976. With the president-elect and Mexico's political destiny now formally in place, many in the private sector sharpened their attacks on Echeverría, a now significantly weakened foe. His economic policies were slandered as "vague and contradictory"; he himself was accused of corruption in relation to personal investments he had in the development of Cancún, a previously unpopulated strip of Caribbean beach in the southeastern state of Quintana Roo. Rumors of a coup d'état scheduled for November 20—the Day of the Revolution—could even be heard circulating among some who feared that López Portillo, in spite of his perceived moderation, would serve as a hand puppet for

Echeverría's continued rule.[21] Fear of a prolonged Echeverria sexenio was exacerbated when the outgoing president embarked on a farewell tour that saw him trace familiar PRI circuits while emphasizing that he was not saying "goodbye" but merely "see you later."

The specter of a continued "echeverrismo" under the guise of a new president spooked domestic and foreign bankers, entrepreneurs, and merchants, who, according to Héctor Aguilar Camín and Lorenzo Meyer, were irate over an "Echeverría populism that was more verbal than real." Many of them decided to withdraw their capital from Mexico, as described above. This "financial coup d'état" squeezed the national treasury and forced the government to remove the fixed exchange rate with the U.S. dollar (which had stood at 12.5 pesos to the dollar since 1954) and let its value be determined on the world market.[22] This move, reasoned secretary of the treasury Ramon Beteta, was necessary to counter the nation's mounting trade deficit (which then stood at USD 3.7 billion), high foreign debt (USD 13 billion), and stubborn inflation that had averaged 15 percent annually in recent years.[23]

Echeverría announced the government's plan to float the peso in his sixth and final annual address, on September 1, 1976—a self-congratulatory speech that lasted six hours and was riddled with references to the Mexican Revolution. The announcement stunned those who heard it and read about it in mainstream newspapers the following day but was generally missed by those who relied on the workers' press for their news. In their coverage *Ceteme* editors praised Echeverría's epic sermon and cited parts of it that were relevant to the cause of the Mexican worker, including a proposed expansion of the National Popular Subsistence Company and a government plan to fight speculation and hoarding in the commercial sector.[24] Nowhere in their coverage, however, did they mention the devaluation plan that was easily the speech's most salient item. Such a topic was likely omitted due to its potential to chip away at the legitimacy of a paternalistic state intent upon presenting an image of revolutionary but responsible authority to its dependents in the working class. Workers, however, need not have heard the speech or read about it to understand the impact of the fiscal reform. They felt it almost immediately at the

market, bank, or anywhere else they transacted business. With the devaluation the price of all goods and especially of imported consumer goods
like refrigerators and color television sets spiked dramatically, rising 20
and 30 percent almost overnight. To ease the burden the government
instituted raises for workers, civil servants, and pensioners in a way that
compounded the nation's already dire inflationary situation.

To employers in the CCE, the Grupo Monterrey, and elsewhere, the
monetary instability, inflation, and unemployment (to say nothing of
the guerrilla movements) that plagued Mexico in the mid-1970s seemed
symptomatic of a larger ailment. As they saw it the revolutionary political economy that had been revived by Echeverría and had drastically
increased government control over industry, created new state agencies
to distribute goods and regulate their prices, and produced a new labor
code that empowered (even encouraged) workers to challenge their
employers had revealed itself as an archaic and destructive model for
Mexico. Instead of bringing the redemption of the working class, as
evangelists like Echeverría, Jesús Reyes Heroles, and Fidel Velázquez had
so often promised it would, the Mexican Revolution redux had mostly
yielded class conflict, exaggerated labor militancy, and now, recession.

With his regime's fiscal acumen called into question, Echeverría took
to the circuit once again, preaching a gospel that stressed the beneficial
connection between the Revolution and the Mexican people. On October 15 he trekked to the familiar but hostile ground of Monterrey, and
there in the capital of industry he attended numerous groundbreakings,
oversaw a highway construction project, and visited the Monterrey
Technological Institute, one of the nation's premier universities. A trip
he made to Fomerrey #3, a former shantytown on the outskirts of the
city since converted into a government housing project, made the most
headlines. He spoke off-the-cuff, praising the community's residents
for improving their lives through common work and class solidarity.
All that stood in the way of prosperity for the people of Fomerrey, he
insisted, were the "rich and the powerful" who refused to channel their
resources toward the public good. "Great concentrations of capital," he
felt, were not justified, morally speaking, if they were not oriented toward

bettering society. It was not enough "to create effective factories"; it was also necessary that the industrialists and bankers of Monterrey channel their resources toward solving the problems of their fellow man. Those who denied this moral function were "profoundly reactionary"; they were enemies of the people's progress who could not be called Christians.[25] This was a message, the president reminded listeners, that he had first articulated as a candidate, repeated in his inaugural address, and still espoused with conviction at the end of his presidency.

Public responses to the Echeverría challenge immediately emerged. A coalition of business groups led by the Monterrey chapter of the National Chamber of Commerce jointly published a letter in city newspapers denying that they were selfish, that they were enemies of progress, and that they were, somehow, un-Christian. They stressed their efforts to work productively with the state's governor and cited fiscal statistics showing that Nuevo León patrones shouldered an inordinate portion of the nation's tax burden.[26] Their impassioned response garnered them strange bedfellows. Manuel Salazar Ávila, who wrote for *Presente!* (not an outlet known to sympathize with patrones) questioned whether Echeverría's efforts to keep Mexico in a permanent "state of undoing" were deliberate. How else, he reckoned, could one make sense of the "cordial" speech delivered by the president and filled with such "caring" adjectives as "reactionaries," "enemies of progress," "emissaries of the past," and "egoists."[27] Salazar stressed that in criticizing Echeverría he wanted only to emphasize that all Mexicans suffered equally under the weight of an authoritarian regime bent on forcing its personal convictions on all.

Echeverría's tongue-lashing of the Grupo Monterrey also inspired shows of support. Napoleón Gómez Sada, the leader of the Mexican Mining and Metalworkers' Union, believed, as did Echeverría, that Monterrey was filled with "enemies of progress" who threatened not just Nuevo León but the entire country. He warned these "enemies" against thinking that the outgoing administration was powerless; the incumbent government had until its final minute to act in the nation's interests and nationalize their companies.[28] Raúl Caballero Escamilla, secretary general of the Nuevo León State Workers' Federation, also defended the president's remarks and challenged the "lie" that local employers paid an unfair amount of taxes. The riches produced in the state, he contended, came from the efforts of its workers and not from the vanity and delusions of its industrialists and bankers.[29] Fidel Velázquez referred to the speech with a similar air of approval. The men of the Grupo Monterrey, he grumbled, "only think of their personal interests and never of that of the collective," and rather unsurprisingly, given that there was little perceptible difference between the current regiomontano employers and those reprimanded by Cárdenas forty years earlier. "In spite of everything," the labor principal pronounced as the Echeverría administration entered its final month and as he prepared for a new phase at the top of the labor bureaucracy, "the Revolution continues its march."[30]

Conclusion

The Revolution Redeemed (But for Whom?)

Rhetoric, Reality, and the Salvation of the Revolutionary Metonym

If the Revolution that Velázquez identified was still on the march, did it still benefit the Mexican worker to whom it was so often ascribed? Certainly it did, at least according to the workers' press. *Ceteme* writers were careful as the presidential term approached its end to reference recent gains in a way that emphasized the CTM's continued relevance to the cause of the Mexican unionist. They wrote on October 2, 1976, eight years to the day after the country suffered its painful episode, but made no mention of the tragic anniversary. Instead they devoted space inside their publication to trumpeting advances the working class had made in recent years. The New Federal Labor Law was described as a crowning achievement, although it hardly signified the end of workers' gains; much more had been won since May 1, 1970. The Echeverría government, they reported, had also addressed the needs of workers via the creation of the National Workers' Housing Institute and by expanding the National Popular Subsistence Company. Similarly, the purview of the Federal Consumer Advocate's Office, which monitored aspects of the production, distribution, and commercialization of goods in the country, was also broadened in the period.[1] Finally, wages were raised by presidential decree three times during the period: by 18 percent in 1973, by 17 percent in 1974, and by 23 percent following the devaluation of 1976.[2] These increases, wrote *Ceteme* editors, benefited not only *cetemistas* but all of the nation's six million workers (unionized or free) who labored under the minimum wage guidelines.[3]

More changes spearheaded by the regime after 1970 and beneficial to the working class could have honestly been cited as the end of the sexenio approached. Presidential support was crucial in the creation of new federal labor tribunals in late 1974, something the labor bureaucracy had long clamored for. Public sector employment was increased by 60 percent during Echeverría's tenure, a change that dramatically raised public expenditures on health and education benefits for state workers and extended medical coverage as provided by the Mexican Social Security Institute from 24 to 36 percent of the population. These and other federal measures were major policy concessions on the part of the state toward the Mexican working class and were not merely rhetorical gestures. Responding directly to the demands of leaders of powerful national and regional labor organizations, the measures expanded the reach of the federal government into people's lives in a way that increased political support for the regime of the Mexican Revolution.

Still, was the typical Mexican worker better off in 1976 than he or she had been in 1968? No, or at least not according to economic data. The Echeverría administration's penchant for expanding the public sector and spending freely during the period 1972–75 revived Mexico's economic growth temporarily but at the cost of the stability of the national currency. The nation's external debt surged after 1973, making its much lauded price stability impossible to sustain. Inflation ensued, and rates that had averaged 5 percent during the years 1971 and 1972 skyrocketed upward, reaching 12 percent in 1973 and 24 percent in 1976. Many of the labor battles this book describes were generated by inflation and the challenges it posed to workers' wages. Joblessness peaked during this period as well despite the growth of numerous industrial sectors. Employment gains brought about through the creation of large factories in the expanding maquiladora sector, for example, were offset by the loss of employment in small shops that were driven out of existence by larger enterprises.[4] At the end of the day, the economic goals of the Echeverría government, though infused with the watchwords of *mixed, equilibrium*, and *social justice*, closely resembled the capital-intensive, output-maximizing strategies of yesteryear that privileged the needs of employers over employees. Workers were thus left to militate simply to procure working conditions already guaranteed them by law, all the while abiding inflation and feeling their standard of living precipitously decline.

Even unionists, those "privileged" elements of the working class, felt their standing vis-à-vis *patrones* worsen in the post-Tlatelolco period. Despite legal guarantees outlined in the NLFT and elsewhere, the Mexican unionist struggled to exercise even some of his most basic rights. Recall that no discernible difference was noticeable in the percentage of labor suits decided in favor of petitioners (employees) over respondents (employers) during the Echeverría and earlier presidencies, nor were strike petition approval rates higher than seen before. In fact, strikers' statistical chances for government approval were better during the Díaz Ordaz sexenio (1964–70) than during the Echeverría term that followed it, at 3 percent and 1.9 percent, respectively.[5] This data, in short, challenges any assumption that the percentage of strikes recognized as legal was, as a rule, higher during "liberal" than during "conservative" presidencies. No strict correlation, it appears, may be made between the perceived ideology of a regime and its support for workers' rights as demonstrated by labor arbitration and strike statistics.[6] Unfortunately, it thus appeared that the perceived radicalism and bias of the regime for labor very seldom translated into real gains for workers when workplace conflicts arose.

How may we understand the paradox, then, that saw unionists bringing labor suits and filing strike petitions at record rates despite diminished prospects for victory? This phenomenon, I believe, is at least partly explainable by returning to one of this study's principal contentions: *words mattered.* The perpetual war of words waged between politicians and the ownership class during the 1970s strengthened the leaders of the labor bureaucracy by publicly aligning the government with the cause of the Mexican unionist. Moreover, proworker maxims inscribed in the NLFT on topics such as "equilibrium" signaled to many a new era of worker vindication that emboldened them to confront their employers at record levels. Proworker rhetoric, in short, spurred a discourse that heightened class animosity and led to conflict. Patrones, in contrast to their employees, decried the discourse for the ways that it furthered the notion that workers were special and deserved extra rights and privileges. They complained that workers (unionists in particular) were too litigious: that in their zeal to further their individual interests they were obstructing the advancement of the Mexican economy to the detriment of all. Those same owners were also likely to scoff at the process of tripartite labor arbitration out of a belief that it was biased or weighted in favor of the worker or workers who raised the suit.

In all, the rhetoric espoused by politicians and reproduced in the workers' press brandished a reputation for the regime that was a salient factor in the story of post-Tlatelolco tripartite relations. Ultimately, most Mexican unionists perceived their union and political leaders as committed to revolutionary ideals and harbored great expectations of rights they believed could be achieved via activism. It was the expectation of state support and not the proven existence of it that drove unionized workers continually to seek gains even as their prospects for success in arbitration dwindled to historically low levels. It was rhetoric as much as reality that guided the majority of organized labor activity in the era. Rhetoric—that which was spoken, printed, and depicted visually—had real influence over the thinking, actions, and lives of the millions of men and women who formed themselves into the unions of post-Tlatelolco Mexico.

Religion and the Savior Complex in Post-Tlatelolco Mexico

Wielding class-based and revolutionary rhetoric as their primary weapon, redeemers walked the political landscape after Tlatelolco on a mission to save the historical legacy that formed the basis of the only nation most living Mexicans had ever known. There were lesser redeemers, but the path trodden by Echeverría most closely followed the salvation matrix.

Salvation is a complicated structure that need not connote a religious meaning in postrevolutionary Mexico. Organized religion nevertheless played a role in this tale of redemption. Echeverría, we recall, was raised Catholic and pondered entering the seminary as a young man. As president and as the standard bearer of a social movement with a historical anticlerical bent, Echeverría obeyed custom and refrained from practicing his faith in public. He raised eyebrows, however, in 1974 when he visited the Vatican to thank Pope Paul VI for supporting the Declaration of Rights and Economic Duties of the States, a circular that articulated the goals of his third-worldist agenda.[7] This first public contact in the postrevolutionary era between the heads of the Mexican government and the Roman Catholic Church was not the extent of church-state relations in the period. Echeverría vigorously supported the archdiocese's construction of the Basilica of Our Lady of Guadalupe, which houses Mexico's most important religious relic, and was pleased to see the project completed under his mandate.[8] Church support for the Echeverría government was forthcoming as well. Prelates offered their support for the quashing of arrest warrants in the wake of the Corpus Christi massacre of June 10, 1971. The strong anticommunist stance taken by the Mexican Church and the blanket pardons that many clerics issued government officials from their pulpits led many to see a degree of state-church collusion in the military repression of the period. All of this suggested that, as with organized labor, Echeverría saw in the Catholic Church a powerful social institution that could serve as an important (albeit ironic) ally in his quest to restore the legitimacy and authority of the revolutionary regime.[9]

Redeemers, religious or secular, need not be loved. Many, in fact, are destined to suffer in their quests to save their people from perdition. Marjorie Becker believes that to be a redeemer one must endure the kind of pain that Jesus suffered at the end of his life. In some ways the end of a presidential term in Mexico is a metaphorical dying, and she recounts this process during the latter third of the Cárdenas presidency (1939–40), when the president's Christ-like abilities were undermined by disaffected landowners, foreign capitalists, and right-wing groups that opposed his programs. Facing such formidable opposition, Cárdenas was forced to make compromises in order to preserve some revolutionary gains.[10]

Applying this metaphor to the period under review makes Echeverría's presidency (1975–76) appear as a veritable passion play of suffering, temptation, and resolve. During this period he, like Cárdenas, endured tribulations as he battled landowners, withstood pressure from employers' organizations, and subdued threats from armed opposition groups. Add to the mix that he never truly solved Mexico's "student problem" and felt the derision of disaffected students throughout his presidency, in one case quite literally, as he was hit by a rock that caused him to bleed profusely during a March 1975 visit to the UNAM campus.

Key factors, however, produced vastly different outcomes for the redeemers in their missions. Cárdenas, in contrast to Echeverría, greatly improved his and the federal government's relationship with organized labor during his last years in office. For Echeverría, support from the nation's labor bureaucracy was seriously tested due to the rhetorical support he offered for independent unionism and union democratization. Cárdenas's strategy to preserve portions of his revolutionary program by selecting a moderate successor also proved more successful than Echeverría's. Both legacy-conscious leaders considered lifelong friends for the role, but unlike Cárdenas, who selected Manuel Ávila Camacho instead of the more radical Francisco J. Múgica, Echeverría succumbed to personal loyalties by tapping López Portillo—a good choice, he reasoned, because he had "come up through the ranks," but someone who ultimately reneged on his promised moderation and continued the expansion of the para-state sector in a way that exacerbated fiscal problems, increased internal party and state-business rancor, and paved the way for the privatization of the economy after 1982.

Accepting that Echeverría was a less effective and certainly less beloved defender of the revolutionary legacy than was Cárdenas, does the savior suit then fit? No scholar who has yet assessed the man and his era believes that it does. Echeverría barely merits a mention in George Grayson's monograph *Mexican Messiah*, and the nationalist and populist stances he took had no bearing on the actions of Andrés Manuel López Obrador, a one-time *priísta* who defected from the party in the 1980s over its divergence from revolutionary principles and has ever since challenged the political status quo in Mexico.[11] Ironically, though, Echeverría becomes partly deserving of the title of messiah when one runs his credentials through a checklist of six factors that Grayson says explain messiahs' appearances in Mexican history. Certainly Echeverría emerged from a weakened political institution that was widely criticized for being unrepresentative, and yes, he tackled these issues by lowering the voting age from twenty-one to eighteen, responding to student concerns in the areas of university autonomy, and decreasing the minimum percentage of the vote a party needed to have representation in the lower house of Congress.[12] Additionally, he was adept at capturing media attention, as he, along with Fidel Velázquez, who convened a weekly press conference each Monday morning at CTM headquarters, took full advantage of the media and used the theater of mass politics to mold the discourse and espouse state-affirming values of class and revolution. Finally, and most importantly, Echeverría relied heavily on vague proposals complemented by symbolic acts that responded to the needs of the masses to advance his mission. Many of the initiatives described herein, most notably his *tercermundismo* and democratic opening, fit this mold perfectly, as they were largely populist offerings designed to appeal to numerically large but politically weak segments of the voting public. Other measures proved more substantial, certainly, but even the celebrated NLFT occasionally descended into the realm of symbolism, as many of its de jure prescriptions went unenforced or were ignored in practice.

Echeverría failed to meet Grayson's messiah standards in other ways as well, as he did not respond to a lack of confidence in traditional politicians nor did he fulfill a widespread yearning for a message of hope. He was unique among Mexican presidents in that he had not previously held elected office, but this consummate insider who had navigated the channels of the one-party system all the way to its pinnacle inspired very few dreams of change. How could he? He was, after all, the individual after Díaz Ordaz most associated with October 2, 1968, and the abuses, crimes, and excesses of a regime that seemed destined to remain in power forever.

Moreover, Echeverría failed to ingratiate himself in people's hearts and in the national consciousness, despite his immense efforts to do so. His public relations team tried exceptionally hard to present him as someone who, like Cárdenas, was unafraid to shake up the establishment and take on the entrenched and powerful enemies of the working class. He was lauded as both a regular person (he did not hide the fact that he was monolingual, speaking only Spanish) and an exceptional man—a father of eight whose honesty, responsibility, physical strength, and unmatched work ethic made him a natural leader for the Mexican people. But what the government and the PRI judged was evidence of Echeverría's social crusade, others saw as a product of his vanity or worse. A lengthy intelligence cable to the U.S. State Department in August 1975 understood the Mexican president's "frenetic schedule" in a way many Mexicans would have agreed with:

> An objective observer can hardly escape the eventual conclusion that the flurry of activity becomes an end in itself just as Echeverrria has come to love the sheer excitement, color, and cheering crowds of state visits, all questions of substance aside. Obviously, Echeverria is capable of enduring more stress in terms of workload than most men, but this is a self-imposed burden. None of his predecessors over the past two or three decades has found it necessary to expend quite so much energy, put in so many hours on the job, make so many speeches, or engage in such frequent travel at home and abroad in order to govern this long-stable country.

The cable concluded in a fairly prescient manner, stating, "More than one close observer since Echeverria's accession to the presidency has noted a 'touch of megalomania' in Echeverria and a possibly growing 'messianic' aspect to his character. That observation probably has more validity today than ever."[13] Mexicans of the time concurred, evidence showed. A public opinion poll administered in May 1975 revealed that of the 75 percent of respondents who were not in agreement with the Echeverría government, 11 percent listed its "demagoguery" as constituting their number-one complaint. The same survey also conveyed more discouraging news to the regime: 86 percent of all respondents, and 90 percent of those listed as being of the lower middle (i.e., working) class, believed that "definitive changes" were needed in society—a belief that had grown consistently while Echeverría held office, up from 70 percent in September 1972 and 85 percent in May 1974.[14]

With this, quantitative data buttressed anecdotal evidence suggesting that in spite of immense rhetorical efforts on the part of the president, and in spite of some real positive attributes he possessed, Echeverría could never successfully paint himself as a "man of the people" of the ilk of Tata Lázaro. Nor could he cast himself as a social crusader in the mold of Fidel Castro, a man author Gabriel García Márquez once praised for having achieved the "'coveted and elusive' dream of all rulers: 'affection.'"[15] In the end, the guayabera shirts he donned and the native cuisine he had served at state functions were not enough to link him with those titans of the redemptionist and revolutionary narratives. Perhaps he was born too late, suggests historian Alan Knight, for whereas "Cárdenas was a pup (*cachorro*) of the armed revolution; literate but lacking a university degree; Echeverría was a cachorro of the of the institutional revolution (an oxymoron which, of course, found its way into the ruling party's nomenclature)."[16] And his social background was similarly problematic, for never it seemed could he shake his image as a bureaucrat and a "chemically pure" product of the Federal District, to paraphrase the eminent historian Daniel Cosío Villegas, who was his close confidante.[17] Mexico's next messiah, one may have concluded, could not emerge during peacetime and not from the comforts of the urban bourgeoisie and political class.

The last and most damning factor in Echeverria's quest to establish messiah credentials was that he did not ultimately become a "leader of the masses unrestrained by institutional fetters." He undoubtedly challenged the status quo, and at the end of the day even his most ardent critics conceded that he demonstrated strength in not publicly kowtowing to opponents in his party, on the left, or in the business sector. Still, when push came to shove, and when forced to negotiate outside of the public spotlight, Echeverría usually opted for conciliation over outright war. Patrones grouped into large commercial organizations still pushed their weight around in the 1970s and were more often rewarded than thwarted in their dealings with the government. The conciliatory and accommodating approach that the post-Tlatelolco state maintained with these powerful sectors proved that even though changes were implemented in the international, economic, and governmental spheres, *dictablanda* and not blatant force remained the modus vivendi of state-business relations.

Ultimately, the chief protagonists of the drama that produced the social crises of the late 1960s and early 1970s went largely unscathed by them. *Charros*, for example, who personified to many the cooptation, corruption, and authoritarianism of the workers' movement in Mexico, remained firmly in control of it after 1976. Patrones in the Grupo Monterrey and around the nation, too, emerged from the sexenio more unified and wealthier than before. All of this while unionists, the most publicized beneficiaries of post-Tlatelolco reform, enjoyed only some of the benefits promised them and actually felt their economic status decline vis-à-vis patrones during the period. "Whoever falls, falls," Echeverría's famous threat to the perpetrators of the Corpus Christi massacre of June 10, 1971, thus was little more than rhetorical bluster and hot air to many in Mexico's disaffected masses.

If not a messiah, then, does Echeverría qualify as a redeemer? Not according to Enrique Krauze, who has written on the redeemer in Mexico and does not include Echeverría in that taxonomy. As Krauze sees it, Bishop Samuel Ruiz, Subcomandante Marcos, Octavio Paz, and José Vasconcelos all—unlike Echeverría—walked the redeemer's path in twentieth-century Mexico to defend traditional values in certain segments of the society (Ruiz, Marcos) or to instill new ones in all of it (Paz, Vasconcelos) in order to save it.[18] Undoubtedly it is difficult for Krauze, who is a member of the "Generation of '68," which came of age during that era and subsequently dominated cultural production in Mexico, to include the reviled Echeverría in such a grouping. Even so, there were undeniable redeeming qualities in the actions of a president and his acolytes who so vigorously sermonized to reestablish the links that had once bound their government with the legacy of the Mexican Revolution.

Commercial and guerrilla opposition notwithstanding, this strategy succeeded for the short term to restore the legitimacy and fortify the authority of a one-party system that had been weakened by prolonged societal unrest and government abuses. This was a common conclusion reached by outsiders near the end of the Echeverría presidency. Returning to the August 1975 intelligence report referenced above, a U.S. agent summarized the Mexican president's effectiveness in office like so: "A second generation revolutionary . . . a product of the system and devoted to preserving it . . . he has achieved some success (degree is debatable) in improviing [sic] the lot of Mexican poor. But there is no evidence that Echeverria ever rebelled against the innate hypocrisy and corruption of the Mexican system—one which presents a facade of 'revolutionary democracy' to the world and its own constituency while constituting in fact a system designed or adapted to concentrate political power and . . . wealth within the hands of a small establishment."[19] The agent was essentially correct. The PRI benefited from the efforts of post-Tlatelolco redeemers, and only because of Echeverría and Reyes Heroles did it become the "great organizer of the masses." If the PRI had once been an enormous electoral machine, write party historians, "after the seventies it acquired a profile inclusive of the diverse social groups. On these it based its capacity to mobilize people for public government acts and to legitimize its policies."[20]

Nonetheless, the post-Tlatelolco mandate for social inclusion benefited only some privileged elements of the body politic as it created opportunities for labor organizations to mobilize and demand improvements in wages, working conditions, and social security provisions in the years that followed. Echeverría, the new president, elected after intense social conflicts, faced heightened demands for benefits or concessions from popular classes and needed to respond in a way that would rebuild their support for the ruling regime.[21] This study reveals that the results were many, although the benefits and concessions that were granted went unevenly distributed.

Tlatelolco as Historical Watershed and the Necessity of "Preemptive" Reform

In the nearly five decades since the tragic happenings witnessed on October 2–3, 1968, in the Plaza de las Tres Culturas, the status of Tlatelolco as a *parteaguas* or watershed moment in Mexican history has been vigorously disputed. Overall most scholars believe that the student movement created an opening—be it social, political, or both—for a generation of Mexicans to exploit, although there is disagreement over the size of those openings and the extent to which they were exploited in the ensuing period.

Elaine Carey affords the student movement of 1968 great social salience for the ways it questioned presidential authority and challenged ingrained discourses that made women subservient to men and youth to elders, thus spawning future social movements that tested traditional family structures and raised cultural issues once deemed taboo.[22] Like Carey, Sergio Aguayo also sees 1968 as transformative but mainly for the political changes it provoked. Reviewing declassified intelligence files from the era, Aguayo demonstrates how a gradual public awareness of the state's misdeeds after Tlatelolco was a crucial factor in forcing eventual political reform in Mexico.[23] Even Amelia Kiddle and María Muñoz, the editors of a 2010 volume comparing the outcomes of the "popular" (i.e., authentic) measures employed by Cárdenas with the "populist" (demagogic) ones of Echeverría, ascribe Tlatelolco a genuine transformative role, writing, "Tlatelolco not only served as a political watershed, but also a social and academic one. While the legacy of the revolution and the sanctity of the revolutionary family were on the verge of cracking, Echeverría made a misguided and failing attempt to harness mass mobilizations, appease social demands, and control political openings in an effort to salvage what he could from a fractured political legitimacy." Echeverría himself, say the authors, was transformative and "made his mark" even if "its nature is not as clear as Cárdenas's because it is deeply rooted in Tlatelolco, Corpus Christi, a dirty war, and economic calamity."[24]

Conversely, there have been scholars who have ascribed Tlatelolco less clear-cut historical significance, arguing, in the case of Enrique Krauze, that the legacy of 1968 was "uncertain" for the ways its ideological inheritors failed to consolidate its potential. Krauze granted that those events contributed to democratizing the country, although he felt that the "irreverent" qualities of the historic movement coupled with the riddled state of the twenty-first-century Left in Mexico prevented crediting the students of 1968 with any significant achievements.[25] This message echoed one conveyed earlier by Eric Zolov, who viewed 1968 as a "turning point" in modern Mexico but cautioned that to lionize the students as "heroic youth doing battle against antiquated, reactionary systems of thought and power" risked overlooking the "messiness" of the movement.[26]

The conclusions I present herein align me with scholars in the affirmative camp, as I too view the sequence of events that culminated on October 2–3, 1968, as a decisive moment that altered the nation's political culture. I am comfortable in periodizing Mexican history using pre-Tlatelolco and post-Tlatelolco divisions, even if I do not view reforms enacted after 1968 as particularly revolutionary. Ultimately I believe, much like Lorenzo Meyer, Héctor Aguilar Camín, and Michael Snodgrass, that the changes promised and the laws passed in the wake of Tlatelolco were part of a reformist mission spearheaded by a politician who, to quote Snodgrass, "practiced a more calculated populism, one meant to restore ruling party legitimacy rather than transform the socioeconomic structures and political culture of Mexico."[27] Changes, to be sure, did come, but this study primarily (and rather uniquely) demonstrates that political reform implemented after Tlatelolco conveyed the state's deep-seated desire to counter threats to its authority not from university students but from other societal sectors and, most importantly, from organized workers who had militated at heightened levels since the late-1950s. Mexican workers were not the primary victims of government repression in 1968, and Mexican unionists even less so. They were, however, the primary beneficiaries of the government's extensive efforts to reestablish its right to rule the Mexican people in the post-Tlatelolco period.

In a similar vein this book differentiates itself from extant studies through its attention to spectacle and rhetoric in the post-Tlatelolco state's campaign for redemption. Returning to the examples of the massive First of May parades that were held in the period is useful because in those state-sanctioned episodes of mass politics the dynamics of collaborationism were most clearly displayed. On May 1, 1970, the nation's organized labor infantry was mobilized in Mexico City to march in support of the New Federal Labor Law—a major piece of legislation that stood to benefit their lives directly. Put another way, unionists were required to undertake a mass action to show, in the most public way imaginable, their great appreciation to their political leaders for their heartfelt efforts to improve the lives of the Mexican working class.

Granting that the basic operating dynamic of collaborationism was at work on May 1, 1970, an interesting question becomes *What prompted the Mexican state to create a new labor code in the first place?* In this regard political scientists Kenneth M. Coleman and Charles L. Davis's concept of preemptive reform as "a co-optative response by political elites to their fears of uncontrolled political mobilization by the less advantaged elements of society" seems tailor-made for this analysis. Viewing Tlatelolco as the catalyst for future change, one might then wonder *What, if anything, did the state's creation of new legislation intend to preempt?* Here again Coleman and Davis's structure is applicable, as preemptive reform "reflects an intention to institute that degree of change, apparent or real, necessary to preserve essential features of the existing institutional order." Preemptive reform, they qualify, need not imply any profound vision or unity on the part of the ruling regime. At most it can be the product of "a group of decision-makers who share the belief that to do nothing may be to do too little."[28]

Clearly the compulsion to act among Mexico's decision makers and for Luis Echeverría in particular was the product of their familiarity with the workings of an authoritarian system that put reciprocal agreements in place to govern relations between the state and the most crucial sectors of civil society. For decades the system had proven its efficacy but by the late 1960s the nation's political elites recognized that stability could be preserved only by balancing coercion "with at least a modest response to the grievances of those who might act against the 'institutional norm.'"[29] Guarantees were made to workers, policies implemented, and patronage distributed in ways that appeased organized labor's leadership and rank and file to varying extents. Reforms like the NLFT smoothed over kinks in the collaborationist relationship that had long allied organized labor with the Mexican state, even if they had little positive impact on the day-to-day lives of most Mexican workers. Reforms indeed came to Mexico after Tlatelolco, but in a way that primarily ensured the future viability of the labor bureaucracy and the postrevolutionary system at large.

The Bible informs us that Jesus saw the crowd that had assembled around him and addressed them on a mountainside. Included in his famous sermon on the mount was a message to believers that assuaged their fears by stressing continuity and peace. Matthew 5:17–18 reads, "17: Do not think that I have come to abolish the Law or the Prophets; I have not come to abolish them but to fulfill them. 18: For truly I tell you, until heaven and earth disappear, not the smallest letter, not the least stroke of a pen, will by any means disappear from the Law until everything is accomplished."[30] Though he ignored some of Christ the Redeemer's lessons, Echeverría obeyed this one. The law and the prophets were fulfilled; the Mexican revolutionary state in which he was reared emerged from his mandate stronger than it was before he took office in 1970. Plutarco Elías Calles, who laid the groundwork for an all-powerful nation of institutions and laws, must have rested easy knowing that the hegemony of the official party that he created was secured. Lázaro Cárdenas, who put the tenets of revolutionary ideology into action, might have smiled from above as Echeverría the preacher of revolutionary gospel pursued a model of interventionism that expanded the parastate sector and increased the government's control over labor-capital relations and the workings of the economy. And even Fidel Velázquez, who more than anyone else was responsible for the condition of the working class in postrevolutionary Mexico, nodded and mumbled in approval as the labor bureaucracy was bolstered through legislation, economic and political structural reform, and a clear rhetorical alliance with the government.

Calles, Cárdenas, Velázquez, and now Echeverría—redeemers and revolutionary prophets past and present—could honestly rejoice in 1976 that neither the social unrest, the economic distress, nor the *independentista* movement that surged in the post-Tlatelolco period fundamentally upset the collaborationist dynamic that had tied the organized labor movement to the state since 1920. Neither inflation, nor unemployment, nor authoritarianism deterred the labor bureaucracy from assembling its troops in shows of mass support for the regime.

On a cold evening on December 1, 1976, a large group of unionists gathered outside the National Auditorium to cheer on the transfer of power that was occurring inside. After the ceremony many bade farewell to Echeverría, now the former president, as he descended the building's stairwell, thanking him for his efforts "to realize revolutionary works." Such a show of patriotism and solidarity, *Ceteme* reported, was only possible among a people who enjoyed economic stability and had not suffered the ill fates of neighbors who had fallen into militarism and fascism and had toiled without the ability to live a life of dignity and justice as was purportedly enjoyed in Mexico.[31]

Thus things appeared to the bastion of the workers' press on the eve of another presidential succession. The virtual reality crafted in official words and imagery that narrated a heroic tale of vindication for the Mexican working class and the redemption of the revolutionary regime was embraced wholesale. Unpleasant subjects of dirty war, the repression of independent unionists, and the declining social status of the working class, in contrast, were denied. With the transfer of power, the collaborationist machinery had been activated and the acceptable limbs of civil society welcomed the ostensibly moderate but sufficiently *obrerista* López Portillo to the presidential chair with open arms. In all the time elapsed since the watershed events of 1968 had exposed the ruling regime to unprecedented criticism and demands for reform, its hierarchical and undemocratic labor structure was largely unchanged. Fidel Velázquez, the CTM, the charros, and the majority of players in the labor bureaucracy endured. The metonym that linked the nation with modern Mexico's formative event persisted. The Revolution appeared saved, its corpus intact for the foreseeable future.

13. "Deservedly . . ." An illustration in a Monterrey newspaper ridicules workers on May 1, 1970. *El Norte*, May 1, 1970, 2-A. Courtesy of Hemeroteca Nacional.

14. National Union of Mexican Women march in Mexico City in support of students murdered by the regime on October 2, 1968. IISUE/AHUNAM/ Colección Manuel Gutiérrez Paredes "Mariachito"/Expediente 60/3150.

15. First Lady María Esther Zuno de Echeverría's passionate advocacy for women's causes allowed her an independent voice in her husband's administration. Nevertheless, her feminism was not radical, and she presented a picture of gender complementarity, as seen here (*in striped suit*) during a donation drive for the Mexican Red Cross, n.d. AGN Fototeca, Archivo Fotográfico Hermanos Mayo, Luis Echeverría Alvarez, Expediente 35/1.

16. Gender complementarity in the workers' movement on display at a First of May parade in Mexico City, ca. 1975. AGN Fototeca, Archivo Fotográfico Presidencia de la República, Luis Echeverría Alvarez, Expediente 69/5.

17. "David versus Goliath Once Again, Rivetex vs. Female Workers." Hodiac, illustration. *Presente!*, September 24, 1972, 1. Courtesy of Hemeroteca Nacional.

18. "Power outages 45 days before the [president's] annual address? Right, Rafa, why not?" The CTM gloats after its defeat of the Democratic Tendency. *Ceteme*, no. 1276 (April 3, 1976). Courtesy of Hemeroteca Nacional.

19. (*left*) Luis Echeverría and another "redeemer," Fidel Castro, meet in Havana, Cuba, on August 17, 1975. AGN Fototeca, Archivo Fotográfico Hermanos Mayo, Luis Echeverría Alvarez, Expediente 067-1/s.n.

20. (*above*) A healthy collaborationism thrived during the presidency of José López Portillo (1976–82), Mexico's last "nationalist" president. Here López Portillo (*right of center*) marches in lockstep with Fidel Velázquez during a First of May parade in Mexico City, 1978. AGN Fototeca, Archivo Fotográfico Presidencia de la República, José López Portillo, Expediente 724/3.

21. An SME banner expresses the union's energy sector demands in Mexico City, August 2013. Courtesy of author.

22. A bronze Cárdenas endorses the "transformation" of the Revolution at PRI headquarters, August 2013. Courtesy of author.

23. Ignacio Zúñiga (*left*) with Fidel Velázquez, ca. 1991. Courtesy of Ignacio Zúñiga González.

Epilogue

Death and Resurrection

On September 1, 1982, President Jose López Portillo delivered the speech of his life, sending his listeners on an emotional roller coaster that first heard him extol the comprehensive electoral reform law passed under his watch and then shed tears over his failure to help the poor. Looking to exculpate himself for those failures, the outgoing head of state cast blame about, seething that the private banks in Mexico "had betrayed us" by taking "more money out of the country than all the empires that have exploited us since the beginning of our history."[1] It was the nation's private banks, therefore, and not his economic policies that had caused some USD 23 billion in bank deposits and other capital to flee the country in recent years. Speaking to the "traitors" who had "looted" the country, he commanded them to reconvert their assets to Mexican pesos by the end of the month or risk public exposure.[2] To the banking institutions that had enabled such treason, he offered no similar ultimatum. The president punctuated his address with a historic decree: all domestic private banks operating in Mexico were henceforth property of the republic, a measure effective immediately.

López Portillo's dramatic announcement caused a stir reminiscent of March 1938 when demonstrations arose in support of Lázaro Cárdenas's oil expropriation decree. Newspapers reported that schoolchildren in Mexico City received uniform lessons about the revolutionary significance of the act and praised it by creating drawings, murals, and essays. On September 3 a coalition of unionists, teachers, and students over two thousand strong celebrated the measure in Oaxaca and demanded the future nationalization of the food and pharmaceutical industries.[3] The following day, September 4, produced a much larger show of support on the streets of the capital, where fifteen thousand representatives of the Unified Socialist Party of Mexico and twenty-one independent unions exhibited a level of government support from organized labor's left not seen since the oil expropriation.[4] Supporters in Mexico City and elsewhere saw revolutionary significance in the president's measure and believed that the move "open[ed] the path toward a more independent social, political, and cultural life."[5] Daniel Dueñas, who covered the story for *El Universal*, heartily agreed. He echoed the regime's rationale and contended that the decision would strengthen the partnership between the government and private industry and create a golden opportunity to unite Mexico again. The bank nationalization, he confidently predicted, was "only the beginning."[6]

Unlike schoolteachers and other unionists, Mexican bankers and others in the business sector viewed the measure negatively—as an audacious act in a comedy of errors committed by the regime in the area of economic policy. And it was not the first of its kind; *patrones* had watched in horror for nearly six years as the López Portillo administration, seemingly drunk on increased oil revenues (real or projected), spent recklessly and purchased hundreds of unprofitable businesses whose main purposes were to provide jobs and paychecks regardless of productivity. By the time the number of state-run entities in Mexico peaked at an all-time high of 1,155 in 1982, few could remember the political and economic moderation that López Portillo had promised as a candidate. In business representatives' view, the bank nationalization decree was not an affirmation of Mexican sovereignty but a crass attempt on the part of the president to salvage his legacy and shift blame for the nation's severe economic problems from himself to the banks.

Eventually history would prove Daniel Dueñas wrong; the bank nationalization was not "the beginning" but the last, dying gasp of economic nationalism as a governmental imperative. The ensuing change of direction was largely due to the dismal performance of Mexican banks during the period of national control (1983–91). Unfortunately for most Mexicans, national control neither improved banking services nor prevented future capital flight. The number of bank branches increased only nominally (0.7 percent), providing residents only one branch per 19,000 persons, compared to one per 1,930 in Europe.[7] Moreover, the number of accounts dropped 32 percent while the number of administrative workers not involved in banking operations rose 65.5 percent. Statistics hence confirm that the federal government, which hesitated to build new branches out of fear of increasing government bureaucracy, further bureaucratized the system while decreasing public access to banking services.[8] Not surprisingly, this systemic failure spooked domestic and foreign capital, and another USD 20 billion left Mexican banks before reprivatization in 1991.

Heresy and Schism in the Revolutionary Family

The adventure of the banking system in Mexico was emblematic of the experience of hundreds other industries that would abide the push-and-pull processes of revolutionary redemption and abandon in the period, and the debate that the nationalization invited exposed the major ideological rifts that divided members of the revolutionary family. In short, a philosophical divide rooted in generational and cultural factors surfaced in the 1970s that placed individuals into opposing camps known as *políticos* ("politicians," or old-style *priístas* who had parlayed or expected to parlay loyal party service into government positions) and *técnicos* ("technocrats," or government employees with administrative expertise and autonomy in the decision-making process). Políticos and técnicos of the 1970s and 1980s could also be differentiated by their education and, consequently, by their exposure to outside ideas. Men like Echeverría, Reyes Heroles, and López Portillo embodied the standard político, as they had enjoyed comfortable urban upbringings and ease of access into the political class. They, like thousands of other elite beneficiaries of the Revolution, were educated in Mexico and obtained a degree in law, which was seen as a natural stepping-stone to public service. Their successors de la Madrid, Salinas, and Zedillo, on the other hand, constituted the prototypical técnicos, as they were schooled at elite foreign institutions and obtained degrees in business or economics. The physical and intellectual separation from Mexico that they experienced during their formative years distanced them from the discourse of the Revolution and reduced their commitment to preserving its ideology once they held political power.

The técnico/político divide tested the fabric of the Mexican one-party system as técnicos echoed patrones and opposed the expansion of the parastate sector that Echeverría and López Portillo oversaw. Initially, however, theirs was a minority voice that was drowned out by party and union leaders who overwhelmingly supported a course of action deemed revolutionarily compliant. Certainly, López Portillo's nationalization decree delighted políticos who had smarted over his decision to name as his successor the Harvard-educated Miguel de la Madrid, who headed the planning and budget ministry and was a favorite of the técnicos. Out of gratitude, politicians suddenly hailed López Portillo as their champion and "as the man who 'rescued' the party's long-forgotten revolutionary traditions by nationalizing the banks."[9] Moreover, the labor bureaucracy applauded López Portillo, seeing his economic nationalism as adding to a proworker portfolio already bolstered by the hard line he had taken against independent unionists and particularly against workers in the electrical power sector.[10] This latter stance greatly distinguished López Portillo from his predecessor and helped him enjoy a kind of friendly state-organized labor collaborationism never truly present during the Echeverría sexenio.

Again, however, dreams of renewed revolutionary redemption were *naïve*. Miguel de la Madrid acted quickly and decisively once in office to sever himself from the policies of prior administrations. Most famously, he oversaw a massive sell-off or dissolution of state-run entities, a process rapidly accelerated by his successor, Carlos Salinas de Gortari, president of Mexico from 1988 to 1994. Under Salinas's guidance the sale of all commercial banks under government control was completed in 1991, reaping the state a combined USD 11 billion. The bank reprivatization was a model copied hundreds of times thereafter, and by 1993 the government had overseen "one of the most sweeping sales of state companies in the world," relieving itself of 80 percent of the businesses it had operated in 1982, to the tune of USD 21 billion.[11]

Critiques filtered in, but the relatively smooth experience of bank privatization in Mexico and the proceeds gained from the sale of parastate companies—which in part funded the National Solidarity Program, an enormously popular government patronage program—suggested that the free trade and technocratic-inspired strategies adopted by the de la Madrid and Salinas governments were in the nation's best interests. Support for this position even came from Fidel Velázquez, the grizzled veteran of decades of battles to "mexicanize" industry. The CTM heaped praised on López Portillo for the bank nationalization but tacitly condoned through its silence the government's later sell-off of parastate companies that used to be bastions of *charro* power and providers of well-paid union jobs.[12] Rank-and-file unionists, in fact, shouldered the true burden of this support, as they were ordered to table any demands for improved working conditions and even accept wage deductions as part of the austerity policies enacted by the government. Mexican workers overall endured a 43 percent drop in their real income during the period 1982 to 1987, all while Velázquez defended the técnicos and their privatization policies at his Monday morning press conferences.[13] This contradiction did not surprise longtime observers, who understood well that the labor leader's adherence to collaborationism had always trumped his commitment to workers' practical objectives.

But while old allegiances endured, others perished. To those bound to revolutionary ideals the technocrats' free trade position was nothing short of heretical, as it advocated the end of government intervention in the economy. As the 1980s, the "Lost Decade" as some termed it, painfully progressed, and as heresy became orthodoxy, a schism formed in the one-party system. Led by Cuauhtémoc Cárdenas, the son of Lázaro, a coalition of disaffected priístas and members of urban community groups came together in 1987 to challenge the PRI for electoral hegemony. In the eyes of Velázquez and other bulwarks of the government, Cuauhtémoc Cárdenas was not a redeemer but another enemy of the institution. And much like Vicente Lombardo Toledano, Demetrio Vallejo, Rafael Galván, and many others who had challenged the political status quo, Cárdenas appeared a dangerous radical—a communist, said Velázquez—committed to sowing social discord. The label *apostate* was even thrown at Cárdenas, as he was seen as akin to someone who had lost his religion by virtue of defecting from the PRI, the "church" of the Revolution.

Cárdenas, of course, lost the presidency in 1988 to Carlos Salinas in one of the most fraud-filled contests in electoral history. Widespread indignation over the scurrilous incident, however, enabled Cárdenas's challenge to continue beyond 1988 through the creation of the Party of the Democratic Revolution (PRD). Since its establishment in 1990, the PRD has been a permanent opposition force capable of contesting the PRI politically and challenging its monopoly on the revolutionary legacy. Two decades onward, the PRD understood its emergence and continued mission as the product of myriad failures on the part of the PRI to serve Mexico's popular classes. A lavish textbook-style manifesto published in November 2010 explains that the PRD was formed to be an alternative to the corroded PRI-state, one that had been corrupted by neoliberalism and whose failings brought about economic crisis, decreased governability, and greater poverty.[14] To combat this corruption and defend the revolutionary principles of national patrimony, democracy, and social justice, *perredistas* (PRD members) constantly militated to prevent the privatization of Pemex, to combat the electoral fraud perpetrated against them, and to oppose the persecution of Zapatista sympathizers, among other causes.

Additionally, the PRD claimed to pursue continued revolution through its solidarity with Mexican workers. In an essay titled "The Left in Mexico," Rogelio Hernández listed Vicente Lombardo Toledano, Rafael Galván, and the Democratic Tendency as crucial antecedents to his party's creation, thus establishing PRD support for workers and labor organizations that operated outside of the labor bureaucracy and PRI control. The modern PRD also stressed the continued salience of radicalism in social thought and saw the contemporary working class as still rooted in the ideals of the Mexican Communist Party of the 1950s and 1960s, which was unified in its "profession of Marxist faith, a Soviet version of socialism, and the general cult of the Mexican Revolution." A clear solidarity bound the cause of the modern perredista with the martyrs of Tlatelolco, wrote Hernández, as it was the social movement of 1968 that, "although defeated," first opened the possibility of oppositional politics and "unleashed a popular urban movement of the left."[15] Following the Corpus Christi massacre of 1971 another "oppositional political effervescence" purportedly appeared that inspired small trade unions in crucial industrial sectors to separate themselves from official control. In light of such important gains the blood spilled by past social warriors had not been in vain, felt the author, blood and sacrifice, after all, being necessary parts of any redeemer's quest for his people's salvation.

The Quest Transformed

Like his father before him Cuauhtémoc Cárdenas devoted much of his life to defending the ideals of the Mexican Revolution. But unlike the general and president, Cárdenas the younger spent the bulk of his career as a political outsider who thrice ran for president (in 1988, 1994, and 2000) and lost to opponents who advocated the dismantling of programs that revolutionaries had worked so strenuously to implement. In 2013 the quest of Cárdenas continued but under the leadership of a different redeemer, Andrés Manuel López Obrador, who had also pursued the presidency multiple times (2006 and 2012) on the PRD ticket. Like Cárdenas, López Obrador walked along a path motivated to restore ideals such as economic nationalism, workers' rights, and social justice to government. And like Cárdenas's quest after 1988, López Obrador's was (and continues to be) inspired by a healthy dose of electoral indignation, as he was denied the presidency in a 2006 contest that wrote another inglorious chapter in the anthology of electioneering in Mexico. But even with widespread outrage over the "Fraud of 2006," López Obrador's second attempt at the presidency, in 2012, was not as threatening as his first, and he could not prevent the PRI from reclaiming the presidency that year via the victory of its candidate Enrique Peña Nieto in the July election by over three million votes and nearly 7 percentage points.[16]

That the presidency has proven unattainable to those on the political left in Mexico attests to the power of the nation-Revolution metonym established by the PRI in the twentieth century. Success in the 2012 election and the resurrection of the PRI under Peña Nieto was partly due to the party's renewed use of revolutionary discourse, a rhetorical line that contrasted it with the probusiness PAN, which held the presidency from 2000 to 2012. Nothing has irked perredistas more than the reverence priístas from Echeverría to Salinas have feigned toward preserving the "sacred cows of revolutionary iconography" while enacting reforms that effectively "slaughter" them.[17] This kind of revolutionary lip service was audible yet again on August 12, 2013, when Peña Nieto announced a plan to reform Articles 27 and 28 so as to permit private, even foreign, investment in Pemex. Speaking from Los Pinos, Peña Nieto defended the plan's specifics, stressing that the initiative would "retake 'word for word' the text of Article 27" so as to ensure that Mexico's oil and natural gas resources remained the "exclusive patrimony" of the nation.[18] Immediately following the announcement employers and politicians in the PAN applauded the president for presenting a plan that could improve the nation's economic competitiveness and create jobs.[19] PRD officials, on the other hand, viewed the plan as antirevolutionary and began to mobilize their people to combat "the theft of the century" and prevent a return to a prerevolutionary state of affairs, as López Obrador had warned against.[20]

Ground troops were dispatched around Mexico City in the days after the announcement to distribute leaflets that denigrated the proposal. To "privatizate petroleum," the leaflet cautioned, would bring higher taxes, gasoline and natural gas prices, and rates of poverty and violence while incurring a reduction in health, education, housing, and transportation services. On the leaflet's reverse was a historical analysis that ascribed the country's precipitous social decline to the privatization of Mexican industries in the 1980s. It stated, "Mexico is living the greatest political, economic, social, and security decay in its history. This is the result of its governments that have for thirty years looted the assets of the nation and deprived Mexicans of their rights." Oil, it elaborated, represented the principal source of national wealth and was the last industry that remained in public hands. "Everything else has been delivered to private businesses, national and foreign."[21]

Alejandro Rendón, an electrician who belonged to the Mexican Electrical Workers' Union, articulated similar sentiments to me on August 14, 2013, while he manned a table in the Zócalo collecting names for a petition to stop the proposed reform and soliciting money for the nearly forty-five thousand SME members who had lost their jobs following the liquidation of their primary employer, Central Light and Power Company, by presidential decree on October 10, 2009. Affixed to Rendón's table was a crude brown-paper banner depicting the closed fist and lightning bolts, the familiar shield of the SME. In large, hand-painted letters it read, "RE-NATIONALIZATION OF THE ELECTRICAL AND PETROLEUM SECTORS, NO TO PRIVATIZATION!" When I asked Rendón why the cause of the *electricistas* was tied up with the campaign against energy reform, he was blunt. "The petroleum is ours!" he declared. "It does not belong to the rats in government."[22]

Rendón was not simply being hyperbolic; the current crisis of the SME was directly tied to the status of energy sector ownership and control in Mexico. Two days earlier, on the morning of the reform announcement, I sat with SME official Eduardo Bobadilla Zarza in his Mexico City office. Bobadilla was candid in explaining his union's opposition to the past and present governments. The liquidation of his company in 2009, he believed, was designed to expand the Federal Electric Commission's operations into the Federal District and other central states that used to be the exclusive turf of Central Light and Power and the SME. Furthermore, the liquidation of the company and the expansion of the CFE benefited the SUTERM, the union that had the exclusive contract with the CFE and had always been a more pliable labor partner with the government than the SME. With his union out of the way, believed Bobadilla, it became easier for the next administration—be it PAN or PRI—to amend constitutional

Articles 27 and 28, advance the neoliberal agenda, and move toward the complete privatization of the nation's petroleum, natural gas, and other electrical energy-producing resources. "And what of the charros in the SUTERM and their response to the president's reform proposal?" he asked me, rhetorically. "They've kept silent."[23]

Proponents of the energy reform carried out their own public relations campaign in the days that followed. Better financed, they flooded the airwaves, newspapers, and social media with propaganda in favor of the reform. The federal government purchased a week's worth of full-page ads in major Mexico City dailies conveying messages and presenting images that stressed the reform's singular purposes of improving the sector's efficiency and maintaining national control over oil and natural gas resources.[24] The state also blitzed television viewers and radio listeners with a ten-minute spot called "So That They Don't Fool You," designed to debunk "thirteen myths" that were circulating about the reform. Among these myths, the narrator explained, were the false beliefs that with the reform private investors would acquire all the national oil profits; Pemex would transfer control of strategic development areas to private individuals; and the nation would stray from the ideals of Lázaro Cárdenas, a president who had "implemented reforms that indeed permitted the participation of individuals in distinct areas of the oil production process."[25]

To stress the latter point, Peña Nieto gave stump speeches throughout the week explaining how the improvement of the nation's electrical power industry would increase Mexicans' access to low-cost energy, a "Cardenist" act.[26] The PRI, too, trumpeted the reform's consistency with the memory of Cárdenas. The former president's agreement with the proposed reform was tacitly conveyed by an enormous banner that draped the wall behind the statue of him in the stone patio of PRI headquarters. "Mexico Is Transformed with Energy," it read, and it depicted two children clothed in PRI colors running to the viewer's left. Pedestrians and motorists who could view the statue and banner as they passed along Avenida Insurgentes were invited to learn more about the reform by joining a Twitter conversation with the hashtag #TransformandoMexico (Transforming Mexico).

As much as the president and others touted the reform's revolutionary credentials, their arguments fell upon many deaf ears. Some in the press were repulsed by the audacity of linking what they saw as the "privatization" of the oil industry to the heroic measures of Cárdenas to wrest it from foreign hands. A cartoon printed in *La Jornada* on August 15 mocked the historical aptitude of Peña Nieto and criticized his servility to famous PRI oligarchs. Entitled "The Great Historian," the image showed him speaking to an unnamed figure but one recognizable as Carlos Salinas by his cartoonish ears. Peña Nieto, apparently oblivious to history, complained to his colleague, "I don't understand: my historical justification for the energy reform is impeccable. Isn't it, Licenciado Lázaro Cárdenas?" Salinas said nothing in response. He merely giggled and put his hand over his mouth to hide his laughter.[27] And more than just leftists in Mexico were uncomfortable with the administration's use of Cárdenas to justify the measure. Writing in the PRI-friendly *El Universal*, Katia d'Artigues jested that while Cárdenas expropriated the oil industry, Peña Nieto succeeded mainly in expropriating Cárdenas.[28]

By Monday, August 19, the PRD had organized its ranks and was ready to fight the president's efforts to reform Pemex and, as importantly, to expropriate one of the Revolution's most revered icons. It organized a march and demonstration that would best illustrate the antirevolutionary qualities of the president's proposal by culminating in the Plaza de la República and in the shadow of the Monument to the Revolution—the massive four-columned arch that houses the remains of revolutionary titans under its pillars. In another symbolic act, the PRD invited its founder and former standard-bearer Cuauhtémoc Cárdenas to headline the demonstration, a logical move given his unmatched connection to the oil expropriation of 1938. That morning at about 10:45 a.m. a train of marchers appeared on Avenida Ignacio Ramírez and slowly moved toward the monument, repeating chants along the way. Inside the square, large video screens showed footage of revolutionary-era marches, and huge banners lined the plaza's sides, displaying the stern image of Lázaro Cárdenas above the slogan "No to the privatization of petroleum!" On the scene was a man dressed as Father Miguel Hidalgo, the father of

Mexico's independence, who had by then become a familiar presence at PRD events. He posed for photographs with demonstrators in front of a painting of the Virgin of Guadalupe, another icon of Mexican nationalism. Another PRD fixture was present as well, a man who called himself the Rayito de Esperanza, meaning the "Little Ray of Hope." He wore the yellow mask of the *luchador* and held a lightning bolt of cardboard and gold paper in his hand. Shouting into a megaphone, the folksy superhero promised that he, like the PRD, would continue to exist as long as there was inequality in Mexico.

The meeting officially began when Celeste Cárdenas, wife of Cuauhtémoc, laid a wreath at the foot of her father-in-law's enormous tomb. Following this solemn moment her husband, the day's lone speaker, took to the podium. Not being visible to those behind a partition that secluded PRD bigwigs from the general public, the guest of honor had to deliver his speech to most of those in the plaza via video screens. He voiced potent rhetoric that criticized the "sell-out government" and took umbrage at Peña Nieto's use of his father's memory. He then summarized the main points of an alternate proposal he had prepared that would "modernize not privatize Pemex." The speech's conclusion provoked only a tepid response, largely due to a sound deficiency and the large number of induced activists in the crowd. The national anthem played, and many filed out behind Cárdenas, who led them down Paseo de la Reforma en route to the federal senate building, where he hand-delivered his proposal.

The demonstration was not covered kindly in the press the following day, August 20. Reporting in *La Jornada*, Arturo Canó rejoiced that "Cuauhtémoc Cárdenas, moral leader of the Party of the Democratic Revolution [was] back!," although he could not help but describe the event with pity. He related that the start of the proceedings was delayed to let the venue fill in and that its most significant outcome was that it reminded its participants of the good old days.[29] Others were even less forgiving in their coverage. Ricardo Gómez ridiculed the event in *El Universal*, remarking that the PRD remembered its "DNA" and brought in "cheerleaders" to defend the petroleum industry.[30] Ricardo Alemán, writing in the same edition, skewered the event, saying that it barely convoked one thousand people and estimating that, of those who attended, 80 percent were *acarreados* who did not know what sort of event they had been brought to. None of this signified to Alemán a real popular opposition to the president's reform proposal. "Where are the multitudes," he asked, "that in the imagination of a handful of directors and leaders of the Mexican left would take to the streets to defend the ownership of petroleum, to vindicate nationalism and the memory of the general and ex-president Lázaro Cárdenas?" Where was this "wild Mexico" that the PRD and its chief "evangelist [López Obrador]" predicted would arise to defend this "betrayal of the nation?"[31]

Columnists for *El Universal* and other PRD opponents had a point; the demonstration was not successful and had all the vitality of a Sunday mass in the Metropolitan Cathedral, Mexico City's beautiful but remarkably gloomy basilica. Moreover, the presence of induced political activists there was obvious. The harsh criticism of the event emitted by PRI and PAN supporters surprised few political observers and certainly not Guillermo Flores Velasco, a top PRD advisor with whom I spoke two days after the demonstration. "The newspapers have liberty to write what they want," he reminded me, before proceeding to explain the methods by which the PRI and PAN dominate the media. "The PRI" he continued, "is not connected to revolutionary ideology." "The country is not like it was before," he concluded, although he did not preclude the possibility that some continued trace of revolutionary principles were at work. As he saw it, "a thesis of revolutionary nationalism still exists in some sectors of our party, as it does in the PRI, although their policies are more pragmatic."[32]

The Redeemers' Messengers

As "pragmatic" as its commitment to revolutionary principles may have been, the political economy practiced and the rhetoric forwarded by party leaders in 2013 suggested that the PRI still understood its legitimacy and future viability to be rooted in the legacy of the Mexican Revolution. To better understand this relationship I went to PRI headquarters and spoke with Alicia Sánchez Jara, who then, although ninety-two years old, still reported to work every day in her position as the party's official historian. After I met Jara in her office, we were escorted to the press room, where we were seated in the reporters' section and had our meeting recorded for posterity by a photographer. While we got to know one another, Jara, who is nearly blind, asked for my name and affiliation repeatedly, finally asking me to write down my information in large print with a marker so that she could see it and refer to it during our discussion.

A beloved figure who is widely referred to as *la abuelita del* PRI (the little grandmother of the PRI), Jara is an ambassador who relates to visitors a mix of national history, party lore, and personal anecdotes with the kindness and wisdom of a grandparent. She beamed with joy as she showed me a scrapbook with press clippings and pictures of her with various Mexican presidents and other officials. Born in 1921, she is a daughter of the Revolution and royalty at that, as she is the granddaughter of Heriberto Jara Corona, who was a partner of Madero, a general, an author of the Constitution of 1917, a state governor, and a man so vital to the story of the PRI that the auditorium in the party's headquarters is named in his honor. Jara's father also fought in the Revolution and later worked as an engineer for Ferrocarriles Nacionales de México, a company that based its operations just a few blocks from where the PRI compound now sits. Her father's employment with the railroad led to her involvement in the world of trade unionism, and she served for many years as the national director of the female section of the Mexican Union of Railroad Workers. As the union's representative for women, Jara distinguished herself advocating for the needs of office workers, nurses, and other female employees. Her work as a unionist continued, she told me, and she was proud of having marched that very year in a First of May parade at the front of a column of *ferrocarrileros*.

More than simply an heiress of the revolutionary family, Jara wrote her own chapters in the narrative through her work as a unionist and through the contribution she made to the cause of women's suffrage in Mexico. Jara's role as a primary protagonist of the women's vote, in fact, was a better-known facet of her story and garnered her commendations from Mexican presidents, regular interviews, and praise from feminist groups in Mexico. Despite this public acclaim, she described her role in the process to me with an air of modesty. "We, Mexican women, began to integrate ourselves in the revolutionary ranks after the path to education was opened. Then many women entered schools and we became doctors, chemists, teachers of course, and engineers. We became part of Mexican society. Other women joined the ranks of the PRI."[33] After women received the right to vote on October 19, 1953, Jara used her union position to mobilize the female vote in national elections spanning the period 1958 to 1994. Women's loyalty to the party, it seemed to Jara, was henceforth assured, given that it was the PRI that opened the door for their professional advancement and bestowed political rights upon them.

Jara's diminishment of her role in procuring the women's vote makes sense in the sociopolitical context of corporatism. In her mind the importance of her corporate group in the history of her nation trumped her individual contribution. To her, in fact, the PRI's place in Mexico transcended politics, and after discussing her life's details, she delved into a summary of the Revolution and her party's creation with the kind of detail and reverence befitting a historian and preacher. "When the people advanced in their triumph this party was born with another name, the National Revolutionary Party" she began. "Its founder was Plutarco Elías Calles, whose full-bodied monument we have here in our courtyard. The statues and busts that we have here are like the four cardinal directions of our facilities." In this regard, Jara saw even the city block upon which the PRI's buildings are located as endowed with revolutionary symbolism, and she described for me how each of its abutting streets—Avenida Insurgentes to the west, Calle Luis Donaldo Colosio to the north, Calle Jesús García to the east, and Calle de Heroes Ferrocarrileros to the south—were named for heroes of the Revolution or martyrs of the people's struggle for social justice.

As for her opinion of her party's transgressions, Jara expressed to me a belief similar to one she had stated before. Speaking to a reporter in 2012 she reasoned, "It's very easy for some to say that the PRI's seventy years were shameful, but those who do so forget that during this period the principal institutions of the country were established."[34] When I moved the topic of our discussion to the repression of students and unionists in the sixties and seventies she became a bit defensive, never apologizing for the violence but still rationalizing it as a necessary security measure. She explained, "There are phases of ours that I respect a lot because of the strength the party showed. We militants have had presidents from our party who have been very valuable, who have known the political terrain very well, and have been very disciplined."[35] When I broached the specific subject of Luis Echeverría, Jara was less enthusiastic. After some reflection, however, she affirmed her respect for him. He was "a valuable and disciplined member of the party," she felt, thus tacitly endorsing the line of support shown him by her decades earlier via *La maquinita* (the didactic children's book she published in the early 1970s) and by the PRI and the organized labor sector after the massacres at Tlatelolco and Corpus Christi.

Above all else Jara is a true believer in the goodness of her party and its inextricability from the fate of her nation. She admitted to crying when learning of the PRI's loss of the presidency in 2000 and was enthralled by the emergence of Peña Nieto as the presidential frontrunner in 2012. While glued to the television, she told an interviewer just prior to his election that "our candidate Peña is the only one who can save us and help us return [to the presidency]." After Peña Nieto's victory in the July election, she compared the PRI's resurrection to that experienced by her grandfather, whose career had been effectively ended by Calles but was redeemed when Cárdenas appointed him army inspector general and later had him lead the official party from 1939 to 1940. Shortly after Peña Nieto assumed office in December 2012 she was interviewed again and confirmed her belief in the redeeming powers of the new president. "He will comply," she predicted, in the face of criticisms that he was not moving fast enough to clean up corruption in Pemex and the Mexican Petroleum Workers' Union.[36] She showed the same faith in Peña Nieto some eight months later when I sat with her, assuring me as debate swirled around his energy reform proposal that "the great president that we have now has promised to return the government's focus on our needs. We know that he's going to comply."[37]

If Alicia Sánchez Jara was the PRI's messenger emeritus in 2013, Ignacio Zúñiga González fulfilled the same role for the party's organized labor sector. I met Zúñiga, who was then the CTM's director of communication and information, in the lobby of CTM headquarters on Monday, August 19, the day of the PRD's anti-energy-reform rally. Then seventy-three years old, he appeared much older and admitted as much with the explanation that "I've put myself in many fights for the working class." He was thin and had no hair and poor teeth, but despite his outward appearance he described himself as "skinny but very strong."[38] Like doña Alicia, don Nacho was loved by many and praised profusely by those who worked with him. Although his mind was sharp, I wondered upon meeting him how he handled the tasks demanded of someone in his position. He worked only afternoons and had no computer on his desk but only an ancient Remington typewriter that was missing the upper part of its encasement. Written on a piece of masking tape on the typewriter was PRENSA, meaning "press." There was also PRESA, which means "prisoner," written in marker below it, causing one to speculate whether the strange label was a misprint or otherwise.

When I first sat down with Zúñiga he was very preoccupied with the PRD demonstration that had occurred that morning in the Plaza de la República, just feet from the CTM's front steps. He was dismissive of the PRD and its tactics, calling its leaders "ambitious" (an insult in Mexico) and the policies it had implemented over two decades of governing the Federal District manipulative. Clearly nostalgic for the old days when the PRI governed the nation unilaterally, he fretted that libertinism was running wild in the city and that today's youth were lazy and filled with vice. "My generation wanted to serve the public, not take drugs." He also opposed the assault on unionism in recent times. "They [the PAN and the neoliberals] have tried to destroy unionism. We won't let it happen!" he pledged, ever confident in the ability of the CTM to defend Mexican workers from the abuses of the wealthy.

Following this treatment of current events our discussion turned toward historical topics. Zúñiga was enamored with Ricardo Flores Magón, a fellow journalist whom he praised for founding the Mexican

Liberal Party, leading the anti-Díaz movement, and dying in a pestilential cell for his beliefs. To Zúñiga, Flores Magón was incorruptible and a true redeemer of the Mexican working class. Another redeemer in his estimation was Fidel Velázquez, with whom he had worked closely for thirty-seven years. "Fidel Velázquez was a milkman," he reminded me. "He was very kind, intelligent, and he knew how to organize and unify workers." He was also "very animated in his style of giving speeches, although he spoke softly." "I was very fond of Fidel," he admitted, and he was almost giddy when showing me the objects in the "museum" that he had made in his office out of photographs, plaques, and a framed birth certificate of Velázquez. Focusing on a photograph showing Velázquez giving his weekly interview, surrounded by microphones, Zúñiga waxed hypothetically. "He was very nationalistic. If interviewed today he would say, 'We can't touch Article 27 because the subsoil resources are property of the Mexican people!' That's what Fidel would say," he presumed, while wagging his finger in the air for effect.

Zúñiga had reason to admire Velázquez, who was a powerful patron to him during his long career as a unionist, journalist, and politician. Zúñiga was just thirteen and working as a waiter when he joined his first trade union. After entering UNAM and earning a bachelor's degree in journalism, he joined the ranks of the Industrial Union of Graphic Arts Workers, an affiliate of the CTM. As a young journalist he wrote for *El Universal* and *El Día*, among other Mexico City dailies, until he was hired by Velázquez to be chief editor of *Ceteme* in 1974. Like many good *cetemistas*, he parlayed his connection to the labor monolith into a political position, winning office and serving a term in the Chamber of Deputies from 1979 to 1982. However, his undisputed role of a lifetime was his twenty-six-year stint (1974–2000) at the helm of *Ceteme*, through which he became the primary propagandist for the nation's most important labor organization. "How was it working with Velázquez?" I wanted to know. "Did there exist any differences in your opinions?" Zúñiga chuckled, then remarked self-deprecatingly, "He always saw my point of view."

Two days later we resumed our discussion over *molletes* and *limondadas* at a nearby VIPS, a popular chain restaurant. Turning to topics germane to this book, I asked Zúñiga to describe the relationship between the CTM and the government after 1968. His response was declarative: "Full solidarity." With this established, it became easy for him to demonstrate for me how the Díaz Ordaz and Echeverría governments felt compelled to give workers what they wanted and, most importantly, the New Federal Labor Law of 1970. The workers' press assumed an immensely important role following the implementation of the NLFT, said Zúñiga, as it "analyzed, renounced, and described violations of the law on the part of patrones." Additionally, it helped bolster workers' support for the regime during difficult times. Certainly *Ceteme* was supportive of Echeverría during Zúñiga's tenure, although I was curious about his impression of the ex-president nearly four decades onward. "What about Echeverría?" I asked him. "Did you know him? What was he like?" Yes, he assured me, "I knew him. He was very leftist, but for the nation. He was dynamic, as was his wife doña María Esther. He was progressive and he didn't let the millionaires run amok." Apparently Zúñiga was as impressed by Echeverría's class-based rhetoric in 2013 as he was in the 1970s, when he repeated it almost verbatim in the pages of *Ceteme*. When wage increases were won by the CTM in the mid-1970s, he called them victories over "ownership's vanity."[39] "This does not happen anymore," he regretted. "Today the consortiums come and destroy everything." Protectionist programs of the era like CONASUPO, which he praised as "great instruments for the sustenance of the family," had, he lamented, also gone out of existence. "They disappeared with [Vicente] Fox, with his ideas of Coca-Cola."[40]

Intentionally or unintentionally, Zúñiga ascribed Echeverría redeemer qualities for his defense of revolutionary ideals. Still, his admiration for the Mexican president was sterile when juxtaposed against his affection for Velázquez. I fleshed this difference out a bit, discovering that it was the sensitive issue of independent unionism that besmirched Echeverría in his view. The independent unionist movement led by electricistas in the 1970s, he told me, "was bad. It was Marxist." So too did he disdain the movement's leader, Rafael Galván, a man he believed "was never honest with the masses; he only wanted to reap advantages to turn his workers communist." In all, Zúñiga derided the Democratic Tendency and other independent labor organizations of the era for the ways they weakened workers' unity. Moreover, he did not view the organization's internal selection process, then or now, as undemocratic or corrupt. He felt in 2013 largely as he did in May 1974 when he wrote that a "democratic action ... marked by the vote and the will of the majorities" was exercised inside the ranks of the ten thousand unions affiliated with the CTM.[41]

Independent unionism still confounded CTM goals, but it was the economic policies ushered in by the técnicos in the 1980s, Zúñiga reckoned, that had done more harm to the working class than anything else. He roiled with anger when describing the North American Free Trade Agreement and its effects on Mexico. "NAFTA benefited the United States and Canada but not Mexico," he stated, because free trade did not mix with unionism because of its imperative to reduce labor costs and outsource jobs.[42] He corroborated his analysis with examples, describing for me how a Japanese entrepreneur had stolen the secrets of Mescal and sold a "Japanese tequila" that produced no profits for Oaxaca. Since NAFTA's implementation, he continued, farmers in Quintana Roo had been driven from their lands and were now taxi drivers in Cancún. Even narcotraffickers had been victimized by free trade, as they sprung from pools of potential workers who lost employment opportunities because of the failed policies of recent decades.

All of this analysis made Zúñiga, a lifelong priísta who for the better part of three decades shaped the terms of organized labor's discourse, sound exactly like the canvassers who were distributing anti-energy-reform leaflets on the steps of his building. Like those PRD partisans he viewed the changes ushered in thirty years before with the selling-off of the parastate companies as a turning point in the revolutionary narrative. And he too believed that economic nationalism was the ticket to Mexican prosperity. "It is not socialism!" he declared, referring to the state's ownership of natural resources. "It is a sharing of the natural forces ... of the primary natural materials of the country." Zúñiga's adherence to the ideals of the PRD did not end with this, and he rated Mexico's presidents in a way that most perredistas would concur with. Mexico's most proworker president, in his opinion, was Lázaro Cárdenas, because "he formed the unions." Its least worker-friendly leader, then, was not Vicente Fox or Felipe Calderón—the PAN presidents whom he judged had presided over Mexico's "long dark night of twelve years"—but Carlos Salinas, the priísta who "impulsed neoliberalism, undid the gains of the workers' movement, and allowed patrones to have more power than before."

His enmity toward some in the PRI notwithstanding, Zúñiga remained loyal to the system in which he was reared. On his office wall was even a photograph showing him shaking hands with Salinas as Velázquez stood nearby. When referring to Peña Nieto, he confirmed to me that he had voted for him in a way that would have been unnecessary for a cetemista and priísta twenty years earlier. Turning his attention to the energy reform proposal then under consideration, he again confirmed his party affiliation by asserting, "I am not with the men of the left. I support the president's reform proposal." His compliance, however, did not preclude him from expressing his own opinion—and frustration. "We have our own technology. It's pathetic that we're importing gas from India. In spite of all of this, we're third in the world in oil production. With reform we could be first." Constitutional reform hence was not a change that Zúñiga welcomed but a bitter pill the nation had to swallow if it wished to save its petroleum industry.

Our chat continued into the late evening, finally moving us from the restaurant into the Plaza de la República, which remained brightly lit because of a Youth Week concert that had just ended. We stopped to conclude the interview in that most appropriate venue—a place that had itself undergone a redemption of sorts through the recent additions of modernist lighting, a family-friendly splash pad, and an elevator to take visitors to the dome of the Monument to the Revolution. Scanning his surroundings, Zúñiga commented on the gentrification of the plaza and the adjoining neighborhood in recent years, almost drawing an analogy between the changing place and the PRI's latter-day embrace of middle- and upper-class priorities. Ever true to the revolutionary narrative, he was obligated, apparently, to stress the party's continued popular roots. He energetically protested my contention that the CTM's best days had passed but could not help but pine for a return of some of the organization's traditional values. Unionists in 2013, he believed, needed to militate as vigorously as had their predecessors to assert their constitutional rights and defend previously won benefits. They also stood to benefit from returning to the example set by Fidel Velázquez, that "self-taught milkman" who labored for decades and delivered to Mexican men and women life-altering laws and programs like the NLFT and the National Workers' Housing Institute. Finally, with a priísta reinstalled in Los Pinos and the PRI back in charge of the nation, he longed for the restoration of a vigorous collaboration between his organization and the government. Militancy, Fidel Velázquez, and a healthy collaboration between organized labor and the regime thus were tools that in Zúñiga's estimation could be used as effectively by workers in 2013 as they were by those who fought similar battles after 1968 to resist exploitation and realize the rights afforded them by the institutions and laws of the Mexican Revolution.

INTRODUCTION

1. "Redimir," in Real Academia Española, *Diccionario de la lengua española*.
2. "Redención" and "Redentor," in Real Academia Española, *Diccionario de la lengua española*.
3. See Becker, *Setting the Virgin on Fire*; and Krauze, *Redeemers*.
4. Joseph and Henderson, *Mexico Reader*, 422.
5. Suarez-Potts, *Making of Law*, 105.
6. Suarez-Potts, *Making of Law*, 107.
7. Chasteen, *Born in Blood and Fire*, 283.
8. Wasserman, *Mexican Revolution*, 112.
9. Wasserman, *Mexican Revolution*, 112–13.
10. Suarez-Potts, *Making of Law*, 136.
11. Middlebrook, *Paradox of Revolution*, 57.
12. Stevens, "Mexico's PRI."
13. Grayson, "Mexico, the PRI, and López Obrador," 287.
14. Santiago, *Ecology of Oil*, 240.
15. Middlebrook, *Paradox of Revolution*, 77.
16. Middlebrook, *Paradox of Revolution*, 80.
17. Aguilar Camín and Meyer, *In the Shadow of the Mexican Revolution*, 77.
18. Middlebrook, *Paradox of Revolution*, 80.
19. Santiago, *Ecology of Oil*, 324.
20. Gónzalez Casanova, *La democracia en México*, 233.
21. Instituto Nacional de Estudios Históricos de la Revolución Mexicana, *La constitución*, 34–35.
22. Instituto Nacional de Estudios Históricos de la Revolución Mexicana, *La constitución*, 41.

23. Spalding, *Organized Labor in Latin America*, 122.
24. Ashby, "Dilemma of the Mexican Trade Union Movement," 284.
25. Spalding, *Organized Labor in Latin America*, 124.
26. Snodgrass, "We Are All Mexicans Here," 328–29.
27. Snodgrass, "How Can We Speak of Democracy," 229.
28. Middlebrook, *Paradox of Revolution*, 94.
29. Middlebrook, *Paradox of Revolution*, 5–10.
30. My comfort with the term *collaborationism* also emanates from the work of Arnaldo Córdova and other Mexican labor scholars, who have used *colaboracionismo* (instead of the more generic *colaboración*) as a proper noun to refer to the reciprocal relationship that blossomed in the 1920s between the state and a privileged component of the organized labor movement. See Córdova, *La reforma del poder político en México*.
31. Mallon, "Reflections on the Ruins," 70.
32. Dion, *Workers and Welfare*, 19.
33. See Gillingham and Smith, *Dictablanda*.
34. Clark and Kaiser, *Culture Wars*, 36.

1. TLATELOLCO!

1. This summary of the events of August 27–28, 1968, is drawn from Gustavo Castillo García, "A 40 años: Persecución militar y desalojo del Zócalo," *La Jornada*, October 2, 2008, http://www.jornada.unam.mx/2008/08/27/index .php?section=politica&article=012n1pol.
2. Poniatowska, *Massacre in Mexico*, 45.
3. This summary of the events of 1968 is drawn from Carey, *Plaza of Sacrifices*; Poniatowska, *Massacre in Mexico*; Gómez Bonilla, "Cronología de movimiento estudiantiles"; and Gustavo Castillo García, "Tlatelolco, el infierno," *La Jornada*, October 2, 2008.
4. Ángeles, *El PRI en el gobierno*, 120–21.
5. Hernandez Juárez and Xelhuantzi López, *El sindicalismo*, 23.
6. Hernandez Juárez and Xelhuantzi López, *El sindicalismo*, 31.
7. See Benjamin Smith's chapter, "Building a State on the Cheap: Taxation, Social Movements, and Politics," in Gillingham and Smith, *Dictablanda*.
8. Rousseau, *México*, 66.
9. Dan La Botz, "Fidel Velazquez Sanchez: Embodiment of State Unionism," *Mexican Labor News and Analysis*, special issue: Fidel Velazquez Obituary, June 22, 1997, http://www.ueinternational.org/MLNA/old/vol2spec.html.
10. Sánchez González, *Los primeros cien años de Fidel*, 19.
11. Trueba Lara and BEF, *Fidel Velázquez*, 23–24.

12. Trueba Lara and BEF, *Fidel Velázquez*, 25–28. In addition to Velázquez, other notables among the five little wolves included Jesús Yurén Aguilar, the *lobito financiero*, who never wavered in his loyalty to Velázquez and led a long and fruitful life in the labor bureaucracy as head of the Federation of Federal District Workers' Unions, and Fernando Amilpa, the *lobito intelectual*, who initially rivaled Velázquez inside the labor bureaucracy and was a hero to some on the left.

13. See Sánchez González, *Los primeros cien años de Fidel*, chapter 1.

14. In total, Velázquez took charge of the CTM on ten separate occasions, having been elected secretary general nine times, serving 1941–44, 1944–47, 1956–62, 1962–68, 1968–74, 1974–80, 1980–86, 1986–92, and 1992–97, the year of his death; he also held the position in a nonelected way from 1950 to 1956. See Mejía Prieto, *Fidel Velázquez*.

15. Middlebrook, *Paradox of Revolution*, 113.

16. Middlebrook, *Paradox of Revolution*, 99–101.

17. Spalding, *Organized Labor in Latin America*, 129.

18. Middlebrook, *Paradox of Revolution*, 113–14.

19. Reyna and Trejo Delarbre, *La clase obrera*, 19–20.

20. Sánchez González, *Los primeros cien años de Fidel*, 107. According to the author this change signified the cancellation of whatever leftist influence the CTM claimed, even on paper. "The end of the original CTM," he writes, "was approaching"—a shift in values that tolled the bell for Lombardo, whose open rift with Amilpa made clear that the Marxist ideals he had instilled in the CTM had by 1947 become passé.

21. Middlebrook, *Paradox of Revolution*, 118.

22. Middlebrook, *Paradox of Revolution*, 143.

23. The most important of the groups created to serve as counterweights to growing CTM power was the CROC, sponsored by the state in 1952 and intended to be both loyal to the PRI and hostile to the CTM. See Middlebrook, *Paradox of Revolution*, 150–51.

24. Spalding, *Organized Labor in Latin America*, 132.

25. Spalding, *Organized Labor in Latin America*, 139.

26. Spalding, *Organized Labor in Latin America*, 135.

27. Female railway workers, called *rieleras*, formed an important part of the railway workers' challenge of the late 1950s. For more information, see Alegre, "*Las Rieleras.*"

28. Dan La Botz cites totals showing that sixty thousand of the one hundred thousand eligible workers voted in the contest, with the final (improbable) tally showing 59,749 votes for Vallejo and just 9 votes for the government candidate. See La Botz, *Mask of Democracy*, 72.

29. La Botz, *Mask of Democracy*, 70–72.
30. Spalding, *Organized Labor in Latin America*, 140.
31. Editorial, "A la clase trabajadora, al pueblo de México, al comité nacional del Partido Revolucionario Institucional," *Ceteme*, October 25, 1969, 5.
32. Trueba Lara and BEF, *Fidel Velázquez*, 72. The authors quip that for his attack on railway workers Velázquez was rewarded with a seat in the Senate.
33. Confederation of Mexican Workers, letter to the editor, *Tribuna Obrera*, October 21, 1968.
34. Sector Obrero, Sector Agrario, and Sector Popular de la Partido Revolucionario Institucional, letter to the editor, *Tribuna Obrera*, October 21, 1968, 2.
35. Editorial, "Ocurrirán asambleas cetemistas de orientación en todo el país," *Tribuna Obrera*, October 14, 1968, 4.
36. Editorial, "Misión cumplida," *Tribuna Obrera*, October 14, 1968, 3.
37. Carlos Monsiváis et al., letter to the editor, *El Día*, September 20, 1968, 6.
38. See Gómez Bonilla, "Cronología de movimiento estudiantiles."
39. See editorial section in *Por Qué?*, November 29, 1968, 4. The analogy had a more literary quality in its original Spanish, as "Plaza de las Tres Culturas" rhymed well with "Plaza de las Sepulturas."
40. Urbano Cortés, "El aparato oficial está en quiebra," *Por Qué?*, November 29, 1968, 10.
41. Editorial, "La Constitución ha muerto," *Por Qué?*, December 27, 1968, 3–9; and Carlos Ortega G., "¿Estamos en visperas de un nuevo 1910?," *Por Qué?*, February 7, 1969, 6–8.
42. See Blanche Petrich, "¡Prensa vendida!," *La Jornada*, October 2, 2008.
43. Sánchez González, *Los primeros cien años de Fidel*, 168.
44. Sánchez González, *Los primeros cien años de Fidel*, 170.
45. See Gómez Bonilla, "Cronología de movimiento estudiantiles."
46. See Gómez Bonilla, "Cronología de movimiento estudiantiles."
47. Archivo Histórico de la UNAM, Manuel Gutiérrez Paredes "Mariachito," Expediente 58/2840.
48. Archivo Histórico de la UNAM, Manuel Gutiérrez Paredes "Mariachito," Expediente 58/2897.
49. De Garay, Salazar, and Vega, *PNR, PRM, PRI*, 171.
50. See Gómez Bonilla, "Cronología de movimiento estudiantiles."
51. Middlebrook, *Paradox of Revolution*, 164–65.
52. Editorial, *Ceteme*, January 11, 1969, 2.
53. See editorial, "La Nueva Ley Federal del Trabajo vendrá a reafirmar el progreso socio-económico del país," *Ceteme*, November 8, 1969.

54. Editorial, "El PRI respalda a los trabajadores en su petición de una nueva ley del trabajo," *Ceteme*, February 26, 1969, 4.

55. Editorial, "El PRI respalda a los trabajadores en su petición de una nueva ley del trabajo," *Ceteme*, February 26, 1969, 4.

56. Demetrio Bolaños Espinosa, "Presentan la ley laboral: Primera lectura ante los diputados que la discutirán el próximo martes," *El Universal*, October 31, 1969, 13.

57. The final version of the NLFT included 890 articles, not 889, in addition to 12 transitory articles at the end of the code.

58. Secretaría del Trabajo y Previsión Social, *Ley Federal del Trabajo*, 275.

59. Bolaños Espinosa, "Presentan la ley laboral: Primera lectura ante los diputados que la discutirán el próximo martes," *El Universal*, October 31, 1969, 15. See Article 163 in the NLFT.

60. Secretaría del Trabajo y Previsión Social, *Ley Federal del Trabajo*, 268.

61. Editorial, "Año 1936: La historia vuelve a repetirse," *Ceteme*, November 8, 1969, 2.

62. Editorial, "Es ya tradicional la inconformidad del sector patronal en todos los tiempos," *Ceteme*, November 8, 1969, 2.

63. See editorial, "Primero de mayo," and editorial, "'Presidente Obrerista de México' así lo afirmaron los trabajadores," *Ceteme*, May 2, 1970, 1–12. First celebrated in Chicago on May 1, 1887, and proclaimed the International Day of Labor by the Second International Socialist of Paris in 1889, May 1 has since been used as an opportunity to take to the streets to honor the sacrifice of the "Haymarket Eight," those workers punished in Chicago, some executed, for their participation in events that followed a national strike waged on May 1, 1886, and to advocate for contemporary causes of workers everywhere.

64. Enrique García Bernal, "750 mil trabajadores en la imponente y brillante parada obrera de ayer," *El Nacional*, May 2, 1970, 4.

65. Guillermo Velarde, "Tardó tres horas en pasar la columna de trabajadores," *Excélsior*, May 2, 1970, 9.

66. Enrique García Bernal, "750 mil trabajadores en la imponente y brillante parada obrera de ayer," *El Nacional*, May 2, 1970, 4. The banners read: "La nueva Ley Federal del Trabajo, una conquista más de los regimenes de la Revolución que ha merecido el aplauso y reconocimiento de los trabajadores del D.D.F."; "Así se honra a los Mártires de Chicago"; "Así se cumple con México"; "Gracias, señor Presidente Díaz Ordaz."

67. Guillermo Velarde, "Tardó tres horas en pasar la columna de trabajadores," *Excélsior*, May 2, 1970, 9.

68. Enrique Garcia Bernal, "750 mil trabajadores en la imponente y brillante parada obrera de ayer," *El Nacional*, May 2, 1970, 4.

69. Mexico's participation in the *Apollo 11* moon landing was a significant point of national pride.

70. "750,000 trabajadores en un desfile grandioso y emotivo," *El Universal*, May 2, 1970, 1.

71. Juan Chávez Rebollar, "Presidente Obrerista, lo declaron los trabajadores," *El Nacional*, May 2, 1970, 1.

72. "Patrones y obreros deberán usarla y cumplirla con cabal honestidad," *El Universal*, May 2, 1970, 7.

73. Guillermo Velarde, "Mensaje a patrones y obreros, tras el desfile," *Excélsior*, May 2, 1970, 13.

74. Juan Chávez Rebollar, "Patriótica exhortación del primer mandatario," *El Nacional*, May 2, 1970, 1.

75. Editorial, "Primero de mayo," *Ceteme*, May 2, 1970, 1.

76. Editorial, "¿Qué es el Partido Revolucionario Institucional?," *Ceteme*, May 30, 1970, 4.

77. Editorial, "Después del campeonato de fútbol: Se emplezará a huelga a las líneas de autobuses de Distrito Federal," *Ceteme*, May 30, 1970, 4.

2. ON THE REDEEMER'S TRAIL

1. Editorial, "Síntesis biográfica del hombre revolucionario que regirá el destino de nuestra nación," *Ceteme*, October 25, 1969, 1.

2. At the time Mexico's secretary of internal affairs was charged with overseeing the electoral system and preserving domestic security. The exception was Adolfo López Mateos (president, 1958–64), who served as secretary of labor and social welfare in the administration of Adolfo Ruiz Cortines.

3. Antonio Lara Barragán, "Según industriales, comerciantes y artesanos, se ha logrado un acierto," *El Universal*, October 23, 1969, 1.

4. Demetrio Bolaños Espinosa, "Echeverría, precandidato: Simultáneamente manifestaron ayer su decisión los tres sectores del P.R.I.," *El Universal*, October 22, 1969, 1.

5. José Rigoberto López, "Apoyos de los estados," *El Universal*, October 22, 1969, 17.

6. Jorge Coca P., "Datos biográficos," *El Universal*, 17.

7. Elias Chávez, "La opinión del pueblo," *El Universal*, October 22, 1969, 1.

8. "Luis Echeverria Alvarez," Encyclopedia.com, http://www.encyclopedia.com/.

9. Cosío Villegas, *El estilo personal de gobernar*, 16.

10. Archivo General de la Nación (hereafter AGN), Dirección General de

Investigaciones Polítícas y Sociales (hereafter DGIPS), Fondo Secretaría de Gobernación (hereafter SG), box 867, folder 1, volume 1, "Indice Cronologico de Discursos, Alocuciones y Entrevistas. Precampaña Presidencial de Luis Echeverría Álvarez, 21 Oct–15 Nov 1969, Discurso Ante los Corresponsales Extranjeros, 21 October," 1.

11. AGN, DGIPS, SG, box 867, folder 1, volume 1, "Indice Cronologico de Discursos, Alocuciones y Entrevistas. Precampaña Presidencial de Luis Echeverría Álvarez, 21 Oct–15 Nov, 1969," 6–7.

12. AGN, DGIPS, SG, box 862, folder 5, volume 32, "Indice Cronologico de Discursos, Alocuciones y Entrevistas. Campaña Presidencial de Luis Echeverría Álvarez, Morelos, 4–9 Junio, 1970," 79.

13. AGN, DGIPS, SG, box 862, folder 5, volume 32, "Indice Cronologico de Discursos, Alocuciones y Entrevistas. Campaña Presidencial de Luis Echeverría Álvarez, Morelos, 4–9 Junio, 1970," 80.

14. AGN, DGIPS, SG, box 867, folder 1, volume 1, "Ante una comisión del Sindicato de Trabajadores Ferrocarrileros de la Republica Mexicana, 22 Oct.," 12.

15. See editorial, "Luis Echeverria A. candidato de los trabajadores cetemistas," and editorial, "Nuestro partido, postulará a la presidencia de la república al Lic. Luis Echeverría Álvarez," *Ceteme*, October 25, 1969.

16. Editorial, "Con los obreros a la vanguardia nuestro candidato confía en el desarrollo económico-social del país," *Ceteme*, October 25, 1969, 16.

17. Editorial, "'Unidos con nuestro partido y con ud. México continuará adelante' . . . F.V.," *Ceteme*, October 25, 1969, 4.

18. Editorial, "Echeverría, el hombre," *Ceteme*, October 25, 1969, 4–5.

19. Editorial, "Cumpliré lo que ofrezco: Apasionada fe obrerista manifestó LEA en el VIII Congreso FTDF-CTM," *Ceteme*, November 1, 1969, 5.

20. See Luis Echeverría Álvarez, "Protesto como candidato del PRI a la presidencia de la República," in Partido Revolucionario Institucional, *Pensamiento y doctrina*.

21. De Garay, Salazar, and Vega, *PNR, PRM, PRI*, 174–75.

22. AGN, DGIPS, SG, box 862, folder 1, volume 23, "Indice Cronologico de Discursos, Alocuciones y Entrevistas. Campaña Presidencial de Luis Echeverría Álvarez, Nuevo Leon, 12–17 Abril, 1970," 1/7.

23. AGN, DGIPS, SG, box 1107A, folder 2, "Estado de Baja California, Información Periodística," June 10, 1970.

24. Editorial, "Mañana: Fiesta civica del pueblo. Los mexicanos votaremos en favor de los candidatos del P.R.I. por ser garantes de los ideales de la Revolución Mexicana. En las urnas arrasaremos a la reacción y a sus candidatos," *Ceteme*, July 4, 1970, 2.

25. Editorial, "La abstención política debilita la fuerza ciudadana y frena el progreso del país," *Ceteme*, July 4, 1970, 1–2.

26. Carlos Arreguín, "Porqué es inútil votar," *Por Qué?*, July 2, 1970, 8.

27. AGN, DGIPS, SG, box 1107A, folder 2, "Estado de Baja California, Información de Tijuana," May 4, 1970.

28. AGN, DGIPS, SG, box 1128, folder 2, "Estado de Chiapas, Información de Tuxtla Gutiérrez," July 2, 1970.

29. AGN, DGIPS, SG, box 1128, folder 2, "Estado de Chiapas, Información Periodística," June 7, 1970.

30. De Garay, Salazar, and Vega, *PNR, PRM, PRI*, 176.

31. AGN, DGIPS, SG, box 1122A, folder 3, "Noticias Especiales," July 16, 1970.

32. Editorial, "La patria de luto," *Ceteme*, October 24, 1970, 1.

33. Editorial, "Lázaro Cárdenas: Una lagrima, Un impulso," *Ceteme*, October 24, 1970, 5.

34. Froylan M. López Návarez, "Los dolientes," *Excélsior*, October 21, 1970, 7.

35. *Excélsior*, October 20, 1970, 14.

36. See the photograph in *Ceteme*, October 24, 1970, 3, for a characteristically stern and strong visual of this.

37. *Excélsior*, October 21, 1970, 29.

38. Fernando del Collado, "El árbol genealógico de los herederos de Los Pinos," November 29, 2012, Quién. com, http://www.quien.com/espectaculos/2009/09/09/ el-arbol-genealogico-de-los-herederos-de-los-pinos.

39. Augustín, *Tragicomedia mexicana 2*, 15.

40. "Biografía de Zuno Arce, María Esther," Omnibiografia.com, http://omnibio grafia.com/biografias/biografia.php?id=179 (site no longer available).

41. Rafael Tinoco "El verdadero Cárdenas," *Por Qué?*, November 5, 1970, 3.

42. Rafael Tinoco, "El verdadero Cárdenas," *Por Qué?*, November 5, 1970, 3–6.

43. In a 2008 documentary several survivors of the massacre expressed a belief in Echeverría's primary culpability. See Gueilbert, *La masacre de Tlatelolco*.

44. Barreto, "México disfruta de una revolución actuante!" (illustration), *Por Qué?*, December 4, 1969, 24.

45. Barreto, "México disfruta de una revolución actuante!" (illustration), *Por Qué?*, December 4, 1969, 24–25.

46. Demetrio Vallejo, "Habla Echeverría: ¿Demagogia o realidad?," *Por Qué?*, December 18, 1969, 19.

47. Augustín, *Tragicomedia mexicana 2*, 18.

48. "President Echeverria's .N. Aspirations," August 1, 1975, History Lab, http://www.history-lab.org/documents/1975MEXICO06867.

49. Aguilar Camín and Meyer, *In the Shadow of the Mexican Revolution*, 207.
50. For an analysis that describes Echeverría's policy toward students and intellectuals as highly contradictory but generally more permissive of dissent, see Camp, *Intellectuals and the State*.
51. Zolov, *Refried Elvis*, 191–92.
52. Aguilar Camín and Meyer, *In the Shadow of the Mexican Revolution*, 208.
53. Zabludovsky asked Echeverría, "Caiga quien caiga?" to which the president answered, "Categóricamente sí, Jacobo."
54. See Laura Itzel Castillo Juárez, "Recordando a heberto," *La Jornada*, April 5, 2002.
55. Carey, *Plaza of Sacrifices*, 165.
56. Editorial, "Respaldo absoluto al régimen de la revolución mexicana," *Ceteme*, June 12, 1971, 8.
57. See photograph in *Ceteme*, June 19, 1971, 7.
58. Editorial, "Se manifestó el pueblo ante su presidente leal a México," *Ceteme*, June 19, 1971, 7–8.
59. Editorial, "¡Ni un paso atrás! México no retrocederá . . . ," *Ceteme*, June 19, 1971, 4.

3. "THE GOVERNMENT OF THE REPUBLIC"
1. Editorial, "Cambios en el Comité Nacional de Nuestro Partido," *Ceteme*, July 29, 1972, 4.
2. Editorial, "El C. Fidel Velázquez opinó: El nuevo dirigente del P.R.I. continuará la obra del partido," *Ceteme*, February 24, 1972, 4.
3. Editorial, "PRI: Hora del realismo," *Excélsior*, February 22, 1972, 6; editorial, "Cambios en el PRI," *El Universal*, February 22, 1972, 6.
4. Reyes Heroles also oversaw the creation of the Mexican Institute of Petroleum to study the scientific and technological development of the industry, and research conducted there yielded techniques that reduced production costs.
5. Alejandro Sobarzo Loaiza, "Jesús Reyes Heroles y su paso por petróleos Mexicanos," in Reyes Heroles, *Jesús Reyes Heroles y el petróleo*, 14. Also see works and commentaries included in Meyer, *Jesús Reyes Heroles*, vol. 2.
6. Ruiz Naufal, *La industria petrolera en México*, 423.
7. Alejandro Sobarzo Loaiza, "Jesús Reyes Heroles y su paso por petróleos Mexicanos," in Reyes Heroles, *Jesús Reyes Heroles y el petróleo*, 12.
8. Ferry, *Not Ours Alone*, 10–13.
9. Santiago, *Ecology of Oil*, 296–97.
10. Ferry, *Not Ours Alone*, 338.
11. Ferry, *Not Ours Alone*, 201.

12. Carlos Ortega G., "El petróleo mexicano: 225 millones para una 'nacionalización' fraudulenta," *Por Qué?*, June 27, 1969, 7.

13. Enrique Galván Ochoa, "Guia para entender el proyecto de reforma energetica," *La Jornada*, August 15, 2013, 8. Cárdenas's intentions would be debated again in 2013 upon the presentation of President Enrique Peña Nieto's energy sector reform proposal. Peña's proposal included similar shared profit contracts that he contended Cárdenas had authorized during his presidency. See this study's epilogue for additional analysis.

14. Ruiz Naufal, *La industria petrolera en México*, 424.

15. Galeano, *Open Veins of Latin America*, 169.

16. Galeano, *Open Veins of Latin America*, 219.

17. AGN, LEA, Secretaría de Programación y Presupuesto 658 (hereafter SPP), La Política de Inversiones Públicas en México, Primer Seminario para el Estudio del Desarrollo Económico y Reforma Administrativa, IEPES, PRI, por Fernando Paz Sánchez, November 13, 1974, 2–3.

18. Condumex, Fondo CMXV-3, Impresos de Federico González Garza, 1930–1931, folder 1; Juan Sánchez Azcona, "Los postulados internacionales de la Revolucion," *Gráfico*, June 9, 1930.

19. See Córdova, *La reforma del poder político en México*.

20. Quintero Ramírez, *La sindicalización*, 38–39.

21. Quintero Ramírez, *La sindicalización*, 40.

22. For an example of the former kind, see Carlos Ortega G., "Santa Annas del siglo XX: México en manos extranjeras," *Por Qué?*, December 25, 1969, 7. For an example of the latter, see editorial, "El estado ha superado los anacrónicos principios del liberalismo económico," *Ceteme*, November 15, 1969, 5.

23. Editorial, "Nuestra economía va hacia el monopolismo," *Ceteme*, May 2, 1970, 3.

24. Partido Revolucionario Institucional, *Reunión nacional*, xxv–xxvi.

25. Partido Revolucionario Institucional, *Reunión nacional*, xii.

26. Johnson, *Tercer mundo vs. imperialismo*, 30–31.

27. Jorge Coca P., "Reivindicación del cobre: La Compañía Minera de Cananea quedó ayer mexicanizada," *El Universal*, August 28, 1971, 11.

28. AGN, LEA, SPN, box 862, folder 766/170, "Mexicanización de Cananea, 27 Agosto 1971," 3.

29. "Manifestaciones de júbilo en todo Sonora," *El Universal*, August 28, 1971, 1, 11.

30. Roberto Elzy Torres, letter to the editor, *El Heraldo de Cananea*, August 28, 1971, 1.

31. Editorial, "A propósito de la mexicanización de la empresa mineral local," *El Heraldo de Cananea*, September 1, 1971, 1.

32. See Marcelo Carrillo, "Razonando," *El Heraldo de Cananea*, September 8, 1971, 1, 6.

33. Cámara de Comercio de Cananea, "Referente a la mexicanización de la cía: Minera de Cananea, S.A. de C.V.," *El Heraldo de Cananea*, September 11, 1971, 1.

34. See "Cámara Minera de México Asamblea General 1971," *Boletín Financiero y Minero de México*, pt. 3, August 26, 1971, 1, 5; pt. 4, August 27, 1971, 1, 11–12.

35. "Volumen y valor de la exportacion minero metalurgica de Mexico—1970," *Boletín Financiero y Minero de México*, August 27, 1971, 11.

36. Jorge Coca P., "Reivindicación del cobre: La Compañia Minera de Cananea quedó ayer mexicanizada," *El Universal*, August 28,1971, 1, 11.

37. Passages are taken from editorial, "Ni un paso atrás en materia de nacionalizaciones," SUTERM, October 1973, 4–5.

38. Editorial, "Tarifas electricas con justicia social," SUTERM, October 1973, 21.

39. Editorial, "La prensa nacional comenta lo dicho por el SUTERM," SUTERM, June 1973, 14–15.

4. RESTORING THE REVOLUTIONARY CORPUS

1. *Excélsior*, February 22, 1972, 1, 24.

2. Aquinas, *De regimine principum*, bk. 1, chap. 1.

3. Dealy, "Tradition of Monistic Democracy," 627.

4. Dealy, "Tradition of Monistic Democracy," 631.

5. See Aquinas, *De regimine principum*, bk. 1, chap. 5.

6. Dealy, "Tradition of Monistic Democracy," 629–30.

7. 1 Corinthians 12, New International Version Online Bible, http://www.biblica.com/en-us/bible/online-bible/niv/1-corinthians/12/.

8. Dion, *Workers and Welfare*, 25.

9. "Antecedentes Históricos," Junta Federal de Conciliación y Arbitraje, http://www.stps.gob.mx/bp/secciones/junta_federal/secciones/quienes_somos/antecedentes.html.

10. Spalding, *Organized Labor in Latin America*, 124.

11. Editorial, "Como se integran las juntas de conciliación y arbitraje," *Ceteme*, August 2, 1969.

12. Basurto, *La clase obrera*, 37–38.

13. Santiago, *Ecology of Oil*, 324.

14. Reyna and Trejo Delarbre, *La clase obrera*, 19–20.

15. Basurto, *La clase obrera*, 36.

16. Basurto, *La clase obrera*, 78.

17. Editorial, "En una reunión de nueve horas, no es posible resolver problemas que por muchos años no han tenido solución," *Ceteme*, May 22, 1971, 2.

18. Editorial, "Ante el presidente del CEN del PRI: 'La CTM reclama el primero puesto para luchar contra los enemigos de la Revolución y de México'—F. Velázquez," *Ceteme*, February 26, 1972, 1.

19. Schers, *Popular Sector*, 174.

20. Editorial, "El PRI contra quienes poseen bienes en exceso: Reyes Heroles," *Ceteme*, July 29, 1972, 1.

21. "Fondo mutualista del SUTERM," *SUTERM*, May 1973, 6–7.

22. See photo in *SUTERM*, June 1973, 24.

23. Spalding, *Organized Labor in Latin America*, 138.

24. Consult *Ceteme*, 1970–76, for numerous reprints of this message.

25. Middlebrook, *Paradox of Revolution*, 154.

26. Ángeles, *El PRI en el gobierno*, 14.

27. See *El Día*, April 24, 1974.

28. *El Universal*, May 18, 1971, 1.

29. See Instituto Nacional de Estadística y Geografía, Dirección General de Estadísticas, VI Censo General de Población (1940); and Instituto Nacional de Estadística y Geografía, Dirección General de Estadísticas, IX Censo General de Población y Vivienda (1970). Note that these figures do not include people who resided in communities that adjoined the Federal District and came into the city on a daily basis for work. With them included, the real population of the megalopolis in 1970 was much higher, at about 8.8 million.

30. See *Ultimas Noticias*, May 14, 1974.

31. See *El Día*, April 24, 1974.

32. Editorial, "Hombre y mujer, deben tomar conciencia para tener un hijo," *Ceteme*, February 15, 1975, 1.

33. Moreno, *Yankee Don't Go Home*, 34–36.

34. Sherman, "Mexican Miracle and Its Collapse," 575.

35. Suárez, *Echeverría en el sexenio*, 206.

36. Moreno, *Yankee Don't Go Home*, 34.

37. Editorial, "Compañero: Defiende tu salario," *Ceteme*, October 9, 1976, 15.

38. Editorial, "Los electricistas de Celaya contrarrestan la carestia," *SUTERM*, August/September, 1973, 14.

39. AGN, LEA, Banco de México, box 1113, "El Gobierno Mexicano," September 1–30, 1976, 49.

40. Editorial, "El Suterm demanda medidas efectivas contra la carestía," *SUTERM*, June 1974, 12–13.

41. See coverage in *El Norte*, June 25, 1974.

42. See coverage in *El Norte*, June 28, 1974.

43. Editorial, "Un positive informe de gobierno del Presidente Luis Echeverría," *Ceteme*, September 7, 1974, 7.

5. "AÑOS DE HUELGA"

1. A *regiomontano* is someone who hails from Monterrey, which literally means "king's mountain."

2. Ramiro Flores, "Así era Eugenio Garza Sada," *El Norte*, September 18, 1973, 2.

3. AGN, DGIPS, SG, box 1206A, folder 3, "Estado de Nuevo León, Información de Monterrey—No Se Ha Establecido El Momento La Identidad de los Individuos," September 17, 1973.

4. See Ortíz Rivera, *Eugenio Garza Sada*.

5. AGN, DGIPS, SG, box 1206A, folder 3, "Estado de Nuevo León, Información de Monterrey—A las 9:00 Hrs. Aproximadamente Fue Muerto Garza Sada," September 17, 1973; AGN, DGIPS, SG, "Estado de Nuevo León, Información de Monterrey—Modesto Torres Briones Chofer de Eugenio Garza Sada, Fallecio a las 9:20 Hrs," September 17, 1973.

6. "Intentan septiembre negro," *El Norte*, September 18, 1973, 1.

7. "Sepultan hoy a don Eugenio Garza Sada," *El Norte*, September 18, 1973, 1.

8. Ramiro Flores, "Así era Eugenio Garza Sada," *El Norte*, September 18, 1973, 2.

9. "Hasta la tumba acompaña su chofer a don Eugenio," *El Norte*, September 19, 1973, 1.

10. The low estimate, 125,000, is given in government intelligence reports. See AGN, DGIPS, SG, box 1206A, folder 3, "Información de Monterrey, El Lic. Luis Echeverria Estuvo Presente en el Sepelio de Don Eugenio Garza Sada," September 18, 1973; 250,000 is the high estimate, cited in "250 mil personas en imponente acto, dicen adiós a don Eugenio Garza Sada," *El Porvenir*, September 19, 1973, 1.

11. "Acompañan millares a D. Eugenio," *El Norte*, September 19, 1973, 1.

12. "Urge poner hasta aquí," *El Norte*, September 19, 1973, 1.

13. The advertisement was printed in full in *El Norte* and other major newspapers across the country on September 19, 1973. It was endorsed by the following organizations: Cámara Nacional de Comercio de Monterrey, José Luis Coindreau, president; Cámara de la Industria de Transformación de Nuevo León, Humberto Lobo, president; Centro Patronal de Nuevo León, Francisco Garza González, president; Centro Bancario de Monterrey, Bernabe A. Del Valle, president.

14. Rocha's letter, along with some others deemed sufficiently critical to be

subversive, were reproduced in full in DGIPS reports on September 20 and September 22, 1973. See AGN, DGIPS, SG, box 1206A, folder 3, "Estado de Nuevo León, Información Periodística," September 20 and 22, 1973. Of particular interest was an "Open Letter" sent to the presidential first couple by a committee of the National Union of Mothers of the Family dated September 20, 1973. In it Mexican mothers posed a hypothetical to the First Lady, asking her what she would do when the terrorism that her husband's regime had permitted touched her personally. "Will it be tomorrow . . . [when you experience] the kidnapping of a son?" they inquired plaintively. Unfortunately, Zuno de Echeverría would face a similar dilemma on August 28, 1974, when her father, José Guadalupe Zuno, was kidnapped in Guadalajara by the same Liga Comunista 23 de septiembre that had earlier hijacked the Mexicana jet and planned the failed abduction of Garza Sada in Monterrey.

15. Guillermo Rocha, letter to the editor, *El Norte*, September 20, 1973.

16. See stories in *El Norte*, September 18, 1973.

17. Guillermo Rocha, letter to the editor, *El Norte*, September 20, 1973.

18. Secretaría del Trabajo y Previsión Social, ed., *Revista Mexicana del Trabajo* 3–4 (July–December 1971): 11. Legal contracts were created when two-thirds of a given sector's registered employees voted in favor of regularizing work conditions for all companies involved in that industry.

19. See Schers, *Popular Sector*, chap. 8.

20. Nuncio, *El Grupo Monterrey*, 13.

21. "¿Monterrey . . . Culpable?," *El Norte*, October 18, 1976, insert.

22. This is according to statistics compiled by the Confederation of Mexican Owners and published on its website, http://www.coparmex.org.mx.

23. *Boletín Financiero y Minero de México*, October 30, 1969, 12.

24. AGN, DGIPS, SG, box 1206A, folder 3, "Estado de Nuevo León, Información de Monterrey—Un Grupo de Aproximadamente 250 Normalistas, Efectuaron una Manifestacion y un Mitin Frente," September 17, 1973.

25. Editorial, "Eficiencia," *El Norte*, May 1, 1974, 1.

26. Nuncio, *El Grupo Monterrey*, 36.

27. For a magnificent case study of these dynamics in action in Monterrey, see chapter 3 of Snodgrass, *Deference and Defiance*, 54–81.

28. Nuncio, *El Grupo Monterrey*, 8.

29. Michael Snodgrass explains that industrial paternalism in Monterrey developed as a tactical response to militant unionism and fears of government regulation. Company funds were established there to rival state-run funds, and well-financed company cooperatives offered genuine rewards that outweighed the risks of labor activism. These developments helped workers in

Monterrey forsake unions in favor of company-sponsored cooperatives and bred a good deal of worker loyalty to their employers. See Snodgrass, "Birth and Consequences," 119–21.

30. Again, see Nuncio, *El Grupo Monterrey*, chap. 1. In his discussion Nuncio draws much information from Carmen Lira, "Férreo control patronal del sindicalismo Monterrey," *Uno Más Uno*, October 4, 1979.

31. See Trueba Lara, *Fidel Velázquez*.

32. "Emplaza más la CTM," *El Norte*, June 22, 1974, 7-B.

33. *Paro* is more literally translated as "work stoppage," although I have opted to use the term *lockout* so as not to confuse an employer's decision to stop production with a workers' strike.

34. *El Sol*, June 7, 1974.

35. *El Sol*, June 10, 1974.

36. *El Sol*, June 11, 1974.

37. *El Sol*, June 10, 1974.

38. *El Sol*, June 11, 1974.

39. *El Sol*, June 14, 1974.

40. "Protesta por huelgas masivas: Parará el comercio el Martes," *El Sol*, June 15, 1974, 1.

41. "Paro comercial habrá el martes," *El Norte*, June 16, 1974, 1-B.

42. *El Norte*, June 17, 1974.

43. *El Norte*, June 18, 1974.

44. *El Norte*, June 19, 1974.

45. *El Norte*, June 18, 1974.

46. *El Norte*, June 20, 1974.

47. Editorial, "La C.T.M. contra quienes pretenden mantener sus privilegios, a costa de los trabajadores," *Ceteme*, June 22, 1974, 1.

48. Editorial, "Ante el problema de las gasolineras: Los trabajadores cetemistas, jamás renunciarán al derecho de huelga: Licenciado Raúl Caballero," *Ceteme*, June 22, 1974, 8.

49. *El Norte*, June 20, 1974.

50. *El Norte*, June 21, 1974.

51. *El Norte*, June 22, 1974.

52. *Cachirul*, according to the Royal Spanish Academy's *Diccionario de la lengua española*, is a distinct Mexicanism derived from *cachirulo*, but it specifically means (a) little comb; or (b) illegitimate child. It is from the latter definition that I derive my understanding of the term.

53. *El Norte*, June 22, 1974.

54. "Denuncian maniobras," *El Norte*, June 22, 1974, 7-B.

55. Editorial, "Fin al conflicto de gasolineros de Monterrey," *Ceteme*, June 29, 1974, 6.

56. *El Norte*, June 23, 1974.

57. Ramón Garza, "Perdiendo gana la CTM," *El Norte*, June 23, 1974, 1-B.

58. *El Norte*, June 25, 1974.

59. *El Norte*, June 27, 1974.

60. See reprint of Ernesto Leal Flores, "El convenio gasolinero, monumento de confusiones y violaciones a la Ley," *¡Óigame!*, featured in *El Norte*, June 25, 1974, 5-A.

61. Editorial, "Convenio o burla," *El Norte*, June 25, 1974, 1.

62. Editorial, "En 1974 se repite la rebelión patronal en Monterrey," *Ceteme*, June 29, 1974, 6.

63. See *Ceteme*, June 29, 1974.

64. See *El Norte*, June 26, 1974.

65. See *El Norte*, June 27, 1974.

6. "THE FALSE REDEMPTION OF MAY 1"

1. Editorial, illustration, "Dignamente . . . ," *El Norte*, May 1, 1970, 2-A. The caption reads, "Pos, Aquí no más mano . . . festejando el Día de Trabajo."

2. "La falsa redención del 1º. de Mayo . . . ," *¡Óigame!*, May 1, 1970, insert.

3. Ramírez Fonseca, *Obligaciones y derechos*, 7.

4. Trueba Urbina and Trueba Barrera, *Ley Federal del Trabajo*, 15–17.

5. Secretaría del Trabajo y Previsión Social, *Ley Federal del Trabajo*, 8.

6. Secretaría del Trabajo y Previsión Social, *Ley Federal del Trabajo*, 302.

7. Cavazos Flores, *Manual de aplicación*, 338.

8. Cavazos Flores, *Manual de aplicación*, 308.

9. Cavazos Flores, *Manual de aplicación*, 267.

10. Secretaría del Trabajo y Previsión Social, *Ley Federal del Trabajo*, 286.

11. Trueba Urbina and Trueba Barrera, *Ley Federal del Trabajo*, 33.

12. Secretaría del Trabajo y Previsión Social, *Ley Federal del Trabajo*, 296.

13. See Title 2, Chapter 10, Modifications to Labor Contracts, in the 1931 Federal Labor Law. See Trueba Urbina and Trueba Barrera, *Ley Federal del Trabajo*, 76.

14. Secretaría del Trabajo y Previsión Social, *Ley Federal del Trabajo*, 297.

15. Trueba Urbina and Trueba Barrera, *Ley Federal del Trabajo*, 77.

16. Secretaría del Trabajo y Previsión Social, *Ley Federal del Trabajo*, 298.

17. Secretaría del Trabajo y Previsión Social, *Ley Federal del Trabajo*, 286.

18. AGN, Secretaría del Trabajo y Previsión Social (hereafter STPS), Junta Federal de Conciliación y Arbitraje (hereafter JFCA), No. 12-1973, box 1310,

folder "Emplazamiento a Huelga planteado por el Sindicato Librado Rivera Conexos y Similares de Aluminio Vs. Las Empresas Aluminio Inmobiliaria Aluminio," Collective Contract, "Contrato Colectivo del Sindicato Librado Rivera de Trabajadores en General Conexos y Similares de Aluminio, S.A. de C.V. y las Cmpñías Aluminio, S.A. de C.V. e Inmobiliaria Aluminio, S.A. de C.V.," December 11, 1972, 1, 13.

19. Cavazos Flores, *Manual de aplicación*, 266.

20. Cavazos Flores, *Manual de aplicación*, 281.

21. Barona de la O and Huerta Cruz, "Consideraciones sobre la contratación colectiva," *Revista Mexicana del Trabajo* 1, no. 5 (January–March 1975): 128.

22. This conclusion is drawn from an evaluation of documents contained in AGN, STPS, Dirección General de Inspección Federal del Trabajo (hereafter DGIFT), boxes 1641–44, 1646, report, "Departamento Seguridad Industrial, Visitas de Inspección de Seguridad Industrial. Acta Num. XXXXX. Fecha XX/XX," 1970–71.

23. AGN, STPS, DGIFT, box 1079, folder 13/100D-VII-75-11/1, reports, "Informe de Labores Correspondiente al Mes de Noviembre Uno y Dos.—Deleg.— Puebla, Pue" and "Acta de Inspeccion Inicial a la Empresa 'Productos Alimenticios la Morena, S.A.,'" November 3, 1975.

24. AGN, STPS, Delegación Federal del Trabajo (hereafter DFT) No. 4, box 1200, folder D.IV/201;700(16) "75"/29, "Empacadora Regiomontana," S.A., Inspeccion Inicial Ordenada por el Director de Inspeccion del Trabajo, Inspección Inicial, December 15, 1975, 1–7.

25. AGN, STPS, DFT No. 4, box 1200, folder D.IV/201;700(16) "75"/15, Report, "Productora de Papel, S.A. Inspeccion Inicial Ordenada por el Director General de Inspeccion Federal del Trabajo. Inspeccion Inicial," 1.

26. AGN, STPS, DGIFT, box 1082, folder 13/106-D.X-"75"-9/1/2, Ignacio Olvera Quintero to José María Esquivel Torres, July 21, 1975, 1–2.

27. See "Contrato colectivo de trabajo: Comision Federal de Electricidad & Sindicato Unico de Trabajadores Electricistas de la Republica Mexicana: 1974–1976," SUTERM, April 1974, 5–28.

28. Various labor grievances raised in August 1975 with JFC No. 1 by widows of ex-SUTERM members based in Mérida saw petitioners press the CFE to follow through with contract obligations and compensate them for their husbands being killed on the job. See AGN, STPS, DGIFT, box 1082, folder 13/106-D.X-"75"-9/1/2, 1975, 1.

29. Editorial, "Comision Nacional de los Salarios Minimos: Salarios minimos generales y del campo que estaran vigentes del 1°. de octubre al 31 de diciembre de 1976," *Ceteme*, October 9, 1976, 7.

30. AGN, STPS, DFT No. 3, box 1183, folder D.III/201:710.I(6)/43, Mauro Muñoz T., Juán Ruiz Jimenez, and Cayetano Cárdenas Estrada to Juán Antonio Morales Gomez, October 24, 1974.

31. AGN, STPS, DGIFT, box 1081, folder 106-DI "75"/9/1-2, 1975, I, affidavit submitted by Raul Marmolejo Lozano, September 10, 1975.

32. See Secretaría del Trabajo y Previsión Social, *Ley Federal del Trabajo*, 198–99.

33. AGN, STPS, DFT No. 3, box 1180, folder "Clasificación: D.III/201.I. Generalidades Asuntos Laborales—Comparencia," report by José Santos Reyes Gaytán, September 5, 1973, I.

34. *Trabajadores de raya* refers in this case to the fact that the men were awarded temporary employment by the government because they were, metaphorically, at the front of a line of available workers.

35. AGN, STPS, DFT No. 3, box 1180, folder "Clasificación: D.III/201.I. Generalidades Asuntos Laborales," Diego Beltrán Rodríguez, Zeferino Beltrán Rodríguez, et al. to Salvador Castillo Rivera, September 5, 1973.

36. AGN, STPS, DFT No. 3, box 1180, folder "Clasificación: D.III/201.I. Generalidades Asuntos Laborales—Acta de Investigación," report by José Santos Reyes Gaytán, September 5, 1973, 2–3.

37. AGN, STPS, DFT No. 3, box 1180, folder "Clasificación: D.III/201.I. Generalidades Asuntos Laborales—Informe Complementario," José Santos Reyes Gaytán to Salvador Castillo Rivera, September 6, 1973.

38. AGN, STPS, DFT No. 3, box 1180, folder "Clasificación: D.III/201.I. Generalidades Asuntos Laborales," Salvador Castillo Rivera to Diego Beltrán Rodríguez, Zeferino Beltrán Rodríguez, et al., September 11, 1973.

39. AGN, STPS, DFT No. 3, box 1180, folder "Clasificación: D.III/201.I. Generalidades Asuntos Laborales," Zeferino Beltrán Rodríguez et al. to Salvador Castillo Rivera, September 15, 1973.

40. José Murillo Tejeda, "La Empresa no concedío las prestaciones que solicitaron," *Diario Veracruz*, March 3, 1973, I, 15.

41. AGN, STPS, JFCA No. 12, box 1310, folder "Emplazamiento a Huelga planteado por el Sindicato Librado Rivera Conexos y Similares de Aluminio vs. Las Empresas Aluminio Inmobiliaria Aluminio," Moíses Rodríguez Mendoza and Mario Acenjo Carazin to President, JFC No. 12, February 6, 1973.

42. AGN, STPS, JFCA No. 12, box 1310, folder "Emplazamiento a Huelga planteado por el Sindicato Librado Rivera Conexos y Similares de Aluminio vs. Las Empresas Aluminio Inmobiliaria Aluminio," affidavit of Gustavo Ortega O. submitted to President, JFC No. 12, February 8, 1973, I.

43. See AGN, STPS, JFCA No. 12, box 1310, folder "Emplazamiento a Huelga," affidavit of Gustavo Ortega O., 3–4.

44. See AGN, STPS, JFCA No. 12, box 1310, folder "Emplazamiento a Huelga," affidavit of Gustavo Ortega O., 6–9.

45. See AGN, STPS, JFCA No. 12, box 1310, folder "Emplazamiento a Huelga," affidavit of Gustavo Ortega O., 22.

46. See AGN, STPS, JFCA No. 12, box 1310, folder "Emplazamiento a Huelga," affidavit of Gustavo Ortega O., 10–12, 15, 22–23.

47. See AGN, STPS, JFCA No. 12, box 1310, folder "Emplazamiento a Huelga," affidavit of Gustavo Ortega O., 14, 23, 21.

48. See AGN, STPS, JFCA No. 12, box 1310, folder "Emplazamiento a Huelga," affidavit of Gustavo Ortega O., 15–16, 23.

49. AGN, STPS, JFCA No. 12, box 1310, folder "Emplazamiento a Huelga planteado por el Sindicato Librado Rivera Conexos y Similares de Aluminio vs. Las Empresas Aluminio Inmobiliaria Aluminio," tabulador, 1973, 1–3.

50. See AGN, STPS, JFCA No. 12, box 1310, folder "Emplazamiento a Huelga," tabulador, 1–3.

51. See AGN, STPS, JFCA No. 12, box 1310, folder "Emplazamiento a Huelga," affidavit of Gustavo Ortega O., 12–13.

52. José Murillo Tejeda, "La empresa no concedío las prestaciones que solicitaron," *Diario Veracruz*, March 3, 1973, 1, 15.

53. José Murillo Tejeda, "Aumento de sueldo y otras prestaciones lograron los trabajadores de TAMSA," *Diario Veracruz*, March 5, 1973, 1, 15.

54. AGN, STPS, JFCA No. 12, box 1310, folder "Emplazamiento a Huelga planteado por el Sindicato Librado Rivera Conexos y Similares de Aluminio vs. Las Empresas Aluminio Inmobiliaria Aluminio," agreement between Aluminio, S.A. de C.V., and Sindicato Librado Rivera de Trabajadores en General, Conexos y Similares de Aluminio, S.A. de C.V., April 16, 1973, 1.

55. AGN, STPS, JFCA No. 12, box 1310, folder "Emplazamiento a Huelga planteado por el Sindicato Librado Rivera Conexos y Similares de Aluminio vs. Las Empresas Aluminio Inmobiliaria Aluminio," Enrique Arias Solis, Roberto Prado Lovio, and Tomás Torres Damián to President of JFCA (with copy of Convenio attached), Mexico City, May 7, 1973.

56. An article in *El Norte* (Chihuahua, Chih.), August 8, 1972, "Discrimina INFONAVIT a los empleados no sindicalizados," made such a claim. See AGN, DGIPS, SG, box 1133B, folder 2, "Estado de Chihuahua, Información Periodística," August 8, 1972. INFONAVIT, the National Workers' Housing Institute, was created in 1972 at the behest of the CTM and is currently housed in the union's headquarters in Mexico City.

57. Middlebrook, *Paradox of Revolution*, 164.

7. "BEAUTIFUL LITTLE *COMPAÑERAS*"

1. Liliana de Riz, "El problema de la condición femenina en América Latina: La participación de la mujer en los mercados de trabajo. El caso de México," in Secretaría del Trabajo y Previsión Social, *La mujer y el trabajo*, 24.
2. Secretaría del Trabajo y Previsión Social, *La mujer y el trabajo*, 7.
3. See chapter 4 of Olcott's *Revolutionary Women in Postrevolutionary Mexico* for an argument linking women's labor organizing with citizenship in the Comarca Lagunera region.
4. Franco, *Plotting Women*, 102.
5. Porter, *Working Women in Mexico City*, 96–97, 115.
6. Liliana de Riz, "El problema de la condición femenina en América Latina: La participación de la mujer en los mercados de trabajo. El caso de México," in Secretaría del Trabajo y Previsión Social, *La mujer y el trabajo*, 31–39.
7. Vallejo Novelo, *Derechos de la mujer mexicana*, 63.
8. Archivo Histórico de la UNAM, Manuel Gutiérrez Paredes "Mariachito," Expediente 60/3137, 3132, 3134.
9. Archivo Histórico de la UNAM, Manuel Gutiérrez Paredes "Mariachito," Expediente 60/3150.
10. AGN, DGIPS, SG, box 862, folder 1, volume 23, "En la Asamblea Femenil, Monterrey, N.L., 12 Abril."
11. Sánchez Jara, *La maquinita*, 71–72.
12. Inter-American Commission of Women, *News Bulletin of the Inter-American Commission of Women*, no. 25 (June 1964): 8.
13. See, for example, Cristina Tamayo and Soledad Moreno, "Año Internacional de la Mujer: Demagogia o liberación?," *Bandera Roja*, March 1975, 8.
14. "Alternativa mutiladora: La mujer creativa o madre: Abrió la señora de LE la Tribuna Internacional," *Excélsior*, June 20, 1975, 14.
15. Editorial, "Importancia de la Asamblea Femenil en Febrero," *Ceteme*, January 18, 1975, 3.
16. Editorial, "500 mil mujeres explotadas en el comercio, industria del vestido y en los restaurantes," *Ceteme*, January 18, 1975, 4.
17. Centro de Estudios Históricos del Movimiento Obrero Mexicano, *La mujer y el movimiento obrero mexicano*, 7.
18. AGN, STPS, DFT No. 3, box 1183, folder D.III/201:710.1(6)/52, Comparencia de los Representantes de la Compañia Constructora Canales, S.A. y del Sindicato Nacional de Trabajadores de la Construcción, Plomeros, Similares y Conexos de la R.M.—C.T.M.—Presentando Reglamento Interior de Trabajo Para su Remisión a la H. Jta. Fed. de Conc. y Arbitraje. Submitted by

José Muñoz Espinosa, Inspector Federal del Trabajo, Ciudad Juárez, Chih., April 22, 1976, 1–2.

19. Editorial, "1,200 obreros de teleindustria Ericsson en huelga," *Ceteme*, February 15, 1975, 1.

20. Editorial, "Amas de casa ejecutarán una acción concreta contra la carestía de vida," *Ceteme*, June 8, 1974, 8.

21. Editorial, "El SUTERM aportó numeroso contigente en el desfile del 10. de mayo," *SUTERM*, June 1973, 11.

22. AGN Fototeca, Archivo Fotográfico Presidencia de la República, Luis Echeverría Álvarez, Expediente 69/5.

23. Liliana de Riz, "El problema de la condición femenina en América Latina: La participación de la mujer en los mercados de trabajo. El caso de México," in Secretaría del Trabajo y Previsión Social, *La mujer y el trabajo*, 42.

24. "Que la inmadurez de los Líderes de los Trabajadores de la 'Rivetex' solo les ocasionaron innumerables Daños: Hoy finaliza el plazo fijado por la Junta de Conciliación para que retornen a sus labores," *La Voz*, August 23, 1972, 1, 3.

25. *La Voz*, August 25, 1972.

26. "El Dia de Ayer los 310 obreros de la Rivetex fueron dados de baja en el seguro social: La intransigencia de los líderes asi como de sus asesores hizo víctimas a los trabajadores que se dejaron engañar," *La Voz*, August 30, 1972, 2.

27. Fermin Gutierrez V., "Borchornoso espectáculo de los 'rebeldes' frente al Palacio de Gobierno," *La Voz*, September 10, 1972, 1.

28. Hodiac, illustration, "Otra vez David contra Goliat, Rivetex vs Obreras," *Presente!*, September 24, 1972, 1.

8. "YES THIS FIST IS FELT!"

1. For a more detailed discussion about the ways that Mexico's political elite controlled unions, see Ashby, "Dilemma of the Mexican Trade Union Movement."

2. Cavazos Flores, *Manual de aplicación*, 259.

3. See AGN, STPS, Departamento Jurídico, box 1165, folder 9/360(091) "70"/75 for a clear example of how the registration process could be delayed for years on end.

4. UE International, Mexican Labor, "Organizing in Mexico: It's Tough, Often Brutal, and It Means Taking on the State," http://www.ueinternational.org /Mexico_info/index.php.

5. Virgilio Cárdenas García, "Formas de organización sindical," *SUTERM*, July 1973, 5.

6. Hodiac, illustration, "El movimiento obrero de las momias," *Presente!*, October 1, 1972, 1.

7. Tim Rush, "México: Activan a 'charros' agentes; Continúan los intentos de desestabilizar a Echeverría," *Nueva Solidaridad*, December 1, 1975, 3.

8. Railway workers made waves again in the 1970s, primarily as part of the Railway Workers' Union Movement, an independent coalition that sought to liberate Oaxacan *ferrocarrileros* from STFRM control. Led again by Demetrio Vallejo, the MSF waged a constant struggle against charrismo in the press and in the streets and battled a mix of cetemistas and esquiroles in 1971 when they seized several local offices around Oaxaca in protest of union elections they deemed invalid. See editorial, "Fin del charrismo lideril en México," *Presente!*, November 21, 1971, 3.

9. Rosa Rojas, "Fidel Velázquez, es un defecto de México, dijo el Lic. José Guadalupe Zuno," *Presente!*, January 23, 1972, 7.

10. Abraham López Lara, "Reeleccionistas jurados: Fidel Velázquez, el indispensable," *Excélsior*, January 21, 1972, 5-A. Fernando Amilpa, we recall, was one of the "five little wolves" and one of only two other men to have ever led the CTM at that point.

11. Snodgrass, "How Can We Speak of Democracy," 169.

12. AGN, DGIPS, SG, box 1122C, folder 5, "Estado de Coahuila, Información Periodística," December 23, 1970.

13. Raul Stanford (AMI), "Intimidades políticas," *Presente!*, October 15, 1972, 11.

14. Placards expressing this student-worker unity included, in Chihuahua City (May 1), "Peasants, Workers, Students—United We Will Win" and "Students With Workers for a First of May for the Workers"; in Ciudad Juárez (May 1), "We Support the Student Movement and Its Petitions" and "We Support the Workers in Their Demands"; and in Chihuahua City (May 16), "Students, Peasants, and Workers: United toward Our Destiny." See, respectively, AGN, DGIPS, SG, box 1133A, folder 1, "Estado de Chihuahua, Información de Chihuahua," May 1, 1972; AGN, DGIPS, SG, box 1133A, folder 1, "Estado de Chihuahua, Información de Ciudad Juárez," May 1, 1972; and AGN, DGIPS, SG, box 1133A, folder 1, "Estado de Chihuahua, Informacion de Chihuahua," May 16, 1972.

15. AGN, DGIPS, SG, box 1133A, folder 1, "Estado de Chihuahua, Información de Chihuahua," May 1, 1972.

16. AGN, DGIPS, SG, box 1133A, folder 1, "Estado de Chihuahua, Información de Chihuahua," May 16, 1972.

17. For an example of the events cited, see *Ceteme*, no. 1256, January 24, 1976.

18. See *Ceteme*, no. 1266, April 3, 1976, 1, 8.

19. AGN, DGIPS, SG, box 1122A, folder 3, "Estado de Coahuila, Información Periodística," February 23, 1971.

20. AGN, DGIPS, SG, box 1133A, folder 1, "Estado de Chihuahua, Información de Chihuahua," April 27, 1972.

21. Trejo Delarbre, *¡Este puño sí se ve!*, 67.

22. See editorial, "El SME revisó su contrato colectivo," *SUTERM*, March 1974, 1.

23. Editorial, "Obreros de GE: En lucha contra el imperialismo," *Bandera Roja*, June 30, 1974, 3.

24. Editorial, "La huelga de General Electric REPRIMIDA," *Bandera Roja*, July 20, 1974, 1–2.

25. Trejo Delarbre, *¡Este puño sí se ve!*, 72.

26. Editorial, "Obreros de GE: En lucha contra el imperialismo," *Bandera Roja*, June 30, 1974, 3.

27. Editorial, "Informe sobre el conflicto en la General Electric," *SUTERM*, August 1974, 14–15.

28. Amador Robles Santibañez, "La verdad en el caso de General Electric 'Cerro Gordo,'" *SUTERM*, July 1974, 14.

29. Editorial, "La alternativa de la General Electric," *Bandera Roja*, July 20, 1974, 3.

30. "Como a insectos pide Fidel que se trate a Galván y sus seguidores," *El Universal*, March 22, 1975, 1, 6, 7.

31. Trejo Delarbre, *¡Este puño sí se ve!*, 78.

32. For a characteristic report, see AGN, DGIPS, SG, box 1187A, folder 2, "Estado de Jalisco, Información de Guadalajara—En el Local de la Seccion 73 Galvanistas Celebraron 'Una Asamblea de la Tendencia Democratica Electricista,'" July 21, 1975.

33. Antonio Ortega and Antonio Andrade, "Tres horas de marcha y condenas al 'charrismo sindical,'" *Excélsior*, November 16, 1975, 1, 13.

34. "La grandiosa manifestación del 15 de noviembre," *Bandera Roja*, December 1975, 3; and Antonio Ortega and Antonio Andrade, "Tres horas de marcha y condenas al 'charrismo sindical,'" *Excélsior*, November 16, 1975, 13.

35. "Los gobiernos temen cuando tienen compromisos vergonzantes con minorías," *Excélsior*, November 16, 1975, 1, 8.

36. Francisco Jorda, Jesús Rivera, Ignacio Navarro, and Saul López, "Elecciones directas, sin 'charrismo': TD," *El Universal*, March 21, 1976, 1, 18.

37. For context, see Guillermo Hewett Alva, "Exige Fidel Velázquez: Un cambio radical en la forma de controlar y dirigir a los obreros," *El Universal*, February 25, 1976, 1, 10.

38. Trejo Delarbre, *¡Este puño sí se ve!*, 87.

39. Editorial, "Rotundo Fracaso de Galván," *Ceteme*, July 24, 1976, 3.

40. Editorial, "Los electricistas cetemistas, dispuestos a defender su organización de los provocadores," *Ceteme*, June 19, 1976, 1, 5.

41. For a similar message, see editorial, "Agresion fascista al movimiento obrero y al pueblo de Mexico," *Ceteme*, June 19, 1976, 1, 2.

42. Editorial, "Estamos preparados para las maniobras de la tendencia democrática," *Ceteme*, July 3, 1976, 1, 2.

43. See "El SUTERM y el CT se apoderaron de las instalaciones eléctricas," *El Universal*, July 17, 1976, 1, 8.

44. See Gustavo Escudero, "Unidad de los cetemistas en el edo. de Morelos, contra los provocadores," *Ceteme*, June 19, 1976, 4.

45. See "El SUTERM y el CT se apoderaron de las instalaciones eléctricas," *El Universal*, July 17, 1976, 1, 8.

46. See "En los estados ningún incidente se registró," *El Universal*, July 17, 1976, 8.

47. See articles in *Ceteme*, July 24, 1976.

48. Editorial, "Rotundo Fracaso de Galván," *Ceteme*, July 24, 1976, 10.

49. See reports in *El Universal*, July 26, 1976.

50. Editorial, "La llamada tendencia democrática pro-Izquierdista, se desploma," *Ceteme*, July 31, 1976, 1.

51. Editorial, "Galván, nunca ha sido electricista," *Ceteme*, July 31, 1976, 1, 8.

52. Humberto Aranda, "Si vuelven al trabajo, los de la tendencia tendrán garantías," *El Universal*, August 1, 1976, 1, 20. The figure of ten thousand was challenged by SUTERM officials, who estimated the TD following to be somewhere closer to one thousand.

53. *Ceteme*, August 14, 1976, 3. The image's caption suggests the dazed TD member is Galván, although the drawing is a poor likeness. It reads, "Power outages 45 days before the [president's] annual address? Right, Rafa, why not!"

54. Trejo Delarbre, *¡Este puño sí se ve!*, 90–91.

55. Gómez Sada would head the Mexican Mining and Metalworkers' Union for a quarter century more, until 2001, when in good charro fashion he handed off the reins of power to his son, Napoleón Gómez Urrutia, who continued to preside over the union even after having fled Mexico for Canada to avoid charges of fraud brought against him by federal authorities.

56. Snodgrass, "How Can We Speak of Democracy," 171.

57. For a detailed analysis of independent unionism within the automotive industry, see Middlebrook, "Union Democratization."

58. Hodiac, illustration, "Monstruos de agitación creados por el regimen," *Presente!*, December 17, 1975, 1.

59. See the following works for discussions of the rise of democratic unionism in the automobile, electrical, and steel industries, respectively: Middlebrook,

"Union Democratization"; Trejo Delarbre, *¡Este puño sí se ve!*; and most recently, Snodgrass, "How Can We Speak of Democracy."

9. "THE MEXICAN [REDEEMER] NEVER ASKS!"

1. Aguilar Camín and Meyer, *In the Shadow of the Mexican Revolution*, 203.
2. Nuncio, *El Grupo Monterrey*, 58.
3. Augustín, *Tragicomedia mexicana 2*, 116.
4. Specifically, the CCE petition requested the return to private ownership for certain businesses, including restaurants and steelworks that the federal government had recently taken control of. See editorial, "Congreso del trabajo respalda a Echeverría," *El Norte*, May 14, 1975, 5-A.
5. "Oímos a todos; mayoría prevalece—Echeverría," *El Norte*, May 9, 1975, 1.
6. "Censura Moya a empresarios," *El Norte*, May 10, 1975, 1.
7. "Empresarios refutan a Moya," *El Norte*, May 11, 1975, 1.
8. "Avanza el proceso destructor de la libre empresa mexicana," *El Norte*, May 14, 1975, 5-A.
9. "Sada Zambrano señala error de las empresas," *El Norte*, May 14, 1975, 5-A.
10. AGN, DGIPS, SG, box 1187A, folder 2, "Estado de Jalisco, Información Periodística," August 19, 1975.
11. "President Echeverria's .N. Aspirations," August 1, 1975, History Lab, http://www.history-lab.org/documents/1975MEXICO06867.
12. For a visual description of the parade, see photographs in AGN Fototeca, Archivo Fotográfico Hermanos Mayo, Luis Echeverría Álvarez, Expediente 067-1/s.n.
13. White, *Creating a Third World*, 134.
14. AGN, DGIPS, SG, box 1187A-2, "Vega y Asociados, 'Algunos Problemas Sociales, Políticos y Económicos—Guadalajara,'" May 1975, 18. A similar survey conducted in September 1972 revealed that 42 percent of respondents were receptive to the idea of socialism, a percentage that dropped to 28 percent by 1974 and to 23 percent by the time the Mexican president visited socialist countries on his Third World tour.
15. "Los dirigentes del sector privado expresan confianza en López Portillo," *Excélsior*, September 24, 1975, 14.
16. Augustín, *Tragicomedia mexicana 2*, 58.
17. De Garay, Salazar, and Vega, *PNR, PRM, PRI*, 184.
18. Augustín, *Tragicomedia mexicana 2*, 58.
19. "Ambiciosos, reeleccionistas, indiscretos y con proyectos transexenales, Echeverria y Salinas," Proceso.com.mx, September 24, 1995, http://www.proceso.com.mx/170230/ambiciosos-reeleccionistas-indiscretos-y-con-proyectos-transexenales-echeverria-y-salinas.

20. De Garay, Salazar, and Vega, *PNR, PRM, PRI*, 189.
21. Augustín, *Tragicomedia mexicana 2*, 122.
22. Aguilar Camín and Meyer, *In the Shadow of the Mexican Revolution*, 202.
23. "Mexico: Down Goes the Peso," *Time*, September 13, 1976, http://www.time .com/time/magazine/article/0,9171,914587,00.html.
24. See *Ceteme*, September 4, 1976.
25. "Visita el primer mandatario el fraccionamiento popular fomerrey no. 3: Hace el Presidente Echeverría un llamado a los ricos para que den a su capital un sentido social moderno, a fin de evitar explosiones sociales," *El Norte*, October 16, 1976, 5-A.
26. "¿Monterrey . . . culpable?," *El Norte*, October 18, 1976, 1.
27. Manuel Salazar Ávila, "Echeverría vs. 'ricos de Monterrey,'" *Presente!*, October 26, 1976, 3.
28. "Proponen nacionalizar empresas de Monterrey," *El Norte*, October 19, 1976, 1-A.
29. Editorial, "Los empresarios rezagados, no son ni representan a Monterrey," *Ceteme*, October 23, 1976, 1, 8.
30. Gustavo Escudero Mendoza, "La CTM apoya al Sr. Presidente, en la condena a los patrones de Monterrey," *Ceteme*, October 23, 1976, 1, 8.

CONCLUSION

1. Editorial, "Nuestra central demanda total control de precios," *Ceteme*, October 2, 1976, 1, 8.
2. Coleman and Davis, "Preemptive Reform and the Mexican Working Class," 8.
3. See *Ceteme*, October 2, 1976, 8.
4. Coleman and Davis, "Preemptive Reform and the Mexican Working Class," 7–8.
5. And both of these rates, actually, were dwarfed by the high (although highly anomalous) rates achieved during the conservative presidency of Manuel Ávila Camacho, when 66.3 percent, 66.5 percent, and 40.7 percent of all strike petitions were approved during the years 1943, 1944, and 1945, respectively.
6. See Middlebrook, *Paradox of Revolution*, 165–66.
7. "Presidentes mexicanos y papas: Relaciones de escándalo," Proceso.com.mx, April 29, 2011, http://www.proceso.com.mx/268945/presidentes-mexicanos -y-papas-relaciones-de-escandalo.
8. Bernardo Barranco, "La iglesia ante el bicentenario," September 15, 2010, https://bernardobarranco.wordpress.com/tag/luis-echeverria/.
9. Rafael Azul, "Mexico: Judge Quashes 'Genocide' Indictment of Former President Luis Echeverría," August 21, 2004, World Socialist Website, http://www

.wsws.org/en/articles/2004/08/mexi-a21.html. And as with state-organized labor collaborationism, a renewed church-state alliance reaped rewards for each of the partners. Changes came quickly following this détente. Pope John Paul II was invited to visit Mexico in 1979, leading the apoplectic Jesús Reyes Heroles, who had always pursued the redemption of somewhat different revolutionary values, to resign from the cabinet in disgust. The papal visit in 1979 was merely a portent of larger changes to come. The Catholic Church experienced its own redemption in 1992 when many of the anticlerical provisions written into constitutional Articles 3, 5, 24, 27, and 130 were redacted, thus abolishing several of the most profound revolutionary priorities—a ban on religious education, for example—and permitting the resumption of diplomatic relations between the government and the Vatican.

10. Becker, *Setting the Virgin on Fire*, 157.

11. See Grayson, *Mexican Messiah*.

12. De Garay, Salazar, and Vega, *PNR, PRM, PRI*, 173.

13. "President Echeverria's .N. Aspirations," August 1, 1975, History Lab, http://www.history-lab.org/documents/1975MEXICO06867.

14. AGN, DGIPS, SG, box 1187A-2, "Vega y Asociados, 'Algunos Problemas Sociales, Políticos y Económicos—Guadalajara,'" May 1975, 23, 15.

15. Krauze, *Redeemers*, 353.

16. Alan Knight, "Cárdenas and Echeverría: Two 'Populist' Presidents Compared," in Kiddle and Muñoz, *Populism in Twentieth-Century Mexico*, 17–18.

17. Cosío Villegas, *El estilo personal de gobernar*, 9.

18. Bishop Samuel Ruiz and Subcomandante Marcos were the best-known symbols of the Zapatista guerrilla uprising; Octavio Paz was the country's most celebrated writer, a Nobel laureate, and a diplomat; and José Vasconcelos was the architect of Mexico's public education system and a lightning rod of controversy in the early postrevolutionary period.

19. Again, see "President Echeverria's .N. Aspirations," August 1, 1975, History Lab, http://www.history-lab.org/documents/1975MEXICO06867.

20. De Garay, Salazar, and Vega, *PNR, PRM, PRI*, 180.

21. Dion, *Workers and Welfare*, 106.

22. See Carey, *Plaza of Sacrifices*.

23. See Aguayo Quezada, *1968*.

24. Kiddle and Muñoz, *Populism in Twentieth-Century Mexico*, 7.

25. Krauze, "El legado incierto."

26. Zolov, "Showcasing the 'Land of Tomorrow,'" 187. I garner Zolov's impression of the movement's "messiness" from his review of *Plaza of Sacrifices*, by Elaine Carey, *Americas* 63, no. 1 (July 2006): 161–62.

27. Snodgrass qtd. in Cárdenas, "Populist and Popular," in Kiddle and Muñoz, *Populism in Twentieth-Century Mexico*, ix.
28. Coleman and Davis, "Preemptive Reform and the Mexican Working Class," 3–4.
29. Coleman and Davis, "Preemptive Reform and the Mexican Working Class," 6.
30. This passage is taken from Matthew 5, New International Version Online Bible, http://www.biblica.com/en-us/bible/online-bible/niv/matthew/5/.
31. Editorial, "Los cetemistas de sus vallas, dieron un firme apoyo al Presidente Lic. José López Portillo," *Ceteme*, December 4, 1976, 10.

EPILOGUE

1. Alan Riding, "Mexico Seizing Banks to Curtail Flight of Capital," *New York Times*, September 2, 1982.
2. Alan Riding, "Mexico's Affluent Elite Shudders over Drive on Economic 'Traitors,'" *New York Times*, September 5, 1982.
3. Damián Gomez, "Demanda la COCEO la nacionalización de las industrias alimentaria y farmacéutica," *El Día*, September 3, 1982.
4. Enrique Sánchez Márquez, "Sindicatos independientes y PSUM expresan su adhesión," *El Universal*, September 4, 1982.
5. Editorial, "Apoyo entusiasta," *Excélsior*, September 4, 1982.
6. Daniel Dueñas, "Alacena: (Esto es sólo el principio)," *El Universal*, September 4, 1982.
7. Anthony DePalma, "Mexico Sells Off State Companies, Reaping Trouble as Well as Profit," *New York Times*, October 27, 1993.
8. Germán Seijas Román, "¿Banca nacionalizada or burocratizada?," *El Economista*, October 19, 1992.
9. Alan Riding, "Mexico's Lame Duck Leader: An Audacious Adios," *New York Times*, October 1, 1982.
10. Intelligence reports from 1977 confirm the López Portillo regime's hard line against the Democratic Tendency and other advocates of the independentista cause. See, for example, AGN, DGIPS, SG, box 1553A, folder 3, "Distrito Federal—Aproximadamente 300 Seguidores de la Tendencia Democratica del SUTERM se Encuentran," October 26, 1977.
11. Anthony DePalma, "Mexico Sells Off State Companies, Reaping Trouble as Well as Profit," *New York Times*, October 27, 1993.
12. Dan La Botz, "Fidel Velazquez Sanchez: Embodiment of State Unionism," *Mexican Labor News and Analysis*, special issue: Fidel Velazquez Obituary, June 22, 1997, http://www.ueinternational.org/MLNA/old/vol2spec.html.
13. Tina Rosenberg, "Death Watch in Mexico; Labor Boss Fidel Velázquez," *Nation*, April 18, 1987, http://www.highbeam.com/doc/1G1-4803371.html.

14. Partido de la Revolución Democrática, *20 Años*, 13.
15. Partido de la Revolución Democrática, *20 Años*, 28–31.
16. Mexico's Federal Electoral Institute reported these final results for the first- and second-place finishers in the 2012 presidential contest: Enrique Peña Nieto—19,226,784 (38.21 percent); Andrés Manuel López Obrador—15,896,999 (31.59 percent). See IFE, "Las elecciones del primero de julio: Cifras, datos, resultados," http://www.ine.mx/archivos3/portal/historico /recursos/IFE-v2/CNCS/CNCS-IFE-Responde/2012/Julio/Le010712/Le 010712.pdf.
17. This language is borrowed from Craib, *Cartographic Mexico*, 256.
18. Francisco Reséndiz and Noé Cruz, "Peña va por apertura acotada en Pemex," *El Universal*, August 13, 2013, 1.
19. Karla Paulina Gómez, "Empresarios dan aval a iniciativa," *El Universal*, August 12, 2013, A9.
20. Raymundo León, "AMLO: La reforma de Peña no busca modernizar Pemex," *La Jornada*, August 12, 2013, 5.
21. Morena, *Al Zócalo con AMLO: Domingo 8 de septiembre 10:00AM* (Mexico City: Movimiento de la Regeneración Nacional, 2013).
22. Alejandro Rendón, interview by author, Mexico City, August 14, 2013.
23. Eduardo Bobadilla Zarza, interview by author, Mexico City, August 12, 2013.
24. See "El petróleo es y siempre será nuestro," advertisement, *El Universal*, August 13, 2013.
25. Rosa Elvira Vargas, "Versión oficial: Las críticas a la reforma energética son 'mitos,'" *La Jornada*, August 16, 2013, 7.
26. Rosa Elvira Vargas, "'Ser audaces y atrevernos a acelerar' el desarrollo, plante Peña Nieto," *La Jornada*, August 15, 2013, 5.
27. Hernández, illustration, "Gran historiador," *La Jornada*, August 15, 2013, 10.
28. Katia d'Artigues, "¿Modernizando Pemex? De Lázaro Cárdenas a Enrique Peña," *El Universal*, August 12, 2013, A10.
29. Arturo Canó, "Regresa un grito que hacia tiempo no se oía: '¡Cuauhtémoc, Cuauhtémoc!,'" *La Jornada*, August 20, 2013, 3.
30. Ricardo Gómez, "El PRD no olvida su ADN y llevo porras para defender el petróleo," *El Universal*, August 20, 2013, A7.
31. Ricardo Alemán, "¿Donde están las multitudes?," *El Universal*, August 20, 2013, A8.
32. Guillermo Flores Velasco, interview by author, Mexico City, August 21, 2013.
33. Alicia Sánchez Jara, interview by author, Mexico City, August 21, 2013. Subsequent uncited quotations are from the same interview.
34. Alejandro Sánchez, "La abuelita que conoce el oro y las sombras del PRI,"

Spleen Journal, http://www.spleenjournal.com/index.php?option=com
_content&view=article&id=321.
35. Jara, interview.
36. Alejandro Sánchez, "La abuelita que conoce el oro y las sombras del PRI,"
Spleen Journal, http://www.spleenjournal.com/index.php?option=com
_content&view=article&id=321.
37. Jara, interview.
38. Ignacio Zúñiga González, interview by author, Mexico City, August 19, 2013.
Subsequent uncited quotations are from the same interview.
39. Ignacio Zúñiga González, "Rotundo triunfo de la clase obrera: 22 por ciento
de aumento salarial," *Ceteme*, September 14, 1974.
40. Zúñiga, interview.
41. Ignacio Zúñiga González, "Reelección y democrácia," *Ceteme*, May 4, 1974, 12.
42. Zúñiga, interview. Subsequent uncited quotations are from the same interview.

BIBLIOGRAPHY

ARCHIVAL SOURCES

Archivo General de la Nación (AGN), Mexico City
    Archivo Fotográfico
        Fondo Hermanos Mayo
        Fondo Presidencia de la República
    Biblioteca Ignacio Cubas
    Dirección General de Investigaciones Politícas y Sociales (DGIPS)
    Fondo Secretaría de Gobernación (SG)
    Presidente José López Portillo (JLP)
    Presidente Luis Echeverría Álvarez (LEA)
    Secretaría del Trabajo y Previsión Social (STPS)
        Delegación Federal del Trabajo (DFT)
        Dirección General de Inspeción Federal del Trabajo (DGIFT)
        Junta Federal de Conciliación y Arbitraje (JFCA)
    Secretaría de Patrimonia Nacional (SPN)
    Secretaría de Programación y Presupuesto (SPP)
Archivo Histórico de la Universidad Nacional Autónoma de México (UNAM),
    Mexico City
    Colleccion Manuel Gutiérrez Paredes "Mariachito"
Biblioteca Central Lic. Jesús Reyes Heroles de PEMEX, Mexico City
Biblioteca Miguel Lerdo de Tejada, Mexico City
Centro de Estudios de Historia de México (CONDUMEX), Mexico City
Confederación de Trabajadores de México, Biblioteca Profesor Bernardo Cobos
    Díaz, Mexico City
Fundación Nacional Luis Donaldo Colosio, Mexico City
Instituto de Investigaciones Bibliográficas—Biblioteca Nacional, Mexico City

Instituto de Investigaciones Bibliográficas—Hemeroteca Nacional, Mexico City
Instituto de Investigaciones Dr. José María Luis Mora, Mexico City
Junta Federal de Conciliación y Arbitraje, Archivo Histórico, Mexico City
University of New Mexico, General Libraries, Albuquerque, New Mexico

PUBLISHED SOURCES

Aguayo Quezada, Sergio. *1968: Los archivos de la violencia*. Mexico City: Reforma, 1998.

Aguilar Camín, Héctor, and Lorenzo Meyer. *In the Shadow of the Mexican Revolution: Contemporary Mexican History, 1910–1989*. Austin: University of Texas Press, 1993.

Alegre, R. F. "*Las Rieleras*: Gender, Politics, and Power in the Mexican Railway Movement, 1958–1959." *Journal of Women's History* 23, no. 2 (June 2011): 162–86.

Ángeles, Luis. *El PRI en el gobierno: El desarrollo de México 1930–2000*. Mexico City: Fundación Colosio, 2003.

Aquinas, Thomas. *De regimine principum, ad regem Cypri*. 1267.

Ashby, Joe C. "The Dilemma of the Mexican Trade Union Movement." *Mexican Studies* 1, no. 2 (Summer 1985): 277–301.

Augustín, José. *Tragicomedia mexicana 2: La vida en México de 1970 a 1982*. Mexico City: Editorial Planeta Mexicana, 1992.

Barbosa Cano, Fabio. *La reconversión de la industria petrolera en México*. Mexico City: Instituto de Investigaciones Económicas, Universidad Nacional Autónoma de México, 1993.

Basurto, Jorge. *La clase Obrera en la historia de México: En el régimen de Echeverría: Rebelión e independencia*. Mexico City: Siglo Veintiuno Editores, 1983.

Becker, Marjorie. *Setting the Virgin on Fire: Lázaro Cárdenas, Michoacán Peasants, and the Redemption of the Mexican Revolution*. Berkeley: University of California Press, 1996.

Bonfil Batalla, Guillermo. *México profundo: Una civilización negada*. Mexico City: Random House Mondadori, 2008.

Brachet-Márquez, Viviane. *El pacto de dominación: Estado, clase y reforma social en México (1910–1995)*. Mexico City: El Colegio de México, 1996.

Camp, Roderic Ai. *Intellectuals and the State in Twentieth-Century Mexico*. Austin: University of Texas Press, 1985.

Carey, Elaine. *Plaza of Sacrifices: Gender, Power, and Terror in 1968 Mexico*. Albuquerque: University of New Mexico Press, 2005.

Cavazos Flores, Baltasar. *Manual de aplicación e interpretación de la Nueva Ley*

Federal del Trabajo. Mexico City: Confederación Patronal de la República Mexicana, 1971.

Centro de Estudios Históricos del Movimiento Obrero Mexicano. *La mujer y el movimiento obrero mexicano en el siglo XIX: Antología de la prensa obrera.* Mexico City: CEHSMO, 1975.

Ceteno, Miguel Ángel. *Democracy within Reason: Technocratic Revolution in Mexico.* 2nd ed. University Park: Pennsylvania State University Press, 1997.

Chasteen, John C. *Born in Blood and Fire: A Concise History of Latin America.* 3rd ed. New York: W. W. Norton, 2011.

Clark, Christopher, and Wolfram Kaiser. *Culture Wars: Secular-Catholic Conflict in Nineteenth-Century Europe.* Cambridge: Cambridge University Press, 2003.

Coleman, Kenneth M., and Charles L. Davis. "Preemptive Reform and the Mexican Working Class." *Latin American Research Review* 18, no. 1 (Winter 1983): 1–31.

Cordera, Rolando, and Ricardo Rocha. *México: Los años del cambio.* Mexico City: Editorial Diana, 1994.

Córdova, Arnaldo. *La reforma del poder político en México.* 2nd ed. Mexico City: Ediciones ERA, 1972.

Cosío Villegas, Daniel. *El estilo personal de gobernar.* Mexico City: Editorial Joaquín Mortiz, 1974.

Craib, Raymond B. *Cartographic Mexico: A History of State Fixations and Fugitive Landscapes.* Durham NC: Duke University Press, 2004.

Dealy, Glenn C. "The Tradition of Monistic Democracy in Latin America." *Journal of the History of Ideas* 35, no. 4 (1974): 625–46.

de Garay, Fernando, Alberto Márquez Salazar, and Mariana Vega. *PNR, PRM, PRI: Esbozo histórico.* Mexico City: Biblioteca Fundación Nacional Colosio, 2003.

Díaz Cárdenas, León. *Cananea.* Cuadernos Obreros no. 9. Mexico City: Secretaría del Trabajo y Previsión Social, 1986.

Dion, Michelle L. *Workers and Welfare: Comparative Institutional Change in Twentieth-Century Mexico.* Pittsburgh: University of Pittsburgh Press, 2010.

Ferry, Elizabeth Emma. *Not Ours Alone: Patrimony, Value, and Collectivity in Contemporary Mexico.* New York: Columbia University Press, 2005.

Franco, Jean. *Plotting Women: Gender and Representation in Mexico.* New York: Columbia University Press, 1989.

French, John D., and Daniel James, eds. *The Gendered Worlds of Latin American Women Workers: From Household and Factory to the Union Hall and Ballot Box.* Durham NC: Duke University Press, 1997.

Galeano, Eduardo. *Open Veins of Latin America: Five Centuries of the Pillage of a Continent*. New York: Monthly Review Press, 1997.

Gálvez, Arturo. *La industria petrolera en México: Una crónica*. Vol. 3, *Crisis del crecimiento y expansión de Petróleos Mexicanos (1970–1988)*. Mexico City: Petróleos Mexicanos, 1988.

Gillingham, Paul, and Benjamin T. Smith, eds. *Dictablanda: Politics, Work, and Culture in Mexico, 1938–1968*. Durham NC: Duke University Press, 2014.

Gómez Bonilla, Édgar. "Cronología de movimiento estudiantiles en Puebla y la ciudad de México, 1968." *Tiempo Universitario* 1, no. 20 (October 1998). www.archivohistorico.buap.mx/tiempo/1998/a1g20.html.

Gómez de Silva, Guido. *Diccionario breve de Mexicanismos*. Mexico City: Fondo de Cultura Mexicana, 2001.

Gónzalez Casanova, Pablo. *La democracia en México*. Mexico City: Editorial Era, 1969.

Grayson, George W. *Mexican Messiah: Andrés Manuel López Obrador*. University Park: Pennsylvania State University Press, 2007.

———. "Mexico, the PRI, and López Obrador: The Legacy of Corporatism." *Orbis* 51, no. 2 (2007): 279–97.

Gueilbert, Matías, dir. *La masacre de Tlatelolco*. Anima Films, 2008. DVD.

Haggard, Stephan, and Robert R. Kaufman. *The Political Economy of Democratic Transitions*. Princeton NJ: Princeton University Press, 1995.

Hall, Linda B. *Oil, Banks, and Politics: The United States and Post-revolutionary Mexico, 1917–1924*. Austin: University of Texas Press, 1995.

Hart, John Mason. *Anarchism and the Mexican Working Class, 1860–1931*. Austin: University of Texas Press, 1987.

Hernandez Juárez, Francisco, and María Xelhuantzi López. *El sindicalismo en la reforma del estado: Una visión de la modernización de México*. Mexico City: Fondo de Cultura Económica, 1993.

Instituto Nacional de Estadística y Geografía, Dirección General de Estadísticas. VI Censo General de Población, 1940.

Instituto Nacional de Estadística y Geografía, Dirección General de Estadísticas. IX Censo General de Población y Vivienda, 1970.

Instituto Nacional de Estudios Históricos de la Revolución Mexicana. *La constitución de la Confederación de Trabajadores de México*. Mexico City: INEHRM, 1986.

Inter-American Commission of Women. *News Bulletin of the Inter-American Commission of Women*. Washington DC: General Secretariat of the Organization of American States/Pan-American Union.

Johnson, Kenneth F. *Tercer mundo vs. imperialismo*. Mexico City: Ediciones el Caballito, 1973.

Joseph, Gilbert M., and Timothy J. Henderson, eds. *The Mexico Reader: History, Culture, Politics*. Durham NC: Duke University Press, 2002.

Joseph, Gilbert M., and Daniel Nugent, eds. *Everyday Forms of State Formation: Revolution and the Negotiation of Rule in Modern Mexico*. Durham NC: Duke University Press, 1994.

Kiddle, Amelia M., and María L. O. Muñoz, eds. *Populism in Twentieth-Century Mexico: The Presidencies of Lázaro Cárdenas and Luis Echeverría*. Tucson: University of Arizona Press, 2010.

Krauze, Enrique. "El legado incierto del 68." October 2008. http://www.letraslib res.com/revista/letrillas/el-legado-incierto-del-68.

———. *La presidencia imperial: Ascenso y caída del sistema político mexicano, 1940–1996*. Barcelona: Tusquets Editores México, 1997.

———. *Redeemers: Ideas and Power in Latin America*. New York: HarperCollins, 2011.

La Botz, Dan. *Mask of Democracy: Labor Suppression in Mexico Today*. Boston: South End Press, 1992.

Lear, John. *Workers, Neighbors, and Citizens: The Revolution in Mexico City*. Lincoln: University of Nebraska Press, 2001.

Lenti, Joseph U. "Collaboration and Conflict: Organized Labor, Business, and the State in Post-Tlatelolco Mexico." PhD diss., University of New Mexico, 2011.

———. "'A Revolutionary Regime Must Put the Interests of the Majority First': Class, Collectivism, and Paternalism in Post-Tlatelolco Mexican Tripartite Relations." *Latin Americanist* 54, no. 4 (Winter 2010): 163–82.

Lenti, Joseph U., and Amelia M. Kiddle. "Co-opting Cardenismo: Luis Echeverría and the Funeral of Lázaro Cárdenas." In *Populism in Twentieth-Century Mexico: The Presidencies of Lázaro Cárdenas and Luis Echeverría*, edited by Amelia M. Kiddle and María L.O. Muñoz, 174–89. Tucson: University of Arizona Press, 2010.

Mallon, Florencia E. "Reflections on the Ruins: Everyday Forms of State Formation in Nineteenth-Century Mexico." In *Everyday Forms of State Formation: Revolution and the Negotiation of Rule in Modern Mexico*, edited by Gilbert M. Joseph and Daniel Nugent, 69–106. Durham NC: Duke University Press, 1994.

Mejía Prieto, Jorge. *Fidel Velázquez: 47 años de historia y poder*. Mexico City: Editorial Diana, 1991.

Meyer, Eugenia, ed. *Jesús Reyes Heroles: Obras completas*. Vols. 1–2. Mexico City: Asociación de Estudios Históricos y Políticos Jesús Reyes Heroles, 1995–96.

Middlebrook, Kevin. *The Paradox of Revolution: Labor, the State, and Authoritarianism in Mexico*. Baltimore: Johns Hopkins University Press, 1995.

———. "Union Democratization in the Mexican Automobile Industry: A Reappraisal." *Latin American Research Review* 24, no. 2 (1989): 69–93.

Moreno, Julio. *Yankee Don't Go Home: Mexican Nationalism, American Business Culture, and the Shaping of Modern Mexico, 1920–1950*. Chapel Hill: University of North Carolina Press, 2003.

Murolo, Priscilla, and A. B. Chitty. *From the Folks Who Brought You the Weekend: A Short, Illustrated History of Labor in the United States*. New York: W. W. Norton, 2001.

Murray, R. Emmett. *The Lexicon of Labor*. New York: New Press, 2010.

Nuncio, Abraham. *El Grupo Monterrey*. Mexico City: Editorial Nueva Imagen, 1982.

Olcott, Jocelyn H. *Revolutionary Women in Postrevolutionary Mexico*. Durham NC: Duke University Press, 2006.

Ortíz Rivera, Alicia. *Eugenio Garza Sada*. Mexico City: Planeta de Agostini, 2003.

Partido de la Revolución Democrática. *20 Años: Un futuro con historia*. Mexico City: PRD, 2010.

Partido Revolucionario Institucional. *Pensamiento y doctrina*. Vol. 4. Mexico City: Partido Revolucionario Institucional, 1970.

———. *Reunión nacional para el estudio del desarrollo industrial de México: Ponencias I*. Mexico City: Instituto de Estudios Políticos Económicos y Sociales, 1970.

Paz, Octavio. *The Labyrinth of Solitude*. London: Penguin Books, 1999.

Poniatowska, Elena. *Massacre in Mexico*. Translated by Helen R. Lane. Columbia: University of Missouri Press, 1991.

Porter, Susie S. *Working Women in Mexico City: Public Discourses and Material Conditions, 1879–1931*. Tucson: University of Arizona Press, 2003.

Quintero Ramírez, Cirila. *La sindicalización en las maquiladoras tijuanenses, 1970–1988*. Mexico City: Consejo Nacional Para la Cultura y las Artes, 1990.

Ramírez Fonseca, Francisco. *Obligaciones y derechos de patrones y trabajadores: Comentarios y jurisprudencias*. Mexico City: Editorial PAC, 1985.

Real Academia Española. *Diccionario de la lengua española*. 22nd ed. Real Academia Española. http://rae.es/.

Reyes Heroles, Jesús. *Jesús Reyes Heroles y el petróleo*. Mexico City: Asociación de Estudios Históricos y Políticos Jesús Reyes Heroles, 1992.

Reyna, José Luis, and Raúl Trejo Delarbre. *La clase obrera en la historia de México:*

De Adolfo Ruiz Cortines a Adolfo López Mateos, (1952–1964). 2nd ed. Mexico City: Instituto de Investigaciones Sociales, UNAM, 1996.

Rodríguez, Victoria E., ed. *Women's Participation in Mexican Political Life*. Boulder CO: Westview Press, 1998.

Rousseau, Isabelle. *México: ¿Una revolución silenciosa?: Élites gubernamentales y proyecto de modernización, 1970–1995*. Mexico City: Centro de Estudios Internacionales, 2001.

Ruiz Naufal, Víctor M. *La industria petrolera en México: Una crónica*. Vol. 2, *Gestación y consolidación de Petróleos Mexicanos (1938–1970)*. Mexico City: Petróleos Mexicanos, 1988.

Safa, Helen I. *The Myth of the Male Breadwinner: Women and Industrialization in the Caribbean*. Boulder CO: Westview Press, 1995.

Sánchez González, Augustín. *Los primeros cien años de Fidel: La historia controvertida de la figura política mas duradera del siglo XX en México*. Mexico City: Editorial Patria, 1997.

Sánchez Jara, Alicia. *La maquinita*. 2nd ed. Mexico City: Editorial Patria, 1977.

Santiago, Myrna I. *The Ecology of Oil: Environment, Labor, and the Mexican Revolution, 1900–1938*. Cambridge: Cambridge University Press, 2006.

Schers, David. *The Popular Sector of the Partido Revolucionario Institucional in Mexico*. Tel Aviv: Tel Aviv University, the David Horowitz Institute, 1972.

Secretaría del Trabajo y Previsión Social. *Estatutos CROC, 1952–1980*. Mexico City: STPS, 1987.

——. *La mujer y el trabajo en México (antología)*. Mexico City: STPS, 1986.

——. *Ley Federal del Trabajo*. 2nd ed. Mexico City: STPS, 1970.

——, ed. *Revista Mexicana del Trabajo*. Mexico City: STPS.

Sherman, John W. "The Mexican Miracle and Its Collapse." In *The Oxford History of Mexico*, edited by William H. Beezley and Michael C. Meyer, 537–68. Oxford: Oxford University Press, 2000.

Snodgrass, Michael. "The Birth and Consequences of Industrial Paternalism in Monterrey, Mexico, 1890–1940." *International Labor and Working-Class History* 53 (Spring 1998): 115–36.

——. *Deference and Defiance in Monterrey: Workers, Paternalism, and Revolution in Mexico, 1890–1950*. Cambridge: Cambridge University Press, 2003.

——. "'How Can We Speak of Democracy in Mexico?': Workers and Organized Labor in the Cárdenas and Echeverría Years." In *Populism in Twentieth-Century Mexico: The Presidencies of Lázaro Cárdenas and Luis Echeverría*, edited by Amelia M. Kiddle and María L. O. Muñoz, 159–73. Tucson: University of Arizona Press, 2010.

——. "'We Are All Mexicans Here': Workers, Patriotism, and Union Struggles in Monterrey." In *The Eagle and the Virgin: Nation and Cultural Revolution in Mexico, 1920–1940*, edited by Mary Kay Vaughan and Stephen E. Lewis, 314–34. Durham NC: Duke University Press, 2006.

Spalding, Hobart A. *Organized Labor in Latin America: Historical Case Studies of Urban Workers in Dependent Societies*. New York: Harper Torchbooks, 1977.

Stevens, Evelyn P. "Mexico's PRI: The Institutionalization of Corporatism?" In *Authoritarianism and Corporatism in Latin America*, edited by James Malloy, 227–58. Pittsburgh: University of Pittsburgh Press, 1977.

Suárez, Luis. *Echeverría en el sexenio de López Portillo: El caso de un expresidente ante el successor*. Mexico City: Editorial Grijalbo, 1983.

Suarez-Potts, William. *The Making of Law: The Supreme Court and Labor Legislation in Mexico, 1875–1931*. Palo Alto CA: Stanford University Press, 2013.

Trejo Delarbre, Raúl. *¡Este puño sí se ve! Insurgencia y movimiento obrero*. Mexico City: Ediciones el Caballito, 1987.

Trueba Lara, José Luis, and BEF. *Fidel Velázquez: Una biografía*. Mexico City: Times Editores, 1997.

Trueba Urbina, Alberto, and Jorge Trueba Barrera. *Ley federal del trabajo reformada y adicionada*. 63rd ed. Mexico City: Editorial Porrua, 1969.

Vallejo Novelo, José, ed. *Derechos de la mujer mexicana*. Mexico City: XLVII Legislatura del Congreso de la Unión, 1969.

Vernon, Raymond. *The Dilemma of Mexico's Development: The Roles of the Private and Public Sectors*. Cambridge MA: Harvard University Press, 1963.

Wasserman, Mark. *The Mexican Revolution: A Brief History with Documents*. Boston: Bedford/St. Martin's, 2012.

White, Christopher M. *Creating a Third World: Mexico, Cuba, and the United States*. Albuquerque: University of New Mexico Press, 2007.

Witherspoon, Kevin B. *Before the Eyes of the World: Mexico and the 1968 Olympic Games*. DeKalb: Northern Illinois University Press, 2014.

Zolov, Eric. *Refried Elvis: The Rise of the Mexican Counterculture*. Berkeley: University of California Press, 1999.

———. "Showcasing the 'Land of Tomorrow': Mexico and the 1968 Olympics." *Americas* 61, no. 2 (October 2004): 159–88.

France, 215
Franco, Francisco, 241
Franco, Jean, 320
Frankenstein, 249
"Fraud of 2006," 285
Frayre, Claro, 195–96
freedom of labor, 5–6
free workers, 134, 181, 192, 197, 201, 207–8
Frutería La Victoria, 166
FSTDF, 36, 63, 66, 135, 221, 303
FSTSE, *fig. 16*, 63, 97, 155, 222
FTNL, 162–68, 171–74, 260

Galeano, Eduardo. See *Open Veins of Latin America*
Galván, Rafael, *fig. 18*, 115, 236–37, 240–41, 243, 247–48, 257, 284, 297, 324
Gálvez Betancourt, Carlos, 246
García, Manuel, 163–64
García Barragán, Marcelino, 78, 85
García Márquez, Gabriel, 271
Garza Sada, Eugenio: accomplishments of, 148, 150, 159; birth, family, and upbringing of, 147; condolence letters for, 150; funeral of, 151–53; and Monterrey Technological Institute, 148; murder of, 148–49, 154, 158
gasolinera conflict (Monterrey), 161–62, 167–74
gasoline station owners, 163–65, 167, 170–71
Generation of '68, 272
gender: and complementarity, *fig. 15, fig. 16, fig. 17*, 217–19, 222; and revolution, 212–16, 223–26
General Directorate of Political and Social Investigations. See DGIPS
General Electric, 86, 221. See also Cerro Gordo strike
General Packing Industry and Affiliated Workers' Union of Puebla, 187
Gillingham, Paul, 23

glassworkers' strike (1936), 61
God, 124–25
Gómez, Ricardo, 290
Gómez Sada, Napoleón, 249, 260, 324
Gómez Urrutia, Napoleón, 324n55
Gómez Z., José Luis, 42
González Blanco, Salomón, 63
González Morfín, Efraín, 80
Gracida, José, 172
Grayson, George, 268–69
Grupo Monterrey, 78, 159, 167, 173, 259–61, 272
Guadalupe, Our Lady of, 20, 267, 290
Guadalupe Zuno, José, 233, 314n14
guayabera shirt, *fig. 9*, 83, 271
guerrilla movement, 58, 149, 158, 259, 272, 327n18
Guevara, Che, 87
Guevara Botello, Juan, 246
guilds, 125
Gustavo A. Madero, borough of, 131, 134
Gutiérrez, Fermin, 225

Los Halcones, 90–91, 233
Harvard University, 282
Haymarket Eight. See Chicago General Strike (1886)
health and safety provisions, 10, 25, 154–55, 182, 186–89, 198, 202, 211; workers' demands regarding, 34, 196–98. See also safety inspection reports
hegemony: cultural, 22; electoral or political, 21, 26, 34, 78, 229, 277
El Heraldo, vi
El Heraldo de Cananea, 113
Hernández, Rogelio, 284–85
Hernández Ochoa, Rafael, 129
Hidalgo, Fr. Miguel, 289
hoarding, practice of, 128, 258
homework, 214
House of the World Worker. See Casa del Obrero Mundial

To order or obtain more information on these or other University
of Nebraska Press titles, visit nebraskapress.unl.edu.

CPSIA information can be obtained
at www.ICGtesting.com
Printed in the USA
LVOW08s2339140817
544968LV00008B/492/P